Praise for earlier versions of *Vampyres*

'The myth is endlessly adaptable, it will fit in with any culture and its preoccupations. It haunts the European imagination . . . If you care to know in great detail how Bram Stoker put *Dracula* together – what sources he consulted, what libraries he visited – this is the book for you.' Hilary Mantel, *Daily Telegraph*

'Frayling's introduction is an outstanding piece of literary history: he has exhumed all kinds of quaint and curious lore with the indefatigable scholarly diligence of a Van Helsing, and his account of what he found among the dead men is perceptive, absorbing and witty . . . *Vampyres* certainly has the power to grip and enlighten.' Kevin Jackson, *The Independent on Sunday*

'Allows the reader to trace, through the labyrinth of 19th-century popular fiction, the gradual emergence of our standard horror-film-type vampire . . . The vampire-tales Frayling collects illustrate the richness of the genre and resurrect several lost gems . . . A genuine contribution to vampire studies.' John Carey, *The Sunday Times*

'Christopher Frayling's engrossing theme is the dangerous night visitors, the nocturnal missionaries – emissaries one might almost call them – of the Romantic twilight and the midnight glooms of Victorian repression . . . *Vampyres* is a very Baedeker of vampirism . . . a masterly guide-book.' Valentine Cunningham, *Observer*

'*Vampyres* is a capacious book dripping with suspense and replete with horror. Christopher Frayling's excellent introduction tracks the history of vampire treatises from the 18th century to Stoker's 1897 classic . . . The book is sharply written and incisively edited.' Andrew St George, *The Financial Times*

'Christopher Frayling has made a thorough scholarly survey of the vampiric literature of the 19th-century Gothic Revival . . . The book is an enthralling anthology of excerpts from the works of vampirologists . . . Frayling's cogent introductory and explanatory analyses are written with tongue-in-cheek zest: his own tongue, of course, in his own cheek.' Patrick Skene Catling, *Evening Standard*

CHRISTOPHER FRAYLING

VAMPYRES

Genesis and Resurrection
from *Count Dracula* to *Vampirella*

'A VERY BAEDEKER
OF VAMPIRISM'

OBSERVER

 Thames & Hudson

For Dr John William Polidori, who came too close to a vampire

'May 28 – Went to Geneva. Introduced to a room where about 8; 2 ladies. Lord Byron's name was alone mentioned; mine, like a star in the halo of the moon, invisible. . .'   Polidori's *Diary*

p. 2 Odilon Redon's dream lithograph of 1891 – 'Beneath the Shadow's Wing, the Black Creature was Biting Energetically'; p. 10 *The Invisible Giant*, from Bram Stoker's collection of fairy tales *Under the Sunset*, 1881; p. 454 Sixpenny paperback edition of *Dracula*, 1901, featuring the first published image of the Count.

Vampyres: Genesis and Resurrection from Count Dracula to Vampirella
© 2016 Thames & Hudson Ltd, London
Main text © 2016 Christopher Frayling

This book is a revised and expanded edition of *Vampyres: Lord Byron to Count Dracula*, published in 1991 by Faber & Faber. A considerably shorter version, *The Vampyre*, was published in 1978 by Gollanz.

The Author hereby asserts his right to be identified as the author of the text of the work in accordance with the Copyright Designs and Patents Act 1988.

The extracts from *Stone Cottage: Pound, Yeats and Modernism* by James Logenbach (1988), pp. 108–9, © 1988 Oxford University Press, Inc., are reproduced by permission of Oxford University Press, USA.

The lines from *The Waste Land* by T. S. Eliot from *Collected Poems 1909–62*, Faber & Faber Ltd, 1922, were originally reprinted by courtesy of Mrs Valerie Eliot.

The Lady of the House of Love from *The Bloody Chamber* by Angela Carter. Published by Vintage, 1995. © Angela Carter. Reproduced by permission of the Estate Angela Carter c/o Rogers, Coleridge & White Ltd, 20 Powis Mews, London W11 1JN.

First published in 2016 in hardcover in the United States of America by Thames & Hudson Inc., 500 Fifth Avenue, New York, New York 10110

thamesandhudsonusa.com

Library of Congress Catalog Card Number 2016931243

ISBN 978-0-500-25221-5

Printed and bound in India by Replika Press Pvt. Ltd

CONTENTS

PREFACE TO
THE NEW EDITION

References to bloodsuckers of various descriptions go right back to classical times, and in some myth cycles to the Garden of Eden. But the literary vampire was born two hundred years ago, in June 1816, in a holiday villa overlooking Lake Geneva. Incessant rain – it was the worst summer on record – encouraged Lord Byron, Percy Shelley, Mary Godwin and Dr John Polidori to scare each other with ghost stories late at night as a kind of family bet. After Mary Godwin had read out the 'operation' scene of her *Frankenstein*, Lord Byron began a tale about a blue-blooded aristocrat who dies in a Turkish graveyard – and promises to return. Some of the participants in the session had been reading about the vampires of folklore, and the still-active controversies surrounding the epidemics of vampirism which were said to have spread through peasant societies in Eastern Europe and Greece since the early eighteenth century. The story told by Lord Byron that night in June was subsequently rewritten and expanded by Dr Polidori, Byron's physician during the Geneva summer, and published without permission in 1819 under the title *The Vampyre*. Byron was furious. But it was too late to stem the flow. *The Vampyre* was a runaway bestseller, instantly copied and adapted for the stage. Not only did some editions of the story bear the tantalizing initials 'L. B.' on the title page, but Goethe – no less – considered it 'the English poet's finest work'. The aristocratic literary vampire had been well and truly launched, with the best possible calling-card.

This book explores the bloodline of the literary vampire, from June 1816 back to the agricultural specimens who haunted the Age of Enlightenment, and forward to the novels, penny-dreadfuls, stories and poems that bookended the century between *The Vampyre* (1819) and Bram Stoker's *Dracula* (1897), still the most celebrated novel of them all. Usually, in fiction at any rate, the undead creatures tended to be aristocratic, sometimes male (loosely based on the mean, moody and magnificent image of Byron), sometimes the female of the species – a more personalized form of sexual predator 'with a strawberry mouth', often originating in bohemian Paris. At the height of the Victorian craze, the art critic Walter Pater even saw a hint of the blood-sucker in the best-known portrait of a woman in Western art, Leonardo's *Mona Lisa*: 'Like a vampire, she has been dead many times, and learned the secrets of the grave.'

New elements had been added to the literary formula, new locations explored, new characteristics invented, new remedies tested as the century progressed. By the time *Dracula* was published, most pre-Freudian variations on the theme had been tried out – one of the very first examples of the concerns of 'high culture' being transmitted into the culture of the increasingly crowded and print-hungry inner cities, a special effect that lasted the best part of a century. An article in *The Bookman* magazine suggested that it was high time to get away from forests and castles and crucifixes and decadent aristos of both genders who liked their drink to be served at body temperature: 'We need horrors that survive modern plumbing and the brilliance of electric light.'

Enter the cinematic vampire – with *Nosferatu* (1922) and *Dracula* (1930) leading the card-carrying variety – and, in printed form, the pulp magazines of the interwar years, the sci-fi vampires of the 1950s, the sado-sensual versions of the 1960s and early 1970s, Stephen King's *Salem's Lot* (1975), which has small-town America as its setting, and Anne Rice's *Interview with the Vampire* (1976), which blends latter-day romanticism with a narrator-vampire, and gives one of the creatures an inner-life as an addict. The stage had by then been set for *Buffy the Vampire Slayer* on television, and the phenomenally successful *Twilight Saga* on the big screen, where the pallid vampire plays to the desires – and repressions – of its adolescent audience; as much a herbivore as a carnivore.

Today, with the enduring appeal of Goth fashions and the journey of horror fiction and film (for all ages) from margin to mainstream, the vampire seems to be everywhere. As are the zombie and the werewolf. Reboots of *Dracula* are on every bookstall. In the academic world, the undead have become an increasingly popular subset of Gothic Studies – partly stimulated by the original version of this book. So I thought it was an excellent time to revisit my study of vampires, to revise and update it, to add new material arising from the latest research plus a series of visual essays, which run in parallel to the main themes of the written text. And to finish on *The Lady of the House of Love* by my good friend the late Angela Carter, from her now-classic collection of stories *The Bloody Chamber*. *The Lady of the House of Love* (which was based on Angela's radio play *Vampirella*) is partly about the early research for my *Vampyres*, as I explain; it is also – and more importantly – a brilliant distillation of the main arteries of the vampire theme in literature over the last two hundred years, and a commentary on why vampires entered the cultural bloodstream in the first place. A very suitable climax to this new edition, which is now about resurrection as well as genesis.

Christopher Frayling

PART ONE
A LITERARY HISTORY

LORD BYRON
TO COUNT DRACULA

'If Lord George Selwyn returns, let him in by all means. If I am still alive
I shall be pleased to see him; if not, he will be pleased to see me.'

Lord Holland on his deathbed,
as reported by Horace Walpole

The modern vampire story was born – in suitably oral circumstances – inside a villa overlooking Lake Geneva rented for the holidays on the night of 17 June 1816, when the weather was unusually wet and the atmosphere unusually tense. The birth coincided with that of *Frankenstein*, and their paths were destined to cross over the next two hundred years, many, many times. The modern vampire arrived in the world, fully formed, as a fashionably pallid aristocrat, complete with seductive voice, pouting lips, blue blood and mean, moody and magnificent personality.

A month before the night of the birth, on 13 May 1816, Percy Shelley, eighteen-year-old Mary Wollstonecraft Godwin, their five-month-old son William and Mary's stepsister Claire Clairmont (who was eight months younger than Mary) had checked into Monsieur Dejean's fashionable Hôtel d'Angleterre facing the Alps on the north side of the lake, just outside the city of Geneva. They were tired out. Mary had been seasick and coach-sick for most of the ten-day journey from London, via Paris.

The Hôtel d'Angleterre, a large three-storey stone building set back from the lakeside, with a park leading to the road from Geneva to Lausanne, was a stopover favoured by the well-heeled British starting on their grand tours. It was the first coaching inn on the way out of the austere walled city, which shut its gates at 10 p.m. sharp.

A week later, Lord Byron and his personal physician/travelling companion Dr John Polidori, accompanied by a *valet de chambre*, two servants and two drivers, arrived at the hotel in Sécheron. Before he left England at the end of April, Byron had given Claire Clairmont (then known as Clara, or to her family as Jane) his address as 'Milord Byron, Poste Restante, Genève', which was why she had managed to persuade Percy Shelley and Mary Godwin to go to Geneva. For, in April 1816, Claire briefly – in a characteristically impetuous move which, she later wrote, gave her ten minutes of pleasure and a lifetime of pain – had become Byron's mistress.

Unknown to his noble employer, twenty-year-old Dr Polidori, who had recently graduated in medicine from the University of Edinburgh with a thesis on sleepwalking, had been offered 500 guineas to produce a publishable diary of their adventures, so he noted the Byron party's movements in some detail. It is the only surviving diary of June 1816 to have been written on the spot and at the time – albeit published with 'peccant passages' removed by Polidori's aged aunt Charlotte. The entries for that crucial month in Mary Godwin's *Journal* have disappeared, and only a few of her relevant letters have survived. Polidori was, in the words of his acquaintance Harriet Martineau, 'a handsome, harum-scarum young man'. He also had painful ambitions to be a poet rather than a medical man, and a thin skin. But, as his *Diary* amply shows, it has to be said he was not a very gifted writer:

> May 26 – Went to the house beyond Cologny that belonged to Diodati. They ask five-and-twenty louis for it a month ... The view from this house is very fine; beautiful lake; at the bottom of the crescent is Geneva. Returned ...
>
> May 27 – ... L. B. met M. Wollstonecraft Godwin, her sister [in fact stepsister] and Percy Shelley. I got the boat into the middle of Leman Lake, and there lay my length, letting the boat go its way ... Dined; P. S., the author of [the poem] *Queen Mab* came; bashful, shy, consumptive; twenty-six [in fact only twenty-four]; separated from his wife, keeps the two daughters of Godwin, who practise his theories [of the emancipation of women, and of open marriage; evidently Byron had been gossiping]; one L. B.'s [Claire Clairmont] ...

A few days later, the Shelley party – now with a Genevan nursemaid called Louise Duvillard but known as 'Elise' – moved across the lake to the smaller of two secluded properties owned by a M. Jacob Chappuis, below the Villa Diodati on the sloping shore of Lake Geneva. The address was 'Maison Chappuis, Montalègre', but Mary Godwin referred to it as 'Chapuis'. The square, stone-built, two-storey 'cottage' set among vineyards near the winding lake road had access to a small harbour, which belonged to Chappuis. Mary Godwin wrote to her half-sister about the weather on 1 June, from 'Campagne C, near Coligny':

Unfortunately we do not now enjoy those brilliant skies that hailed us on our first arrival to this country. An almost perpetual rain confines us principally to the house; but when the sun bursts forth it is with a splendour and heat unknown in England. The thunder storms that visit us are grander and more terrific than I have ever seen before. We watch them as they approach from the opposite side of the lake, observing the lightning play among the clouds in various parts of the heavens, and dart in jagged figures upon the piny heights of Jura, dark with the shadow of the overhanging cloud . . .

Mary Godwin was beginning to share Shelley's 'enjoyment' of storms, though she still preferred 'sunshine and gentle breezes' to the extremes of the sublime, which were his preference. Byron, too, was busy exploring the impact of the increasingly extreme weather conditions on his emotions. In Canto the Third (92 & 93) of *Childe Harold's Pilgrimage*, which he wrote at this time, he described a heavy storm he had experienced on 13 June:

Thy sky is changed! – and such a change! Oh night,
And storm, and darkness, ye are wondrous strong.
Yet lovely in your strength, as is the light
Of a dark eye in woman!

The year 1816 has subsequently become known as 'the year without a summer' – a meteorological freak in Europe, resulting in widespread harvest failures and even famine.

Lord Byron had moved into the Villa Diodati on 10 June. Its original name had been the Villa Belle Rive. This villa, which had belonged to the family since Gabriel Diodati supervised its construction in 1710, was not occupied: Edward Diodati and relatives lived in a smaller house near the village of Cologny, and rented out the main house to visitors. It was a two-storey grey stone villa with a substantial porticoed basement, surrounded on three sides – at first-floor level – by a large balcony with an elaborate iron balustrade. The Byron party were under the impression that John Milton once stayed there. He didn't, for the simple reason that the villa was not built in his lifetime. Maybe the Milton connection had been stressed as part of the sales pitch. There *were* some family connections between the Diodatis and John Milton. Certainly, the Satan of *Paradise Lost* (1667) would have felt very much at home in the villa by mid-June. The villa was a few minutes away from the Maison Chappuis, and in the evenings the Shelley party would walk up the slope to join Lord Byron.

Earlier that month, Claire Clairmont had discovered that she was pregnant, but waited a while before breaking the news to Byron. His response was: 'Is the brat mine?' In the meantime, he continued to have sex with 'that odd-headed girl' ('if a girl of eighteen comes prancing to you at all hours of the night – there is but one way'). And he used her to copy out Canto the Third of *Childe Harold's Pilgrimage* (which he had finished by 27 June) for despatch to his publisher in London.

Mary Godwin also copied verses – a job she enjoyed, since she, too, evidently felt an attraction for Byron (though not always for his behaviour) and was impressed by his staggering 'intellectual energy'. When Byron later made his announcement to Claire Clairmont and Percy Shelley that his relationship with Claire was over, he specifically asked that Mary should *not* be present to hear the news. This confused but did not surprise her, for Byron had made it abundantly clear, since their meeting on 27 May, that he preferred to have conversations about important matters with men rather than women. As Mary was to recall, in October 1822:

> I do not think that any person's voice has the same power of awakening melancholy in me as [Byron's] – I have been accustomed when hearing it to listen and to speak little – another voice, not mine, ever replied … Since incapacity and timidity always prevented my mingling in the nightly conversations of Diodati – they were as it were entirely tête-à-tête between my Shelley and [Byron] …

Polidori's *Diary* also makes it clear that Byron preferred to dine and talk with Shelley alone – 'Dined with S …', 'Then to see Shelley …', 'Thence to Shelley …', 'To Shelley in boat …' – and that the ladies were expected to amuse themselves with less grown-up pursuits. Being excluded from these intimate *tête-à-têtes* was a new and possibly disturbing experience for Mary

Godwin. From her earliest conversations with Percy Shelley in June 1814 – in front of the tomb of her mother Mary Wollstonecraft in St Pancras Cemetery – she had come to expect her relationship with him to be a communion of equals, a meeting of like-minded individuals who had freely chosen to live together outside the conventions of society. She was the daughter of Shelley's two favourite political philosophers – 'a child of love and light' he called her – and the most impressive scholar of any woman he had ever encountered.

In her *Journal* for October 1822, Mary wrote that Percy brought out the best in her: 'I thought how superiorly gifted I had been in being united to one to whom I could unveil myself, and who could understand me.' He was the *only* person who could achieve this: she tended to feel much less 'natural' with his friends and acquaintances, and sometimes felt upset when he discussed their intimate affairs with them. In other words, her life had become sharply focused on his. So when she found herself excluded from the 'nightly conversations of Diodati', it must have come as a shock. It told her a lot about Lord Byron, and maybe a little about Percy Shelley as well. Dr Polidori, on the other hand, had been relentlessly teased and patronized by Lord Byron from the moment they landed in Ostende on 25 April. As Byron wrote:

> I never was much more disgusted with any human production – than with the eternal nonsense – and tracasseries – and emptiness – and ill-humour – and vanity of that young person; he was exactly the kind of person to whom, if he fell overboard, one would hold out a straw to know if the adage be true that charming men catch at straws.

It seems from his *Diary* that the doctor was acting as Byron's accountant as well as his physician and companion, perhaps at the publisher John Murray's request. If so, it was a role that was unlikely to endear him to his employer.

The earliest published account of the circumstances in which the first modern vampire – and *Frankenstein* – were born comes from Percy Shelley's Preface to the first (anonymous) edition of *Frankenstein*, dated September 1817. This was presented 'as if' by Mary, but was in actual fact subtly diminishing of her efforts (in comparison with those of her two better-known friends, Byron and Shelley):

... this story was begun in the majestic region where the scene is principally laid, and in society which cannot cease to be regretted. I passed the summer of 1816 in the environs of Geneva. The season was cold and rainy, and in the evenings we crowded around a blazing wood fire, and occasionally amused ourselves with some German stories of ghosts, which happened to fall into our hands. These tales excited in us a playful desire of imitation. Two other friends (a tale from the pen of one of whom would be far more acceptable to the public than any thing I can ever hope to produce) and myself agreed to write such a story, founded on some supernatural occurrence. The weather, however, suddenly became serene; and my two friends left me on a journey among the Alps, and lost, in the magnificent scenes which they present, all memory of their ghostly visions. The following tale is the only one which has been completed.

But a fuller and much better-known account comes from Mary Shelley's own Introduction to the 1831 popular edition of *Frankenstein* – written some fourteen years after Shelley's, and fifteen years after the events it purported to describe. This account has been retold and embellished, over and over again, ever since.

But it proved a wet, ungenial summer, and incessant rain often confined us for days to the house. Some volumes of ghost stories, translated from the German into French, fell into our hands. There was the *History of the Inconstant Lover*, who, when he thought to clasp the bride to whom he had pledged his vows, found himself in the arms of the pale ghost of her whom he had deserted. There was the tale of the sinful founder of his race whose miserable doom it was to bestow the kiss of death on all the younger sons of his fated house, just when they reached the age of promise . . . I have not seen these stories since then; but their incidents are as fresh in my mind as if I had read them yesterday.

'We will each write a ghost story,' said Lord Byron; and his proposition was acceded to. There were four of us. The noble author began a tale, a fragment of which he printed at the end of his poem of *Mazeppa* [1819]. Shelley, more apt to embody ideas and sentiments in the radiance of brilliant imagery, and in the music of the most melodious verse that adorns our language, than to invent the machinery of a story, commenced one founded on the experiences of his early life. Poor Polidori had some terrible idea about a skull-headed lady, who was so punished for peeping through a keyhole – what to see I forget – something very shocking and wrong of course . . . The illustrious poets also, annoyed by the platitude of prose, speedily relinquished their uncongenial task.

I busied myself to think of a story – a story to rival those which had excited me to this task . . . I thought and pondered – vainly. I felt that blank incapacity of invention which is the greatest misery of authorship, when dull Nothing replies to our anxious invocations. Have you thought of a story? I was asked each morning, and each morning I was forced to reply with a mortifying negative . . .

Many and long were the conversations between Lord Byron and Shelley, to which I was a devout but nearly silent listener. During one of these, various philosophical doctrines were discussed, and among others the nature of the principle of life, and whether there was any probability of its ever being discovered and communicated. They talked of the experiments of Dr [Erasmus] Darwin (I speak not of what the Doctor really did, or said that he did, but, as more to my purpose, of what was then spoken of as having been done by him), who preserved a piece of vermicelli in a glass case, till by some extraordinary means it began to move with voluntary motion. Not thus, after all, would life be given. Perhaps a corpse would be reanimated; galvanism had given token of such things; perhaps the component parts of a creature might be manufactured, brought together, and endued with vital warmth. Night waned upon this talk, and even the witching hour had gone by, before we retired to rest. When I placed my head on my pillow, I did not sleep . . . On the morrow I announced that I had thought of a story. I began that day with the words, It was on a dreary night in November, making only a transcript of the grim terrors of my waking dream.

At first I thought of but a few pages – of a short tale; but Shelley urged me to develop the idea at greater length. I certainly did not owe the suggestion of one incident, nor scarcely of one train of feeling, to my husband, and yet but for his incitement, it would never have taken the form in which it was presented to the world. From this declaration I must except the preface. As far as I recollect, it was entirely written by him.

And now, once again, I bid my hideous progeny go forth and prosper...

All agree that the dramatic events had started with a two-volume collection of ghost stories, *Fantasmagoriana ou Recueil d'Histoires d'Apparitions, de Spectres, Revenants, etc.*, translated into French from the original German by Jean-Baptiste Benoît Eyriès. A copy of the book was found in Geneva, and Lord Byron read it aloud while they sat around the ornate fireplace, and – taking his cue from the second story in the collection, *Les Portraits de Famille* – suggested in a playful spirit that they should each have a go at writing a tale of terror: 'Every one is to relate a story of ghosts, or something of a similar nature,' said a character in *Les Portraits de Famille*, '...it is agreed amongst us that no one shall search for any explanation, even though it bears the stamp of truth, as explanations would take away all pleasure from ghost stories.'

If we compare Dr Polidori's *Diary* written at the time with Mary Shelley's version, there are significant variations in their accounts of what happened next. Mary's is the much better read. It successfully promotes the book it is prefacing, skilfully manipulates Gothic clichés (the extreme weather, the ghost stories, the discussion beyond 'the witching hour', the nightmare) and contains a thrilling cliff-hanger ('Have you thought of a story?'), but the events it describes probably did not happen like that at all.

There was, she says, in the *Fantasmagoriana*, 'the *History of the Inconstant Lover* ... [and] the tale of the sinful founder of his race whose miserable doom it was to bestow the kiss of death ...' – these were, in fact, called *La Morte Fiancée* and *Les Portraits de Famille*, and Mary's summaries of them are not very accurate; it is interesting, though, that she remembered them as stories about a) a man who is pursued by the ghost of his deserted wife and b) a family whose 'younger sons' are doomed to die, because she was troubled by the fate of Harriet Westbrook Shelley – Percy's deserted wife – who was to drown herself in the Serpentine at the end of that same year of 1816; and she had had personal experience of what it was like to lose her baby (in March 1815). Evidently, these distressing incidents, which were 'as fresh in my mind as if I had read them yesterday', had chimed with her own deepest concerns, and subsequently may have become confused in her mind with the collection of ghost stories.

'There were four of us' – in fact, there were *five* people present; as usual in her reminiscences, Mary omits Claire Clairmont.

'Poor Polidori had some terrible idea about a skull-headed lady . . .' In fact, the doctor told the story which was to become his *Ernestus Berchtold* (1819) about the love-affair between a Swiss patriot and a lady who turns out to be his sister and which, in the published version, he referred to as 'the one I began at Cologny, when *Frankenstein* was planned'; maybe the incest theme was thought by participants to be too near the knuckle, given the (perhaps) malicious rumours circulating in England at the time about Byron's relationship with his half-sister. The story Mary refers to, about a lady who peeps through the keyhole and sees something she shouldn't, was possibly told by Claire. Polidori's contribution was not spooky at all: as he rather pompously wrote, 'I had agreed to write a supernatural tale, and that does not allow of a completely everyday narrative.' He was a literal sort of person . . .

'The illustrious poets . . . speedily relinquished their uncongenial task' – in fact, Lord Byron and Percy Shelley took a lot longer to become bored with the game than she suggests. Mary also implies that they disliked the prospect of sitting indoors and chatting (when they could be out in the boat exploring Jean-Jacques Rousseau territory): in Canto the Third (98) of *Childe Harold*, though (which was completed about ten days after the ghost-story session), Byron felt that 'confinement' might stimulate them all to 'find room/And food for meditation, nor pass by/Much, that may give us pause, if pondered fittingly'. According to Thomas Moore's *Letters and Journals of Lord Byron* (1830), Byron said to Mary about the ghost-story session: 'you and I will publish ours together'.

Mary's account of what happened then – 'Many and long were the conversations between Lord Byron and Shelley, to which I was a devout but nearly silent listener' – may not be strictly accurate either: the conversation in question was probably between *Polidori* and Shelley. For his *Diary* entry for 15 June, the physician describes a conversation with Shelley about 'principles – whether man was to be thought merely an instrument', a subject on which Polidori was something of an expert: not only had he published his thesis on sleepwalking and mesmeric trances the previous year, as recently as 12 June he had discussed these and related matters with a Dr Odier (another graduate from the University of Edinburgh) who happened to live nearby. It is possible, of course, that the Polidori conversation with Shelley stimulated *another* one, later in the evening – involving Byron, Shelley and Mary Godwin – with the physician no longer in the room. But the likelihood is that the conversation involving 'various philosophical doctrines', about 'the nature of the principle of life' and whether human beings were free agents, was with Dr Polidori.

The family ghost-story game seems at the time to have been far less genial and playful than Mary recalls. Polidori was at his most pretentious and vulnerable. Claire had just announced that she was pregnant. Byron, feeling competitive and sensitive to the slightest criticism, was making his views about strong intellectual women more and more apparent. Percy was feeling highly strung. On the night of 18 June, all these factors turned the ghostly talk into a bizarre encounter group: the 'tempestuous loveliness of terror' – as Shelley was to call it, in his poem *On the Medusa* (1819) – was getting seriously out of hand. Polidori noted:

> June 18. . . Shelley and party here . . . Began my ghost-story after tea. Twelve o'clock, really began to talk ghostly. L. B. repeated some verses of Coleridge's *Christabel*, of the witch's breast; when silence ensued, and Shelley, suddenly shrieking and putting his hands to his head, ran out of the room with a candle. Threw water in his face, and after gave him ether. He was looking at Mrs S, and suddenly thought of a woman he had heard of who had eyes instead of nipples, which, taking hold of his mind, horrified him. – He married; and, a friend of his liking his wife, he tried all he could do to induce her to love him in turn. He is surrounded by friends who feed upon him, and draw upon him as their banker. Once, having hired a house, a man wanted to make him pay more, and came trying to bully him, and at last

challenged him. Shelley refused, and was knocked down; coolly said that
would not gain him his object, and was knocked down again . . .

The lines from Coleridge's *Christabel* (1797) that had pushed Shelley over the
edge and sent him shrieking from the room were these:

> Then drawing in her breath, aloud,
> Like one that shuddered, she unbound
> The cincture from beneath her breast:
> Her silken robe and inner vest
> Dropped to her feet, and full in view,
> Behold! Her bosom and half her side,
> Hideous, deformed, and pale of hue –
> A sight to dream of, not to tell!
> And she is to sleep by Christabel!

This horrifying image, in a dramatic poem of love between women, confused
with a fantasy that was already on his mind, was the one that Percy Shelley
projected on to 'Mrs S' (Mary Godwin).

Mary had informed him, the previous year, that Coleridge's concept of
the 'hideous, deformed' bosom had originally been more specific: 'two eyes
in her bosom'. The image had evidently 'taken hold', as well it might. And
so Shelley put his hands to his head, thinking perhaps that he had gone
mad, shrieked, and rushed out of the room. The image of Mary as a harpy
– 'hideous, deformed and pale of hue' – was too much for him. What *she*
thought of the attribution, neither Polidori nor Mary recorded. And why
Shelley should suddenly have imagined her as 'a sight to dream of, not to
tell' remains a mystery.

And all *this* happened on the very evening that Mary blandly referred to
as the one when 'Shelley . . . commenced [a story] founded on the experiences
of his early life'. Polidori's convoluted account of how 'He married; and, a
friend of his liking his wife . . .' related to an incident involving Shelley's friend
Thomas Jefferson Hogg and the poet's first wife Harriet; the reference to
'friends who feed upon him' may have been about William Godwin, Mary's

father, and Charles Clairmont, Claire's brother. If so, Mary later decided to draw a veil over this story of her father as a sort of financial bloodsucker.

Throughout the short-story evenings, Polidori also seems to have been kept busy dispensing ether or laudanum to Shelley (for his nervous headaches and hyperactivity) and Black Drop – a popular compound, which contained opium – to Byron. These were not thought to be *stimulants* – there was more than enough stimulation going on already; they were tranquillizers.

In the Introduction to her book, Mary Godwin externalizes these extraordinary tensions and turns them into the stage-effects of a Gothic melodrama. Just before describing the events of June 1816, she confesses in the same essay that she feels much more at home with 'airy flights of my imagination' than with attempts to describe everyday life and people – 'Life appeared to me too common-place an affair as regarded myself': instead of turning lived experience into prose, she preferred, she says, 'the formation of castles in the air – the indulging in waking dreams ... My dreams were at once more fantastic and agreeable ...'

And this may provide a clue as to the *real* reason why she rewrote the story of what happened at the ghost-story session. She had to contend with notions of feminine literary decorum – readers of the popular edition of *Frankenstein* might have been *truly* shocked if she had been more than 'a devout but nearly silent listener' in such august male company. It would not have been seemly to delve into and write about *their* deepest fantasies. The trappings of the Gothic – where sexuality became a matter of drawbridges and moats and castles – were acceptable, but lived experience was not. She also lacked confidence where writing was concerned, and may even have agreed with Shelley that a tale from the pen of Lord Byron 'would be far more acceptable to the public than any thing I can ever hope to produce' – even though, as her Introduction implies, it might have been better if she had said so herself, rather than publicly admitting it in a 'preface ... entirely written by him'.

So perhaps the key phrase is 'Life appeared to me too common-place an affair as regarded myself'. It was obviously *not* commonplace where Byron and Shelley were concerned. But she couldn't possibly write about that. It was not at all commonplace where she was concerned either, but, for all sorts of personal and social reasons, that's the way it appeared to *her*.

None of this explains why she wrote Claire Clairmont and John Polidori out of the ghost-story sessions, apart from adding 'my readers have nothing to do with these associations'. It may be that she saw herself as one of the keepers of the flame of Shelley's and Byron's posthumous reputations: all the male contributors to the ghost-story session were dead by the time she wrote her Introduction; Claire died in 1879. But another important reason why she rewrote the events – as well as the purpose of introducing the cheap edition of *Frankenstein* and the obvious one of marketing her work to a new generation of readers at a time when she had to rely on her earnings as an author – was that she needed publicly to establish the motherhood of her own 'progeny'.

The first edition of *Frankenstein* had been anonymous. Percy Shelley had, in fact, helped out with the writing style of the second major draft of the novel (and made it more florid – for better or worse), acted as her copy-editor and corrected most of the proofs. Some readers of the first edition, however, thought that *Frankenstein* was *by* Percy Shelley. It certainly attracted more public attention, and was better received, than anything he had written up until then. So, quite rightly, she felt that she had to state loud and clear in her Introduction that she was in fact the mother.

She makes it clear that the pressure on her, in that august company, was intense. Shelley and Byron were being competitive. Byron had offered to share a publication – a fantastic offer, for an apprentice writer. 'As the daughter of two persons of distinguished literary celebrity' – Mary Wollstonecraft and William Godwin – Mary Wollstonecraft Godwin was *expected* by all who knew her to be a writer of significance. This, however, did not come easily: 'In [my early writings – and she *was* only eighteen] I was a close imitator – rather doing as others had done than putting down the suggestions of my own mind'. To increase the pressure, 'my husband ... was from the first, very anxious that I should prove myself worthy of my parentage, and enrol myself on the page of fame'.

Lord Byron would not have had much time for her as a writer even if she *was* able to prove herself worthy of her parentage: where he was concerned, she was better occupied in copying out the manuscript of *Childe Harold*. Shelley was highly supportive, but his kind of Promethean genius tended to unsettle her: her views on over-reachers who aimed to steal the fires from heaven without taking responsibility for the consequences were made abundantly clear in the character, and fate, of Victor Frankenstein. Or maybe, when Shelley supported her, he was just being nice. He was – especially in her reworked popular edition of 1831 – 'always most earnest and energetic in his exhortations that I should cultivate any talent I possessed, to the utmost', but maybe his encouragement – she thought – was 'not so much with the idea that I could produce anything worthy of notice, but that he might himself judge how far I possessed the promise of better things hereafter'. And the pressure of that 'promise' made her frightened of failure, and frightened of not living up to his high expectations of her.

In this atmosphere, Mary busied herself, according to her account of the events of mid-June 1816, to find her own voice – crucially, to think of 'a story to rival those which had excited me to this task'. But it just wouldn't come. Only 'that blank incapacity of invention which is the greatest misery of authorship'. *Have you thought of a story?* she was asked each morning. And each morning the answer was 'a mortifying negative'.

Eventually, following the late-night discussion with Byron and Shelley – and it was important for what she was trying to say that it *had to be* with Byron and Shelley, the illustrious poets who had excluded her from their *tête-à-têtes* about 'the nature of the principle of life', the experiments of the poet-scientist Dr Erasmus Darwin and of Luigi Galvani and his nephew/editor Giovanni Aldini – she had her waking nightmare. And, much to everyone's surprise, came up with the creation sequence of *Frankenstein* in short-story form.

Again, it didn't happen quite like that, but – where the motherhood of the text is concerned – that may not be the point. Polidori's *Diary* reveals that Mary was almost certainly the *first*, not the last, to tell her story. He was likely to register that kind of detail, and write it down. After all, she was a fellow 'outsider' in this game. Mary had evidently been mulling it over in her mind for some time. But her story *was* triggered by that principle-of-life chat at 'the witching hour' – the chat that finally released her writer's block. As Polidori wrote:

> June 15 – . . . Shelley etc. came in the evening; talked of my play etc., which was worth nothing [Polidori had written a drama called *Cajetan*, which had already caused much hilarity]. Afterwards, Shelley and I had a conversation about principles – whether man was to be thought merely an instrument.
>
> June 16 – Laid up. Shelley came, and dined and slept here, with Mrs S and Miss Claire Clairmont. Wrote another letter.
>
> June 17 – . . . Dined with Shelley etc. here . . . The ghost-stories are begun by all but me.
>
> June 18 – . . . Shelley and party here . . .

So the conversation about 'the nature of the principle of life' (or, in Polidori's version, about 'principles – whether man was to be thought merely an instrument') took place on the evening of 15 June. Two days later, 'The ghost-stories are begun by all but me.' If the conversation was the immediate stimulus to Mary's waking nightmare – as she was to recall so vividly – the dream must have happened either on the night of the 15th or 16th – most probably the 16th when the Shelleys slept at the Villa Diodati. In this case the ghost-story session happened on 17 and 18 June (when Polidori told *his* story, and Shelley lost control of himself). Byron's uncompleted story – later published with his *Mazeppa* (1819) – was indeed dated 17 June 1816. And, when Mary described the physical surroundings of her nightmare – 'the dark *parquet*, the closed shutters . . . the glassy lake and white high Alps' – she was maybe describing her room in the *Villa Diodati*, rather than in the Maison Chappuis. The description still fits. So the 'creation' scene of *Frankenstein* was told on 17 June. And so was Byron's contribution. It was *Polidori* who – predictably – had problems answering the question 'Have you thought of a story?'

From the point of view of the history of literature, it is unfortunate that Mary Godwin surrounded the events of 17 and 18 June 1816 with Gothic stage-effects and tacky stories about skull-headed ladies, because thereafter these tended to associate Frankenstein and the vampire with the bandits and necromancers who had been fashionable since the late eighteenth century, and which Jane Austen was about to satirize in *Northanger Abbey* (published just three months before *Frankenstein*). Rather than with the *future* of horror, science fiction and the rise of popular culture. This, despite the fact that Percy Shelley wrote that his wife's novel was far more than 'a mere tale of spectres and enchantment'. It raised much more interesting issues, and was based on Mary's lived experience. It also took a long time to turn into a novel, rather than emerging fully-fledged from a nightmare. Dr Polidori seems to have written an 'outline' of Mary's story – together with Lord Byron's and his own – and turned himself into something of a social celebrity at Genevan dinner parties by retelling all the stories for the rest of that summer. The 'outline' of the story told by 'Miss M. W. Godwin' eventually found its way to the editor of the *New Monthly Magazine*, together with Polidori's *Vampyre*, which was very loosely based on Byron's story (see page 31). It had probably been sent by one of Polidori's dinner-party hosts, whose identity remains a mystery. But this outline has since disappeared. Evidently, the events of mid-June 1816 in the Villa Diodati became all the rage among upmarket grand tourists, and prim dinner guests in and around Geneva.

In the days immediately following Mary Godwin's nightmare at the Villa Diodati, rumours of bizarre goings-on were beginning to circulate among the English tourists on the other side of the lake at the Hôtel d'Angleterre, Sécheron. The *maître d'hôtel* Monsieur Déjean began to hire out telescopes, so that his guests could get a closer look. One tourist – Sylvester Douglas, Lord Glenbervie – picked up some juicy stories while dining at Sécheron on 3 July. He wrote in his diary:

> Among more than sixty English travellers here, there is Lord Byron, who is cut by everybody. They tell a strange adventure of his, at Déjean's Inn. He is now living at a villa on the Savoy side of the lake with that woman, who it seems proves to be a Mrs Shelley, wife to the man who keeps the Mount Coffee-house.

This gives some idea of the kind of gossip that was circulating among those 'sixty English travellers'. The final sentence gets every single detail hilariously wrong. Byron was *not*, of course, living with 'a Mrs Shelley', who in any case was still Mary Godwin at the time. The man who kept the Mount Coffee-house was John Westbrook, father of Harriet Westbrook, who was Shelley's first (and only, in 1816) wife. So Lord Glenbervie had succeeded in confusing Mary Godwin with both Claire Clairmont *and* Harriet Westbrook, Percy Shelley with Harriet's father, and Shelley with Lord Byron. Never mind – there was obviously *something* nasty going on in the Villa; probably group sex and/or a league of incest involving Percy, Mary, George and Claire. When tablecloths were seen drying on the iron balcony, they were rumoured to be girls' knickers.

One reason the gossip then proceeded to spread from English tourists to citizens of Geneva was that the behaviour of the tenants of the Villa Diodati had come to the attention of the local police. In the Genevan police records (among the Archives d'État), I have found ample evidence that Lord Byron and Dr Polidori, at least, were becoming known to the local constabulary.

On one occasion, Byron reported that his boat's anchor and some fixtures and fittings had been stolen from the harbour near Maison Chappuis, and then took the law into his own hands by noisily threatening some completely innocent local residents. On another, Polidori roughed up a local apothecary – breaking his spectacles and throwing his hat into the gutter – because he had supplied him (or rather Lord Byron) with some substandard drugs: this resulted in a warrant for the doctor's arrest, to add to his many other difficulties. But the most interesting case was a bungled breaking-and-entering attempt at the Villa Diodati itself which, according to the *rapport de police*, resulted in a lieutenant suggesting that the neighbouring cabarets should be placed under observation to see if any 'étrangers et gens suspects' (foreigners or strangers and suspicious-looking people) were hanging around: the Genevans do not seem to have been too keen on strangers; it had not occurred to the lieutenant that the culprits might be *citizens*.

In summer 1816, Geneva seems from the documents to have been swarming with top-of-the-range English tourists. Some of them were associated with the allied troops who had recently defeated Napoleon, others stopping over on their grand tours, others still coming to see the latest discovery (or invention) of the Romantics – the magnificent Alps. This was, after all, the first time for fifteen years that tourists could travel freely around the continent. Tourism and Switzerland were beginning to become as synonymous as Lord Byron and scandal.

Mary Shelley's Introduction – and the subsequent success of her novel, especially in its cut-down version of 1831 – has tended to associate that year without a summer exclusively with *Frankenstein*. The ghost-story session long ago entered literary mythology, the subject of several feature films (three in the 1980s alone) and of countless references in fantasy novels. For many, it is far better known than the novel it introduced. And yet, an equally significant association – if not a *more* significant one, in the light of subsequent developments in cultural history – was with the birth in prose of the *literary* vampire, as distinct from his/her folkloric forebear. Because just after Mary Godwin started *her* story, Lord Byron began a tale about a blue-blooded aristocrat of an ancient family called Darvell, who accompanies a young man on a trip to Turkey and dies in a graveyard there – having promised to return from the dead a month later. The published version, a 'fragment', ends on that promise:

> As he sat [in a Turkish burial ground], evidently becoming more feeble, a stork, with a snake in her beak, perched upon a tombstone near us; and, without devouring her prey, appeared to be steadfastly regarding us. I know not what impelled me to drive it away, but the attempt was useless; she made a few circles in the air, and returned exactly to the same spot. Darvell pointed to it, and smiled – he spoke – I know not whether to himself or to me – but the words were only, "Tis well!'
>
> 'What is well? What do you mean?'
>
> 'No matter; you must bring me here this evening, and exactly where that bird is now perched. You know the rest of my injunctions.'
>
> He then proceeded to give me several directions as to the manner in which his death might be best concealed. After these were finished, he exclaimed, 'You perceive that bird?'
>
> 'Certainly.'
>
> 'And the serpent writhing in her beak?' . . .

He smiled in a ghastly manner, and said faintly, 'It is not yet time!' As he spoke, the stork flew away . . .

Mary Shelley in her Introduction states that 'the noble author [Byron] began a tale, a fragment of which he printed at the end of his poem of *Mazeppa*'; the inference being that Byron told only the *beginning* of his tale, and that he always intended to publish a 'fragment' of it. In fact, Byron only appended his *Fragment* in *Mazeppa* in self-defence, after the pirate publication of *The Vampyre*, a story based on an idea by Byron but entirely written – without permission – by Polidori. Polidori's summary of the story Byron told on 17 June 1816 suggests that rather more of Byron's story was told than Mary Shelley recalled. 'It depended for interest upon the circumstances of two friends leaving England, and one dying in Greece, the other finding him alive, upon his return, and making love to his sister.' The published *Fragment* refers only to 'two friends leaving England, and one dying in Greece'. Polidori must have remembered Byron telling the rest of the story (the part that shows it to have been a vampire tale *before* he began his process of adaptation); presumably, Byron omitted the 'vampire' elements from his *Fragment* in order to make the story he told seem as far removed as possible from *The Vampyre*.

Polidori had rewritten, and expanded, Byron's story during 'two or three idle mornings' to while away the time in summer 1816, while Byron and Shelley were otherwise engaged. He left his manuscript behind in Geneva and thought no more of it. Someone then sent this to a publisher in London, without his consent, or so he subsequently claimed. So although he had rewritten the story, under the title *The Vampyre*, he was not responsible for *publishing* it. The publisher was Henry Colburn, who had had a success with Lady Caroline Lamb's *Glenarvon* of 1816: he acquired and issued *The Vampyre*, complete with a new Introduction about the Noble Lord who 'never went to sleep without a pair of pistols and a dagger by his side', and about the rumour that Byron had procured 'in his house two sisters as the partakers of his revels' (a rumour that was, as the Introduction hastened to point out, 'entirely destitute of truth'). So three years after the Geneva summer, in April 1819, *The Vampyre* was resurrected back in London just like Polidori's revamped vampire Lord Ruthven – with his 'dead grey eye' and 'the deadly hue of his face' – who returns from Turkey to bite his way through London society during the season. The story began:

> It happened that in the midst of the dissipations attendant upon a London winter, there appeared at the various parties of the leaders of the *ton* a nobleman, more remarkable for his singularities than his rank. He gazed upon the mirth around him, as if he could not participate therein. Apparently, the light laughter of the fair only attracted his attention, that he might by a look quell it, and throw fear into those breasts where thoughtlessness reigned. Those who felt this sensation of awe, could not explain whence it arose: some attributed it to the dead grey eye, which, fixing upon the object's face, did not seem to penetrate . . . His peculiarities caused him to be invited to every house . . .

The story ended not with a snake in a stork's beak, but with the marriage of Lord Ruthven and the narrator's sister, a marriage that ends in tears because the narrator, bound by oath, is unable to tell anyone about Ruthven's guilty secret: 'when they arrived, it was too late. Lord Ruthven had disappeared, and Aubrey's sister had glutted the thirst of a VAMPYRE!'

The slim volume became an instant bestseller, partly because everyone thought it was by Byron himself. Some editions even bore the tantalizing initials 'L. B.' on the title page, though most were anonymous, and Goethe thought it 'the English poet's finest work'. Polidori – rather than his employer – had in fact written every word of it. So he then started petitioning for an author's fee. He did not like the attribution to Byron, he had not written the new Introduction, but if the story *was* to be published, he understandably wanted some credit for it. Eventually, he was paid £30 in retrospect for his pains – £30 for a little book that launched a thousand imitations.

Even after the question of authorship had been cleared up, publishers of Byron's works were reluctant to let *The Vampyre* slip away: in Paris, there were so many complaints by subscribers when the story was dropped from the second edition of Byron's *Works* in 1820 ('we did not wish to speculate with the name of the English Lord') that a corrected and revised version of

Polidori's tale was reinstated in the third edition a few years later ('we have decided to give way to the pressure of numerous subscribers by resuscitating *The Vampyre*').

It was ironic, said one literary critic of the day, that it took 'an absurd story, not even by him' finally to establish the reputation of Lord Byron on the continent of Europe. Byron, meanwhile, was furious – 'I have besides a personal dislike to Vampires', he wrote, 'from the little acquaintance I have with them' – and urged the publisher John Murray to issue his *Fragment of a Story* (appended to his poem *Mazeppa*) as quickly as possible, in self-defence. 'Damn the Vampyre – what do I know of Vampyres?'

Polidori was disgraced, and died two years later – at the age of twenty-five – of brain damage, following a carriage accident. Byron, among others, immediately put it around that the doctor had committed suicide. Even in death, Dr Polidori was not to be allowed any dignity. He had been fired by Byron at the end of the Geneva summer. Since then, he had published an essay 'Upon the Source of Positive Pleasure' (1818), which denounced rank, wealth and power as empty illusions.

For the first thirty years of its literary life, between roughly 1820 and 1850, the vampire was to be indelibly associated with the public image of Lord Byron. This association tended to limit the possibilities of character development within the *genre*, but it did help to reinforce the malodorous reputation of the British aristocracy on the continent. Charles Robert Maturin began his Gothic novel *Melmoth the Wanderer* (1820) with an old Spanish crone screaming 'No English . . . Mother of God protect us . . . Avaunt Satan', which would suggest that Byron wannabes wandering around Europe had a similar reputation to some of today's Goth-attired, tattooed bikers.

The aristocratic vampire had been launched with the finest credentials.

A RED SEA

The vampire is as old as the world. Blood tastes of the sea – where we all come from. Although we normally associate the myth with Eastern Europe or Greece, probably because of epidemics that emanated from those regions in the eighteenth century, traces of vampirism are to be found in most cultures. Blood drained by the Lamiae, emissaries of the Triple Goddess Hecate; blood sucked by Lilith, the other woman in Adam's life; blood shed for dead Attis and mourning Cybele, the Great Mother; blood as taboo (the book of Genesis warns us not to eat 'flesh with the life thereof, which is the blood thereof'); blood for healing, for fertility, for rejuvenation; blood as unclean; blood sacrifices to the Nepalese Lord of Death or the Mongolian Vampire God. The pelican feeding her young with blood from her own breast. Drink ye all of this in remembrance of me . . .

Attempts to trace the origins and early development of the vampire myth have seldom been successful, perhaps because the lore is so synthetic. Montague Summers tried in two influential books – *The Vampire, His Kith and Kin* (1928) and *The Vampire in Europe* (1929) – to write a history of vampirism from earliest times to the present day, but succeeded only in showing how difficult it is to define the characteristics that exclusively belong to the vampire. The laboured analysis contained in these books was strangely digressive (this was not helped by the fact that Summers believed in vampirism 'to the letter') and the sources embroidered beyond all recognition (on one famous occasion, he mistook a popular penny-dreadful article for a scholarly dissertation). So Summers ended up telling a series of more or less nasty stories, with a couple of major detours to take in the complete works of Shakespeare and his beloved Restoration theatre. 'Of recent years,' he concluded, 'the histories of vampirism in England are perhaps few, but this is not so much because they do not occur as rather that they are carefully hushed up and stifled.' As a man who professed to be 'no votary of the cinematograph', he would presumably have found the current worldwide interest in vampirism utterly baffling.

But the family tree of the card-carrying vampire of modern European fiction – the *grand saigneur*, combining the beauty of Milton's Satan with the haughtiness of Byron's Fatal Man – as opposed to the genesis of the myth itself, is much more accessible. Some of the early Romantics, such as Goethe, Gottfried August Bürger and John Keats, based their vampire visions (loosely) on classical Greek and Roman manifestations. More often, vampire tales and poems in the nineteenth century (when the genre developed in two distinct directions, represented in this book by 'Lord Ruthven and his Clan' and 'The Tempestuous Loveliness of Terror'; see pages 149–278) were derived from folktales and eyewitness accounts of 'posthumous magic' in peasant communities, which dated from the period 1680–1760. Somehow, the inarticulate peasant vampires described by the commentators Joseph Pitton de Tournefort and Dom Augustin Calmet, Folkloric Vampires who attacked sheep and cows as often as their relatives, became the aristocratic hero-villains (like Milton's Satan, they tend to get all the good lines) of the Romantics. In the eyewitness accounts, the chubby vampires tended to have florid complexions – as if they had been drinking too much – swollen bodies, skin slippage, wide-open mouths full of blood and a halitotic stench. In Romantic fiction, they tended to be fashionably pallid and clean-shaven, with seductive voices and pouting lips, and they were always sexually attractive. In folklore, the vampire was likely to hurl himself or herself at the victim's chest or arm – to smother, as well as to suck. In fiction, the preferred erogenous zone was invariably the neck. It was quite a transformation: a special effect that lasted for the best part of a century.

THE NOBLE LORD

Some commentators have attributed the upward social mobility of the vampire, in a general way, to mythologies surrounding certain members of the British aristocracy in post-Enlightenment Europe, and especially France. The stereotype can be traced to various sources: anecdotes about Lord Rochester and the Restoration Court (Byron listed the plays of Thomas Otway as one of the key influences on the public image he chose to adopt); tales about George Augustus Selwyn, MP, whose hobby it apparently was (in an 'amateur' way, and for 'delight' rather than 'pleasure') to watch gruesome executions and tortures; or about the banker Sir John Lambert, who was said to have had bizarre views about cadaverous women ('he could only love girls who were dangerously thin ... and he had a private collection of mummified ladies') and to have combed revolutionary Paris for suitable specimens. The behaviour of these men could, at a stretch, be legitimized in theory by Edmund Burke's philosophical principle that 'the passions which turn on self-preservation, turn on pain and danger; they are delightful when we have an idea of pain and danger without being actually in such circumstances . . . Whatever excites this delight, I call *sublime*.'

More crucial than all these examples was the public image of Lord Byron himself (a calculated image, enshrining the principle that life could be treated as theatre, complete with satanic scowl, which he admitted was lifted from the Gothic villains of Mrs Radcliffe). In Paris, at the time Polidori's *Vampyre* was first published, boulevard gossips were unwittingly contributing to the sales of the book by spreading the rumour that the English Milord had murdered his mistress and 'enjoyed drinking her blood, from a cup made of her cranium'. Goethe is on record as having suggested offhandedly that 'there were probably one or two dead bodies in that man's past'. The phenomenal sales in Paris of Lady Caroline Lamb's novel *Glenarvon* (her revenge, after a much-publicized affair with Byron which went spectacularly wrong), with an Introduction that made explicit the association between the satanic Clarence de Ruthven, Lord Glenarvon, and Lord Byron ('Woe be to those who have ever loved Glenarvon!'), simply reinforced such rumours. So did editions of Lady Blessington's *Conversations with Lord Byron* (1834), which claimed that Byron had said, 'Do you know that when I have looked on some face that I love, imagination has often figured the changes that death must one day produce in it – the worm rioting on lips now smiling, the features of health changed to the livid and ghastly tints of putrefaction . . . this is one of my pleasures of imagination.' When Peter Schlemihl lost his shadow to the Devil in Adelbert von Chamisso's novella of 1814, it can have surprised no one that it was at a party arranged by a member of the English aristocracy.

Lamb's *Glenarvon* had been published in England on 9 May 1816, shortly after Byron left England for Geneva. Throughout the summer of 1816, Byron (who did not have immediate access to a copy) was increasingly apprehensive about what exactly she had written about their affair: on 23 June he asked, 'What – and who – the devil is *Glenarvon*?'; on 22 July he added, 'I have not even a guess at the contents – except for the very vague accounts I have heard – and I know but one thing which a woman can say to the purpose on such occasions and that she might as well for her own sake keep to herself

– which by the way they very rarely can.' He was particularly worried about the motto she had apparently chosen for her novel (adapted from his own *The Corsair* of 1814):

> He left a name to all succeeding times,
> Link'd with one virtue and a thousand crimes.

'If such be the posy,' he wrote, 'what should the ring be?'

By the beginning of August 1816, he had read the book; his immediate reaction was to consider himself 'libelled by her hate'. But by December of the same year, he had distanced himself enough from the whole affair to seem amused: 'It seems to me that, if the authoress had written the *truth*, and nothing but the truth – the whole truth – the romance would not only have been more *romantic*, but more entertaining. As for the likeness,' he added, rather uncharitably, 'the picture can't be good – I did not sit long enough.' Clearly, the question of the character of Clarence de Ruthven, Lord Glenarvon, had often been discussed during that extraordinary summer, and, for once, Byron was worried about what the public might make of his image. The association between Ruthven Glenarvon and the Satanic Lord is never made explicit in the book (at least, not in the English edition), but by making her hero-villain pay for his 'thousand crimes' (at the end of the story, he is pursued by a phantom ship), Lamb was, as Byron feared, enjoying her revenge:

> ... the heart of a libertine is iron, it softens when heated in the fires of lust, but it is cold and hard inside ...

> It was one of those faces which, having once beheld, we never afterwards forget. It seemed as if the soul of passion had been stamped and printed upon every feature. The eye beamed into life as it threw up its dark ardent gaze, with a look nearly of inspiration, while the proud curl of the upper lip expressed haughtiness and bitter contempt; yet, even mixed with these fierce characteristic feelings, an air of melancholy and dejection shaded over and softened every harsher expression.

> *Glenarvon*

This, as much as all the other villains, with their 'gaunt faces' and 'piercing eyes', who epitomized the metamorphoses of Satan in the Gothic novel, represents the prototype for the Byronic vampire. When Polidori wrote *The Vampyre*, he simply transposed the description to fit his 'Lord Ruthven' (history does not record what James, the real fifth Baron Ruthven, thought about all this). In *The Vampyre*, the character of Lady Mercer seems to have been based on Caroline Lamb, while the unstable relationship between Aubrey and Ruthven during and after their grand tour (admiration, disillusionment, disgust) mirrors closely what Polidori felt about Lord Byron's treatment of him in the summer of 1816. He may also have remembered one of the tales in the *Fantasmagoriana* – *La Morte Fiancée* – which featured a villainous Italian Marquis: 'His long and wan visage, his piercing look, had so little of attraction in them, that everyone would certainly have avoided him, had he not possessed a fund of entertaining stories.' Like Ruthven, the Italian Marquis of the ghost story specializes in destroying lesser mortals at the gaming table.

The contribution of this image in all its various incarnations – from Mrs Radcliffe's villains to the Byronic hero, from George Selwyn to Lord Byron himself – to the popular success of the vampire theme in the Paris and London of the 1820s was clearly decisive, and set the tone for the more ephemeral works in the genre. Works such as Cyprien Bérard's two-volume *Lord Ruthwen ou les Vampires* (Paris, 1820), which chronicled the adventures of 'ce Don Juan vampirique' (or, as a contemporary critic put it, 'ce Lovelace des tombeaux') on a bloody grand tour around Venice, Florence, Naples, Modena, the Tyrol, Poland, Moravia, Athens, Benares (Varanasi) and Baghdad. Each of these stopovers gave the wicked Milord a chance to return from the dead to debauch a blushing bride, before moving on to the next, and the novel finished with the threat, 'We could perhaps publish Lord Ruthwen's *History of My First Life*, if we are encouraged to do so by some success with this publication.' A postscript referred to *The Vampyre* as 'without doubt the most extraordinary of all Lord Byron's compositions – extraordinary in the germ of his idea rather than in the execution, where we do not recognize his touch'. Needless to say, this tale of 'exquisite debauchery' had only the remotest connection with 'the mad superstition of vampirism, a disorder of the imagination of ignorant people, which is maybe only the result of an illness not yet understood'. This disclaimer was echoed by the *London Magazine*'s review of St John Dorset's *The Vampire: A Tragedy in Five Acts* (April 1821, set in ancient Egypt), which the anonymous critic reckoned had little to do with either the Folkloric Vampire or 'the revolting egotism which pervades every page of Lord Byron's works'. 'That such compositions as Lord Byron's could retain their popularity', the critic concluded, 'was impossible: they are the children of a diseased imagination and came into the world bearing within them the seeds of early dissolution.' He couldn't have been wider of the mark if he had tried.

For the vampire genre in the nineteenth century was to grow in two distinct but related directions, both very fruitful. One owed much to Polidori's *Vampyre* (thus to the Byronic legend, as filtered through boulevard gossip), the other to Shelley's 'tempestuous loveliness of terror' (thus to the kind of psychosexual trauma that Byron's reading of *Christabel* – an archetypal *femme fatale* – induced; see pages 22–23). The Polidori strain was to be reincarnated in French and English melodramas of the 1820s, in a marathon penny-dreadful in the 1840s, as Count Azzo von Klatka in Karl von Wachsmann's *Mysterious Stranger* (1844, tr. 1854) and, eventually, as Count Dracula himself. The Shelley strain was to be reincarnated in works by E. T. A. Hoffmann, Théophile Gautier, the decadents Charles Baudelaire and Lautréamont, and, eventually, Bram Stoker. *Dracula*, as we shall see, represents a *synthesis* of the two main developments in the genre and more besides.

Edmund Burke had written: 'to make anything very terrible, obscurity in general seems to be necessary'. The painter Henry Fuseli went further when, in 1802, he defined the difference between the legitimate depiction of terror and the inadmissible depiction of horror: 'We cannot sympathize with what we detest or despise, nor fully pity what we shudder at or loathe . . . mangling is contagious, and spreads aversion from the slaughterman to the victim.' The Polidori/Byron/Ruthven vampire was to show that 'mangling' was not necessarily detestable or despicable (it could even be fun), although its possibilities for development were limited, and it could too easily be parodied. The Christabel/Shelley/Gautier vampire was to show that maybe Burke and Fuseli had a point after all.

Before the events of 1816, there had been some isolated references to vampirism, or to the iconography of vampirism, in prose literature – such as the Ogre's seven little daughters, with their fresh complexions and 'very big mouths, with long teeth, very sharp, very far apart', in Charles Perrault's version of *Hop O' My Thumb* (1697); or the lost race of people at the earth's core in *Protocosmos* who feed on the blood of their marital partners, in Giacomo Casanova's *Icosameron* (1788); or the Baron d'Olnitz, who believes (literally) that 'love is like rabies' in Jacques-Antoine de Révéroni Saint-Cyr's Sadian novel *Pauliska* (1798); or the obese Count de Gernande, who in his remote château near Dijon bleeds his wife to death to satisfy his gourmet's appetite for blood, in the Marquis de Sade's *Justine, or the Misfortunes of Virtue* (1791); or the Ghoul in Nights 945–48 of the *Thousand and One Nights*, who is dispatched in a way that is (to my knowledge) unique in the literature, by a sharp kick in the testicles – and even more sustained attempts to visit classical variations on the myth, by early Romantics from Germany. But those who were involved in that 'wet, ungenial summer' succeeded in fusing the various elements of vampirism into a coherent literary genre for the first time. The long-term consequence can still be seen today, any night, especially at the 'witching hour', all over the Western world.

LIGHTEN OUR DARKNESS

Eyriès's collection of ghost stories *Fantasmagoriana* did not, of course, conjure up the 'kiss of death' theme of *Les Portraits de Famille* – the story that inspired the ghost-story competition in the Villa Diodati – from out of thin air. The Gothic novelists had sometimes referred *en passant* to the theme of vampirism, but they did not exploit the idea in a thoroughgoing way. So the source, as Eyriès acknowledged, was from an earlier period, predating the burning of the Gothic flame – a period when philosophers of the Age of Reason in France, Germany and Italy were trying to come to grips with well-publicized epidemics of vampirism emanating especially from Eastern Europe. The Preface to *Fantasmagoriana* refers specifically to the work of

Dom Augustin Calmet and his critics, as well as to Voltaire's *Dictionnaire Philosophique* (1764) and to more credulous works by cranky scientists dating from the more recent age of illuminism. The anonymous Introduction to Polidori's *Vampyre* (written for the *New Monthly Magazine*, April 1819) also refers to Calmet's 'great work upon this subject', but adds 'the veracious Tournefort's' account of his travels in the Levant to its list of sources. There is no record of any discussion about these books having taken place in summer 1816 (although Robert Southey was discussed, and he had appended both the French botanist Tournefort's account and an anecdote from Calmet *in extenso* to his vampire poem *Thalaba the Destroyer* some fifteen years before), but the 'epidemics' they analysed must nevertheless bc considered as crucial stimuli to the success of the vampire genre in the nineteenth century.

In his *Dictionnaire Infernal* (published in the 1820s), Jacques Collin de Plancy came to this ironic conclusion about the vampire epidemics of the early eighteenth century:

> The most astonishing thing about these accounts of vampirism is that they shared the honour of astounding the eighteenth century with our greatest philosophers. They terrified Prussia, Silesia, Bohemia and the whole of northern Europe, at precisely the same time as wise men in England and France were attacking superstition and popular error with the utmost confidence.

These epidemics had occurred in the interior of the Istrian peninsula (1672); in East Prussia near the Baltic coast (1710 and 1721); Hungary, along the Carpathian Basin (1725–30); in the Habsburg kingdom of Serbia (1725–32); in East Prussia again (1750); in the Prussian province of Silesia (1755); Ottoman Wallachia (1756) and Russia (1772). But the 'wise men' were only interested in those manifestations which involved named individuals, or which were the subject of formal government reports 'duly attested' – the cases of Giure Grando (in Khring/Kringa, Istria); Peter Plogojowitz/Petar Blagojevjch (in Kisilova, possibly modern Kisiljevo, in Austrian Serbia); Arnold/Arnod/Arnaut Paole (in Medvegia/Medvegna, also in Austrian Serbia); and the vampires of Olmutz/Olomouc in the Habsburg Margraviate of Moravia. Of these, the example that attracted the most interest (even Louis XV of France and, according to Horace Walpole, George II of England took note) was that of Arnold Paole – an ex-militiaman from Serbia – in 1731–32. Walpole was to write of the Hanoverian monarch to his regular correspondent Anne Fitzpatrick, Lady Ossory, 'I know that our late King, though not apt to believe more than his neighbours, had no doubt of the existence of vampires, and their banquets on the dead.'

So serious were reports of mass hysteria from the village of Medvegia, near Belgrade in Austrian Serbia, that the Austrian government 'felt obliged to intervene'. Parts of Serbia had been ceded to Austria as recently as 1718, at the Peace of Passarowitz. Two public inquiries were launched by the Emperor – the first in December 1731 led by infectious-diseases specialist Glaser, the second in January 1732 under the supervision of a Regimental Field Surgeon of a Foot Regiment, Johannes Flückinger. The Austrians were occupying substantial parts of both Serbia and Wallachia, and they evidently wanted to find out more about the bizarre local customs near their garrison towns – particularly if these customs led to breaches of the peace. It was the direct involvement of Austrian authorities that gave the 'epidemics' international visibility. The findings of the public inquiry have often been embellished beyond all rec-ognition (by various periodicals in the eighteenth century, by Dr Herbert Mayo in his *Letters on the Truths Contained in Popular Superstitions*, 1847, and by Dudley Wright and Montague Summers in the twentieth century), but the document itself, published in Belgrade and Nuremberg in 1732, under the title *Seen & Discovered*, requires no such embroidery.

> Having heard from various quarters that . . . so-called vampires have been
> responsible for the death of several persons, by sucking their blood, I have
> been commissioned by a local Honorable Supreme Commander to throw
> some light on this question . . . This report has been compiled with the help
> of the captain of the Stallath Company of *heyduks*,* the standard-bearer,

---

*A *heyduk* (or *haiduk*) was originally a robber or brigand or, in more modern terms, a social bandit. The term was still used in this sense in parts of Serbia at that time, but in Hungary and Austrian Serbia *heyduk* had come to signify a company of foot soldiers (who were granted some social status and control over a tract of land in return for services rendered). In Poland the term meant personal attendants of the nobility. Here, *heyduk* seems to have the Hungarian and other of the most respected *heyduks* of the neighbourhood. After much questioning, these *heyduks* have declared unanimously that *about five years ago a* heyduk *of the area, named Arnold Paole, broke his neck, falling from a hay wagon.* The said Arnold Paole had told various people, in the course of previous years, that he had been troubled by a vampire, near Gossowa,† in Turkish Serbia.

(a) That is why he himself ate earth taken from the tomb of a vampire, and smeared himself in the blood of a vampire (as is the custom) to cleanse himself of its cursed influence. However, twenty or thirty days after his death, several persons complained that the said Arnold Paole had come back to torment them, and that he had caused the deaths of four others. In order to put a stop to this danger, their *hadnak* – who had been present at such events before – suggested that the vampire be disinterred: this was duly done, forty days after his death, and he was found to be perfectly preserved. His flesh had not decomposed, his eyes were filled with fresh blood, which also flowed from his nose, mouth and ears, soiling his shirt and funeral shroud. His fingernails and toenails had dropped off, as had his skin, and others had grown through in their place, from which it was concluded that he was a true vampire. So, according to the custom of those regions, a stake was driven through his heart. But, as this was being performed:

(b) He gave a great shriek, and an enormous quantity of blood spurted from his body. The body was burned that same day and the ashes cast into his tomb. But the people in these parts claim that all those who are tormented and killed by a vampire become vampires in turn when they die. That is why it was decided to disinter and execute the four corpses

---

meaning (hence, 'the captain of the Company of *heyduks*'). Paole, as a *heyduk*, had moved to the village from the Turkish-controlled part of Serbia, 'where he had been bitten'. In a later account (as we shall see) he was accused of being a 'Ministerial Tool'. The interesting ambiguity of the term (in annexed and 'free' Serbia) may have something to do with the projection of vampiric characteristics on to so many *heyduks* by Serbian peasants ('vampire' equals 'collaborator', perhaps). Or with confusion over national identity.

†The spelling (and location) of Gossowa varies through all the accounts. Sometimes it is 'Cassowa in Turkish Servia'; sometimes 'Cashaw, upon the borders of Turkish Servia'. I have left the spelling and location as in one of the original accounts. It is perhaps today's Kosovo.

mentioned above, in the same way. The affair went even further: for it had been argued persuasively that the said Arnold Paole had not only attacked human beings, but cattle as well, and sucked out their blood.

(c) Those who were said to have eaten meat from these contaminated beasts, and who had died as a result, were presumed vampires in turn; in the space of three months, seventeen persons of various ages had died within two or three days, some of them without any previous illness. Further:

(d) The *heyduk* Jowiza [or Jobira] let it be known that his daughter-in-law [or stepdaughter] Stanacka [or Stanjoika], having gone to bed a fortnight before, in perfect health, had woken up at midnight screaming horribly; terrified, she claimed that she had been *touched on the neck* by a man who had been dead for more than nine weeks, the son of a *heyduk* called Milloe [or Milloje]. From that moment, she became weaker and weaker from pains in the chest and died on the third day. That is why this same afternoon, after hearing various witnesses, we went to the cemetery, accompanied by the village *heyduks*, in order to open the suspect tombs and examine the corpses inside. This examination and dissection revealed the following facts to us:

(1) A woman named Stana, who died in childbirth at the age of twenty, three months ago, after a three-day illness, had claimed that she washed in the blood of a vampire to cleanse herself from all possible taint. Otherwise both she and her child – who had died just after birth and because of careless burial had been half-eaten by dogs – would also become vampires. She was in an excellent state of preservation. Cutting open her body, we found much fresh blood . . . her intestines, lungs, liver, stomach and spleen were as fresh as those of a healthy, living person. Her vessels were not filled with clotted blood, as is usual . . . fresh and living skin had grown recently, as had finger and toenails.

(2) A woman named Miliza [or Milica], aged sixty, dead after a three-month illness and buried for some ninety days, still had much liquid blood in her chest, and the other *viscera* were like those mentioned above, in a fresh condition. During the dissection, the *heyduks* present were astonished to see that her body had become much plumper since her death, and were unanimous in affirming, knowing her as they had done since her youth, that

in her lifetime she was extremely thin . . . They also affirmed that it was she who had started the spread of vampires this time, for she had eaten some mutton previously contaminated by vampires.

(3) A child of eight days old, buried for ninety days, was also judged to be in a vampiric state.

And so on, with similar descriptions of eleven more corpses, including an eighteen-day-old child and mother Ruscha [or Ruzica], a *heyduk*'s son Milloe [or Milloje] and the son's victim Stanacka [or Stanjoika]. Of these eleven, eight were 'judged to be in a vampiric state'; the rest had decomposed, although with some 'the earth and graves were like those of the nearby vampires'. Stanacka still bore the marks of her night visitor; 'Under her right ear, we could clearly make out a bluish scar, about the length of a finger.'

> After the examinations had taken place, we ordered the heads of all these vampires to be cut off by some local gypsies, their bodies to be burned, and their ashes scattered in the River Morava, while the corpses found to be in a state of decomposition were returned to their graves. I affirm – together with the assistant medical officers dispatched to me – that all these things took place just as we have reported them at Medvegia, in Serbia, on 7 January 1732. Signed: Johannes Flückinger, Regimental Field Surgeon (and four others).*

Predictably enough, this unusually detailed report caused a sensation. At the annual Leipzig fair in 1732, a cheap version of the Arnold Paole story became an instant bestseller. On 3 March the *Dutch Gleaner* (which was very popular in Versailles court circles) ran a detailed and suitably embellished account. This stimulated a lively correspondence, so the journal featured another article a fortnight later, summarizing the various views expressed. (Some English periodicals, including the *London Journal*, the *Gentleman's Magazine, Applebee's*

---

*This report was compiled on the orders of the local Austrian Supreme Commander, acting on behalf of the Emperor. It is perhaps significant – as was later pointed out – that all the 'suspect' *heyduks* and their families were Slavs belonging to the Orthodox Church, for the report was launched by an Imperial power which was, of course, Roman Catholic.

Journal and *The Craftsman*, cobbled together translations or adaptations, which appeared between 11 March and 27 May 1732.) The two *Gleaner* articles were both reprinted in the *Mercure Historique et Politique* for October 1736. Dom Augustin Calmet, Benedictine Abbot of Senones, anthologized most of these articles in his full-length *Treatise on the Apparitions of Spirits and Demons, and on the Revenants and Vampires of Hungary, Bohemia, Moravia and Silesia* (Paris, 1746), later to be known in England as *The Phantom World*. This book attracted a lot of attention among the chattering classes. Eventually, King Louis XV (always one to keep up with changes in fashion) took a personal interest and asked the Duc de Richelieu to find out as much as he could about 'these vampires' and what lay behind the Austrian reports. This, too, may have had a political motive. In 1750, four years after the first publication of Calmet's *Treatise*, there was a serious riot in Paris which began because of rumours about why so many children had recently become missing persons: the rumour was that Louis XV had in fact kidnapped them in order to drink their blood, a prescription suggested to him by the royal physicians to keep him young and healthy. In such a social atmosphere, it was important for the King to find out exactly what had occasioned such rumours.

The fashionable journals in London as well made much of the Arnold Paole story for a season or two. When the poet Alexander Pope was writing to Dr William Oliver of Bath (he of Bath Oliver biscuit fame) in February 1740 about a recent illness, and various embellishments he was making to the design of his grotto in Twickenham, it seems to have been *de rigueur* for him to make reference to the activities of the Eastern European bloodsuckers. In the letter Pope's illness became his 'death', the grotto his 'burial' and the favours he was asking of his friends (such as Dr Oliver) – for 'Marbles and Minerals' and other grotto materials – his 'plague':

> Since his Burial (at Twitnam) he has been seen sometimes in Mines and Caverns and been very troublesome to those who dig Marbles and Minerals: if ever he has walked above ground, he has been (like the vampires in Germany) such a terror to all sober and innocent people, that many wish a stake were drove thro' him to keep him quiet in his Grave.

But the interest aroused in intellectual circles by this prototypical example of 'peasant superstition' lasted much longer. Between the late 1720s and the 1760s learned essays on questions relating to superstition were by no means uncommon, for those philosophers in Europe who were pledged to the idea of progress clearly enjoyed amassing evidence about what they called the 'primitive' or 'dark' areas. The reports of 1731–32 directly stimulated at least twelve treatises and four dissertations; at one time or another the debate involved such leading figures of the Enlightenment as the Marquis d'Argens, Voltaire, Denis Diderot, Jean-Jacques Rousseau, Gerhard van Swieten (Empress Maria Theresa's personal physician and adviser) and the Chevalier de Jaucourt (a prolific contributor to Diderot's and D'Alembert's great *Encyclopedie*). The era known in the textbooks as the Age of Reason, and seen by many historians as the origin of the modern secular mind, was much perplexed by the question of vampirism.

Of the serious works that were published immediately after the reports of 1732, some sought the origins of vampiric manifestations in 'the work of Satan', suggesting that vampires were reanimated by the Devil himself. Others adopted a more reductionist or naturalistic stance, stressing that there *must* be some natural explanation (medical, that is) to account for the state of the corpses, the superstition *and* the reaction of the local community. An anonymous doctor suggested that 'the devil was possessing these corpses, and using them for supernatural purposes'; Michael Ranft, a rather humourless German theologian, opined that the dead *could* sometimes influence the living but that they could *never* take the form of resurrected corpses (this, in a book with the deathless title *That Dead Men Chew in Their Coffins*, 1729/1734). A pamphleteer from Leipzig preferred to believe that this was a simple case of food poisoning ('which would be contagious'), and a German philosopher blamed the whole thing on the effects of opium ('and other drugs') which could apparently cause collective nightmares, especially in Turkey.

Jean-Baptiste de Boyer, the Marquis d'Argens, in his *Lettres Juives* (1738), attempted to explain away the symptoms of vampirism in corpses ('systemati-cally', as he put it) by proving that the fresh blood that was reported to have been found in vampires' tombs was, in fact, nothing of the sort: 'Juices in the dead Body by nitreas and sulphureous Particles fermenting with them, may furnish a Liquor nearly *resembling* blood.' D'Argens reckoned that his conclusions about 'the physical reasons for all this' had been confirmed by a simple experiment, for which he thoughtfully included the recipe: take an ovenware dish and mix one part milk with two parts oil of Tartar; bring to the boil; the liquor will change colour, from white to red, as the salts in the oil of Tartar begin to dissolve the fatty substances in the milk, and the contents of the dish will eventually be converted into '*une espèce de sang*' (at least, the consistency and colour will *look like* blood). Thus, by extension, it was not beyond the bounds of possibility that juices in a dead body had been converted into a liquor 'nearly *resembling* blood', as the heat of the sun fermented the nitrous particles in the soil of the grave, and at the same time caused these nitrous particles to insinuate themselves into the corpse. This reaction, or fermentation, could have dissolved the coagulum occasioned by death, and made it gradually become liquid in the veins. Calmet later repeated the experiment. D'Argens's empirical argument was intended to prove that one need not deny all the facts contained in the 'attested' certificates in order to rid oneself of a belief in vampires – a simultaneous acceptance of the documentation (after all, the reports had been signed by notable people) and *rejection* of the 'supernatural' account. These reports were indeed describing what the officials had seen with their own eyes – it was just that they did not know how to interpret or explain phenomena that could be natural. They attributed them to an *external* invigorating force.

Other explanations of the Paole phenomenon (and of less well-publicized vampires) over the years covered the whole spectrum of 'reasonable' arguments (and, incidentally, set the tone for future discussions of the subject, right up to the present day). They included:

Premature burial – evidence of vampirism might, it was thought, be evidence of the last struggles of those we would now call cataplectics to free themselves from their premature graves;

Unnaturally well-preserved corpses – perhaps the result of soil conditions or the absence of air, which could delay corruption, the 'great shriek' that was heard during the staking ritual being simply the explosion of gas from such a corpse; thin people were thought to decompose more slowly than others;

Natural growth of nails and skin after death, and the failure of flesh to decay in certain circumstances – for example, after a very sudden death without illness; the falling away of nails and skin was seen as the growth of *new* nails and skin;

Plague – the symptoms of the victim – pallor, listlessness, fever, nightmares – were thought to be those of the plague. The transmission of the 'vampire's curse' from predator to victim, who then became predator in turn, was a graphic way of explaining the rapid spread of plague germs. Vampires and rats tended to be close companions in European folklore from an early stage, and there *was* an epidemic of the plague in East Prussia in 1710. The initiator of the plague could become the vampire scapegoat for medically inexplicable phenomena;

Rabies, in particular, was to become a later variation on this theme: there were well-documented epidemics of rabies in Hungary (1721–28), Saxony (1725–26) and Prussia (1785–89), and the analogies between the two types of infection – biting, followed by animal-style behaviour and an unquenchable thirst – were to be the subject of considerable research in the twentieth century;

Theological confusion, for example in those areas where the Greek Orthodox Church was making inroads on Roman Catholicism, and the Church's ruling on the corruption of the body had become ambiguous; or where old folkloric survivals were in conflict with the Christian church. Belief in vampirism predated Christianity, but Christianity added many elements to the lore and rituals;

Heresy, in the form of a satirical reversal of the Roman Catholic Communion service, with the vampire as a hellish imitation of Christ (Diderot's *Encyclopédie* was later to extend the application of this in its famous index entry 'Cannibalism: *see* Eucharist');

A type of 'community superstition' about some incident in the past which tended to manifest itself in times of national defeat or foreign occupation. Medvegia was, as we have seen, annexed to Austria in 1718, and in some accounts Arnold Paole, like the Seven Sleepers of Ephesus or Rip Van Winkle, wakes up to find himself under a new regime;

Corrupt priests – Pope Benedict XIV, Prospero Lambertini, for example, is alleged to have been convinced that the real source of the trouble was 'those priests who give credit to such stories, in order to encourage simple folk to pay them for exorcisms and masses'. Lambertini had inserted a reference to the Paole controversy in the second edition of a text he wrote on canonization, which was published in Venice in 1766. There is no such reference to vampires in the original edition (Bologna, 1734), so it is fair to assume that Pope Benedict had first been introduced to them by reading Dom Calmet's work on the subject in the interim. In Chapter 21 of *On Canonization* (the return of the dead to life), Lambertini summarizes the story of Arnold Paole and concludes that:

> Whether the discussion is about corpses found in a state of incorruption, or about the blood which flows from them or about the growth of hair and nails after death, or about the decapitation of vampires or the cremation of their bodies, with the scattering of their ashes in water, *everything* seems to depend on how much faith, or trust, we have in those who witnessed the events.

These 'so-called vampires' (*'vampiros dictos'*) may, in fact, be simply attributable to over-active imaginations, or to blind terror about something else – something more tangible, such as the plague perhaps. For the Pope, the problem was not so much the interpretation, as the *facts* described in the reports. In Louis Antoine de Caraccioli's *Life of Pope Benedict XIV* (Paris, 1783), Lambertini is said to have told an archbishop of the Greek Orthodox Church that the real source of the trouble was some unscrupulous priests in remote rural areas. 'The Pope,' adds Caraccioli, 'too enlightened not to know for sure that vampirism is a work of ignorance and superstition, hastened to reply in these terms.' Some twentieth-century scholars have, however, questioned this attempt to present Pope Benedict as a card-carrying figure of the Enlightenment, and the evidence on which it is based.

It should be added that the most recent analyses of the eyewitness accounts of 1731–32, by professional folklorists and specialists in 'vampire forensics', have concluded that the 'manifestations' represent attempts by preliterate communities to make sense of what we would today call 'contagion', 'decomposition', 'funerary customs' and 'apotropaics' (ways of keeping evil at bay), to make sense of the normal processes associated with death and decay, such as the bloating of corpses, skin slippage, the falling away of nails and skin, the temporary nature of *rigor mortis*, the emission of blood from the mouth and nose, and decomposition at different rates. But, such analyses add, before we dismiss these preliterate attempts at cause and effect – which tend to emphasize 'who did it' rather than 'how it can possibly have happened' – perhaps with an early twenty-first-century enlightened shrug of the shoulders, it is as well to consider the initial reactions of post-literate societies to something like the Aids epidemic, or Ebola. The resemblances can be startling.

At the time, there were so many of these 'explanations' going the rounds that a contemporary article entitled 'Political Vampyres', reprinted from *The Craftsman* in the London *Gentleman's Magazine* (May 1732), commonsensibly decided to send up the whole business of explanation, while making a few new suggestions in the process:

> This account of *Vampyres*, you'll observe, comes from the Eastern Part of the World, always remarkable for its *Allegorical Style*. The States of *Hungary* are in subjection to the *Turks* and *Germans*, and govern'd by a pretty hard Hand; which obliges them to couch all their Complaints under *Figures*. This Relation seems to be of the same kind.
>
> These *Vampyres* are said to torment and kill the *Living* by *sucking out all their Blood*; and a *ravenous Minister*, in this part of the World, is compared to a *Leech* or *Bloodsucker*, and carries his Oppressions beyond the Grave, by anticipating the *publick Revenues*, and entailing a Perpetuity of *Taxes*, which must gradually drain the Body Politick of its Blood and Spirits. In like manner, Persons who groan under the Burthens of such a *Minister*, by selling or mortgaging their estates, torment their *unhappy Posterity*, and become *Vampyres* when dead. Paul Arnold, who is call'd a Heyduke, was only a *Ministerial Tool*, because it is said he had kill'd but 4 Persons; whereas, if he had been a *Vampyre* of any Rank, we should probably have

heard of his *Ten Thousands ... As to the driving A Stake through the Heart of Arnold, at which he gave an horrid Groan,* this seems an argument that the whole Story is a Fable, us'd to convey a satirical Invective against some *living Oppressor ...* The Blood which Arnold lost might figurate the making him refund the *corrupt Wages* which he had suck'd out of the Veins of his Countrymen. History, especially our own, supplies us with so many Instances of *Vampyres*, in this Sense, that it would fill Volumes to enumerate them ... Private Persons may be *Vampyres*, or *Blood-Suckers*, i.e. *Sharpers, Usurers, and Stockjobbers, unjust Stewards* and *the dry Nurses of the Great Estates*; but nothing less than the Power of a *Treasury* can raise up a compleat *Vampyre.*

Oddly enough, Dr Johnson missed a trick when he omitted vampires altogether from his *Dictionary* (1755). (The word, incidentally, first entered the English language in print in 1734 – probably as a direct result of Arnold Paole's fall from that hay wagon.) But this satirical line of thought was to run and run. In October 1785, for example, the *Universal Register* featured a short tale in which a get-rich-quick narrator is robbed of his profits by thieves he calls 'vampires'. The word still required a footnote, though, in which Western Europe could express superiority over the East:

> In Poland and some other countries, a notion is entertained that some persons after they are dead and buried, have the power of sucking others till they die and to them they give the name 'vampire'.

In the Introduction to his gory poem *The Vampyre* (1810), John Stagg suggested that 'If it had not been for a lucky thought of the clergy, who ingeniously recommended staking them in their graves, we should by this time have had a greater swarm of blood-suckers than we have at present, numerous as they are.'

Even in 1746, when Dom Augustin Calmet first published his famous *Treatise,* the original vampire anthology, he was criticized by (among others) fellow members of his Benedictine Order for bothering to substantiate, or refute, bedtime horror stories. Calmet was probably France's most respected biblical scholar of the eighteenth century, renowned for his attempts to popularize scriptural exegesis – he also put together a forty-nine-volume study of the Bible – and it was felt by many that the time and effort he had devoted to compiling anecdotes about vampires were evidence of senility (he was seventy-four), intellectual decay or both. This response (which did nothing to stop the various editions of his *Treatise* from becoming bestsellers) combined with Voltaire's later remarks to create an image of Calmet as a plodding, credulous and over-literal crank. In fact, the *Treatise* took full note of current 'explanations' (premature burial, soil conditions, rats and mice chewing on funeral shrouds, normal growth of hair and nails after death, differing rates of decay in corpses, regional superstition and so on) and his conclusion is studiously open-ended:

> Thanks be to God, we are by no means credulous. We avow that all the light which science can throw on this fact discovers none of the causes of it. Nevertheless, we cannot refuse to believe that to be true which is juridically attested by persons of probity . . .
>
> But the stories told of these apparitions, and all the distress caused by these supposed vampires, are totally without solid proof. I am not surprised that the Sorbonne has condemned the bloody and violent retribution wrought on these corpses; but it is astonishing that the magistrates and secular bodies have not employed their authority and legal force to put an end to it.
>
> This is a mysterious and difficult matter, and I leave bolder and more proficient minds to resolve it.

Calmet deplores the hysteria that had surrounded outbreaks of vampirism, if only because there was always the possibility of decapitating or hammering a stake through the heart of a living person for unwittingly spreading the plague. And he points out that even in the original report of 1732, there are certain clues that provide ammunition for a 'reasonable' analysis: Paole told various people *before* he died that he thought he must be in danger of becoming a vampire; the events are closely associated with the incidence of 'animal disease'; and there are internal inconsistencies in the account. But most of Calmet's other judgments were later thought to have been *too* open-ended. His argument was that either there *were* vampires – in which case there must be 'solid proof', and also, Calmet added, some reference in Scripture which would locate this proof within an equally solid theological context – or there were not – in which case there was no point at all in studying them. Calmet's *Treatise*, like most of the ponderous theological and philosophical theses it anthologized, assumed an unproblematic relationship between the subject (vampiric manifestations) and the evidence (eyewitness accounts and scriptural legitimization of them). He could not see the difference between the 'attested' facts and their interpretation.

In the end, he said, 'We must remain silent on this matter, since it has not pleased God to reveal to us either the extent of the demon's power, or the way in which such things may come to pass.' And then, 'Supposing there be any reality in the fact of these apparitions of vampires, shall they be attributed to God, to angels, to the spirits of these ghosts, or to the devil?' Saints, as well as vampires, had bodies that were immune to decay.

Nevertheless, on *first* publication, the *Treatise* represented a tentative step towards the critical method that a little later in the century was to become more commonplace; by the time the great *Encyclopédie* was published, Calmet's caution and circumspection seemed out of date, and his subject matter not worthy of such a 'proficient mind'. Under 'Vampire' (*Hist. des Superstit.*), Louis de Jaucourt wrote: 'Father Calmet has written an absurd book on this subject, a book one would not have thought him capable of writing. It only goes to show how far the human mind is prone to superstition.' And in his *Historical Treatise on Apparitions* (Paris, 1751), Nicolas Lenglet Dufresnoy challenged Calmet's uncritical presentation of second-hand anecdotes ('the true, the doubtful and the false are all put together, without any coherent principle for distinguishing them') and expressed concern about some of Calmet's theological judgments (for example, his ruling on 'the resurrection of infidels'). Dufresnoy concluded that Calmet should have thought more about the possible impact of some of his bizarre anecdotes on 'feeble minds – the number of which greatly exceeds clever ones'.

However, another wave of vampirism, this time on the Silesian border, was reported just as the Calmet controversy was at its height. Empress Maria Theresa had been so shocked that another 'barbarous trial of poor dead men' had taken place, and 'so profoundly indignant' about the 'dark, disturbed

imagination of the common people', that she had sent her personal physician and adviser, Gerhard van Swieten, to prepare a survey on 'posthumous
magic'. This medical survey, which was written in 1755, adopted a stance that
was far removed from the hint of defensiveness contained in the report of
1732. It was later published under the title *Vampyrismus*.

> Posthumous magic is to be found where ignorance reigns, and is very prob-
> ably the work of the Greek schismatics . . . One of the vampires 'executed'
> was said to have been swollen with blood, since the executioner, a thoroughly
> reliable man, no doubt, in matters concerning his trade, claimed that when
> he cut up bodies which were sentenced to be burned, a great quantity of
> blood gushed forth. Nevertheless, he afterwards modestly agreed that this
> great quantity was about a spoonful – and this is a very different matter . . .
> One would have to be an ignorant quack to find evidence of the supernatural
> merely in the presence of such facts, which are actually very common . . .
> Sacrilege was committed, the sanctity of tombs was violated, the reputation
> of the dead and their families was sullied, the bodies of children who died
> in innocence were put into the hands of the executioner . . . Where are the
> laws that authorize such anomalies? What a tragedy! This makes me so
> angry that I see I shall have to end here in order not to become carried away.

The immediate result of this survey was a series of forceful legislative measures taken by Maria Theresa to combat the spread of 'so-called vampires and
posthumous magic' (March 1755) and 'superstition and magic' (August 1756).
These removed from the parish priests, inquisitors and local authorities all
power to deal with alleged vampires. In future, central government officials
would handle any such manifestations – especially if they seemed to threaten
public order. The long-term result was to rekindle the philosophical debate on
the subject in Germany, France and Italy. One Italian commentator blamed
'vampirism' on 'a certain contagious disease'. Another, Giuseppe Davanzati,
the Archbishop of Trani and a friend of Prospero Lambertini, asked, 'Why
is this demon so partial to base-born plebeians? Why is it always peasants,
carters, shoemakers and innkeepers? Why has the demon never been known
to assume the form of a man of quality, a scholar, a philosopher, a theologian,

a landowner or a bishop? I will tell you why. It is because men of education and men of quality are not so easily deceived as idiots and men of low birth and therefore do not so easily allow themselves to be fooled by appearances.' It was up to the educated and the enlightened (such as the Archbishop) to take the place of ignorant, credulous parish priests as 'examples to the half-witted and the ignorant'. Eventually, this type of élitism was to be turned on its head by a characteristic contribution from Voltaire, in the supplement to his *Dictionnaire Philosophique*:

> What! Vampires in our Eighteenth Century? Yes ... in Poland, Hungary, Silesia, Moravia, Austria and Lorraine – there was no talk of vampires in London, or even Paris. I admit that in these two cities there were speculators, tax officials and businessmen who sucked the blood of the people in broad daylight, but they were not dead (although they were corrupted enough). These true bloodsuckers did not live in cemeteries: they preferred beautiful places ... Kings are not, properly speaking, vampires. The true vampires are the churchmen who eat at the expense of both the king *and* the people.

And in the *Salon of 1767*, Diderot criticized 'the vermin which devours and destroys our vampires, by pouring out – drop by drop – the blood they have sucked from *us*'.

But against the icy blasts of d'Argens, de Jaucourt, van Swieten, Voltaire, Diderot and others, Jean-Jacques Rousseau alone continued to take Calmet's anthology seriously. He was not so much concerned (as the others were) with 'explaining' peasant superstition from a distance, naturalistically, or with the pedantry of churchmen (how many vampires could stand on the head of a pin, perhaps); his concern was with the way in which Calmet had argued his point.

In one sense, surely, there could be no doubt that vampires really did exist – that is, in the minds of those army officers, civil servants and priests who solemnly swore after they had examined the post-mortem evidence that they had witnessed their presence. For 'if there is in this world one story that has been attested, it is just that of vampires', Rousseau wrote in his open *Letter to Christophe de Beaumont, Archbishop of Paris* (1762). 'No evidence is lacking – depositions, certificates of notables, surgeons, priests and magistrates. The proof *in law* is utterly complete . . . Yet with all this,' he continued, 'who actually *believes* in vampires? Will we all be condemned for not believing in them?' In an unpublished note on 'attested vampirism', which he drafted following the *Letter to Beaumont* (preparing himself for further attacks from the clergy), Rousseau reiterated this point and referred to an article in the *Gazette des Gazettes* of 1 November 1765 for further endorsement.

That article had supplemented a fairly standard (and fairly inaccurate) account of the vampire epidemics – in particular, the stories of Arnold Paole and Peter Plogojowitz – with a critical commentary on the evidence which once again raised the question of how such evidence might be judged or attested. The anonymous Berlin correspondent of the *Gazette* had concluded:

> This opinion – that the epidemics happened exactly as reported – strange as it may seem, is proved by so many facts that no one can reasonably doubt its validity, given the quality of the witnesses who have certified the authenticity of those facts . . . *I am a far from credulous man*; but it seems to me that one *cannot* refuse to believe a thing which is of such *public* notoriety, attested with due formality of law and by men of probity – above all in the light of the fact that there have been so many examples, or repetitions, all equally supported by witnesses.

The *Gazette* article ended on the following challenge: 'It is up to the *philosophes* to seek out the *causes* which can produce events so little in accord with nature.' For Rousseau, doubts about the existence of vampires persisted, not for lack of witnesses (even if the 'due formality' had sometimes occurred up to *five years* after the event) but for want of any plausible and available explanation of the alleged facts. He did not take up the challenge implied by the *Gazette*, however, perhaps because his main reason for addressing himself to the subject went far beyond that of establishing what constituted a rational explanation of its causes or origins. From the few direct references in his works to the phenomenon of vampirism, it is clear that the question of the existence of vampires was of no special importance to him. They might be real creatures; they might not. But it was futile, he argued in a draft of the fourth book of *Émile* (his treatise on education, written in 1758–59) to suppose that their reality could be confirmed by arguments analogous to those employed in, for example, discussions of miracles.

> For some time now, the public news has been concerned with nothing but vampires; there has never been a fact more fully proved *in law* than their existence, yet despite this, show me a single man of sense in Europe who believes in vampires or who would even deign to take the trouble to check the falseness of the facts ... Who will venture to tell me exactly how may eyewitnesses are needed to make a phenomenon credible?

He went on to ask about both miracles and vampires, 'Of what use are miracles as proof of your doctrine if the miracles themselves require so much proof?' The more interesting question was why the vampire (or miracle) should have become such an important article of popular belief in the first place. Eyewitness accounts were unconvincing, not because they were indubitably false or illusory – as the *philosophes* supposed – but because no rational explanation of the existence of these monsters had as yet been offered. Like Calmet, then, though for very different reasons, Rousseau kept an open mind about the status of the testimony of vampire epidemics. The essential point was that neither the exegesis of Scripture nor the rationalists' attempts to explain paranormal phenomena could really teach us anything about the nature of vampires, or about the manifest nightmares those creatures represented to us.

For Rousseau evidently regarded such popular beliefs – so widely dismissed by the *philosophes* – as of the utmost importance in themselves. The point he made about them was that however little so-called 'attested histories' instructed us about the status of vampires, they revealed much about the nature of authority in civilized society. In the outspoken *Letter to Beaumont* Rousseau observed that vampires were miraculous phenomena that required obscurantist dogmas to explain them just *because* common sense was at present insufficient. Miracles remain an extraordinary feature of our fears and hopes about the world only so long as a special place in the community is entrusted to their interpreters, and at the same time the authority that is wielded over us by these interpreters of Scripture depends upon our faith in their ability to grasp the sense of miracles better than we can ourselves. Vampires are thus yet another manifestation of the sombre and nefarious tyranny of opinion exercised by priests over the minds of men. In the *Letter*, Rousseau described miracles as 'scholarly subtleties in Christianity' which require above all else that the flock of believers should submit to principles they cannot grasp by reason and sense. Miracles are an instrument for the enforcement of duties employed by the purveyors of a Gospel unfathomable to ordinary people, and in that context he would perhaps, on this rare occasion, have agreed with Voltaire that the true vampires are the churchmen. For Rousseau, *both sacred and secular authority* derived their strength from popular superstitions, and fear of a miraculous monster such as the vampire helped to underpin respect for and submission to the worldly agents of an omnipotent God. In this way the dreaded superhuman force of vampires transforms the divinity of God into the wretched practice of obedience to his temporal ministers, and vampires – whether they be real or unreal creatures – wield a sinister power over men which is plain enough. If people are expected to believe in miracles, then why are we surprised that they also believe in vampires?

Rousseau's second, related, point about vampires draws its force essentially from the context in which he placed his remarks about them. This is that the relations between vampires and their prey are an extremely potent symbol for characterizing even the ordinary ties of dependence that bind individuals together in civilized society. Not only temporal rulers but their subjects as well had come to behave as vampires do, according to Rousseau, for 'Dependence on men,' he wrote in the second book of *Émile*, 'being out of order, gives rise to every kind of vice, and through this the master and the slave become mutually depraved.' Modern man is both predator and quarry to other members of his own species in a war of each against each which is all the more terrible because it is contrary to his nature. For every one of us, *Le vampire, c'est les autres*. Anatomical evidence of our teeth and intestinal tract showed that we must originally have been frugivores like the horse, sheep and rabbit, but civilization had made us carnivores with an appetite for conquest and blood in addition to food. There had been two causes of this development, Rousseau believed: on the one hand, the artificial cultivation of the soil, which slowly depleted the natural resources of the earth and unavoidably brought men into conflict over the vegetation that remained; and on the other, the institution of private property, which turned strangers into enemies and made each of us a predator not just of the diminishing produce of the soil but of the degraded humanity of our neighbours too. So, with the birth of property and the growth of agriculture we had transfigured ourselves into masters and slaves in turn, everyone moved by contempt for the person and lust for the goods of the next man, so that we had finally become a species of animal which in its totality is self-destructive. Like Karl Marx after him, Rousseau may have been attracted to the vampire image because it offered a vivid means of symbolizing modes of mutual dependence in society which were not benign – as many of their contemporary social theorists argued – but benighted, parasitic and grotesque – a master-slave dialectic, with teeth.

Whether or not the demonic creature of our worst fears existed in fact, if we only looked into ourselves – and into our society – we should find the demon there already. In zoology the *genus vampiricus* had already been identified, processed, tabulated and labelled. Carl Linnaeus had, in fact, mistakenly applied the label to a harmless fruit bat in the 1758 edition of his *System of Nature* – which must have given the inhabitants of the South of France some interesting nightmares – but at least this meant that vampires were *in the system*. The label 'Linnaeus's false vampire bat' is in fact still in use! A rather different type of science was needed to help us understand their meaning, and why they were so attractive as an explanation.

Rousseau's points were certainly lost on the popular French gazettes: by the 1770s they had simply substituted for the credulous coverage of the 1730s and 1740s a post-Enlightenment sense of Parisian superiority over the primitive rural communities of Eastern Europe. The *Gazette Française* of 26 October 1770 contained a representative piece:

> The madness of Vampires, which caused such a sensation in Hungary many years ago, has just broken out again in a little town on the borders of Moldavia, accompanied by events which are as horrible as they are bizarre. The plague having entered the town, a few imposters persuaded some of

the lower class of persons that a sure way of keeping the contagion under control was to tear out the teeth of the plague-ridden corpses and suck the blood out of the gums. This disgusting practice caused many people to perish, despite the care that the Police took to prevent it from taking place. *This* fact – however incredible it may appear – is attested by very reliable witnesses.

The punch-line was that the behaviour of the locals required as much believing as the original 'madness of vampires'.

However, in the decade immediately preceding the French Revolution, advanced thinking in France – at least among certain factions of the second generation of *philosophes*, whose main ambition was to become as famous as the first – took a rather different direction. For it was during the 1780s that the cult of Rousseau grew among believers in mesmerism, spiritualism, physiognomy and animal magnetism, and the Genevan philosopher's more balanced statements were usually jettisoned in favour of those aspects of his thought that were judged to be 'romantic'. As a member of a mesmerist lodge in Paris put it, 'The reign of Voltaire and of the *Encyclopédistes* is collapsing. One finally gets tired of cold reasoning. We must have livelier, more delicious delights. Some of the sublime, the incomprehensible, the supernatural.' Not only did an interest in vampirology – as part of a wider concern with the exotic and the occult – become fashionable in such circles, but certain Parisian newspapers exploited this interest by featuring reports of vampire-like monsters which had been 'sighted' in South America.

The *Courier de l'Europe* of October 1784, for example, hailed the capture of a Chilean creature – part-man, part-bat, part-lion – and reflected solemnly that this only proved the truth of ancient fables about vampires, harpies and sirens ('heretofore considered legendary'); 'a beautiful opportunity for the naturalists of the New and Old Worlds'. Although an attempt to capture a female of the species, and thus to breed vampires in French zoological gardens, failed miserably (they could not find another one), stories of this kind seem to have been fairly widely exploited in certain publishing circles, and even believed. They did not, in fact, appear so absurd at a time – as historian

Robert Darnton has observed – when ovists, preformationists and panspermatists 'outdid each other in speculation about sexual generation'; when Honoré, Count Mirabeau, later a revolutionary hero, professed to believe 'that Frederick the Great had produced centaurs and satyrs' by controlled experiments involving his courtiers and an assortment of animals; when Jacques-Pierre Brissot, later to be another revolutionary leader, feared that bestiality would disfigure the human race, noting that 'everyone has heard of the child-calf and the child-wolf'; when fully developed donkeys were seen, through microscopes, kicking around in donkey semen, at a reputable laboratory in Paris; when Linnaeus's works were still in print, including illustrations of an ejaculation of semen from a pollen grain that he had observed through a microscope; and when a legal dictionary permitted itself some doubts about the illegitimacy case in which a woman claimed to have conceived a child by her husband, whom she had not seen for four years, in a dream. If everyone had heard of the child-calf and the child-wolf, why not the man-bat? Why not indeed! In the light of eighteenth-century theories of sexual generation and the cross-breeding of the species, the question was not quite as idiotic as it may now seem. No doubt this debate contributed to the sales of artists' impressions of the Chilean vampire, which were available in kiosks on the streets of Paris. In the era of Cagliostro and de Sade, such 'attested' stories could be believed, explained and celebrated all at the same time. Plus, the image of the giant Chilean harpy-vampire could be adapted to fit the dreaded Austrian Archduchess Marie Antoinette – in a folk memory, perhaps, of the rumour that had set Paris murmuring way back in 1750. Eventually, it took Charles Darwin to set the record straight: the vampire bat did *not* have the face of a man, it lived in Central and South America rather than the South of France, and it was tiny – so tiny, in fact, that intercourse with a human being would have proved something of a technical problem.

As Darnton discovered, scientists working on cross-breeding of the species in pre-revolutionary Paris had to call upon their imaginations to make sense of, and even to *see*, the data revealed by their increasingly sophisticated microscopes, telescopes and dissections. What they saw was a different world from the one we see today, and they made it out as best they could with a collection of organizing theories, many inherited from their predecessors. In the 1780s the latest line in *haute culture* was no longer cynically to explain away attested 'facts', reducing the data about vampires to a set of rational precepts; rather, it was to collect information about the general science of teratology, or monsters, and to use laboratory research in order to *extend* the boundaries of the 'natural' to incorporate as many enjoyably 'paranatural' phenomena as possible. And that included vampires . . .

LORD RUTHVEN AND HIS CLAN

Robert Southey transcribed both the Arnold Paole story and Joseph Pitton de Tournefort's adventures on the island of Mykonos, in the notes to his 'rhythmical romance' *Thalaba the Destroyer* (1801); the Introduction to Polidori's *Vampyre* refers to the same sources. The Preface to Eyriès's *Fantasmagoriana* provides a brisk survey of the philosophical controversy, concluding with a quote from Voltaire: 'It is by no means rare for a person of lively feeling to fancy he sees what never really existed.' Byron had already exploited the vampire theme before summer 1816, in the curse sequence of his poem *The Giaour* (1813). And Shelley was on record as having discussed (also before 1816) 'the Turkish opinion that men that are buried have a sort of life in their graves'. So, not only was the vampire genre at first inhibited by its association with the Ruthven/Byron image; it was also, until much later in the nineteenth century, based on a very limited frame of reference, defined by the critical controversy surrounding Calmet's work in France, and by the misrepresentation of this controversy in the pre-Romantic atmosphere of 1780s Paris.

All the various plays, poems, stories and operas that exploited the commercial potential of Polidori's *Vampyre* (by authors such as Charles Nodier, James Planché, James Malcolm Rymer, Alexandre Dumas and Dion Boucicault) simply reworked the Ruthven plot, or used the 'historical background' contained in the anonymous Introduction (which was possibly by Polidori's publisher). As late as 1872, a burlesque opened at the Royal Strand Theatre, London, sending up the whole *Vampyre* genre. According to the author, it was based on 'a German legend, Lord Byron's story, and a Boucicaultian drama', and the central character was a plagiarist who derives nourishment from other people's ideas. The story concerned this incompetent vampire's attempts to steal notebooks belonging to two Romantic novelists, so that he can use their ideas for the next weekly instalment of his penny-dreadful. In Germany and France, E. T. A. Hoffmann, Prosper Mérimée and Théophile Gautier were quicker to transcend the limitations imposed by this popular 'model', but in London, and on the Paris boulevards, Lord Ruthven was so successful that he would not lie down.

If by chance the theatre-going public began to find his adventures *too* predictable, he could always join forces with his fellow monster from June 1816 to keep the box office busy. In 1826, for example, a visiting German princeling drifted into the English Opera House, in London, searching for something typical of the region:

> 'There was no opera, however,' he later recalled with surprise. 'Instead we had terrible melodramas. First *Frankenstein*, where a human being is made by magic, without female help – a manufacture that answers very ill; and then *The Vampire*, after the well-known tale falsely attributed to Lord Byron. The principal part in both was acted by Mr T. P. Cooke, who is distinguished for a very handsome person, skilful acting and a remarkable dignified, noble deportment. The acting was, indeed, admirable throughout, but the pieces so stupid and monstrous that it was impossible to sit out the performance.'

A very early example of the horror double bill, with the same star – and presumably sets and special effects – in both halves of it. Others followed suit. Others still imported European versions such as Ernst Raupach's *Wake Not the Dead* (1822, tr. 1823), which were adapted for the London stage. Operatic horror shows were so popular by autumn 1826 that the journal the *Opera Glass* ran a ten-stanza poem entitled *The Devil Among the Players*, which described how even the best singers seemed to have become diabolically possessed by *The Vampyre*, *Frankenstein* and *Faust*.

In 1846 *Knight's Penny Magazine* (a purveyor of 'wholesome mental nutriment') lashed out at the 'cheap weekly sheets' which were foisting trashy tales and tired vampire stories on 'the working people, and especially the young': 'The less informed readers, who most need sound knowledge, are reading such things as *The Spectre at the Hall* or *The Feast of Blood*.' But the moralists had to accept defeat, and on the principle 'If you can't beat them, join them', various worthy causes decided to harness the obvious commercial potential of the vampire myth. Pamphlets on temperance (*The Vampire* by 'the wife of a medical man', in which the Vampyre Inn sucks unwary alcoholics to their doom), on the dangers of overcrowding in the vast new metropolitan graveyards (*The Cemetery*, in which 'earth gives up her injured dead, unbid'), on the horrors of premature burial (compiled by the pro-cremation lobby), on the evils of gambling (*Ye Vampires* by 'The Spectre'), on the propagation of Christian knowledge (*A Vampire* by A. L. G.), or simply on the advantages of having 'pure thoughts' (the extraordinary *Modern Vampirism: Its Dangers and How to Avoid Them* by A. Osborne Eaves), all postdating the period of Ruthven's greatest success, made their polemicism more accessible to the 'less informed', by using the 'feast of blood' formula. The vampire-equals-plagiarist equation well sums up the popular aspects of the genre in nineteenth-century France and England.

James Malcolm Rymer's *Varney the Vampyre* (1845–47), a marathon penny-dreadful of 868 double-column pages, exemplifies the inflationary processes at work in the period of the vampire industry's peak production. It was subtitled *The Feast of Blood* (and, as we have seen, was singled out for a special mention by the moralists of the same year). The plot of *Varney* (lifted straight out of Polidori and derivatives) contains three main ingredients: Sir Francis Varney's attempts to seduce the innocent heroine; the local villagers' realization that Varney is a vampire and organization of a mass counter-attack; and a wedding scene, where Sir Francis is denounced in the nick of time and chased out of the area. This extremely simple story is rewritten at least five times in the course of the book. After he has been chased away Sir Francis turns up elsewhere in some disguise, and the reader is (presumably) expected to guess which character in a given episode he really is. Since Sir Francis's habits include 'hissing', haunting 'bone houses' and cemeteries, and attacking eligible young girls, it does not take a genius to discover who done it. Eventually, in a scene that was lifted from the melodramatization of *Frankenstein*, Sir Francis Varney, exhausted by his unsuccessful endeavours and disillusioned by an unsympathetic world, leaps into Mount Vesuvius, never to be heard of again.

If Rymer makes full use of Polidori, he also invents new variations on the theme, variations that will be reworked by later writers including Bram Stoker. *Varney* includes an original sub-plot concerning a Hungarian vampire count (the first in English literature); comic relief (straight out of the music hall) in the irrepressible double act of Admiral Bell and Able-Seaman Jack Pringle; and a whole series of scenes set in and around country churchyards, crypts, charnel houses and undertakers' parlours, the atmospheric detail of which was evidently based on close observation of early Victorian funerary customs. More significantly, unlike Byron's Augustus Darvell ('of considerable fortune and ancient family') and Polidori's Lord Ruthven (with his 'dead grey eye' and the 'deadly hue of his face'), Sir Francis Varney of Ratford Hall is an *unpredictable* hero-villain: his vampiristic moon-madness is more of an addiction than a built-in character trait. Anne Rice's *Interview with the Vampire* (1976) starts here. On one occasion, he even begs forgiveness of his intended victim in advance, knowing that at any moment the blood lust will possess him, and that he will be powerless to control himself. For the first time, the aristocratic vampire is not a figure of fashion in high society: Sir Francis is a scruffy, shambling, misunderstood, dirty old man; the Bannerworth family (his main victims) are embarrassed to be seen near him, even when his blood addiction has been repressed.

Rymer may have resurrected Lord Ruthven (in particular, the idea that a vampire can be revived by the moon's rays goes back to Mary Shelley's interest in galvanism as a means of giving life to dead limbs), but in the process of expanding Polidori's twenty-page story to over 850 pages, he gave new life to the genre as well, and enabled it (eventually) to shed the restricting characteristics that Ruthven had bequeathed. And he even managed to send up the tradition he had exploited: one of the funnier sub-plots in *Varney* concerns a Venetian nobleman named 'Count Polidori', and Sir Francis himself is 'killed' so often that the interest becomes purely technological – how will it be done this time? These 'camp' aspects seem to have been part of Rymer's original plan. *The Feast of Blood* was so successful that a play was rushed on to the London stage while the penny parts were still coming out: in it, the first plot cycle was expanded to fill a whole evening.

Nearly fifty years later, Ruthven (or rather Sir Francis) was to rise yet again from the dead. For, surprising as it may seem, Bram Stoker seems to have owed a great deal to *Varney the Vampyre*. *Dracula* may be a world away from the horror comic gore of Rymer's masterpiece, but among the plot motifs that Stoker sucked (and digested) from *Varney* – none of which had appeared so explicitly in Polidori's *Vampyre* – are:

1   The 'initiation' of the heroine, through contact with the vampire.
2   The suggestion of sexual attraction, followed by revulsion, followed in turn by attraction again, between female victim and tormenting vampire.
3   The *incongruity* of a central European folk-myth in an English rural setting.
4   The respect of the hunter for the hunted.
5   The Bannerworths' methodical, scientific approach to dealing with the vampire. This foreshadows Bram Stoker's treatment of the Dutch vampire-hunter Professor van Helsing 'MD, D.Ph., D.Litt., etc. etc.' – only the D.Litt. from Oxford seems a trifle far-fetched, given his shaky command of the English language – who is prepared to use everything from blood transfusions to the more traditional sacred wafers and crucifixes, and even some survivals from the old religion, in his battle of wits with the Count (who also proves to be fairly versatile, using folklore rather than science). This aspect of both *Varney* and *Dracula* may perhaps be taken to represent the conflict between Victorian scientific positivism (or 'expertise') and the forces of the unknown – a new addition to the genre.
6   Some more specific motifs, including a vigil at the witching hour by the tomb of a suspected vampire (involving the victim's fiancé), the vampire's transmutation into a wolf, the arrival of a deserted ship and the chase to the vampire's resting-place.

Further evidence that Bram Stoker had read *Varney* may be embodied in the name he chose for Lucy's fiancé. In *Varney*, one of Sir Francis's victims,

Clara Crofton, is engaged to a man named Ringwood; in *Dracula*, Lucy Westenra (another victim) is engaged to a man named Holmwood, who lives in a family house called Ring. Among the various candidates for the origin of 'Holmwood', this remains the most convincing.

However, connections of this kind – some trivial or doubtful, others perhaps more significant – show only where Stoker found his literary antecedents. As the literary scholar Leonard Wolf has said, 'There is nothing in *Varney*, nothing at all, that is capable of sounding anything like the chords of dark understanding that reverberate in page after page of Stoker's *Dracula*.' Before examining these 'chords of dark understanding' (and suggesting how an ex-civil servant from Dublin arrived at them), it is worth pausing to look at the vampire mosaic which had been pieced together throughout the nineteenth century, to greater or lesser effect, and which *Dracula* somehow succeeded in completing.

For, there were, of course, many other variations on the *genus vampiricus* in the nineteenth century and the turn of the twentieth, including assorted vampire plants (such as Phil Robinson's *Man-Eating Tree* in a Nubian forest, 1881, and H. G. Wells's *Strange Orchid*, 1895), psychic sponges (such as Arthur Conan Doyle's *The Parasite*, 1891, and Mary E. Wilkins-Freeman's *Luella Miller*, 1903), vampire houses and portraits (such as in *The Desires of Men* by L. T. Meade, 1899), evil scientists posing as vampires to keep the peasants

A VAMPIRE MOSAIC Vampires in folklore, prose and poetry, 1689–1913

Date			
Vampire	*Source*	*Preferred Victims*	*Distinguishing Features*
1689			
Giure Grando: male peasant, Khring, Istria (1672).	Johann von Valvasor: *Die Ehre den Hertzogthums Crain*	Relatives – men or women.	Likes to be invited across the threshold, after knocking on the door.
1728/1732			
Peter Plogojowitz: male peasant, Kisilova, Austrian Serbia (1725).	Michael Ranft: *De Masticatione Mortuorum in Tumulis*	Acquaintances – men or women.	Lies on top of his victims, and either throttles them or bites their chests.

away (such as in *Carpathian Castle* by Jules Verne, 1892) and even a 'winged kangaroo with a python's neck' (Phil Robinson's *Last of the Vampires*, 1893). Significantly, most of these bizarre variants date from the 1890s, when the genre had either to diversify or to repeat itself. And my chart, 'A Vampire Mosaic', does not include detailed references to Heinrich von Kleist's *Penthesilea* (1808), in which the wild Amazon queen bites into the living flesh of her victim and lover, Achilles, or to Lautréamont's strange pyrotechnical display of vampire imagery in Song One of the *Songs of Maldoror* (1868), or to Ivan Turgenev's delicate prose-poem about the vampire Alice, who guides the narrator through the skies and eventually vanishes in the rays of the sun after meeting the serpentine creature of death ('the more horrible because it had no shape') – *Phantoms*, also 1868 – largely because these three works defy categorization. Nor does it deal with the vampiric significance of Coleridge's Ancient Mariner, Wordsworth's Leech Gatherer, Blake's flea, Byron's Manfred, Shelley's the Cenci, Keats's Lamia, Emily Brontë's Heathcliffe and Charlotte Brontë's Bertha Rochester (These have been studied in great detail for traces of the vampire virus by James Twitchell, who interprets the theme as *any* example in Romantic literature where Coleridge's 'desire and loathing strangely mixed' are to be found.) But the 'Vampire Mosaic' does include all the key *explicit* developments in the genre – according to the latest research by specialists in the field.

Vampires of special interest are marked with an asterisk.

Remedy	Comments
Decapitation (the stake would not penetrate).	'Characteristic of the area.'
Staking and burning.	The first case to arouse official (Austrian) curiosity.

Date *Vampire*	*Source*	*Preferred Victims*	*Distinguishing Features*
1732 *Arnold Paole: male *heyduk*, Medvegia, Austrian Serbia (1731).	Johannes Flückinger: *Visum et Repertum*	Acquaintances – men, women and children. Also sheep and cattle.	Bitten by a vampire (perhaps in Turkey) before accidental death.
Between AD 117 and 138; 1797 *Philinium: female, 'The Bride from Amphipolis', Corinth.	Phlegon of Tralles: *Fragmenta Historicorum Graecorum*; Johann Wolfgang von Goethe: *The Bride of Corinth*	Machates, a young man.	Returns from the grave after six months to sleep with the youth by night.
Between AD 200 and 245; 1797, 1820 *The Empusa: female, 'The Bride of Corinth', 'The Lamia'.	Philostratus: *Life of Apollonius of Tyana*; Goethe: *The Bride of Corinth*; John Keats: *The Lamia*	Menippus, a young man 'with beautifully proportioned physique'.	'A Phoenician woman' who wishes to 'fatten up' a young man with pleasures, then 'devour his young and beautiful body'.
1805 Count F . . .: Russian Count, northern Italy.	Heinrich von Kleist: *The Marquise of O. . .*	The Marquise.	'To the Marquise, he seemed (at first) a very angel from heaven.' 'He was as handsome as a young God, even if his face was rather pale.' He is rumoured dead, then returns. After he has confessed that it was *he* who made her pregnant, 'he would not have looked like a devil to her then, if he had not seemed like an angel to her at his first appearance'. Her first response is to throw holy water at him.
1819 *Lord Ruthven: English Lord, Athens and London.	John William Polidori: *The Vampyre*	Impressionable society ladies and innocent girls.	'Dead grey eye'; 'deadly hue of his face'.
1819–20 *Aurelia: Baroness from 'the most beautiful country imaginable'.	E. T. A. Hoffmann: story in *The Serapion Brethren*	Men, including her husband.	'Marvellously charming and beautiful.' 'Darksome fire in her eyes, and deathlike pallor.'

Remedy	Comments
Staking and burning.	The subject of government reports, and the cause of a long-lasting philosophical controversy.
Interrupted by her parents, she becomes a corpse. To prevent her return, the corpse is burned to ashes outside the city wall, and sacrifices are made to the guardians of the underworld.	An indirect influence on Goethe (1797), who was the first to make the vampire respectable in literature. In Goethe's version, the girl dies of grief because her parents have refused to let her marry the man she loves. She returns – 'Still to love the bridegroom I have lost / And the lifeblood of his heart to drink' – only finding sexual release when freed by death from her parents' control. In the original, Machates has never met the girl before. Gautier was to use the motif again, in *Arria Marcella*.
Apollonius – representing Greek rationalism – discovers her true purpose before the wedding, and tells the guests that the fine decorations 'exist yet do not exist'. At that moment, they 'flutter away' and the lamia collapses.	In Philostratus's version, Apollonius's intellect breaks through the barrier of illusion. In Keats's version, Apollonius's 'eye severe' and 'calm-planted steps' are treated less sympathetically, and the lamia's motives towards Lycius (Menippus) are never spelled out; after the 'foul dream' is banished, Lycius dies. Another influence on Goethe (and Hoffmann). These two stories represent the main classical bases of the literary vampire, and the wedding motif was to recur in many of the Ruthven derivatives (on several occasions in *Varney*).
To recognize each other as normal human beings, with failings.	Hoffmann reckoned that Kleist did not need to 'raise a vampire out of the grave' to achieve his effect. For Ernest Jones, 100 years later, *The Marquise*, because of its powerful association of love and death, and its clear reference to the incubus, was an archetypal vampire story (especially given Kleist's recurring concerns – for example in the play *Penthesilea*, 1808, where the female vampire bites her lover to death).
None.	The first Byronic vampire, and the foundation of the genre.
None.	Her vampirism is associated both with her mother and with a diabolical 'stranger'. She usually goes to the graveyard for sustenance. Partly of classical origin, partly an attempt to explore the relationship between the 'craze' and the principle of 'Serapionism'.

Date *Vampire*	*Source*	*Preferred Victims*	*Distinguishing Features*
1820 *Lord Ruthven: '*un seigneur Anglais*'; Italy, Greece, India and Eastern Europe.	Cyprien Bérard: *Lord Ruthwen ou les Vampires*	Young brides. One of these, Bettina, becomes a benevolent vampire.	Poses as 'Lord Seymour', Prime Minister of Modena, and claims to have 'served in the army of Scotland'.
1820 Oscar Montcalm, demoniac vampire, who has taken on the *appearance* of the late Lord Ruthven, Earl of Marsden, at the moment of the aristocrat's death, in order to woo Lady Margaret. It is all 'in the Scotch annals'.	J. R. Planché: *The Bride of the Isles, a Tale* (by 'Lord Byron')	Every All Hallows E'en, he must 'legally wed in all due form' a chaste virgin, before the 'setting of the moon', to renew his undead existence for another year: he must then kill her and drink her 'heart's blood'. The vampire can inhabit many different bodies, but only one at a time.	'A tongue to charm his victims, and eyes like the fascination of a basilisk'; a 'pallid hue – the invariable case with vampires, their blood not flowing'; a face 'the image of death itself'. Wears a kilt and 'does not eat salt on his trencher'.
1821 *Smarra (or the Nightmare): associated with fantasies about a female, Thessaly, Greece.	Charles Nodier: *Smarra ou les Démons de la Nuit*	The narrator, a young man named Lucius (or Lucian), who recounts a dream of his friend Polémon, a Scythian warrior.	'Méroé, the most beautiful of all the beauties of Thessaly, took off her turquoise ring and pressed it with her finger, to raise the enchanted stone, and reveal a creature – colourless and formless – which snarled and growled and fell on to the breast of the sorceress. "Go," she cried, "spectre of love, go and torment the victim I have chosen for you ... If you do this, faithful slave of love, you may, when the time for dreams is over, return to the arms of the queen of nightly terrors" ... So saying, she released the monster from her blazing hand, and it began to spread its strangely coloured wings: it was like a deformed, laughing dwarf, whose hands were armed with the finest metal which could cut into the skin without tearing it, and it began to drink my blood. As it bit into my heart, it grew in size, raised its enormous head, and laughed.'

Remedy	Comments
A hot iron stake through the heart, and through the eyes as well.	Two-volume variation on the Ruthven theme (the first vampire novel), with long sub-plots which read like a bloody grand tour. Aubrey (from *The Vampyre*) joins in. This was rumoured to have been written by Charles Nodier (who denied it, and wrote the influential play *Le Vampire* in revenge).
Prevent the vampire from completing the marriage ceremony (as happens three times in the story); but be sure not to cast his twisted gold ring into the well at Fingal's Cave, as he will survive even that.	A souvenir tie-in with the play *The Bride of the Isles*; since the king-vampire has strong supernatural powers and as many lives as 'the Witch of Endor's tabby cat' – albeit in different corporeal forms – the possibilities for sequels were rich. *The Bride* is 'based on a popular superstition still extant in the southern isles of Scotland'. Celtic revival meets *The Vampyre*.
To wake up, after various other fantasies, to reality.	One of Nodier's more bizarre concoctions, loosely based on the work of Apuleius of Carthage (*c.* AD 114–91) – especially *The Golden Ass* – but also owing much, according to the author, to 'Homer, Virgil, Catullus, Dante, Shakespeare (*The Tempest*), Milton and others'. The narrator falls asleep while riding through an enchanted forest near Thessaly and, in his dream, imagines that he is watching the nightmare of another, but is unable to move or intervene. The nightmare itself is a vampiric version of Fuseli's painting (and when Tony Johannot illustrated Nodier's story, he based his *Smarra* on Fuseli's incubus). Apart from the central episode (involving Méroé, the *Smarra*, and the other victim, Polémon), the story seems to have been something of an academic exercise for Nodier and, because the references to other authors are so dense, the *Prologue, Récit, Epode* and *Epilogue* are all extremely difficult to follow. When the story was first published, Nodier appended some notes on vampirism, and a discussion of the travels of the Abbé Fortis in Dalmatia. He was also to jump on the Ruthven bandwagon, by writing the most successful of the first batch of French melodramatizations, *Le Vampire*.

| **Date** | | | |
Vampire	*Source*	*Preferred Victims*	*Distinguishing Features*
1822 (tr. 1823) *Brunhilda: female noble, Burgundy, France.	Ernst Raupach: *Wake Not the Dead/Let the Dead Rest*	Children ('the veins of youth'). Finally, her husband.	'Her tresses – dark as the raven face of night – set off to the utmost advantage the beaming lustre of her slender form.' Can cause transmutation into a serpent.
1827 The Bey of Moina: male aristocrat, Illyria.	Prosper Mérimée: *La Guzla*	His bride, La Belle Sophie.	Ice-cold to the touch.
1827 'The cursed Venetian': male aristocrat, Illyria.	Prosper Mérimée: *La Guzla*	Illyrian yeomen and *heyduks*.	Blue eyes; 'a smile like a man who sleeps and is tormented by a hideous love'.
1828 Bertha Kurtel, a beautiful undead peasant girl reanimated by Count Rudolf, who has made a pact with the Devil and lives in Ravensburg Castle near Heidelberg; he turns into a 'fleshless skeleton' every night in return for 'almost eternal life'.	Elizabeth Caroline Grey: *The Skeleton Count or the Vampire Mistress*	Bertha's former companions Minna Klaus (a little girl) and Theresa Delmar ('a lovely maiden'). According to Father Ambrose, 'they generally attack females and children'.	An 'angelic countenance' with long black hair and 'a wild and stolid glare'; abstains from food; after being shot and falling into the Rhine, is revived by the beams of a full moon.
1833 *Berenice: female aristocrat, 'ancestral estate at Arnheim'.	Edgar Allan Poe: *Berenice*	'Egaeus', her cousin.	Once 'agile, graceful and overflowing with energy', she becomes emaciated with disease: 'The eyes were lifeless, and lustreless, and seemingly pupilless ... the lips thin and shrunken.'
1835 *No name: daughter of a wealthy Cossack, countryside near Kiev.	Nikolai Gogol: *Viy*	Men, especially Homa Brut, a philosopher.	Appears as a witch on a phantom horse; changes into a 'terrible beauty, with eyelashes that fell like arrows on the cheeks, and glowed with the warmth of secret desires'.

Remedy	Comments
Murder – but the memory remains.	Brought back to life by sorcery, Brunhilda represents the first example, in prose, of the 'vampire as sexual allegory', and the first sustained example in any medium.
None.	Associated with the suicide of Sophie's lover. Political allegory, with folktale presentation.
None.	Also political, with folktale presentation. The 'cursed Venetian' is killed for burning the *heyduks'* property and for 'corrupting' a local girl, but returns to have his revenge on the Illyrians. Byronic overtones.
Either set fire to her or 'peg her down with a stake', the infuriated villagers reinter her in her empty coffin and stake her in the abdomen.	A resurrection experiment 'ends no her with the nature of a vampire'. This penny-dreadful 'story of the skeleton Count and his vampire mistress' fuses *Frankenstein* with *The Vampyre*, as had already happened in a double bill on the stage. Elizabeth Grey's aunt had actually appeared in *The Bride of the Isles*.
Remove her teeth, to exorcize the obsession.	The characteristic Poe themes of premature burial, guilt feelings about the death of a mistress and incest are here interwoven with an obsession about vampirism.
Exorcism keeps her at bay – temporarily.	She has 'power over monstrous winged creatures' but is herself controlled by Viy, chief of the gnomes. A sub-plot concerns a dog which transmutes into a beautiful girl, who then snatches babies and vampirizes them. Folktale, with subtle political overtones.

Date Vampire	Source	Preferred Victims	Distinguishing Features
1836 *Clarimonde: female, royal courtesan, a parish near the Concini Palace (not far from Venice).	Théophile Gautier: *La Morte Amoureuse*	Her lovers, and especially Romuald, a 'simple' country priest.	'A beauty beyond the divine portrait of the Madonna.' 'Sea-green eyes and teeth of the purest Orient pearl.'
Early 1840s *Gorcha and Sdenka: male and female peasants, a village in Moldavia.	Alexis Tolstoy: *The Family of the Vourdalak*	Relatives – men, women and children.	Gorcha: 'waxen features', pressed against the window; 'corpse-like appearance'. Sdenka: naive and innocent, becomes provocative and wanton.
1844 (tr. 1854) *Count Azzo von Klatka: aristocrat, Carpathian Mountains.	Karl von Wachsmann.: *The Mysterious Stranger*	Women, especially Franziska von Fahnenberg, 'a dazzling beauty'.	'It was a man about forty, tall, and extremely thin ... There was contempt and sarcasm in the cold, grey eyes, whose glance, however, was at times so piercing, that no one could endure it long.'
1845–47 *Sir Francis Varney: English Lord, Ratford Hall (Yorkshire), London and Italy.	James Malcolm Rymer: *Varney the Vampyre*	'Innocent' young girls.	'Tall, gaunt figure' with cadaverous features, much given to scratching his fingernails along window-glass.
1848–51 (tr. 1910) Kostaki: male aristocrat ('accustomed to command'), Carpathian Mountains, Moldavia.	Alexandre Dumas: *The Pale-Faced Lady*	Women, especially his brother's fiancée, Hedwige.	'Pale as death; his long black hair, scattered over his shoulders, was moist with blood ... his eyes alone, those fearful eyes, were living!'
1853 Etherial Softdown: shoemaker's daughter, New England and New York.	Charles Wilkins Webber: *Spiritual Vampirism*	Men with vitality, especially husbands.	'An oaf-like person, with a hungry sharpness in her eye that made people shrink.'

Remedy	Comments
Holy water.	Power to release repressions, in a dream state. First seen at the 'simple' priest's ordination, she gradually brings out a side of his personality that resembles 'a dissolute, supercilious young lord'.
Staking; trampling under horses' hooves.	Folktale presentation modelled on eighteenth-century accounts, with Arnold Paole especially in mind. Gogol and Mérimée were the main literary influences. Tolstoy wrote several other stories about the weird and the folkloric at this time, including *The Vampire* ('Upyr'), which takes place in contemporary Moscow 'society'. The affair between the Duchesse de Gramont and the rakish d'Urfé (mentioned in *The Family*) is the subject of another fantastic tale, *Le rendezvous dans trois cents ans*.
To hammer three long iron nails into his coffin lid (with the Count inside). Once bitten, the victim must bathe her wound in the vampire's blood.	The setting, and the behaviour of the Count, make this seem a direct (if rather 'innocent') precursor to the opening of *Dracula*. Azzo even has power over wolves
Hanging, shooting, drowning and staking do not work, so the vicar suggests, 'Have you tried prayer?' Varney eventually destroys himself by jumping into Vesuvius.	Revived by the moonlight (a legacy of Mary Shelley on galvanism). Attacks of blood lust come on unexpectedly (even Varney is surprised when he discovers his affliction). Towards the end he becomes more animal-like and no longer represses his problem: when the landlord asks what he would like in the morning, he replies, 'Blood.' Starts operating during the Restoration, and knows all about Rochester.
Protection: a consecrated twig of box tree, still moist with holy water. Once bitten, the victim must rub mould, soaked in the vampire's blood, into the wound. Destruction: a consecrated sword, used as a stake.	Detail of Moldavian life used to give colour to an adventure story (in *Corsican Brothers* style). The vampire originates, predictably enough, with a curse: 'The race of Brancovan is already cursed, because Brancovan killed a priest.'
Overcome by a more powerful personality, Humility Barebones Stout, a fanatical Puritan who wishes to rule the world by the 'power of cant'.	Prefaced by a dissertation on mesmerism, this bizarre novel (the first to feature a 'psychic sponge') contains much satire on various religious sects of the period. 'Vampirism', it is concluded, 'is clearly a disease of the nervous system.' To prove the point, Etherial saps the vitality of all around her, by a 'cannibalism of the soul'. 'And what of the victim if she dragged him down into idiocy?' adds Webber. 'Served him right!'

Date Vampire	Source	Preferred Victims	Distinguishing Features
1857 *"The woman with the strawberry mouth': French.	Charles Baudelaire: *Les Métamorphoses du Vampire*	The poet, who much appreciates the experience.	'Squirming like a snake upon the coals / Kneading her breasts against the iron of her corset…'
1859 *A 'something': (male?), New York.	Fitz-James O'Brien: *What Was It?*	Those who sleep in a certain room, especially men.	'There was a mouth; a round smooth head without hair; a nose, which, however, was little elevated above the cheeks; and its hands and feet felt like those of a little boy.'
1865 Elizabeth (or Erzsebet) Báthory: aristocrat (blood-relative of royalty), the foothills of the Carpathians; the lowlands of Hungary.	Rev. Sabine Baring-Gould: *The Book of Were-wolves*	650 young virgins (mainly peasants).	'On one occasion, a lady's maid saw something wrong in her headdress, and as a recompense for observing it, received such a box on the ears that blood flowed from her nose, and spurted on to her mistress's face: when the blood drops were washed off her face, her skin appeared much more beautiful.'
1865 *Mary Stuart: Queen of Scots.	Algernon Charles Swinburne: *Chastelard*	The men closest to her – Darnley and Chastelard among them.	'For all Christ's work, this Venus is not quelled / But reddens at the mouth with blood of men / Sucking between small teeth the sap o' the veins …'
1867 Teresa Biffi, a farmer's daughter, who returns as 'the Lady Teresa'.	William Gilbert: *The Last Lords of Gardonal*	Baron Conrad, feudal lord of the Engadin, who ordered her family – and accidentally herself – to be burned to death.	'The hideous face of a corpse that had remained some time in the tomb'; 'she placed her clammy hand upon her victim's mouth, and threw him with great force upon the floor'.

Remedy	Comments
She appears to change from a beautiful vampire to 'an old leather bottle with sticky sides and full of pus', to 'the remains of a skeleton', as the poet awakens to a 'clear reality'.	The archetypal incarnation of the *femme fatale* (from *Les Fleurs du Mal*), whose bite sends the poet into an ecstasy of agony: 'She sucked the pith from my bones, and, drooping, I turned towards her to give her the kiss of love ...'
Blood-starvation.	A short-story equivalent to Fuseli's painting, *The Nightmare* (and to Tony Johannot's book illustrations on the same theme in the 1820s). Very reminiscent of Poe at times but in a realistically 'domestic' setting (the bohemian world of New York writers). Like Le Fanu and Stoker, O'Brien was Irish. Unlike them, he was a Roman Catholic.
Her accomplices were executed, and she was imprisoned (at home) for the rest of her life.	'It shows how a trifling matter may develop the passion, in its most hideous proportions ...' Assisted by 'two old women', the bloody Countess takes a sadistic pleasure in torturing, and bathing in the blood of, young virgins: 'She once bit a person who came near her sick-bed as though she were a wild beast.' The first full account of Báthory's activities had been published (in Latin) in 1729. Baring-Gould's was the first major treatment in English – a rather disingenuous account.
History takes care of this particular incarnation.	Mary cannot weep, but enjoys the spectacle of suffering. Chastelard wants nothing more than to become her victim, to contribute to her beauty: 'His heart feels drunken when he thinks that her sweet lips and life will smell of his spilt blood.' Swinburne was reading the works of de Sade at the time, although this acted only as a catalyst. In *Juliette*, and especially *Justine*, de Sade had explored the relationship between blood and sexuality (adding blood to his already extensive list of aphrodisiacs and stimulants for men).
When she has had her revenge, 'she was never heard of afterwards'.	The setting – Switzerland and northern Italy at the time of the Reformation, when the local peasants seem deeply confused – is unusual. The author was W. S. Gilbert's father.

Date Vampire	Source	Preferred Victims	Distinguishing Features
1870 The Baital: a vampire, ghoul or evil spirit that animates corpses; male (?), Benares, India.	Richard Burton: *Vikram and the Vampire* (dating from early in the Christian era)	Enjoys baffling Raja Vikram.	'Its eyes, which were wide open, were of a greenish brown, and never twinkled; its hair also was brown, and brown was its face. Its body was thin, and ribbed like a skeleton; blood it appeared to have none.'
1872 *Countess Carmilla Karnstein (once called 'Millarca'): aristocrat ('of very ancient and noble family'), Styria.	Sheridan Le Fanu: *Carmilla*	Sensitive young girls, especially the narrator.	'Except that her movements were languid – *very* languid – there was nothing in her appearance to indicate an invalid. Her complexion was rich and brilliant; her features were small . . . her eyes large, dark and lustrous . . . I never saw hair so magnificently thick and long when it was down about her shoulders . . . in colour, it was a rich, very dark brown.'
1872 *Fanny Campbell, a veritable 'English rose', is suspected.	Eliza Lynn Linton: *The Fate of Madame Cabanel*	The housekeeper's little nephew Adolphe, who is really dying of the plague.	'The plump form, tall figure and fresh complexion of the Englishwoman', as distinct from the 'swarthy, ill-nourished' inhabitants of a Brittany village.
1887 *The Horla ('a visitor'): encountered in an 'ancestral home' by the Seine, near Rouen.	Guy de Maupassant: *The Horla*	Convinces the (male) narrator that 'my mind has become the serf of some other being'.	The invisible Horla is first *felt* 'squatting on my chest . . . drinking my life from between my lips'.
1887 Vespertilia the blood-drinker: buried in a crypt, since Roman times.	Anne Crawford: *A Mystery of the Campagna*	Impressionable young men, staying in the Vigna Marziali.	Lives in a sarcophagus, wrapped in a winding-sheet, where 'her red lips seem to grow redder' and 'the blue veins on that divinely perfect bosom hold living blood'.

Remedy	Comments
To solve one of the Baital's riddles.	The chronicle of various attempts by Raja Vikram and his son to bring the talkative Baital (a bat-like creature, who likes to hang upside down on a tree) to the jogi (or magician) who is four miles away. The various adventures of this selection (in which the Baital tries, on the whole successfully, to distract the Raja) have little to do with vampirism, despite the title (even the Baital seems to resemble a giant fruit bat). But there are references to Hindu devotees 'in a state of mesmeric catalepsy'. Burton himself was later to claim that *Vikram* was a major stimulus to vampire literature.
Staking, decapitation, and her remains burned.	Le Fanu's masterpiece concerns the strange and very beautiful lesbian relationship between Carmilla and the narrator; the supernatural elements play a peripheral role. Although Carmilla is aware that the relationship must be destructive (in the event, it destroys her as well), Le Fanu's finest touch is the *sympathy* she feels for her victim: 'Think me not cruel because I obey the irresistible law of my strength and weakness . . . In the rapture of my enormous humiliation, I live in your warm life, and you shall die – die, sweetly die – into mine. I cannot help it . . .'
To take her to 'the old pit' outside the village and there thrust a stake through her body.	An interesting study of mob violence and petty jealousy, set in northern France. 'Vampire' characteristics are projected on to an innocent foreigner, to 'explain' her behaviour.
The obsessed narrator tries iron bars on the windows and doors, then decides to get rid of 'Man's new master' by setting fire to the house (and, by a terrible mistake, the servants). After that inevitably fails, there 'is nothing left for me but to kill myself'.	A weird fusion of O'Brien's *What Was It?* and Gogol's *Diary of a Madman*, this story concerns 'that horrible impotence which paralyses us in our dreams'. Sub-plots include a mesmerist seance, and a visit 'to the Théâtre Français to see a play by Alexandre Dumas' (to take the narrator's mind off things – a nice in-joke). The narrator's mistake is to confuse something that is going on inside his mind with something that is going on outside it.
A sharpened stake made out of a garden pickaxe handle.	The vampire becomes a metaphor for the creative process – as the young victim tries to compose an opera and the narrator to finish a painting. The author was F. Marion Crawford's sister.

Date Vampire	Source	Preferred Victims	Distinguishing Features
1887 Ethelind Fionguala, the 'white shouldered', 300-year-old vampire bride who haunts a graveyard in County Cork.	Julian Hawthorne: *The Grave of Ethelind Fionguala*	Possessors of the 'ring of the Kern – the fairy ring', who also have vivid imaginations, such as the suggestible artist Kerringale.	'... there was, in her aspect and bearing, something familiar in the midst of strangeness, like the burden of a song heard long ago': she wears a jewelled bridal dress, has a mocking laugh, and allows her victims to rest their heads against her white shoulders.
1890 Ariadne Brunnell, whose nocturnal visits to the bedroom induce sexy dreams of flying, enveloped by silken tresses in 'an inky cloud', followed by 'drowsy delight' and erotic languor.	Hume Nisbet: *The Vampire Maid*	Romantic young visitors to a remote stone moorland cottage on the Westmoreland coast. The vampire's widowed mother, the landlady, prepares a drugged sleeping draught to ease the process.	'... her hair and eyes seemed too black with that strangely white skin, and perhaps her lips too red for any except the decadent harmonies of Aubrey Beardsley.'
1891 Gilles de Rais: male aristocrat ('the richest baron in France'), the Châteaux of Tiffauges and Machecoul, France.	J. K. Huysmans: *Down There*	Over 150 children.	'A robust, active man, of striking beauty and rare elegance.' Durtal, the historian and central figure, lives 'in perfect accord, and even mischievous amity' with his subject.
1893 *Catherine Larue (née Frayser): 'well-to-do' society lady, Napa Valley, near San Francisco.	Ambrose Bierce: *The Death of Halpin Frayser*	Her son, Halpin Frayser.	A slighted, possessive mother, she destroys the dreamy Halpin by taking the form of 'a creature of his dreams'.

Remedy	Comments
Not to pass the house of the Kern of Querin by night, not to sing or play a traditional tune beneath the latticed casement and, above all, not to kiss her cold lips. For if you do, she will live for another 100 years. Avoid rural graveyards on Halloween.	Irish folkloric yarn, told by Nathaniel Hawthorne's son – an acquaintance of Oscar Wilde at this time. Although several vampire *authors* were Irish, the story's location ('not many miles from Ballymacheen') is an unusual one. Irish-American atmosphere. Vampirism is said to be a neglected but 'prominent feature among the troubles of Ireland'.
To escape from the cottage before it is too late, after waking up when 'in her eagerness she had bitten a little too deeply', interrupting a dark nightmare of 'a line of dead bodies of young men on the floor'.	Ariadne bites the arm rather than neck; in dreams she appears as 'a monster bat'; she creates the impression in the victim that 'she is mine' when in fact 'I am hers'. She is *not* a good conversationalist.
Executed 'in a state of grace'.	Part of Huysmans's rejection of the contemporary scene (both social and literary) and consequent attraction for 'the soul of the Middle Ages in its white splendour'. 'You abandon the eternal triangle and the other stale subjects of the modern novelists,' the historian is told, 'to write the story of Gilles de Rais.' Durtal (thus Huysmans) sees Gilles's repentance (under the guidance of the Catholic Church) as genuine. Gilles's crimes are described with an almost sensuous fascination for detail. During his researches, Durtal has a destructive affair with Hyacinthe Chantelouve, a glacial, dominating lady (and a practising Satanist) who can get excited only 'when the bed is strewn with fragments of the blessed Host'.
None: 'a low, deliberate, soulless laugh' remains. But it seems that her one purpose – complete possession of her son – has been achieved.	Catherine Frayser is murdered by her second husband. The husband (Branscom) visits her by night in an old graveyard. Perhaps the dead woman mistakes her victim; more likely, Halpin's fantasy about his clinging mother (which destroys him) is intended to represent a vampiric variant on the Oedipus motif. Very reminiscent of Poe.

Date Vampire	Source	Preferred Victims	Distinguishing Features
1893 *Isaac Lebedenko: male 'in very well-to-do circumstances' (who reincarnates as a female vampire), Constantinople and the Karpak Mountains, Moldavia.	'X.L.' (Julian Osgood Field): *A Kiss of Judas*	Those who have deeply offended (in this life) are attacked, in revenge, by some incarnation of the 'Children of Judas'. The victim of this particular incarnation is Colonel 'Hippy' Rowan, a hearty English clubman.	'He has the eyes of a lunatic, and there is evidently something horribly the matter with his face.' 'His eyes glared with exceptional ferocity from between the red bare lids, and the diamond-decorated claw-like hand grasped convulsively at his soiled white muffler.' Then he resurrects (after suicide) as 'the strange lady with the Madonna face' ('with lustrous violet eyes'). The Kiss of Judas can be the kiss of rabies, of cholera or of affection. In this case, it is affection.
1894 Count Vardalek: Hungarian aristocrat, Styria ('vampire stories are generally located there – mine is also').	Eric, Count Stenbock: *A True Story of a Vampire*	'Gazelle-like' young men.	'Rather tall with fair wavy hair, rather long, which accentuated a certain effeminacy about his smooth face. His figure had something serpentine about it.'
1895 A beautiful maiden in a robe of crimson, tattered at the edges, who works at her ivory loom in a palace guarded by 'dogs and pigs with human limbs' – where she weaves the threads of men's lives and then wears them.	R. Murray Gilchrist: *The Crimson Weaver*	Mature men in search of romance, who have memories of love which she can rekindle.	Skin of deathly white, lips 'fretted with pain', the gait of a peacock, and the feet and claws of a large vulture – hidden under her splendid robe.

Remedy	Comments
Bullets are useless – she disappears (and only two men have seen her). But her/his one purpose has been achieved.	A strange fusion of a 'clubland' adventure, fascination with the *femme fatale* in exotic settings (Beardsley illustrated the original version in the *Pall Mall Magazine*) and a vampire story with a new (and inventive) twist. The 'clubland hero' is (uncharacteristically) criticized for his behaviour, through the medium of the vampire story. Julian Osgood Field seems to have had some contact with the political 'world' of London society. One of the few genuinely imaginative diversifications of the popular genre in the 1890s.
None: 'he utterly disappears'.	The narrator of this camp story is an old Polish woman who, in memory of her long-dead brother (the vampire's victim and a vegetarian), sets up an asylum for stray cats and dogs in Westbourne Park.
Somehow to resist her charms; once kissed, she never leaves.	Written for *The Yellow Book* in the glittering neo-medieval, Celtic Revival style of 'romances of old'; a curious mixture of John Ruskin and Oscar Wilde, this transports the vampire into the realms of the Aesthetic Movement.

Date Vampire	Source	Preferred Victims	Distinguishing Features
1896 Lady Adeline Ducayne, elderly aristocrat who winters in Cap Ferrino, Italy.	Mary Elizabeth Braddon: *Good Lady Ducayne*	Bella Rolleston, her companion, 'a young woman whose health will give me no trouble'.	A 'parchment complexion', 'claw-like fingers', 'wizened nut-cracker-profile'. She uses one Dr Paravicini to procure for her much-needed young blood, since she was 'born the day Louis XVI was guillotined'.
1897 *Count Dracula: aristocrat (of a ruling military dynasty), Carpathian Mountains; Yorkshire; London.	Bram Stoker: *Dracula*	Female – particularly prim English ladies. (Female victims become vampires in turn.)	See description later in this book. 'The general effect was one of extraordinary pallor.'
1898 The undead Lady Priscilla Marvyn who in life killed the evil Sir Rupert.	H. B. Marriott Watson: *The Stone Chamber*	Those who dare to sleep in the stone chamber of Marvyn Abbey, Utterbourne, Devonshire – with its 'barbaric frescoes' – linked by an underground tunnel to the noble family vault. They include the wealthy young man Warrington, the narrator Ned Heywood and the fragrant Marion Bosanquet.	Transmutes when roused into an 'obscene creature', a bat with 'a horrible face watching me out of black narrow eyes'. Once bitten, the victim undergoes a gradual personality change – towards surliness, instability and 'gross behaviour'.
1899 A Spanish *femme fatale*, Annette, with thin lips, a retreating chin, and oily eyes that shine like an Indian cobra; a charming manner.	Dick Donovan: *The Woman with the Oily Eyes*	Jack Redcar, a fine upstanding civil engineer – and 'a brilliant fellow'.	Haunts spa towns in Germany – and the village of Potes in the Asturian Pyrenees; revels in destroying conventionally happy marriages.

Remedy	Comments
To realize that the wounds on the victim's arm are not *really* mosquito bites, and to get out.	The vampire's mark is made by a syringe, inserted while the patient is chloroformed; a transfusion story, by a friend of the Stokers.
Crucifixes, garlic, the Host and the weapons of modern science (such as blood transfusions) all help in the 'quest' – but Dracula is killed (despite all the films since) by Harker's Kukri knife (in the throat) and Morris's Bowie knife (in the heart – *like* a stake). He crumbles to dust.	A synthesis of three main vampire genres: the Byronic Lord, the *femme fatale* and the Folkloric Vampire. Bram Stoker never wrote anything else of the same quality; his dream (see pages 338–39) must have been very special . . .
Not to sleep in the stone chamber; to set fire to the Marvyn family vault.	Evidently written in the wake of *Dracula*, this story is interesting because the victim wants to restore the deconsecrated Abbey – as a property development – and sees the crypt as just part of 'an old-world look'; and all the evidence points to the vampire being Sir Rupert Marvyn – he of 'the black deeds' – until the final twist.
'Caught by a projecting pinnacle' during a rocky landslide.	Apparently based on 'a tradition current in the Pyrenees', though reference is also made to Sir Richard Burton's *Vikram and the Vampire*. The story begins in 1857, the year of the 'Indian Mutiny'.

Date *Vampire*	*Source*	*Preferred Victims*	*Distinguishing Features*
1899 Three 'huge black' thirsty vampire bats.	Sidney Bertram: *With the Vampires*	Charles Grant, an impetuous explorer.	They live in a cave near the Amazon, a week away from Guatevara; their 'sharp incisor teeth' enlarge a wound on Grant's left leg, and the bodies of the 'voracious vermin' become distended as they gorge.
1900 Countess Sarah, last of the Kenyons: English aristocrat, the West Country.	F. G. Loring: *The Tomb of Sarah*	Anyone who disturbs her rest.	'She looked thin and haggard still, and her face was deadly white; but the crimson lips looked like a hideous gash in the pale cheeks, and her eyes glared like red coals in the gloom of the church.'
1900 'A young woman of uncertain age' imprisoned within an old frame and on canvas.	Hume Nisbet: *The Old Portrait*	An eager conservator, who removes the over-painting of a 'bloated . . . publican', to reveal . . .	'An intent face . . . bloodless lips and eyes like dark caverns . . .' in a frame made of 'snake-like worms twined amongst charnel house bones'.
1902 *Luella Miller, a 'slight, pliant sort of creature', an ex-schoolma'am with curly yellow hair and a pink complexion 'like a blossom' – who persuades others to do all the housework for her, and saps their vitality in a mid-nineteenth-century New England village.	Mary E. Wilkins Freeman: *Luella Miller*	Her helpers (of both genders) include two teaching assistants, her husband and sister-in-law, her aunt, doctor and two neighbours: anyone who falls for her vulnerability. She destroys all of them.	Luella 'seemed to draw the heart right out of you' with her 'doll-child' manner, peaches-and-cream appearance and inability to do anything practical. Is she evil, or is she 'like a baby with scissors in its hand cuttin' everybody without knowin' what it was doin"?

Remedy	Comments
Rescue by two travelling companions: the three bats are by now too heavy to fly, but 'float into the depths of darkness'.	An unusual short story set in the world of real-life vampire bats, far away from European Counts and Countesses.
A 'holy circle' keeps her at bay, as do garlic and dog-roses. A stake does the rest.	The setting and atmosphere of this tale resemble the world of M. R. James. James himself was later to write a vampire story (less 'domestic' than this, but with the usual atmosphere of scholarship and antiquarianism), *Count Magnus* (1905).
Cast the image from one's mind, slash the canvas and throw it onto the gas fire.	A fusion of Poe's *Oval Portrait* and Wilde's *Picture of Dorian Gray* with the 'kisses' sequence from *Dracula*.
To confront her with her laziness – braving her calculated hysterics – and to try to dissuade well-intentioned people from supporting her.	Told by Lydia Anderson, 'well over eighty', who has kept the story alive and who may be an unreliable witness. This outstanding tale, à la Henry James, also relates vampirism to 'fear of ancestors' and to 'the days of witchcraft' among the villagers.

Date Vampire	Source	Preferred Victims	Distinguishing Features
1903 Glamr, the giant undead Icelandic shepherd, in a reworking of the Norse Grettir's Saga.	Frank Norris: *Grettir at Thorhall-Stead*	Sheep and horses to start with, then the replacement shepherd Thorgaut and finally Thorhall and his family in their farmhouse in the Vale of Shadows.	In life, Glamr is an unbeliever, with a surly, bullying personality; in death – on Christmas night – his corpse grows heavier, as his limbs enlarge. He returns 'in the figure of a monster': 'the pupils of his eyes were white, the hair matted and thick'. He has superhuman strength, but is blind.
1905 (first written in the wake of *Dracula*) Cristina, a gypsy girl murdered by Sicilian robbers, the Gulf of Policastro, on the west coast of Calabria, Italy.	F. Marrion Crawford: *For the Blood Is the Life*	Angelo, the only son and heir of Alario, a local miser who has died of the fever and been robbed.	Haunts her own grave, where the treasure is buried, on the hillside, and clings on to passers-by 'pale with starvation, with the furious and unappeased physical hunger of her eyes'.
1907 *Reginald Clarke: successful male writer, New York.	George Sylvester Viereck: *House of the Vampire*	Artistic youths who have talent and ideas, especially Ernest Fielding.	'A suspicion of silver in his crown of dark hair only added dignity to his bearing ... without stretch of the imagination, one might have likened him to a Roman Cardinal of the days of the Borgias.'
1912 The undead Mrs Julia Stone, who has committed suicide in the room – where hangs her diabolical life-sized self-portrait – and who returns in her grave-clothes to feast on visitors.	E. F. Benson: *The Room in the Tower*	The narrator who, for fifteen years, has experienced a recurring nightmare about being offered a room for the night in an old tower, next to a silent dark house. The nightmare comes true, near the Ashdown Forest, East Sussex.	She has the 'odour of corruption' and 'a dreadful exuberance'; her self-portrait bleeds when it is moved and always returns to the room; a Persian cat is attracted to her tomb, while the Irish terrier is terrified of it. Mrs Stone has been waiting for fifteen years ...

Remedy	Comments
The hero Grettir wrestles with him, in the process trashing the family home, and hews off his hand with a sword, then burns his body and buries him in a sheep-walk. But 'Glamr the vampire' curses him, and curses have a habit of coming true.	Written in the *faux* archaic style of a saga, this story locates the Folkloric Vampire in a suitably bleak, barren landscape. 'Never was such a fight as this in all Iceland'. Glamr is strictly a 'revenant' rather than a vampire, and much prefers breaking spines to drinking blood.
Traced to her tomb, and staked with 'a piece of tough old driftwood' as the priest shouts exorcisms to drown the unearthly screams 'of a woman buried deep for many days'.	Written – very well – by a Sanskrit scholar, probably in Sorrento, and published posthumously. This story's title refers both to the Holy Communion service and to the Renfield sub-plot of *Dracula*.
Fielding tries to break a chair over Clarke's head, only to find himself confronted by a being 'all brain'. This being assimilates *him* instead, and he ends up as a 'gibbering idiot'.	Clarke is an 'embezzler of the mind'. He claims that he does not exactly *steal* ideas; he just *absorbs* them. Whenever Fielding is about to have an original thought 'a dream-hand clutches it and tears it away'. Eventually Clarke appears to Fielding as a huge cerebral sponge. Although not a nineteenth-century story, this unusual item contains much satire on the gay 1890s: Clarke is clearly intended to be Oscar Wilde; Fielding is Bosie. Viereck was obviously very bitter about Wilde's behaviour and the influence he had over others.
'I hit wildly with both arms, kicking out at the same moment, and heard a little animal squeal'; then the narrator turns away and slams the door. The vampire is reinterred yet again.	The narrator is presented as a 'habitual dreamer', whose dreams usually have 'no kind of psychical significance'. This was the heyday of Psychical Research.

Date			
Vampire	*Source*	*Preferred Victims*	*Distinguishing Features*
1913			
The Blood-Drinker: daughter of the Chief of the Elders, China.	George Soulié (trans.): *Strange Stories from the Lodge of Leisures* (mid-eighteenth-century Chinese folktales)	Those who disturb her rest, in this case a group of travelling merchants.	The Merchant Wang Fou ('Happiness of Kings') wakes to see 'the eyes, from which a red flame was shining, and sharp teeth, half exposed in a ferocious smile, which opened and shut by turns on the throat of the sleeper' (the second merchant).

In essence, there were four archetypal vampires in nineteenth-century fiction: the Satanic Lord (Polidori and derivatives), the Fatal Woman (Raupach, Hoffmann, Gautier, Baudelaire, Swinburne, Le Fanu, Nisbet, Gilchrist, Watson and Donovan), the Unseen Force (O'Brien, de Maupassant) and the Folkloric Vampire (Mérimée, Gogol, Tolstoy, Turgenev, Linton, Hawthorne, Burton and Norris). One might add also the 'camp' vampire (Stenbock, Viereck and perhaps Rymer), although he is parasitic – in a languid sort of way – on all the rest. Bats in South America make an appearance. The vampire as metaphor of the creative process (writing, painting or composing) also makes an occasional appearance.

Clearly, Polidori's *Vampyre* spawned a fully-fledged literary genre, with well-defined rules and a series of plot formulae which could be manipulated to suit popular taste at any time between 1820 and 1850; the location might change (Ruthven was reincarnated in Greece, Italy, the Balkans, rural England and Scotland – he appeared north of the border, not because of any Byronic associations but because the English Opera House was stuck with an extensive stock of unworn kilts), but the story remained more or less the same. The Ruthven phenomenon (perhaps the first literary formula in

Remedy	Comments
After chasing her victim, the young woman is found wrapped around a huge chestnut tree, 'her nails buried in the bark: from her mouth a stream of blood had flowed and stained her white silk jacket'. Her victim (Wang Fou) is lying on the ground. She has become a corpse again.	The Blood-Drinker is a girl who has been dead for six months, and whose coffin has been placed in a barn awaiting burial on a favourable day to be fixed by the astrologers. The merchants spend the night in that barn. The storyteller concludes: 'The corpse of the young woman evidently had not lost its inferior soul, the vital breath. Like all beings deprived of conscience and reason, her ferocity was eager for blood.' The inferior soul had refused to leave the body and, without the superior soul to control it, had forced the body to prey upon the living. Unlike its European counterpart, the Chinese vampire does not cause its victims to become vampires in turn. Just before Soulié's collection was published, Jan de Groot had included some Chinese vampire anecdotes in his *Religious System of China* (Vol. V, 1907). Soulié's Blood-Drinker represents a fascinating folkloric variant (in an aristocratic setting), which dates from just after the European 'epidemics', and originates in Chantung province.

history to originate with high culture and, eventually, to feed into working-class pulp literature) thus illustrates well what the literary historian Tzvetan Todorov defines as a genre (in his *Introduction à la Littérature Fantastique*, 1970): 'texts which do not represent a significant shift in ideas which are held at a given time about a type of literature' and 'which do not normally qualify for inclusion in the history of literature, and thus pass into another category – known as "popular" or "mass" literature' seem peculiarly appropriate as examples for genre or formula analysis. On the other hand, adds Todorov, notions of genre or formula tell us less about texts that *do* represent such a 'significant shift' and consequently qualify for inclusion in mainstream literary histories ('personal productions' as opposed to 'mechanical stereotypes'); with these texts, the critic may find that an *exclusively* thematic (or generic) approach is not enough – questions about 'the defining characteristics of a *discours fantastique* at any given time', or, in other words, about how the writer's effects are achieved, and at what level they operate, may also need to be asked.

Although the main emphasis of my chart is obviously on recurring motifs and formulae, it nevertheless shows clearly how the differences between the

Satanic Lord and the Fatal Woman in the nineteenth century epitomize Todorov's distinction. There may be rules governing the latter type (the Fatal Woman tends to be aristocratic by origin, and, as Mario Praz argued, she becomes a '*cliché indisputable*' during the aesthetic period in France), but the critic who ignores the modifications to the species which some of the personal productions *within* the type represent (as Praz tended to) is providing only a partial analysis. The Medusa did not become 'a mechanical stereotype' until much later in the century.

Certain fairly obvious generalizations arise from my schema. The Folkloric Vampire, favoured by Russian writers, characteristically has peasant associations and has the strongest political connotation. The Unseen Force (and the psychic sponge, which seems to have made its first appearance with *Spiritual Vampirism*), favoured by American writers, owes a great deal to Poe, and prefers to operate in the bourgeois world of 'bohemian' writers; the locale is varied during the Ruthven phase, but, especially in popular literature, settles down somewhere near the Carpathian Mountains around 1844, becoming a cliché (and one to laugh at) well before *Dracula*, in Stenbock's *True Story*. The vampire story is gradually 'domesticated' throughout the century; as a parallel development, the genre (which became respectable when associated with medieval or classical legends) tends more and more to be set in the 'present' (with a significant break between 1865 and 1887, when historical studies in villainy became fashionable). Only in England and France did the vampire (in all incarnations) cater to the taste of the mass reading public; yet no vampire in nineteenth-century *fiction* can be styled working class – I stress fiction, because the two French necrophiliacs who achieved a measure of notoriety in the nineteenth century (and who for some strange reason were always called 'vampires' in the popular press, although the word means almost exactly the opposite), Sgt François Bertrand (late 1840s) and Victor Ardisson (1890s), were both working class. Their exploits were celebrated in French pulp fiction, and even in music-hall songs (such as 'Le Vampire De Muy ou le violeur de cadavres', Chanson Complainte by Jean Bal, 1901, about Ardisson), but for the purposes of this discussion they do not really count as contributors to the genre. Incidentally, a more interesting reference to the vampire in working-class culture (in this case, Victorian English) occurs in Charles Dickens's magazine *Household Words*, 10 May 1851, as part of an article by the writer and spiritualist William Howitt protesting about the proposed enclosure of Epping Forest; the article refers to 'the old vampire song', which apparently goes 'For when a dead man learns to draw a nail / He soon will burst an iron bar in two'. Presumably, this is a reference to rising from the dead (or drawing the nails from a coffin) and being staked (with an iron bar), expressed in craftsman's language.

One particularly noteworthy feature of the chart is that it demonstrates that Irish/Anglo-Irish writers (Fitz-James O'Brien in 1859, Sheridan Le Fanu in 1872, Bram Stoker in 1897) made important contributions to the continuing vampire story at key moments. One could, perhaps, add Oscar Wilde's *Picture of Dorian Gray* (1891) to the list: a critic has referred to *Dorian* as 'from one of the sources of the Dracula myth'. O'Brien is the odd man out in the group, since he was a Roman Catholic graduate of Dublin University and self-styled 'literary soldier of fortune' who emigrated to America shortly after the Great Exhibition of 1851 (about which he edited a journal), to become a regular contributor to the magazines of the *Harper's* stable. The others in the group were not only from similar Protestant backgrounds – the intellectual, cultural and administrative élite of Dublin society; they were also socially connected. Abraham Stoker, father of Bram, worked as a third-class clerk in the Chief Secretary's office at Dublin Castle at the same time as William Richard Le Fanu, Sheridan's brother, was a Commissioner of Public Works. Thomas Phillip Le Fanu, son of William Richard, became a first-class clerk in the Chief Secretary's office at the same time as Bram Stoker was working in the Petty Sessions office. And Stoker's first published works appeared in the *Dublin Evening Mail*, the newspaper of which Sheridan Le Fanu had been proprietor and co-editor. Perhaps it was Bram Stoker's feeling of being strangled by red tape at the gingerbread court of the Viceroy – his day job in Dublin – that gave him a peculiar sense of affinity with the victims of Count Dracula. It is even within the bounds of possibility that the distance between Dublin Castle and Castle Dracula – at a symbolic level – was not quite as great as the maps show. Certainly, both the ancestral home of the Karnsteins in Le Fanu's *Carmilla* (1872) and Dracula's establishment in the land beyond the forest represent superb metaphors for the court of the Viceroy in the late nineteenth century; tales of bureaucracy and imagination, perhaps.

But the Anglo-Irish connections go deeper. The young Bram Stoker is known to have been a regular visitor at the soirées organized by Oscar Wilde's parents, Sir William and Lady Francesca Wilde, at 1 Merrion Square (at the time when Oscar had just entered Trinity College, Dublin). We know that Stoker knew about Irish folktales, an interest inherited from his Sligo-born mother, Charlotte, and it could be that Lady Wilde, who was to edit and publish the legends and charms gathered by her husband from his ear and eye patients, discussed their mutual interest. Certainly, the characters in some of Lady Wilde's tales – such as the demon bride who was said to haunt a churchyard in County Monaghan and to drain the vitality of passers-by – bear a certain family resemblance to the brides of the Count. Much research has been published on such connections. It was Bram Stoker who successfully put forward Oscar Wilde's name for the Philosophical Society of Trinity College and who, in December 1878, married the 'exquisitely pretty' Florence Balcombe – Wilde's sweetheart, on and off, for the past three years. To complete the picture, Julian Hawthorne – son of American writer Nathaniel Hawthorne – was Wilde's contemporary and friend at Oxford, and was often Bram Stoker's personal guest at the Lyceum Theatre. If vampires like to rise from the dead at twilight, there is a surprising amount of evidence to suggest that the Celtic twilight was particularly congenial to them.

Since the mid- to late 1980s – and increasing academic interest in diaspora, roots, identity and Irish cultural studies – it has become fashionable to reclaim *Dracula* as in some sense an Irish novel, just as the work of other prodigal sons and daughters such as Francis Bacon, Eileen Gray and indeed Oscar Wilde has been brought back into the fold: to be more precise, to make sense of *Dracula* in Irish terms. So Stoker's fears – embodied in his best-known book – have been interpreted as about the decline and fall of feudalism in Ireland; about a besieged Protestant élite post-1870s dramatizing its fears; about an absentee Anglo-Irish landlord who has run out of useable land – and who carries his soil with him; lower down the social scale, about a gombeen man, preying on the peasantry; about a coffin-ship (literally); about the charismatic politician Charles Stewart Parnell as the Count; about Stoker's distant forebear Manus 'the Magnificent' O'Donnell, a warrior clan leader who rebelled against King Henry VIII; about memories of Stoker's Sligo-born mother telling him folktales as a sickly child – or memories of tales he heard on his travels around Ireland as Inspector of Petty Sessions in his late twenties – or memories of Lady Wilde's salon. And – more plausibly perhaps – about a form of Protestant Irish Gothic – in dialogue with Charles Robert Maturin and Sheridan Le Fanu – simultaneously repulsed by and envious of Catholic magic, complete with crumbling big houses and castles, eccentric aristocrats who stay up all night; ancestry, guilt and the occult.

Predictably, some of the more reductive of these 'explanations' have recently themselves been revised: *was* Bram Stoker Anglo-Irish in any significant sense? He certainly was not a landed ascendancy grandee: he was a middle-class Protestant Dublin civil servant. How can Dracula have been an absentee landlord, a gombeen man *and* arrive in England in a coffin-ship, all at the same time? Has the theme of insecurity and guilt been overplayed? And if so, why? Would studies of Bernard Shaw, or Wilde, or Joyce so emphatically feel they had to assert their subjects' Irishness: I think not, because their work is more confidently within the literary canon, because the Irishness of their work almost goes without saying. There is evidently more going on in Bram Stoker studies than questions of national identity . . . And what about Irish *Catholic* contributions to the Gothic? And isn't it somewhat irritating to read, over and over again, how smart *we* are and how benighted the late Victorians were? Have some of these insights been *too* reductive – dealing as they do with a culture that was, in historian Roy Foster's words, 'a very complex intellectual and cultural phenomenon'. Was *Dracula* about magic at all – or rather about typewriters, phonographs, high-speed trains, advanced weaponry, cameras and blood transfusions – a kind of late Victorian techno-fiction, where the tech does not always function?: Stoker's fiction is full of fascination with modern technology. The thing is: there is no real *evidence* for any of them. All we really know for sure is that in the only novel Bram

Stoker *set* in Ireland – the West Coast, by the sea – *The Snake's Pass*, published as a book in November 1890, he showed very little serious concern about the Irish countryside, its folktales or its politics; and although he seems at one stage in his life, over in England, to have favoured Home Rule within the British Empire (he once called himself a 'philosophical Home Ruler' and enjoyed the odd exchange with William Gladstone about Irish politics), this was not by any means at the heart of his interest. At least not at a conscious level. It may have been, or it may not. We do not really know. What we do know is that *Dracula* as myth seems to contain legions.

In general, the Satanic Lord was fashionable (in box-office terms) up to 1847, when he gorged himself to death in Rymer's *Varney the Vampyre*. The Fatal Woman made tentative appearances in Germany and France during the early period of Romanticism, but came into her own during 1840–80, a period of fascination by male authors with the exotic, the aesthetic and the decadent; in box-office terms, the Medusa formula was not to become really successful until the 1880s and 1890s, reaching the early cinema with the 'vamps' well before the Satanic Lord. Goethe, Matthew 'Monk' Lewis, Ernst Raupach and (less directly) Heinrich von Kleist exploited the theme at a time when, according to Mario Praz, 'there was no established type of Fatal Woman in the way that there was an established type of Byronic hero'. Later contributors to this sub-genre (such as Théophile Gautier) were to use Goethe's *Bride of Corinth* (and thus the classical theme of love beyond the grave) and Lewis's *The Monk* as models, but the absence of an 'established type' during the phase of Ruthven's ascendancy is better symbolized by the work of Prosper Mérimée. *La Guzla* (1827), which masqueraded as a collection of Illyrian folktales, is almost exclusively concerned with vampires of the Byronic type: the 'cursed Venetian' is characteristically self-destructive, while the 'Bey of Moina' is equally characteristically a powerful political figure who rides roughshod over the sensibilities of lesser mortals. Yet only a decade later, Mérimée's gypsy girl *Carmen* was to become an early archetype of the exotic Spanish *femme fatale*, the fascinating *sorcière*. Significantly, when Mario Praz summarizes the attributes of the Fatal Woman at this stage, he does not quote from *Carmen*; instead, he quotes from *La Guzla*, reapplying

Mérimée's description of a fatal hero to one of Gautier's (later) black widows: 'His stare was enough to make you scatter your father's ashes to the four winds, trample on the holy images of the gods, and, like Prometheus, steal fire from heaven . . .' For it was not really until 1836, with Gautier's Clarimonde in *La Morte Amoureuse*, that '*la belle dame sans merci*' became a '*cliché indisputable*', whose 'typical features' could be isolated from a wide range of literary sources, for the first time. Praz expresses them thus: 'The lover is usually a youth, and maintains a passive attitude; he is obscure, and inferior either in condition or in physical exuberance to the woman, who stands in the same relation to him as does the female spider to her male: sexual cannibalism is her monopoly . . .' A mid-nineteenth-century male fantasy.

THE TEMPESTUOUS LOVELINESS OF TERROR

Clarimonde's idea of a good time is to introduce an obscure country priest, Romuald, to a world of dreams, where he will become a slave to passions 'so long repressed'; the memory of her 'sea-green eyes' and 'teeth of Orient pearl' easily effaces even the divine portrait of the Madonna. When she dies, after reviving the 'fearful orgies of Cleopatra' for eight days and eight nights, she still exercises an obsessive hold over this priest of the Lord. Like Émile Zola's Abbé Mouret, he does not stand a chance:

> At night, from the moment I closed my eyes, I became a young nobleman, a connoisseur of women, dogs and horses, dicing, drinking, blaspheming; and when I awoke at daybreak, it seemed as if I fell asleep and dreamed I was a priest . . . She would have awakened satiety itself from its slumbers, and kept inconstancy constant. To possess Clarimonde was to possess twenty mistresses, it was to possess all the women in the world, so versatile was she, so changeable, so unlike herself; a veritable chameleon!

The irony is, of course, that Romuald never for one moment possesses her. Gautier's story goes well beyond the established conventions of vampire fiction, to a world of adolescent dreams and archetypal fantasies. Within this dream setting, his discourse explores the relationships between Romuald (as child), Clarimonde (as mother and initiator) and Abbé Serapion (as 'pitiless' father, whose 'hard and savage zeal' in explaining why Clarimonde must be destroyed for ever 'gave him the look more of a demon than that of an apostle or angel').

Like the Cleopatra of the French aesthetes (with whom she is compared), Clarimonde, in her infinite variety, destroys the men she loves – and the more 'obscure' or 'inferior' they are, the better. Mario Praz's other definition of the *femme fatale* locates comparisons of this kind within the same ambiance:

> The fascination of beautiful women already dead, especially if they had been great courtesans, wanton queens or famous sinners, suggested to the Romantics, probably under the influence of the vampire legend, the figure of the Fatal Woman who was successively incarnate in all ages and all lands, an archetype which united in itself all forms of seduction, all vices and all delights.

But it was not until the 1850s and 1860s that the impact of what Praz styles 'these clichés' – 'the green-eyed predator' and 'beautiful women already dead' – altered the whole direction of the vampire tale. This thematic shift was allied, significantly enough, to a new image of the English upper class on the continent. The public image of Byron had been that of a mean, moody and magnificent Milord – dominant, with the power of attracting women as moths to a flame. By contrast, the public image of Algernon Charles Swinburne, according to Guy de Maupassant, was that of a decadent aesthete with a nervous tic and a drink problem, so supine that 'the figure he cut did not seem to belong to his sex'. George Selwyn, epitomizing 'le cool', went to France to watch and enjoy while others turned away; Swinburne preferred to be on the receiving end, indulging in a spot of *le vice anglais* when the torture gardens of London ran out of ideas.

At least, that was the public image. It bore about as much relation to the real Swinburne as Glenarvon did to Byron, but in both cases there were enough indicators in their printed works to encourage the wildest rumour. Baudelaire may have described himself experiencing ecstasies as the woman with the strawberry mouth 'sucked the pith from my bones', but in *Chastelard* (1865) Swinburne seemed to be going one step further. For him (extending what de Sade had written seventy-five years before), '*Nature herself* hungers at all her pores for bloodshed, feeding with fresh blood the innumerable insatiable mouths suckled at her milkless breast.' His *femme fatale* – one of the 'wanton queens' of history, Mary Stuart – does not have to encourage Chastelard to become a martyr to his infatuation: already, his one ambition (as was Swinburne's own, in the poem *Satia Te Sanguine*) is to be 'the powerless victim of the furious rage of a beautiful woman'. Baudelaire's ecstasy was less frenetic and overblown, perhaps because he was fantasizing less. Swinburne seems merely to be using words, where Baudelaire had created images. His world was to enter pulp fiction through cheap pornography in England – such as *The Pearl* (1879), which ran a regular feature on adventures in Miss Flaybum's Academy.

Like Cleopatra, Lucrezia Borgia, Elizabeth Báthory or any other members of the monstrous regiment of women who 'sucked between small teeth the sap o' the veins' of consenting adults during this period, Swinburne's Mary Stuart was intended to show how 'for all Christ's work, this Venus is not quelled'. The Victorian critic and aesthete Walter Pater even saw something of this in the *Mona Lisa*:

> All the thoughts and experiences of the world have etched and moulded there, in that which they have of power to refine and make expressive the outward form, the animalism of Greece, the lust of Rome, the mysticism of the Middle Ages with its spiritual ambition and imaginative loves, the return of the Pagan world, the sins of the Borgias. She is older than the rocks among which she sits; like the vampire, she has been dead many times, and learned the secrets of the grave; and has been a diver in deep seas, and keeps their fallen day about her . . .

That, presumably, was why she was smiling. To hide her teeth . . .

COUNT DRACULA

Dracula's debt to the Byronic vampire is obvious: the Count's appearance – despite his great age of 466 – betrays it ('his eyes were positively blazing. The red light in them was lurid, as if the flames of hell-fire blazed behind them'), and his relationship with the débutante-like Lucy Westenra, fiancée of Lord

Godalming, confirms it. The name of Lucy's more practical friend (and the real heroine of the book) may perhaps have been taken from a Hoffmann-inspired tale of terror told by 'Monk' Lewis later that summer in 1816 and called *Mina*. Bram Stoker's knowledge of the occult interests of the Romantic poets was to feature in a later book, *The Jewel of Seven Stars* (1903). What is not so obvious is the way in which Stoker subsumed two other aspects of the vampire genre into his *Dracula* – the Fatal Woman and the Folkloric Vampire. One clue lies in the following well-known and well-embroidered anecdote from Hall Caine's *Recollections of Dante Gabriel Rossetti* (1882). Rossetti had buried a little book of love poems ('chiefly inspired by and addressed to her') in the tomb of Elizabeth Siddal at Highgate ('he spoke to her as though she heard . . . she must take the words with her'):

> But as one by one of his friends – Swinburne and others – attained distinc-
> tion, he began to hanker after poetic reputation – and to reflect with pain
> and regret upon the hidden fruits of his best effort . . . After an infinity
> of self-communications he determined to have the grave opened and the
> book extracted . . . So, one night, seven and a half years after the burial, a
> fire was built by the side of the grave, and then the coffin was raised and
> opened. The body is described as perfect upon coming to light.

'When the book was lifted,' Caine added later, 'there came away some of the beautiful golden hair in which Rossetti had entwined it.' Dante Gabriel Rossetti was a nephew of Dr John Polidori (of *Vampyre* fame); Dante Gabriel's brother, William Michael, was later to publish Polidori's *Diary* (in 1911), and the whole Rossetti family had access to a bowdlerized version of it transcribed by Aunt Charlotte, Polidori's aged sister. Elizabeth Siddal, Dante's wife for two short years, epitomized the type of sad, fragile beauty to which Rossetti and the Pre-Raphaelites were martyrs: 'a spectral halo seems to radiate from his figures,' writes Praz, 'as it radiates also round certain episodes of his life, in particular that of his marriage, which might have been taken bodily from the tales of Poe.' This spectral halo seems to have been, for Rossetti, a substitute for creating a serious relationship with Elizabeth in this life; certainly, he was much more effective in his relationship with her after death.

Hall Caine's *Recollections* were an attempt to set the record straight about Rossetti's life 'in all love of his memory' – whether or not all his anecdotes were strictly true. Stoker's *Dracula* was dedicated to the Manx novelist, for Hall Caine was one of Stoker's closest friends and his confidant (it has even been suggested that he must have had a hand in the writing of *Dracula*). Stoker had consulted Caine before, and it appears that in 1891 on a visit to Scotland the actor-manager Henry Irving, Hall Caine and Irving's business manager Bram Stoker discussed 'weird subjects' together (see page 108). In 1896, towards the end of the writing of *Dracula*, Stoker borrowed money from Caine – he was experiencing a liquidity crisis – and hoped that the proceeds of his forthcoming novel would help repay the debt. When Bram and his wife Florence moved to 27 Cheyne Walk, Chelsea, in 1881, they discovered that Dante Gabriel Rossetti was their 'close neighbour' at no. 16. The connections between Caine's anecdote and the activities of Lucy Westenra (in her 'Lilith' incarnation) around Hampstead and Highgate seem clear; when Van Helsing goes to visit her in her tomb nearly a week after she has died, she seems to be 'if possible, more radiantly beautiful than ever'.

But there may have been other, more direct, connections between *Dracula* and the *femme fatale*. We now know that during his researches Bram Stoker was reading Sabine Baring-Gould's *Book of Were-wolves* (1865). In that strange collection of nasty stories, he *could* have read about one of the archetypal 'beautiful women already dead' who so fascinated the decadents – Elizabeth Báthory, the bloody countess of Hungary, whose unique ideas about personal hygiene were alleged to have resulted in the deaths of approximately 650 young virgins. He could have, but we do not know that he did. Another link with the *femme fatale* involves the short story *Dracula's Guest* (published 1914), probably pieced together from Stoker's working papers for *Dracula* and published posthumously, which tells of Jonathan Harker's close encounter with the long-dead 'Countess Dolingen of Gratz'; Stoker removed all reference to this from the final draft, maybe because it was too closely modelled on Sheridan Le Fanu's *Carmilla*. Quite apart from discovering the name of his fearless vampire destroyer and father figure in Le Fanu's Dr Hesselius – another possibility – Stoker seems to have been much taken by the strange and beautiful relationship between vampire and victim in *Carmilla*. Lucy and the brides of Dracula court their prey in ways that owe much to Le Fanu's listless *femme fatale*, and the extraordinarily supine response of the victims (who 'seem somehow' to have encountered the archetypal image of the predator before, 'in connection with some dreamy fear') – if I lie still and half close my eyes, I will not *really* be guilty – locates parts of Stoker's book on a similar psychological plane. In Ivan Turgenev's *Phantoms* (1868) also the narrator is struck by the feeling that the beautiful vampire, Alice, 'was a woman I had known at some time or other, and I made tremendous efforts to recall where I had seen her . . . In a flash everything had melted away again like a dream.' It may well have been Le Fanu's story that suggested to Stoker the idea of writing a vampire novel in the first place. *Carmilla*'s dream-like fantasy about sexually aware, and sexually dominant, women – who register as attractive and repellent both at the same time – would seem to have bitten deep into the psyche of two apparently prosaic, not-so-eminent Victorian males: Bram Stoker and his fictional counterpart, Jonathan Harker. In *Dracula* this was a case of 'some longing and at the same time some deadly fear'.

The Folkloric Vampire finds its way into the book through the wealth of detail on topography and gypsy lore that Stoker managed to incorporate – from research sources as wide-ranging as a hunter's memoirs about life in Transylvania, a survey of the region's 'superstitions' by the wife of a serving officer in the Austro-Hungarian army and the more down-to-earth Baedeker's *Southern Germany and Austria* (see 'The Genesis of Dracula', page 333). Their availability in print in the 1890s testifies to the fashion for romantic and usually patronizing travellers' tales about Eastern Europe – written by retired British officials or sometimes their wives – in the last two decades of the century. The works of 'E. D. Gerard', in particular, are the closest in tone to the world of *Dracula*, with their sense of 'leaving the West and entering the East', as Harker puts it at the beginning of the novel. The two sisters who used this pen-name (Emily and Dorothea) wrote a series of books, articles and novels that waxed eloquent about the folktales of the Carpathians: they are full of superstitious gypsies, ancient beliefs based on the seasons of the earth, and magic places. Both had lived in the countries they described, and both were married to army officers (one a Magyar, one a Pole). The two books of theirs that Jonathan Harker was likely to have read in the British Museum Library are *The Waters of Hercules* (1886) and *The Land Beyond the Forest* (1888). From *The Waters of Hercules* he would have learned about the 'Gaura Dracului' (or 'Devil's Hole'), a concealed pit in the wilds of Wallachia, surrounded by exotic foliage ('the beautiful mask of a hideous thing'), which had more than once 'lured a victim into its jaws' and which was said by local peasants to be haunted – an entrance to the other world, a place for giving the Devil (or 'Dracul') his due. In *The Land Beyond the Forest* (which Stoker definitely knew about) he would have found many details about the folktales of Transylvania, and especially about the 'nosferatu, or vampire, in which every Romanian peasant believes as firmly as he does in heaven or hell . . .'. Much of the lore in *Dracula* comes from a chapter in this book, originally published as an article in 1885, sometimes almost verbatim. It did not have much to say about vampires, but Stoker made full use of such references as there were. He was not an experienced writer of fiction when first he embarked on his masterpiece in spring 1890 (he had yet to publish his first full-length novel), and the research sources he was using – their phrases, their information, their ideas – were transposed all too obviously into the finished text. Only when he was writing from his own experience, and about places he knew well, did he manage to cut loose from his research.

The books of 'E. D. Gerard' were in vogue in the mid- to late 1880s, and *Dracula* was eventually published at a time when various derivatives were still on the market to contribute to Bram Stoker's success. These included *The Pobratim, A Slav Novel* (1895) by Professor P. Jones (which has a long chapter about a Montenegrin vampire), *'Midst The Wild Carpathians* (1894) by Maurus Jokai (which was translated from the Hungarian to read like a carbon copy of 'E. D. Gerard' and concerns dark deeds in and around the 'Gradina Dracului' or 'Gardens of the Devil') and *Untrodden Paths in Roumania* (1888) by Mrs Mary Walker (which contains much material on Vlad Dracula – the Impaler – and his 'unimaginable cruelties').

Another main route by which the Folkloric Vampire entered Dracula (apart, possibly, from Stoker's interest in aspects of Irish and Scottish folklore) is represented on my chart by Sir Richard Burton's free adaptation of a portion of the Sanskrit folktales *Vikram and the Vampire* (1870, reissued 1893). The folktales date back to the eleventh century, if not before. Despite the title the book itself would have been of little interest to Stoker, although – characteristically – Burton was later to attribute the growth of a 'facetious, fictitious literature' on the subject of vampires to the inspiration of his *Vikram*. Each story in the collection concerns Raja Vikram's attempts to capture the wily Vetala or Baital, who hangs from a tree like a fruit bat, reanimates corpses and is good at riddles. But when Stoker was actually introduced to Sir Richard Burton (by Henry Irving) in January 1879, and later had a chance to chat with him about his various adventures 'amongst old tombs' near Damascus, 'the man riveted my attention'. '... Burton's face seemed to lengthen when he laughed; the upper lip rising instinctively and showing the right canine tooth. This was always a characteristic of his enjoyment.' And when the two met again, in 1886, Stoker noted once more that as Sir Richard's 'strong, deep, resonant voice' dominated the proceedings, 'the upper lip rose and his canine tooth showed its full length like the gleam of a dagger'. The association between 'old tombs', 'the canine tooth' and Burton's evident ruthlessness may, it has been suggested, have stuck in Stoker's mind, even if Vikram did not. Where the eighteenth-century philosophical debates about the folklore of vampires were concerned, Stoker showed some awareness of them when he was interviewed by a journalist named Jane Stoddard in 1897, shortly after the first publication of *Dracula*.

> She asked him: 'Is there any historical basis for the [vampire] legend?'
>
> He replied: 'It rested, I imagine, on some such case as this. A person may have fallen into a death-like trance and been buried before the time. Afterwards the body may have been dug up and found alive, and from this a horror seized upon the people, and in their ignorance they imagined that a vampire was about ...'

However, Count Dracula himself is not, of course, a figure entirely or even largely out of folklore. His distant literary ancestors have already been mentioned, but there were two more recent literary 'models' at Stoker's disposal. *The Mysterious Stranger* by Karl von Wachsmann, a German tale that dates from around 1844 and was translated in 1854 for *Chamber's Repository*, may well have sown the seeds for the most famous (and most often filmed) section of *Dracula*, set in the Count's Carpathian castle, and Count Azzo von Klatka behaves towards his victims in ways that beg comparison with his more notorious disciple. But the *form* of *Dracula* was clearly derived from another literary source, dating from 1860: Wilkie Collins's *The Woman in White*, a successful attempt to revive the then-unfashionable epistolary novel. Stoker was especially impressed by the technique of presenting records 'which are exactly contemporary', and by a mass of material from a variety of perspectives. The character of the suave, grotesque villain, Count Fosco (the most popular of Collins's inventions, included in the story because 'the crime was too ingenious for an English villain'), may also have impinged on Stoker's imagination. Fosco's physical appearance – he is built like Orson Welles – and bizarre habits (which include talking to 'little feathered children', his beloved caged birds) do not resemble Count Dracula's in the slightest, but his pedantic way of speaking, his rather 'forced' charm ('the magnetic personal influence which I exercise over my fellow creatures') and, above all, the pleasure he takes in destructive relationships (the victim feeling 'a strange, half-willing, half-unwilling liking for the Count') seem nearer to Stoker's characterization. We are never given a direct portrait of Count Fosco; like Count Dracula, he appears to us (with a splendid sense of construction) through his impact on the various narrators, who may or may not be reliable.

In 1887 Wilkie Collins published another story that may have impinged on Stoker's mind – this time a short story in his series of 'little novels' called *Miss Mina and the Groom*. The heroine's full name is Wilhelmina. 'I bear my German mother's Christian name,' she says, '. . . all my friends, in the days when I had friends, used to shorten this to Mina.' The story, which is evidently intended for undemanding railway readers, is about Mina falling under the spell of a mere groom – an experience that leaves her feeling 'like a new woman'. So, perhaps Stoker found *his* heroine's name in Wilkie Collins rather than in 'Monk' Lewis. If so, vampire and victim may both have been inspired by the same literary imagination – Wilkie Collins's. For some reason, many of Stoker's heroines have first names that begin with the letter 'M'.

Yet despite all these connections, Count Dracula was much more than a synthetic literary creation. Bram Stoker *lived* him. Wherever Mina's Christian name came from, her surname was borrowed from Joseph Harker, one of the scene-painting team employed by the actor-manager Henry Irving at the Lyceum Theatre. Harker later recalled that Stoker 'appropriated my surname for one of his characters'. Theatrical legend has it that the *Dracula* project was first suggested to Stoker during long discussions about suitable parts for Irving, conducted in the Beefsteak Room behind the Lyceum. Irving, Stoker and Hall Caine regularly met there after the show to try – over a chop or two – to adapt plays or stories to Irving's inimitable talents: it was unusual for any play to go onto the Lyceum stage unaltered. On one celebrated occasion, on 30 April 1890 – a month *after* Stoker first started his working notes for *Dracula* – they were joined by Arminius (Armin or Herman) Vámbéry, a distinguished Hungarian Orientalist from the University of Budapest. Many of the subjects for discussion on these occasions tended to be concerned with the supernatural – the Wandering Jew, the Flying Dutchman, the Demon Lover, for example – but Irving had already played them all, in one form or another. Stoker – as Irving's most recent (and best) biographer Jeffrey Richards reminds us – was 'steeped in the supernatural atmosphere of such productions as *The Corsican Brothers*, *Faust* and *The Bells*'. In 1894, to give another example, Irving purchased a stage adaptation of *Dr Jekyll and Mr Hyde*, but never performed the parts. As Hall Caine later recalled: 'The truth is, great actor that Irving was, the dominating element in his personality was for many years a hampering difficulty.' According to Stoker, the parts they discussed tended to be 'too young . . . too rough . . . [or] too tall'; nevertheless, they persevered and 'the conversation tended towards weird subjects . . . Irving always said that Caine would write a great work of weirdness some day.' Sadly, though, there is no evidence that Stoker discussed any aspect of vampire lore or even Transylvania with Vámbéry – who never published anything on the subject.

But it may well be that at one stage the character of Count Dracula was considered by Stoker as a possible vehicle for Irving, in a specially written dramatic version: in memory of the night of 30 April 1890, Vámbéry makes a fleeting appearance in *Dracula* as Van Helsing's 'friend Arminius', a world authority on *voïvode* or Prince Dracula and vampires (which he was not – and he did not consider his contribution to the story, if indeed he made any, sufficiently important to merit a mention in his autobiography). Perhaps Vámbéry mentioned *en passant* some conversation he had had with I. Bogdan, a colleague of his at Budapest, who was at that time preparing the first major biography of Vlad Tepes (The Impaler). In the event, Irving was never to play the part of the Count. When Stoker organized a play-reading of the book in a cut-and-paste version in order to protect the theatrical copyright, in May 1897, Irving is said by family tradition to have thought the ramshackle performance 'Dreadful!' Why Irving should have been so tactless was not clear; perhaps it was because the vocal tricks of the vampire Count, as well as aspects of his character and some of his physical mannerisms (particularly his melodramatic habit of holding women at arm's length and shouting at them), resembled more than a little Irving's performances during his twilight years at the Lyceum. (According to one critic of the day, Irving's 'hissing and terrible voice' had become much too much of a good thing; Shaw called his barnstorming Shakespeare performances 'Bardicide'!) If this is so, then the relationship between Jonathan Harker (often Stoker's mouthpiece) and the Count may tell us more about the business manager's relationship with his employer than does Stoker's own (usually gushing) *Personal Reminiscences of Henry Irving*, published in 1906, shortly after Irving's death. *Personal Reminiscences* consists largely of 757 pages of hero-worship mixed with awe. Hall Caine, in his obituary of Stoker, wrote 'never have I seen, never do I expect to see, such absorption of one man's life in the life of another'. Or perhaps Irving was just joking . . .

The relationship had started very strangely. Stoker, then a young Dublin civil servant and part-time drama critic, had been so inspired by Irving's rendition of Thomas Hood's *Dream of Eugene Aram the Murderer* (1831), and especially by 'the sense of his dominance', that as Irving 'collapsed, half fainting' at the end, Stoker had a fit of 'something like hysterics'. This incident apparently helped to convince him that he should abandon his Dublin career and eventually he joined Henry Irving, the Guv'nor, in London as 'his faithful, loyal and devoted servitor' – looking after the accounts, organizing tours and keeping 'illustrious patrons' at bay in the foyer when they made Irving 'depressed and nervous'. But by the time *Dracula* was written, the Lyceum was in trouble and Irving was becoming increasingly difficult to deal with. Stoker was beginning to find that it was a full-time job simply pandering to his gigantic ego. There was a storage fire in 1898, followed by financial collapse in 1902.

The business manager's suggestions during this period (usually about finances, but sometimes about repertoire as well – he even helped with some texts) characteristically met with condescension, if not bland disregard. We have seen how Irving liked to introduce Stoker to illustrious patrons, such as Sir Richard Burton or Arminius Vámbéry, after the show, and the 'devoted servitor' continued to enjoy this aspect of his work with a wide-eyed, scalp-hunting enthusiasm which never left him. *Personal Reminiscences* is full of lists of the names of famous people, some of them running to several pages. But as Irving became more capricious, he also, paradoxically, became more dependent. One of the contributors to the *We Saw Him Act* anthology (1939) on the art of Irving recalls an occasion when the actor-manager broke down in front of his public: 'Please stop. I cannot recite for you – or say a few words for you – or give my name to you. Here Bram, Bram, I say . . .' Because of this, Stoker could no longer be sure of his respect for Irving – and that mattered a great deal to him. The strange mixture of worship and awe that permeates the *Personal Reminiscences* (of twenty-eight years' service) was probably a legacy of this period. It may be that for Stoker, as for Polidori, the vampire as demanding employer was a crucial equation. But the most likely connection between Irving and *Dracula* is that the Count's mannerisms were inspired by the actor's performances on the Lyceum stage, rather than by the person.

Dracula differs from the previous vampire Counts of literature, not simply because he is an old actor past his prime but because he is a *military* figure as well, who periodically reminisces about his military successes in the distant past, in campaigns to drive the Turks out of his territory. And this is where Bram Stoker's historical researches become interesting. *Dracula* owes very little to Tournefort, Calmet and the other sources that had been pillaged during the Ruthven period; but we know that Stoker found the name 'Dracula' in a book he was reading, William Wilkinson's *Account of the Principalities of Wallachia and Moldovia* (1820), in Whitby Museum, Subscription Library and Warm Bathing Establishment on 19 August 1890. Like Jonathan Harker in the story, he may then have gleaned further information from the British Museum. Recent books about the life and times of Vlad the Impaler have implied that Stoker took a research historian's interest in the subject, but one glance at his later book *Famous Imposters* (1910) shows clearly how cavalier Stoker's attitude was towards his sources – and that was when he was trying to write serious history. On this occasion, he was even less interested in historical accuracy; at most, he was looking for a name (which eventually became the title), a past (some reminiscences) and possibly a physical description. The research that he did was always with a view to writing a *novel*.

Stoker gives his Dracula the title of Count, the family tree of a Szekely, plus a home in Transylvania and a castle near the Borgo pass. In fact, Vlad Dracula had the title *voïvode* or prince, the Szekelys hailed from Hungary rather than Transylvania, his home was in Wallachia and his castle in Poenari, nowhere near the Transylvania–Bukovina border. In other words, Bram Stoker was more interested in a fairytale setting (Transylvania, land of 'witches and hobgoblins', according to one of his sources), a Gothic villain with a three-syllable name (they tended to be 'Counts', members of a fading aristocracy, and for some reason often Hungarian as well) and an atmosphere of the exotic. As he wrote at the beginning of *Dracula*, his basic aim was to concoct 'a history almost at variance with the possibilities of latter-day belief'. So a Count, distantly related to Attila the Hun and living in the land beyond the forest was just fine by him. When subsequently asked by an American journalist about whether he actually *knew* anything about Transylvania, Stoker candidly replied: 'Trees are trees, mountains are – generally speaking – mountains, no matter in what country you find them, and one description fits all.'

In any case, of the *many* sources for Vlad's reign that have subsequently been unearthed (including six pamphlets, written at various times and for various purposes) only four were in the British Museum catalogue at the time

Stoker was preparing his novel: an account of Vlad's atrocities, published in Bamberg in 1491, with a woodcut on the cover that bears a certain family resemblance to the *facial* characteristics of Count Dracula; the English translation (1574) of Sebastian Münster's *Cosmographia*, which contains a brief account of Vlad's reign; Richard Knolles's *Generall History of the Turks* (1603), which tells of Vlad's penchant for 'sharpe stakes'; and the record of Vlad's arrest, commissioned by the Pope in 1462. But there is no evidence that Stoker read them, and he much preferred to make up the history (out of bits and pieces) as he went along. Wilkinson's *Account of the Principalities of Wallachia and Moldavia*, the book Stoker read and annotated in Whitby, is noticeably muddled about the history – which Dracula was which – and never mentions the name Vlad.

Vlad IV, or Vlad the Impaler, was *voïvode* of Wallachia in 1448, from 1456 to 1462, and in 1476. Vlad III, the previous *voïvode*, had been known as 'Dracul', or 'the Dragon' – probably because he was a member of the Order of the Dragon, pledged to fighting the Turks. When Vlad the Impaler inherited the name, 'Dracul' also came to mean 'the Devil' – among other reasons, because of the atrocities he committed (impaling, roasting, decapitation, and so on) when fighting the Turks, who had imprisoned him during his youth and had taught him the value of terror tactics. 'Drac' meant dragon, 'ul' meant 'the' and 'a' meant 'son of', so 'Dracula' meant the 'son of the dragon'.

Various legends came to be associated with Dracula, as pamphleteers were commissioned to use the story for different purposes (none of them, incidentally, was concerned with vampirism, and very few with Transylvania). The 1491 Bamberg pamphlet, which Stoker could conceivably have read – if he could manage the High German: he could have looked at the picture – outlines his various atrocities with evident relish, then goes on to tell of Vlad's conversion to Roman Catholicism. In Ivan the Terrible's Russia, Vlad became known as 'a stern but just ruler to his people'. In some pamphlets, Vlad was presented as a once and future prince, like Arthur, Charlemagne or the sleeping Barbarossa, who would rise again from the dead when the nation was threatened – a reputation that has survived to this day. I can well remember when I was visiting Romania in the mid-1970s, when the official Communist

Party commemorations leading up to the five-hundredth anniversary of Vlad's death were being discussed: there was to be a special postage stamp, the late President Nicolae Ceausescu made a major speech about Vlad as national hero (for 'the Turks' read 'the Soviets' *and* 'the West') and there was much talk about how Romanians preferred to think of the *voïvode* of Wallachia as 'the Impaler' rather than as 'Dracula'. The vampire connection, I was solemnly informed, was being emphasized and peddled, with malice aforethought, by 'the West', and, worse still, it most likely originated in Hungary!

In other pamphlets of the early modern period, Vlad was presented as a grotesque, like Richard III of England and Ivan III of Muscovy, to be scorned by some future regime for political purposes, usually to entrench their own position. There was even a Wallachian legend about the previous *voïvode*, Vlad the Dragon, who was said to have risen from his grave at sunset to keep an eye on his territory. Very little about the Vlad legends (or even about the atrocities, which were of a kind normally attributed to tax collectors at the time) was unique – not even his name. The author of *Dracula* successfully managed to confuse the two Vlads, father and son, but he wasn't likely to be particularly interested in all of this; he had other things on his mind.

The critic Ludovic Flow has written about Stoker's work, and about *Dracula* in particular:

> He is the master of the commonplace style in which clichés flow as if they were impelled by the same pressure as genius. I don't say this lightly. There is a semi-heroic, Everyman quality about his intense command of the mediocre – as if the commonplace had found a champion who could wear its colours with all the ceremony of greatness. When such a man, just once, is thoroughly afraid, the charade stops and what you get is *Dracula*.

Literary and historical sources will take us only so far. When the forty-two-year-old Bram Stoker first conceived the novel, he had more than books on his mind. Florence Stoker, his widow, was to recall in 1927 that 'When he was at work on *Dracula*, we were all frightened of him ... he seemed to get obsessed by the spirit of the thing'. Was he, like Jonathan Harker, the supine victim of a seductive vampire he thought he had seen somewhere before? Was he, like Count Dracula, a potent, animal-like creature of instinct who thought he could bring out the latent sexuality of even the most prim English miss? Did he *need* someone like the Count, to keep his sexual drives in order – 'this man belongs to *me*'? Or was he watching, in terror? Most explanations of Stoker's haemosexual trauma (in the form of his nightmare about 'this man belongs to me', see pages 338–39) make him seem like a banal version of one of psychiatrist Richard von Krafft-Ebing's more pathetic case studies, one with the rude passages written in Latin. It was, we are told, something to do with a childhood experience of blood-letting in a Dublin hospital and a fear of doctors; or to do with a childhood illness, and a subconscious desire to eat his baby brothers; or because he caught tertiary syphilis in 1890 (or was it 1897?); or because his wife's frigidity had driven him to consort with prostitutes (so he felt guilty and frustrated at the same time); or because he had a *thing* about menstruation. For none of which is there – so far – a scrap of sustainable evidence.

Bram Stoker himself seems to have thought of *Dracula* as a simple adventure story which was also a Christian allegory – the boarding schools' eleven versus the forces of darkness. The implications of the story clearly run much deeper than he realized (otherwise, apart from anything else, how can one explain its enduring fascination), but how much? The trauma can never satisfactorily be recovered, but sticking to the book the many connections that are made between blood and sexual initiation (connections that are never, needless to say, overtly explored) provide some interesting indicators. One possible (if not particularly original) reading goes like this. When Lucy is bitten by Dracula, it is clear that she has been 'initiated' for the first time. The vampire drinks more than just *her* blood, however, for the men who are in love with her have also had their blood transfused into her veins (Van Helsing sniggers at the thought that they have all really become 'husbands'); as she loses her vitality, so do they. Dracula also tells Mina that she has become 'flesh of my flesh . . . kin of my kin' through intercourse with the vampire, but Van Helsing will not be happy until both Lucy Westenra and Mina Harker are the prim young ladies they once were, so he explains to the other 'husbands' (who are also in danger, in a different way) why it is imperative for them not to be fooled into believing that the desires of the flesh are as much fun as they look. It is too late to save Lucy (for she has 'died' and risen to a new, and extremely seductive, incarnation), but 'that wonderful Madam Mina', who has 'a man's brain ... and a woman's heart' (a combination Stoker himself seems to have found almost as attractive as the ravishing Lucy haunting the cemetery), can still be saved to become a good wife for Jonathan and a good mother to their baby. The trouble is that there is something of Dracula in all of us. 'This evil thing is rooted deep in all good,' says Van Helsing, 'in soil barren of holy memories it cannot rest.'

So, like a Miltonic fallen angel, Dracula may be a metaphor for a choice we all must make. But in this case the weapons of Christianity are not enough, so Van Helsing uses the weapons of folklore *and* the weapons of modern science as well. Modern science, for example, in the form of blood transfusions, is explicitly associated with the dilution of sexual drive – one of the inevitable discontents of civilization. If this reading is correct, then *Dracula* is a manifesto for sexual repression. Whatever Bram Stoker dreamed about, it must have scared the hell out of him.

The trauma may, of course, have concerned a 'nameless fear' of a very different order. Nikolai Gogol, Alexis Tolstoy and Ivan Turgenev all wrote their Folkloric Vampire tales at times when the tsarist censorship was at its tightest, and, by presenting them as peasant folktales, managed to get away with an often explicit association between vampirism and the Cossacks, or the landlords. Clearly, the vampire theme lends itself very well to an exploration of relationships that involve the exercise of power – political and social, as well as psychological – as Jean-Jacques Rousseau pointed out. The master–slave dialectic could, as we have seen, be rewritten as a vampire relationship that is equally degrading for both parties. Reactions to the eighteenth-century peasant vampires may be related to the precarious power and influence of the Roman Catholic Church in areas where Greek Orthodoxy or pre-Christian magic had taken root (the vampire as a satirical projection, a kind of reverse mirror-image of transubstantiation). Existentialists today might interpret the power of the crowd as vampiric (the vampire is other people). The two major developments in the nineteenth-century vampire genre were both associated (at a popular level, especially in France) with the public image of Milord Rosbif on the continent. Whether the Satanic Lord was dominating and self-destructive or supine and self-destructive, the literary (as opposed to the folkloric) vampire he represented may well have had something to do with attitudes towards English imperialism.

The *form*, as well as the content, that *Dracula* took, at a time of high imperialism, would seem to substantiate this last suggestion. The form is a series of (mainly typewritten) documents, arranged in a collage, all representing the views of the 'initiates' and all concerned with the one character who does not contribute a single document himself ('needless matters have been eliminated . . . all the records are exactly contemporary, given from the standpoints and within the range of knowledge of those who made them'). Stoker may even have jettisoned the opening 'Munich' section of the novel – from his working notes, later reworked as *Dracula's Guest* – partly *because* it contains a letter from the Count himself. The 'standpoints' of Stoker's characters – the old (and rather tactless) professor, the deep-thinking doctor (who has the strange belief, derived from Nietzsche, that 'I may be of an exceptional brain, congenitally'), the young solicitor, the English Milord, the upper-middle-class girl (who is not expected to work) and the incredibly competent middle-class girl (who has learned how to earn a living) – are thus built into the form of the book.

The image of society that gradually emerges through this form can be expressed in terms of beliefs held by *all* the 'initiates'. The working class is associated with music-hall accents, drunkenness, money-grubbing and a touching deference to their betters; women are assumed, on the whole, to be flighty and submissive (most of the troubles in the second half of the book arise because Mina Harker has been kept in the dark by the other 'initiates', and everyone expresses surprise at her 'competence') or, after marriage, potential wild beasts (like in the music-hall songs) – even Dracula has to get 'married' to find out; gypsies are despised (and normally associated with Dracula's other friends, the rats and the wolves); anything to do with the East is distrusted on principle, and the 'quest' of the 'initiates' involves an attempt to prevent the Count from colonizing England (his behaviour represents a reverse mirror-image of what the American, Dutch and English 'initiates' have in common). Although they may use the latest developments in science and technology, the 'initiates' seem to be fighting a rearguard action in favour of 'the world we are about to lose', and the trauma is expressed, characteristically enough, as a Christian crusade. The year that *Dracula* came out – 1897, the year of Queen Victoria's Diamond Jubilee – was taken by Lenin to mark the apogee of imperialism, the highest stage of capitalism. In general, Stoker's Protestant Christianity has been downplayed by recent critics, who have tended to focus instead on the incidents in the book that support their theses about gender and identity. It was also the year in which Sigmund Freud commenced his psycho-analytical researches. At first the rational reader thinks that the 'initiates' are quite mad, but gradually, with Dr Seward, he or she comes to recognize that the behaviour of the madmen is truly 'an index to the coming and going of the Count'. And by rooting for their actions, the reader sides with their beliefs. Not for nothing were quests of this kind so often associated with St George, the fearless protector of the unsullied virgin and the slayer of the winged 'Dracul' – the dragon, the Devil or the vampire.

One of the experts consulted by Bram Stoker (with whom he had been in correspondence since the mid-1880s) was the Oxford specialist in Oriental languages and Fellow of All Souls, Professor Max Müller. Indeed, Stoker's research notes suggest that it was after reading a quotation from Müller's work on the Magyar tongue that he first had the idea of making Count Dracula both a 'Szekely' and kin to Attila the Hun. The quotation implied that the Huns had made contact with the Szekely tribes in the fifth century, and this was transformed in the novel into Dracula's claim that 'in our veins flows the blood of many brave races who fought as the lion fights, for lordship . . . what devil or what witch was ever so great as Attila, whose blood is in these veins? . . . Is it a wonder that we were a conquering race; that we were proud? . . . [But] the warlike days are over. Blood is too precious a thing in these days of dishonourable peace; and the glories of the great races are as a tale that is told.' It has been suggested that Professor Müller (born in Dessau) may have been one of the models for Professor Van Helsing (of Amsterdam). Stoker and Müller met at least twice, once at the Lyceum, once at Oxford. It is also possible that in Stoker's mind, hidden beneath the crusade against the empire of the nosferatu, lay some kind of cosmic racial conflict – between the representatives of modern Anglo-Saxon stock, plus an infusion of American, and the representative of the 1,400-year-old line of Attila the Hun. If so, it is interesting that at precisely the time when Stoker started corresponding with Max Müller, the Professor was researching into the origins of the ancient symbol of the swastika as 'universal solar symbol', and was engaged in an Anglo-German debate about whether or not this 'universal symbol' belonged to the history of the 'Aryan peoples'. In Stoker's notes, Van Helsing started life as 'a German Professor of History' by the name of Max. He, too, was to be interested in the degeneration of the stock.

Shortly after *Dracula* was published, Bram Stoker helped to put on a Diamond Jubilee Benefit Performance at the Lyceum on 25 June 1897 for the Indian and colonial troops gathered in London. His comments on the occasion are in this context instructive: 'The troops', he wrote, 'represented every colour and ethnological variety of the human race, from coal black through yellow and brown up to the light type of the Anglo-Saxon reared afresh in new realms beyond the seas.' A subsequent benefit, he added, this time to celebrate the Coronation of Edward VII in 1902, was attended by 1,000 guests 'from every part of the world and of every race under the sun. In type and colour they would have illustrated a discourse on ethnology or craniology. Some were from the centre of wildest Africa, not long come under the dominion of Britain ... one of them a king whose blackness of skin was beyond belief.' It was the swansong of the Lyceum Theatre. Both events were contrasted by Stoker, in Volume One of his *Personal Reminiscences of Henry Irving*, with a visit he made to the United States warship *Chicago*, on 3 June 1894, at the invitation of Admiral Erben:

> If the greeting was hearty, the farewell was touching. We had got into the
> boat and were just clearing the vessel, we waving our hats to those behind,
> when there burst out a mighty cheer, which seemed to rend the air like
> thunder. It pealed over the water that still Sabbath afternoon and startled

the quiet folk on the frontages at Gravesend. Cheer after cheer came ringing and resonant with a heartiness that made one's blood leap. For there is no such sound in the world as that full-throated Anglo-Saxon cheer which begins at the heart – that inspiring, resolute, intentional cheer which has through the memory of 10,000 victories and endless moments of stress and daring become the heritage of the race.

Citing the Admiral's own motto, Stoker concluded – without a trace of irony – that the visit of the *Chicago* illustrated the well-known phrase or saying 'Blood is thicker than water'. It happens to be a fair summary of the story of *Dracula* as well . . .

Karl Marx enjoyed reading the horror tales of Hoffmann and Dumas père for relaxation at bedtime. When he was seeking a compelling image to characterize the attributes of capital, in Chapter X of *Das Kapital* (1867, tr. 1887, on the working day), he chose a whole series of fantasy images, whose unifying theme was blood. 'Capital is dead labour,' he wrote, 'that, vampire-like, only lives by sucking living labour, and lives the more, the more labour it sucks.' He referred to 'the were-wolf's hunger for surplus labour', and to the fact that 'the prolongation of the working day quenches only in a slight degree the vampire thirst for the living blood of labour'. The capitalist process 'swallows up unpaid labour'. What better image to illustrate the theory that the more unpaid labour the capitalist can extract from the worker, the greater his profit? The red sea of the labour market could thus be seen to feed an apparently eternal life. But Marx went further. When (in the same chapter) he sought a comparison between the historical evolution of the English factory system and another set of economic relationships (through history), he turned to the lord-peasant relationship in the Danubian principalities, and epitomized this by the image of 'the Wallachian Boyard'. Who was this 'Wallachian Boyard' who demanded that a large proportion of the peasants' time be devoted to his seignorial estate? The source Marx quotes (Elias Regnault's *Histoire des Principautés Danubiennes*, 1855) provides the answer, and perhaps explains why the image stuck in his mind. The 'Wallachian Boyard' was none other than

Vlad the Impaler, Vlad Dracula, whose story, 'by showing how he treated the rich and powerful, shows also how he treated the humble':

> On one occasion, he had 400 missionaries from Transylvania thrown on the fire – and ordered the impaling of 500 Tziganes – then he plundered their riches. Eventually, the inhabitants of Tirgoviste begged the sultan to intervene. Vlad was told of this, so he immediately rushed to Tirgoviste, surprised the people in the middle of their Easter celebrations, had 300 of them impaled around the city wall, and sent their wives and children to work as slaves on the construction of his fortress ... In these barbarous times, the rights of absolute power, like those of war, were exercised with a ferocity which shows that, in this regard, the Christian princes could not, with justice, complain about the barbarity of the Turks.

The English translation of *Das Kapital* was first published in 1887. Karl Marx's 'Wallachian Boyard' was thus the first reference to Dracula as a symbolic character (rather than an historical one) in the English language.

Bram Stoker had much to dream about ...

Fanciful portrait of George Gordon, Lord Byron, standing by a rocky shoreline with servant and dinghy, by Scottish painter George Sanders: in numerous engravings, this painting of 1807–10 helped to establish Byron's public image.

Top Engravings after Theodor von Holst of the creation scene, and of Victor leaving home, for the first popular edition of Mary Shelley's *Frankenstein* (1831). **Above** The Villa Diodati overlooking Lake Geneva, engraved for *Finden's Illustrations of the Life and Works of Lord Byron* (1833).

Oil portrait by Richard Rothwell of Mary Wollstonecraft Shelley, first exhibited in 1840.

Above Oil portrait of the handsome, vain Dr John William Polidori by F. G. Gainsford, painted *c.* 1816, the year of the Geneva summer. Opposite Front cover of a penny 'people's edition' of Polidori's *The Vampyre*, 1884, still wrongly attributing the story to Lord Byron.

THE VAMPYRE.

BY LORD BYRON.

LONDON: JOHN DICKS, 313, STRAND.

Price One Penny.

WEST'S. Characters in THE VAMPIRE.
Plate 3d Price 1d Plain.
Bridget, Mrs Grove.
Lord Ronald, Mr Bartley,
Andrew, Mr Minton
Mc Swill, Mr Harley,
London, Published March 8. 1824, by W. West, at his Theatrical Print Warehouse, 57, Wych Str.t Strand.

Above Penny-plain toy theatre sheet of 'West's Characters in *The Vampire*', published in March 1824 to cash in on the phenomenal success of the play. **Opposite** Playbill of 1826 advertising a double bill of *The Vampire* and *Presumption!* at the English Opera House: Thomas Potter Cooke played both the vampire and the monster.

POSITIVELY THE LAST NIGHT
Of the Company's Performing this Season.

Mr. T. P. COOKE
This Evening, as **The Vampire;** also as
The Monster, in **PRESUMPTION;** or, the **FATE OF FRANKENSTEIN.**

Theatre Royal, English Opera House, Strand.
This Evening, THURSDAY, OCTOBER 5th, 1826,

Will be presented *(Third Time this Season)* the popular *Romantick Melo-Drama*, in Three Parts, founded on the celebrated Tale, called

THE VAMPIRE:
Or, THE BRIDE OF THE ISLES.

The MUSICK of the INCANTATION composed by Mr. M. MOSS.

CHARACTERS IN THE INTRODUCTORY VISION.

The Vampire, Mr. T. P. COOKE,
Lady Margaret, Miss CARR,
Unda, *(Spirit of the Flood)* Miss BODEN, Ariel, *(Spirit of the Air)* Miss SOUTHWELL.

CHARACTERS IN THE DRAMA.

Ruthven, *(Earl of Marsden)* Mr. T. P. COOKE, Ronald, *(Baron of the Isles)* Mr. BARTLEY,
Robert, *(a Retainer of the Baron)* Mr. THORNE, Mc. Swill, *(Henchman to the Baron)* Mr. W. CHAPMAN,
Andrew, Mr. MINTON, Father Francis, Mr. SHAW.

Lady Margaret, *(Daughter to Lord Ronald)* Miss CARR,
Bridget, *(Housekeeper to Lord Ronald)* Mrs. TAYLEURE, Effie, Miss GOWARD.

After which, BY PARTICULAR DESIRE, *(Fourth Time this Season)*

GRETNA GREEN.

The MUSICK principally composed by Mr. REEVE.

Lord Lovewell, Mr. J. BLAND, Mr. Jenkins, Mr. WRENCH,
Mr. Tomkins, Mr. W. BENNETT, Larder, Mr. POWER,
Waiters, Postillions, &c. Messrs. Coad, East, Lodge, &c.

Emily, Miss BODEN,
Betty Finnikin, Miss KELLY.

In the course of the Evening, Mr. BARTLEY will deliver the

FAREWELL ADDRESS
On the Close of the Season, in the Character of
SIR WILLIAM BUFFER.

To conclude with *(Thirteenth Time this Season)* a Romance of a peculiar interest, entitled

PRESUMPTION!
Or, THE FATE OF FRANKENSTEIN!

Frankenstein, Mr. BAKER,
De Lacey, *(a banished Gentleman)* Mr. W. BENNETT, Felix De Lacey, *(his Son)* Mr. THORNE,
Fritz, Mr. W. CHAPMAN, Clerval, Mr. J. BLAND, William, Master BODEN,
Hammerpan, Mr. SALTER, Tanskin, Mr. MINTON, Guide, Mr. J. COOPER, Gypsey, Mr. J. O. ATKINS,
(------) Mr. T. P. COOKE.

Elizabeth, *(Sister of Frankenstein)* Miss BODEN, Agatha De Lacey, Miss HAMILTON,
Safie, *(an Arabian Girl)* Miss GOWARD, Madame Ninon, *(Wife of Fritz)* Mrs. BRYAN.

WITH AN ENTIRELY NEW LAST SCENE,
Conformably to the termination in the original Story, representing

A SCHOONER IN A VIOLENT STORM!
In which FRANKENSTEIN and THE MONSTER are destroyed.

Stage Manager, Mr. BARTLEY.—— Musical Director, Mr. HAWES.—— Leader of the Band, Mr. WAGSTAFF.
BOXES 5s. Second Price 3s. PIT 3s. Second Price 1s. 6d. LOWER GALLERY 2s. Second Price 1s. UPPER GALLERY 1s. Second Price 6d.
Boxes, Places, Private and Family Boxes, to be taken at the Box-Office, Strand Entrance, from 10 till 4.
Doors open at half-past 6, begin at 7. No Money returned. Vivat Rex! Lowndes, Printer, Marquis Court, Drury Lane.

VARNEY, THE VAMPYRE;
OR,
THE FEAST OF BLOOD.

CHAPTER I.
MIDNIGHT.—THE HAIL-STORM.—THE DREADFUL VISITOR.—THE VAMPYRE.

THE DISCOVERY OF THE DESECRATED CORPSE.

THE VAMPYRE'S MIDNIGHT VISIT.

FLORA ENCOUNTERS VARNEY IN THE SUMMER-HOUSE.

Four lurid pages from the marathon serial penny-dreadful *Varney the Vampyre or the Feast of Blood* (1845–47) by the Scottish former civil engineer James Malcolm Rymer.

PART TWO
AN ANTHOLOGY

1 LIGHTEN OUR DARKNESS

Private persons may be *Vampyres*, or *Blood-Suckers*, i.e. *Sharpers, Usurers, and Stockjobbers, unjust Stewards* and *the dry nurses of the Great Estates*; but nothing less than the Power of a *Treasury* can raise up a compleat *Vampyre*.

Gentleman's Magazine, May 1732

A VOYAGE TO THE LEVANT

JOSEPH PITTON DE TOURNEFORT

Joseph Pitton de Tournefort (1656–1708) was, at the time he wrote this, botanist to King Louis XIV of France. According to Voltaire (*The Age of Louis XIV*), 'in 1700 Tournefort was sent out to the Levant, the object of his voyage being to collect plants for the royal garden, hitherto neglected . . .' But the famous botanist discovered rather more than he had bargained for. His *Voyage to the Levant* (1702) contains this extraordinary account of the mass hysteria which greeted a vampire epidemic on the island of Mycone (or Mykonos). A Jesuit Father who had visited the region in the mid-seventeenth century – François Richard – had also reported the sighting of 'demons who animate human bodies, and preserve them from corruption' and had been surprised to discover that 'either because of their weak faith, or because of the obstinacy of the demon, the Greek Priests could achieve nothing with their exorcisms'. (Tournefort refers to Richard's account, with some scorn.) Despite the detached irony with which he describes the scene, it is clear that Tournefort was frightened enough at the time to remember every single detail.

The extract from the *Voyage* is especially interesting for two reasons. First, it refers to a theological muddle which, from the mid-seventeenth century onwards, the Greek Orthodox Church tried desperately to resolve: they had proclaimed in the past that the rite of excommunication prevented corpses from decomposing, condemning heretics to a permanent state of 'passive vegetation' as *Vrykolakas*, but now that the *Vrykolakas* were (apparently) beginning to behave like their more active Slavic counterparts, the vampires, there was always the danger that the Church would be held in some senses responsible. Gerhard van Swieten (a devout Austrian Catholic) was later to attribute much of the 'ignorance' surrounding alleged vampire epidemics to the teachings of the 'Greek schismatics' who had so confused the issue; on the other hand, Catholics had contributed too, by refusing to bury suicides in consecrated ground. Second, this extract was extremely influential during the revival of interest in vampirism of the early Romantic period. Southey transcribed much of it for the notes to his vampire poem *Thalaba the Destroyer*; the *Fantasmagoriana* (which stimulated the ghost-story session of June 1816) referred to it, as did the anonymous Introduction to Polidori's *Vampyre* (1819). Lord Byron had probably read Tournefort's *Voyage* well before the summer of 1816. This extract is from an early translation.

WE WERE PRESENT AT A VERY DIFFERENT SCENE, and one very barbarous, in the same island of Mycone, which happened upon occasion of one of those corpses,* which they fancy come to life again after their interment. The man whose story we are going to relate was a peasant of *Mycone*, naturally ill-natured and quarrelsome; this is a circumstance to be taken notice of in such cases: he was murdered in the fields, nobody knew how, or by whom. Two days after his being buried in a chapel in the town, it was noised about that he was seen to walk in the night with great haste, that he tumbled about people's goods, put out their lamps, gripped them behind, and a thousand other roguish monkey tricks. At first the story was received with laughter; but the thing was looked upon to be serious, when the better sort of people began to complain of it; the *Papas* themselves gave credit to the fact, and no doubt had their reasons for so doing; masses had to be said, to be sure: but for all this, the peasant drove his old trade, and heeded nothing they could do. After divers meetings of the chief people of the city, of priests and monks, it was gravely concluded, that it was necessary, in consequence of some musty ceremonial, to wait till nine days after the interment should be expired.

On the tenth day they said one mass in the chapel where the body was laid, in order to drive out the demon which they imagined was got into it. After mass, they took up the body, and got everything ready for pulling out

---

*Vrykolakas. A spectre consisting of a dead body and a demon. Some think that *Vrykolakas* signifies a carcass denied Christian burial.

its heart. The butcher of the town, an old clumsy fellow, first opened the belly instead of the breast: he groped a long while among the entrails, but could not find what he looked for; at last somebody told him he should cut up the diaphragm. The heart was pulled out, to the admiration of all the spectators. In the meantime, the corpse stank so abominably, that they were obliged to burn Frankincense; but the smoke mixing with the exhalations from the carcass merely increased the stink, and began to muddle the poor people's minds. Their imagination, struck with spectacle before them, grew full of visions. It came into their noddles that a thick smoke arose from out of the body; we durst not say it was the smoke of the incense. They were incessantly bawling out *Vrykolakas*, in the Chapel and square before it: this is the name they give to these supposed *Revenants*. The noise bellowed through the streets, and it seemed to be a name invented on purpose to rend the roof of the Chapel. Several there present averred, that the wretch's blood was extremely red: the Butcher swore the body was still warm; whence they concluded, that the deceased was a very ill man for not being thoroughly dead, or in plain terms for suffering himself to be re-animated by *Old Nick*; which is the notion they have of a *Vrykolakas*. They then roared out that name in a stupendous manner. Just at this time came in a flock of people, loudly protesting they plainly perceived the body was not grown stiff, when it was carried from the fields to church to be buried, and that consequently it was a true *Vrykolakas*; which word was still the burden of the song.

I don't doubt they would have sworn it did not stink, had not we been there; so amazed were the poor people with this disaster, and so infatuated with their notion of the dead's being re-animated. As for us who were got as close to the corpse as we could, that we might be more exact in our observations, we were almost poisoned with the intolerable stink that issued from it. When they asked us what we thought of this body, we told them we believed it to be very thoroughly dead: but as we were willing to cure, or at least not to exasperate their prejudiced imaginations, we represented to them, that it was no wonder the butcher should feel a little warmth when he groped among entrails that were then rotting; that it was no extraordinary thing for it to emit fumes, since dung turned up from a dung-heap will do the same; that as for the pretended redness of the blood, it still appeared by the butcher's hands to be nothing but a very stinking nasty mess.

After all our reasons, they were of opinion it would be their wisest course to burn the dead man's heart on the sea-shore: but this execution did not make him a bit more tractable; he went on with his racket more furiously than ever: he was accused of beating folks in the night, breaking down doors, and even roofs of houses; clattering windows; tearing clothes; emptying bottles and vessels. It was the most thirsty Devil! I believe he did not spare anybody but the Consul in whose house we lodged. Nothing could be more miserable than the condition of this island; all the inhabitants seemed frightened out of their senses: the wisest among them were stricken like the rest: it was an epidemical disease of the brain, as dangerous and infectious as the madness of dogs. Whole families quitted their houses, and brought their tent-beds from the farthest parts of the town into the public place, there to spend the night. They were every instant complaining of some new insult; nothing was to be heard but sighs and groans at the approach of night: the better sort of people retired into the country.

When the prepossession was so general, we thought it our best way to hold our tongues. Had we opposed it, we had not only been accounted ridiculous blockheads, but atheists and infidels. How was it possible to stand against the madness of a whole people? Those that believed we doubted the truth of the fact, came and upbraided us with our incredulity, and strove to prove that there were such things as *Vrykolakasses*, by citations out of the *Shield of Faith*, written by Pere Richard a Jesuit Missionary. He was a *Latin*, say they, and consequently you ought to give him credit. We should have got nothing by denying the justness of the conclusion: it was as good as a comedy to us every morning, to hear the new follies committed by this night bird; they charged him with being guilty of the most abominable sins.

Some citizens, that were most zealous for the good of the public, fancied they had been deficient in the most material part of the ceremony. They were of opinion, that they had been wrong in saying mass before they had pulled out the wretch's heart: had we taken this precaution, quoth they, we had bit the Devil, as sure as a gun; he would have been hanged before he would ever have come there again: whereas saying mass first, the cunning dog fled for it a while, and came back again when the danger was over.

Notwithstanding these wise reflections, they remained in as much perplexity as they were the first day: they meet night and morning, they debate, they make processions three days and three nights; they oblige the *Papas* to fast; you might see them running from house to house, holy-water-brush in hand, sprinkling it all about, and washing the doors with it; nay, they poured it into the mouth of this poor *Vrykolakas*.

We so often repeated it to the magistrates of the town, that in *Christendom* we should keep the strictest watch a-nights upon such an occasion, to observe what would happen in the town; that at last they caught a few vagabonds, who undoubtedly had a hand in these disorders: but either they were not the chief ringleaders, or else they were released too soon. For two days afterwards, to make themselves amends for the *Lent* they had kept in prison, they fell foul again upon the wine-tubs of those who were such fools as to leave their houses empty in the night: so that the people were forced to betake themselves again to their prayers.

One day, as they were hard at this work of prayer, after having stuck I know not how many naked swords over the grave of this corpse, which they disinterred three or four times a day, for any man's whim; an *Albanian* that happened to be at *Mycone*, took it upon him to say with a voice of authority, that it was to the last degree ridiculous to make use of the swords of Christians in a case like this. Can you not conceive, blind as you are, says he, that the handles of these swords being made like a cross, hinder the Devil from coming out of the body? Why do you not rather take the *Turkish* sabres? The advice of this learned man had no effect: the *Vrykolakas* was incorrigible, and all the inhabitants were in a strange consternation; they knew not now which Saint to call upon, when of a sudden with one voice, as if they had given each other the hint, they fell to bawling out all through the town, that it was intolerable to wait any longer; that the only way left, was to burn the *Vrykolakas* entire; that after so doing, let the Devil lurk in it if he could; that it was better to have recourse to this extremity, than to have the island totally deserted: and indeed whole families began to pack up, in order to retire to *Syra* or *Tinos*.

The magistrates therefore ordered the *Vrykolakas* to be carried to the point of the island *St George*, where they prepared a great funeral pile with pitch and tar, for fear the wood, as dry as it was, should not burn fast enough of itself. What they had before left of this miserable carcass was thrown into this fire, and consumed in a short time: it was on the first of January 1701. We saw the flame as we returned from *Delos*: it might justly be called a bonfire of joy, since after this no more complaints were heard against the *Vrykolakas*; they said that the Devil had now met with his match, and some ballads were composed to turn him into ridicule.

All over the *Archipelago* they are persuaded, that only the *Greeks* of the *Grecian* Rite have their carcasses re-animated by the Devil: the inhabitants of the island of *Santorini* are terribly afraid of these Bulbeggars or were-wolves. Those of *Mycone*, after their visions were clearly dispersed, began to be equally apprehensive of the prosecutions of the *Turks* and those of the Bishop of *Tinos*. Not one *Papas* would be at *St George* when the body was burnt, for fear the Bishop should exact a sum of money of them, for taking up and burning a corpse without permission from him. As for the *Turks*, it is certain that at their next visit they made the community of *Mycone* pay dear for their cruelty to his poor rogue, who became in every respect the abomination and horror of his countrymen. After such an instance of folly, can we refuse to own that the present *Greeks* are not the great *Grecians*; and that there is nothing but ignorance and superstition among them?

TREATISE ON THE...VAMPIRES OF HUNGARY [AND SURROUNDING REGIONS]

DOM AUGUSTIN CALMET

Dom Augustin Calmet, the Benedictine Abbot of Senones since 1729, was the best-known biblical scholar of eighteenth-century France, famed for his attempts to popularize 'literal' biblical exegesis. His *Treatise on the...Vampires of Hungary [and Surrounding Regions]* (from which these extracts have been taken) was really the first vampire anthology: a collection of formal reports, newspaper articles, eyewitness accounts and critical pieces on the various epidemics of vampirism which were said to have swept Eastern Europe and Greece in the late seventeenth and early eighteenth centuries. (Calmet's *Treatise* includes parts of Tournefort's *Voyage*, for example.) Later in the century, Calmet's open-mindedness about such 'bedtime horror stories' was often mocked: his over-tentative criticisms of the various sources were no longer considered intellectually respectable. Despite this (or perhaps because of it), Calmet's *Treatise* – first published in Paris in 1746, and in London in 1759 – became a bestseller by the standards of the time (three full French editions in as many years), and remains the most complete surviving account of 'posthumous magic' in the whole of the eighteenth century. The English translation was reissued in 1850, under the title *The Phantom World*, edited by the Reverend Henry Christmas, complete with eccentric spellings of place-names.

'The affair of vampires,' wrote Calmet, 'having made so much noise in the world, as it has done, it is not surprising that a diversity of systems should be formed upon it.' The following extracts are intended to show the problems Calmet set himself, and the ways in which he attempted to resolve them: if the vampire anecdotes were not true, then Calmet saw little point in pursuing them (he had little time, for example, for what we would now call 'sociological' explanations); if they were true, they had to be explained within the terms of reference of Roman Catholic orthodoxy. I have included some of the extracts from contemporary or near-contemporary accounts which Calmet included in his anthology, to show the criteria he chose to adopt in order to establish 'truth'; and also Calmet's version of the Phlegon of Tralles legend, since it was to have such an impact (via Goethe and Keats) on the Romantic imagination. The context for Calmet's discussion, and the second official report of the most famous vampire manifestation of the time (Arnold Paole), are examined in my opening section, 'Lord Byron to Count Dracula'.

EVERY AGE, EVERY NATION, EVERY COUNTRY, has its prejudices, its maladies, its customs, its inclinations, which characterize it, and which pass away, and succeed one to another; often, that which has appeared admirable at one time, becomes pitiful and ridiculous at another. In this age, a new scene presents itself to our eyes, and has done for about sixty years in Hungary, Moravia, Silesia and Poland; men, it is said, who have been dead for several months, come back to earth, talk, walk, infest villages, ill use both men and beasts, suck the blood of their near relations, destroy their health, and finally cause their death; so that people can only save themselves from their dangerous visits and their hauntings, by exhuming them, impaling them, cutting off their heads, tearing out their hearts, or burning them. These are called by the name of oupires or vampires, that is to say, leeches; and such particulars are related of them, so singular, so detailed, and attended by such probable circumstances, and such judicial information, that one can hardly refuse to credit the belief which is held in those countries, that they come out of their tombs, and produce those effects which are proclaimed of them.

I undertake to treat here on the matter of these vampires, at the risk of being criticized, however I may discuss it; those who believe them to be true, will accuse me of rashness and presumption, for having raised a doubt on the subject, or even of having denied their existence and reality; others will blame me for having employed my time in discussing this matter, which is considered as frivolous and useless by many sensible people. Whatever may be thought of it, I shall be satisfied with myself for having sounded a question which appeared to me important in a religious point of view. For, if the return of vampires is real, it is of import to defend it, and prove it; and if it is illusory, it is of consequence to the interests of religion to undeceive those who believe in its truth, and destroy an error which may produce dangerous effects . . .

REVIVAL OR APPARITION OF A GIRL WHO HAD BEEN DEAD SOME MONTHS

Phlegon, freed-man of the Emperor Hadrian, in the fragment of the book which he wrote on wonderful things, says, that at Tralla, in Asia, a certain man named Machates, an innkeeper, was acquainted with a girl named Philinium, the daughter of Demostrates and Chariton. This girl being dead, and placed in her grave, continued to come every night for six months to see her gallant. One day she was recognized by her nurse, when sitting by Machates. The nurse ran to give notice of this to Chariton, the girl's mother, who after making many difficulties, came at last to the inn; but as it was late, and everybody gone to bed, she could not satisfy her curiosity. However, she recognized her daughter's clothes, and thought she recognized the girl herself with Machates. She returned the next morning, but having missed her way, she no longer found her daughter, who had already withdrawn. Machates related everything to her; how, since a certain time, she had come to him every night; and in proof of what he said, he opened his casket and showed her the gold ring which Philinium had given him, and the band with which she covered her bosom, and which she had left with him the preceding night.

Chariton, who could no longer doubt the truth of the circumstance, now gave way to cries and tears; but as they promised to inform her the following night, when Philinium should return, she went away home. In the evening the girl came back as usual, and Machates sent directly to let her father and mother know, for he began to fear that some other girl might have taken Philinium's clothes from the sepulchre, in order to deceive him by the illusion.

Demostrates and Chariton, on arriving, recognized their daughter and ran to embrace her; but she cried out, 'Oh, father and mother, why have you grudged me my happiness, by preventing me from remaining three days longer with this innkeeper without injury to any one? For I did not come here without permission from the gods, that is to say, from the demon, since we cannot attribute to God, or to a good spirit, a thing like this. Your curiosity will cost you dear.' At the same time she fell down stiff and dead, and extended on the bed.

Phlegon, who had some command in the town, stayed the crowd and prevented a tumult. The next day, the people being assembled at the theatre, they agreed to go and inspect the vault in which Philinium, who had died six months before, had been laid. They found there the corpses of her family arranged in their places, but they found not the body of Philinium. There was only an iron ring which Machates had given her, with a gilded cup, which she had also received from him. Afterwards they went back to the dwelling of Machates, where the body of the girl remained lying on the ground.

They consulted a diviner, who said that she must be interred beyond the limits of the town; they must appease the Furies and the terrestrial Mercury, make solemn funeral ceremonies to the god Manes, and sacrifice to Jupiter, to Mercury, and to Mars. Phlegon adds, speaking to him to whom he was writing: 'If you think proper to inform the emperor of it, write to me, that I may send you some of those persons who were eyewitnesses of all these things.'

Here is a fact circumstantially related, and accompanied with all the marks which can make it pass for true. Nevertheless, how numerous are the difficulties it presents! Was this young girl really dead, or only sleeping? Was her resurrection effected by her own strength and will, or was it a demon who restored her to life? It appears that it cannot be doubted that it was her own body; all the circumstances noted in the recital of Phlegon persuade us of it. If she was not dead, and all she did was merely a game and a play which she performed to satisfy her passion for Machates, there is nothing in all this recital very incredible. We know what illicit love is capable of, and how far it may lead any one who is devoured by a violent passion . . .

THE VAMPIRES OF MORAVIA

I have been told by the late Monsieur de Vassimont, counsellor of the Chamber of the Counts of Bar, that having been sent into Moravia by his late Royal Highness Leopold, first Duke of Lorraine, for the affairs of the Prince Charles his brother, Bishop of Olmutz and Osnaburgh, he was informed by public report, that it was common enough in that country to see men who had died some time before, present themselves in a party, and sit down to table with persons of their acquaintance without saying any thing; but that nodding to one of the party, he would infallibly die some days afterwards. This fact was confirmed by several persons, and amongst others by an old curé, who said he had seen more than one instance of it.

The bishops and priests of the country consulted Rome on so extraordinary a fact; but they received no answer, because, apparently, all those things were regarded there as simple visions, or popular fancies. They afterwards bethought themselves of taking up the corpses of those who came back in that way, of burning them, or of destroying them in some other manner. Thus they delivered themselves from the importunity of these spectres, which are now much less frequently seen than before. So said that good priest.

These apparitions have given rise to a little work, entitled *Magia Posthuma*, printed at Olmutz, in 1706, composed by Charles Ferdinand de Schertz, dedicated to Prince Charles of Lorraine, Bishop of Olmutz and Osnaburgh. The author relates, that in a certain village, a woman being just dead, who had taken all her sacraments, she was buried in the usual way in the cemetery. Four days after her decease, the inhabitants of this village heard a great noise and extraordinary uproar, and saw a spectre, which appeared sometimes in the shape of a dog, sometimes in the form of a man, not to one person only, but to several, and caused them great pain, grasping their throats, and compressing their stomachs, so as to suffocate them. It bruised almost the whole body, and reduced them to extreme weakness, so that they became pale, lean and attenuated.

The spectre attacked even animals, and some cows were found debilitated and half dead. Sometimes it tied them together by their tails. These animals gave sufficient evidence by their bellowing of the pain they suffered. The horses seemed overcome with fatigue, perspired profusely, principally on the back; were heated, out of breath, covered with foam, as after a long and rough journey. These calamities lasted several months.

The author whom I have mentioned examines the affair in a lawyer-like way, and reasons much on the fact and the law. He asks, if, supposing that these disturbances, these noises and vexations, proceeded from that person who is suspected of causing them, they can burn her, as is done to other ghosts who do harm to the living. He relates several instances of similar apparitions, and of the evils which ensued; as of a shepherd of the village of Blow, near the town of Kadam, in Bohemia, who appeared during some time, and called certain persons, who never failed to die within eight days after. The peasants of Blow took up the body of this shepherd, and fixed it in the ground with a stake which they drove through it.

This man when in that condition derided them for what they made him suffer, and told them they were very good to give him thus a stick to defend himself from the dogs. The same night he got up again, and by his presence alarmed several persons, and strangled more amongst them than he had hitherto done. Afterwards, they delivered him into the hands of the executioner, who put him in a cart to carry him beyond the village and there burn him. This corpse howled like a madman, and moved his feet and hands as if alive. And when they again pierced him through with stakes he uttered very loud cries, and a great quantity of bright vermilion blood flowed from him. At last he was consumed, and this execution put an end to the appearance and hauntings of this spectre.

The same has been practised in other places, where similar ghosts have been seen; and when they have been taken out of the ground they have appeared red, with their limbs supple and pliable, without worms or decay; but not without great stench. The author cites divers other writers, who attest what he says of these spectres, which still appear, he says, very often in the mountains of Silesia and Moravia. They are seen by night and by day; the things which once belonged to them are seen to move themselves and change their place without being touched by any one. The only remedy for these apparitions is to cut off the heads and burn the bodies of those who come back to haunt their old abodes.

At any rate they do not proceed to this without a form of justicial law. They call for and hear the witnesses; they examine the arguments; they look at the exhumed bodies, to see if they can find any of the usual marks which lead them to conjecture that they are the parties who molest the living, as the mobility and suppleness of the limbs, the fluidity of the blood, and the flesh remaining uncorrupted. If all these marks are found, then these bodies are given up to the executioner, who burns them. It sometimes happens that the spectres appear again for three or four days after the execution. Sometimes the interment of the bodies of suspicious persons is deferred for six or seven weeks. When they do not decay, and their limbs remain as supple and pliable as when they were alive, then they burn them. It is affirmed as certain that the clothes of these persons move without any one living touching them; and within a short time, continues our author, a spectre was seen at Olmutz, which threw stones, and gave great trouble to the inhabitants . . .

ACCOUNT OF A VAMPIRE, TAKEN FROM D'ARGENS'S JEWISH LETTERS

We find another instance in the *Lettres Juives*, new edition, 1738, Letter 137.

'We have just had in this part of Hungary a scene of vampirism, which is duly attested by two officers of the tribunal of Belgrade, who went down to the places specified; and by an officer of the emperor's troops at Graditz, who was an ocular witness of the proceedings.

'In the beginning of September there died in the village of Kisilova, three leagues from Graditz, an old man who was sixty-two years of age. Three days after he had been buried, he appeared in the night to his son, and asked him for something to eat; the son having given him something, he ate and disappeared. The next day the son recounted to his neighbours what had happened. That night the father did not appear, but the following night he showed himself, and asked for something to eat. They know not whether the son gave him anything, or not; but the next day he was found dead in his bed. On the same day, five or six persons fell suddenly ill in the village, and died one after the other in a few days.

'The officer, or bailiff of the place, when informed of what had happened, sent an account of it to the tribunal of Belgrade, which despatched to the village two of these officers and an executioner, to examine into this affair. The imperial officer from whom we have this account repaired thither from Graditz, to be witness of a circumstance which he had so often heard spoken of.

'They opened the graves of those who had been dead six weeks. When they came to that of the old man, they found him with his eyes open, having a fine colour with natural respiration, nevertheless motionless as the dead; whence they concluded that he was most evidently a vampire. The executioner drove a stake into his heart; they then raised a pile and reduced the corpse to ashes. No mark of vampirism was found either on the corpse of the son, or on the others.'

Thanks be to God, we are by no means credulous. We avow that all the light which science can throw on this fact discovers none of the causes of it. Nevertheless, we cannot refuse to believe that to be true which is juridically attested, and by persons of probity.

'There are two different ways of effacing the opinion concerning these pretended ghosts, and showing the impossibility of the effects which are made to be produced by corpses entirely deprived of sensation. The first is, to explain by physical causes all the prodigies of vampirism; the second is, to deny totally the truth of these stories; and the latter means, without doubt, is the surest and the wisest. But as there are persons to whom the authority of a certificate given by people in a certain place appears a plain demonstration of the reality of the most absurd story, before I show how little they ought to rely on the formalities of the law in matters which relate solely to philosophy, I will for a moment suppose that several persons do really die of the disease which they term vampirism.

'I lay down at first this principle, that it may be that there are corpses which, although interred some days, shed fluid blood through the pores of their body. I add moreover, that it is very easy for certain people to fancy themselves sucked by vampires, and that the fear caused by that fancy should make a revolution in their frame sufficiently violent to deprive them of life. Being occupied all day with the terror inspired by these pretended ghosts or *revenans*, is it very extraordinary, that during their sleep the idea of these phantoms should present itself to their imagination, and cause them such violent terror, that some of them die of it instantaneously, and others a short time afterwards? How many instances have we not seen of people who expired with fright in a moment; and has not joy itself sometimes produced an equally fatal effect?'...

ARGUMENTS ABOUT THE HUNGARIAN GHOSTS

Some advantage of these instances and these arguments may be derived in favour of vampirism, by saying that the ghosts of Hungary, Moravia, and Poland are not really dead; that they continue to live in their graves, although without motion and without respiration; the blood which is found in them being fine and red, the flexibility of their limbs, the cries which they utter when their heart is pierced or their head being cut off, all prove that they still exist.

That is not the principal difficulty which arrests my judgment; it is, to know how they come out of their graves without any appearance of the earth having being removed, and how they have replaced it as it was; how they appear dressed in their clothes, go and come, and eat. If it is so, why do they return to their graves? why do they not remain amongst the living? why do they suck the blood of their relations? why do they haunt and fatigue persons who ought to be dear to them, and who have done nothing to offend them? If all this is only imagination on the part of those who are molested, whence comes it that these vampires are found in their graves in an uncorrupted state, full of blood, supple, and pliable; that their feet are found to be in a muddy condition the day after they have run about and frightened the neighbours, and that nothing similar is remarked in the other corpses interred at the same time and in the same cemetery? Whence does it happen that they neither come back nor infest the place any more when they are burned or impaled? Would it be, again, the imagination of the living and their prejudices which reassure them after these executions? Whence comes it that these scenes recur so frequently in those countries, that the people are not cured of their prejudices, and daily experience, instead of destroying, only augments and strengthens them?

SINGULAR INSTANCE OF A HUNGARIAN GHOST

The most remarkable instance cited by Ranft in his book *That Dead Men Chew in Their Coffins*, is that of one Peter Plogojowitz, who had been buried ten weeks in a village of Hungary, called Kisilova. This man appeared by night to some of the inhabitants of the village while they were asleep, and grasped their throat so tightly that in four-and-twenty hours it caused their death. Nine persons, young and old, perished thus in the course of eight days.

The widow of the same Plogojowitz declared that her husband since his death had come and asked her for his shoes, which frightened her so much that she left Kisilova to retire to some other spot.

From these circumstances the inhabitants of the village determined upon disinterring the body of Plogojowitz and burning it, to deliver themselves from these visitations. They applied to the Emperor's officer, who commanded in the territory of Gradiska in Hungary, and even to the Curé of the same place, for permission to exhume the body of Peter Plogojowitz. The officer and the Curé made much demur in granting it, but the peasants declared that if they were refused permission to disinter the body of this man, whom they had no doubt was a true vampire (for so they called these revived corpses), they should be obliged to forsake the village, and go where they could.

The Emperor's officer, who wrote this account, seeing he could hinder them neither by threats nor promises, went with the Curé of Gradiska to the village of Kisilova, and having caused Peter Plogojowitz to be exhumed, they found that his body exhaled no bad smell; that he looked as when alive, except the tip of the nose; that his hair and beard had grown, and instead of his nails which had fallen off, new ones had come; that under his cuticle, which appeared whitish, there was a new skin, which looked healthy, and of a natural colour; his feet and hands were as whole as could be desired in a living man. They remarked also in his mouth some fresh blood, which these people believed that this vampire had sucked from the men whose death he had occasioned.

The Emperor's officer and the Curé having diligently examined all these things, and the people who were present feeling their indignation awakened anew, and being more fully persuaded that he was the true cause of the death of their compatriots, ran directly for a sharp pointed stake, which they thrust into his breast, whence there issued a quantity of fresh and crimson blood, and also from the nose and mouth. After this the peasants placed the body on a pile of wood, and saw it reduced to ashes ...

REASONINGS ON THIS MATTER

These authors have reasoned a great deal on these events. 1. Some have believed them to be miraculous. 2. Others have looked upon them simply as the effect of a heated imagination, or a sort of prepossession. 3. Others again have believed that there was nothing in them all but what was very simple and very natural, these persons not being dead, but acting naturally upon other bodies. 4. Others have asserted that it was the work of the devil himself; amongst these, some have advanced the opinion that there were certain benign demons, differing from those who are malevolent and hostile to mankind, to which benign demons they have attributed playful and harmless operations, in contradistinction to those bad demons who inspire the minds of men with crime and sin, ill use them, kill them, and occasion them an infinity of evils. But what greater evils can one have to fear from veritable demons and the most malignant spirits, than those which the ghouls of Hungary inflict on the persons whose blood they suck, and thus cause to die? 5. Others will have it that it is not the dead who eat their own flesh or clothes, but serpents, rats, moles, ferrets, or other voracious animals, or even what the peasants call *striges*, which are birds that devour animals and men, and suck their blood. Some have said that these instances are principally remarked in women, and, above all, in a time of pestilence; but there are instances of ghouls of both sexes, and principally of men; although those who die of plague, poison, hydrophobia, drunkenness, and any epidemical malady, are more apt to return, apparently because their blood coagulates with more difficulty; and sometimes some are buried who are not quite dead, on account of the danger there is in leaving them long without sepulture, from fear of the infection they would cause.

It is added, that these vampires are known only to certain countries, as Hungary, Moravia, and Silesia, where those maladies are more common, and where the people, being badly fed, are subject to certain disorders occasioned by the climate and the food, and augmented by prejudice, fancy, and fright, which are capable of producing or of increasing the most dangerous maladies, as daily experience proves too well. As to what some have asserted, that the dead have been heard to eat and chew like pigs in their graves, it is manifestly fabulous, and such an idea can have its foundation only in ridiculous prepossessions of the mind.

The opinion of those who hold that all that is related of vampires is the effect of imagination, fascination, or of that disorder which the Greeks term *phrenesis* or *coribantism*, and who pretend by that means to explain all the phenomena of vampirism, will never persuade us that these maladies of the brain can produce such real effects as those we have just recounted. It is impossible that on a sudden, several persons should believe they see a thing which is not there, and that they should die in so short a time of a disorder purely imaginary. And who has revealed to them that such a vampire is undecayed in his grave, that he is full of blood, that he in some measure lives there after his death? Is there not to be found in the nation one sensible man who is exempt from this fancy, or who has soared above the effects of this fascination, these sympathies and antipathies – this natural magic? And besides, who can explain to us clearly and distinctly what these grand terms signify, and the manner of these operations so occult and so mysterious? It is trying to explain a thing which is obscure and doubtful, by another still more uncertain and incomprehensible.

If these persons believe nothing of all that is related of the apparition, the return, and the actions of vampires, they lose their time very uselessly in proposing systems and forming arguments to explain what exists only in the imagination of certain prejudiced persons struck with an absurd idea; but, if all that is related, or at least a part, is true, these systems and these arguments will not easily satisfy those minds which desire proofs far more weighty.

2 LORD RUTHVEN AND HIS CLAN

Just at that moment Gertrude drew
From 'neath her cloke the hidden light;
When, dreadful! She beheld in view
The shade of Sigismund! – sad sight!

Indignant roll'd his ireful eyes,
That gleam'd with wild horrific stare;
And fix'd a moment with surprise,
Beheld aghast th'enlightening glare.

His jaws cadaverous were besmear'd
With clotted carnage o'er and o'er.
And all his horrid whole appeared
Distent, and fill'd with human gore!

From *The Vampyre*, by John Stagg
(1810)

THE VAMPYRE

JOHN POLIDORI

Written in summer 1816 (during 'two or three idle mornings'), while Polidori's employer was busy elsewhere, *The Vampyre* was not published until April 1819, by which time the author had forgotten all about it. It first appeared in the *New Monthly Magazine* under Byron's name, and was the occasion for a vicious row between the publisher of the magazine, the editor (who resigned as a result) and the other interested parties. Byron, more irritated than he cared to admit, hastily denied all knowledge of the project: 'I have a personal dislike to Vampires, and the little acquaintance I have with them would by no means induce me to reveal their secrets.' But he nevertheless urged John Murray to publish his *Fragment* as quickly as possible. As a result of all this infighting, Polidori was only paid £30 (in retrospect) for what is probably the most influential horror story of all time. The story (which bears little resemblance to Byron's *Fragment*) reflects the strained relationship between Polidori and Lord Byron (or 'Lord Ruthven') throughout the summer of 1816.

John Polidori came from a literary family; his father, Gaetano, was a scholar, poet and translator (he had, for example, translated the complete works of Milton and Horace Walpole's *Castle of Otranto* into Italian). John grew up in the Italian community of Soho. He went to Edinburgh University to study medicine, graduating in 1815 at the remarkably young age of nineteen (his dissertation, on aspects of somnambulism and mesmerism, reveals an interest in the weirder aspects of science some time before he encountered Byron and Shelley). As a Roman Catholic Italian immigrant, he had found it impossible to attract an illustrious patron during his university career, and his is the only dissertation of 1815 not to be dedicated to one. After his brief (and tempestuous) spell as Byron's physician, he returned to England in 1817, hoping to establish himself with a medical practice in Norwich. This provoked a characteristic rejoinder from Byron:

I fear the Doctor's skill at Norwich,

Will hardly salt the Doctor's porridge.

In 1819 he published a novel, *Ernestus Berchtold*, which was expanded from the tale he had originally told at the ghost-story session of June 1816. He died in August 1821, at the age of twenty-five. For some time he had been suffering from brain damage, after a carriage accident, and it was thought he may have committed suicide by drinking prussic acid (this has recently been disputed, however, in a convincing analysis of the medical evidence). In any event, the coroner's jury pronounced a verdict of 'death by the visitation of God', and he was buried in consecrated ground.

The Vampyre was the first story successfully to fuse the disparate elements of vampirism into a coherent literary genre.

IT HAPPENED THAT IN THE MIDST of the dissipations attendant upon a London winter, there appeared at the various parties of the leaders of the *ton* a nobleman, more remarkable for his singularities than his rank. He gazed upon the mirth around him, as if he could not participate therein. Apparently, the light laughter of the fair only attracted his attention, that he might by a look quell it, and throw fear into those breasts where thoughtlessness reigned. Those who felt this sensation of awe, could not explain whence it arose: some attributed it to the dead grey eye, which, fixing upon the object's face, did not seem to penetrate, and at one glance to pierce through to the inward workings of the heart; but fell upon the cheek with a leaden ray that weighed upon the skin it could not pass. His peculiarities caused him to be invited to every house; all wished to see him, and those who had been accustomed to violent excitement, and now felt the weight of *ennui*, were pleased at having something in their presence capable of engaging their attention. In spite of the deadly hue of his face, which never gained a warmer tint, either from the blush of modesty, or from the strong emotion of passion, though its form and outline were beautiful, many of the female hunters after notoriety attempted to win his attentions, and gain, at least, some marks of what they might term affection: Lady Mercer, who had been the mockery of every monster shewn in drawing-rooms since her marriage, threw herself in his way, and did all but put on the dress of a mountebank, to attract his notice – though in vain; when she stood before him, though his eyes were apparently fixed upon hers, still it seemed as if they were unperceived; even her unappalled impudence was baffled, and she left the field. But though the common adultress could not influence even the guidance of his eyes, it was not that the female sex was indifferent to him: yet such was the apparent caution with which he spoke to the virtuous wife and innocent daughter, that few knew he ever addressed himself to females. He had, however, the reputation of a winning tongue; and whether it was that it even overcame the dread of his singular character, or that they were moved by his apparent hatred of vice, he was as often among those females who form the boast of their sex from their domestic virtues, as among those who sully it by their vices.

About the same time, there came to London a young gentleman of the name of Aubrey: he was an orphan left with an only sister in the possession of great wealth, by parents who died while he was yet in childhood. Left also to himself by guardians, who thought it their duty merely to take care of his fortune, while they relinquished the more important charge of his mind to the care of mercenary subalterns, he cultivated more his imagination than his judgement. He had, hence, that high romantic feeling of honour and candour, which daily ruins so many milliners' apprentices. He believed all to sympathize with virtue, and thought that vice was thrown in by Providence merely for the picturesque effect of the scene, as we see in romances: he thought that the misery of a cottage merely consisted in the vesting of clothes, which were as warm, but which were better adapted to the painter's eye by their irregular folds and various coloured patches. He thought, in fine, that the dreams of poets were the realities of life. He was handsome, frank, and rich: for these reasons, upon his entering into the gay circles, many mothers surrounded him, striving which should describe with least truth their languishing or romping favourites: the daughters at the same time, by their brightening countenances when he approached, and by their sparkling eyes, when he opened his lips, soon led him into false notions of his talents and his merit. Attached as he was to the romance of his solitary hours, he was startled at finding, that, except in the tallow and wax candles that flickered, not from the presence of a ghost, but from want of snuffing, there was no foundation in real life for any of that congeries of pleasing pictures and descriptions contained in those volumes, from which he had formed his study. Finding, however, some compensation in his gratified vanity, he was about to relinquish his dreams, when the extraordinary being we have above described, crossed him in his career.

He watched him; and the very impossibility of forming an idea of the character of a man entirely absorbed in himself, who gave few other signs of his observation of external objects, than the tacit assent to their existence, implied by the avoidance of their contact: allowing his imagination to picture every thing that flattered its propensity to extravagant ideas, he soon formed this object into the hero of a romance, and determined to observe the offspring of his fancy, rather than the person before him. He became acquainted with him, paid him attentions, and so far advanced upon his notice, that his presence was always recognized. He gradually learnt that Lord Ruthven's affairs were embarrassed, and soon found, from the notes of preparation in — Street, that he was about to travel. Desirous of gaining some information respecting this singular character, who, till now, had only whetted his curiosity, he hinted to his guardians, that it was time for him to perform the tour, which for many generations has been thought necessary to enable the young to take some rapid steps in the career of vice towards putting themselves upon an equality with the aged, and not allowing them to appear as if fallen from the skies, wherever scandalous intrigues are mentioned as the subjects of pleasantry or of praise, according to the degree of skill shewn in carrying them on. They consented: and Aubrey immediately mentioning his intentions to Lord Ruthven, was surprised to receive from him a proposal to join him. Flattered by such a mark of esteem from him, who, apparently, had nothing in common with other men, he gladly accepted it, and in a few days they had passed the circling waters.

Hitherto, Aubrey had had no opportunity of studying Lord Ruthven's character, and now he found, that, though many more of his actions were exposed to his view, the results offered different conclusions from the apparent motives to his conduct. His companion was profuse in his liberality; the idle, the vagabond, and the beggar, received from his hand more than enough to relieve their immediate wants. But Aubrey could not avoid remarking, that it was not upon the virtuous, reduced to indigence by the misfortunes attendant even upon virtue, that he bestowed his alms; these were sent from the door with hardly suppressed sneers; but when the profligate came to ask something, not to relieve his wants, but to allow him to wallow in his lust, or to sink him still deeper in his iniquity, he was sent away with rich charity. This was, however, attributed by him to the greater importunity of the vicious, which generally prevails over the retiring bashfulness of the virtuous indigent. There was one circumstance about the charity of his Lordship, which was still more impressed upon his mind: all those upon whom it was bestowed, inevitably found that there was a curse upon it, for they were all either led to the scaffold, or sunk to the lowest and the most abject misery. At Brussels and other towns through which they passed, Aubrey was surprised at the apparent eagerness with which his companion sought for the centres of all fashionable vice; there he entered into all the spirit of the faro table: he betted, and always gambled with success, except where the known sharper was his antagonist, and then he lost even more than he gained; but it was always with the same unchanging face, with which he generally watched the society around: it was not, however, so when he encountered the rash youthful novice, or the luckless father of a numerous family; then his very wish seemed fortune's law – this apparent abstractedness of mind was laid aside, and his eyes sparkled with more fire than that of the cat whilst dallying with the half-dead mouse. In every town, he left the formerly affluent youth, torn from the circle he adorned, cursing, in the solitude of a dungeon, the fate that had drawn him within the reach of this fiend; whilst many a father sat frantic, amidst the speaking looks of mute hungry children, without a single farthing of his late immense wealth, wherewith to buy even sufficient to satisfy their present craving. Yet he took no money from the gambling table; but immediately lost, to the ruin of many, the last gilder he had just snatched from the convulsive grasp of the innocent: this might but be the result of a certain degree of knowledge, which was not, however, capable of combating the cunning of the more experienced. Aubrey often wished to represent this to his friend, and beg him to resign that charity and pleasure which proved the ruin of all, and did not tend to his own profit; but he delayed it – for each day he hoped his friend would give him some opportunity of speaking frankly and openly to him; however, this never occurred. Lord Ruthven in his carriage, and amidst the various wild and rich scenes of nature, was always the same: his eye spoke less than his lip; and though Aubrey was near the object of his curiosity, he obtained no greater gratification from it than the constant excitement of vainly wishing to break that mystery, which to his exalted imagination began to assume the appearance of something supernatural.

They soon arrived at Rome, and Aubrey for a time lost sight of his companion; he left him in daily attendance upon the morning circle of an Italian countess, whilst he went in search of the memorials of another almost deserted city. Whilst he was thus engaged, letters arrived from England, which he opened with eager impatience; the first was from his sister, breathing nothing but affection; the others were from his guardians, the latter astonished him; if it had before entered into his imagination that there was an evil power resident in his companion, these seemed to give him almost sufficient reason for the belief. His guardians insisted upon his immediately leaving his friend, and urged, that his character was dreadfully vicious, for that the possession of irresistible powers of seduction, rendered his licentious habits more dangerous to society. It had been discovered, that his contempt for the adultress had not originated in hatred of her character; but that he had required, to enhance his gratification, that his victim, the partner of his guilt, should be hurled from the pinnacle of unsullied virtue, down to the lowest abyss of infamy and degradation: in fine, that all those females whom he had sought, apparently on account of their virtue, had, since his departure, thrown even the mask aside, and had not scrupled to expose the whole deformity of their vices to the public gaze.

Aubrey determined upon leaving one, whose character had not yet shown a single bright point on which to rest the eye. He resolved to invent some plausible pretext for abandoning him altogether, purposing, in the mean while, to watch him more closely, and to let no slight circumstances pass by unnoticed. He entered into the same circle, and soon perceived, that his Lordship was endeavouring to work upon the inexperience of the daughter of the lady whose house he chiefly frequented. In Italy, it is seldom that an unmarried female is met with in society; he was therefore obliged to carry on his plans in secret; but Aubrey's eye followed him in all his windings, and soon discovered that an assignation had been appointed, which would most likely end in the ruin of an innocent, though thoughtless girl. Losing no time, he entered the apartment of Lord Ruthven, and abruptly asked him his intentions with respect to the lady, informing him at the same time that he was aware of his being about to meet her that very night. Lord Ruthven answered that his intentions were such as he supposed all would have upon such an occasion; and upon being pressed whether he intended to marry her, merely laughed. Aubrey retired; and, immediately writing a note to say, that from that moment he must decline accompanying his Lordship in the remainder of their proposed tour, he ordered his servant to seek other apart-ments, and calling upon the mother of the lady, informed her of all he knew, not only with regard to her daughter, but also concerning the character of his Lordship. The assignation was prevented. Lord Ruthven next day merely sent his servant to notify his complete assent to a separation; but did not hint any suspicion of his plans having been foiled by Aubrey's interposition.

Having left Rome, Aubrey directed his steps towards Greece, and crossing the Peninsula, soon found himself at Athens. He then fixed his residence in the house of a Greek; and soon occupied himself in tracing the faded records of ancient glory upon monuments that apparently, ashamed of chronicling the deeds of freemen only before slaves, had hidden themselves beneath the sheltering soil or many coloured lichen. Under the same roof as himself, existed a being, so beautiful and delicate, that she might have formed the model for a painter, wishing to portray on canvass the promised hope of the faithful in Mahomet's paradise, save that her eyes spoke too much mind for any one to think she could belong to those who had no souls. As she danced upon the plain, or tripped along the mountain's side, one would have thought the gazelle a poor type of her beauties; for who would have exchanged her eye, apparently the eye of animated nature, for that sleepy luxurious look of the animal suited but to the taste of an epicure. The light step of Ianthe often accompanied Aubrey in his search after antiquities, and often would the unconscious girl, engaged in the pursuit of a Kashmere butterfly, show the whole beauty of her form, floating as it were upon the wind, to the eager gaze of him, who forgot the letters he had just decyphered upon an almost effaced tablet, in the contemplation of her sylph-like figure. Often would her tresses falling, as she flitted around, exhibit in the sun's ray such delicately brilliant and swiftly fading hues, as might well excuse the forgetfulness of the antiquary, who let escape from his mind the very object he had before thought of vital importance to the proper interpretation of a passage in Pausanias. But why attempt to describe charms which all feel, but none can appreciate? – It was innocence, youth, and beauty, unaffected by crowded drawing-rooms and stifling balls. Whilst he drew those remains of which he wished to preserve a memorial for his future hours, she would stand by, and watch the magic effects of his pencil, in tracing the scenes of her native place; she would then describe to him the circling dance upon the open plain, would paint to him in all the glowing colours of youthful memory, the marriage pomp she remembered viewing in her infancy; and then, turning to subjects that had evidently made a greater impression upon her mind, would tell him all the supernatural tales of her nurse. Her earnestness and apparent belief of what she narrated, excited the interest even of Aubrey; and often as she told him the tale of the living vampyre, who had passed years amidst his friends, and dearest ties, forced every year, by feeding upon the life of a lovely female to prolong his existence for the ensuing months, his blood would run cold, whilst he attempted to laugh her out of such idle and horrible fantasies; but Ianthe cited to him the names of old men, who had at last detected one living among themselves, after several of their near relatives and children had been found marked with the stamp of the fiend's appetite; and when she found him so incredulous, she begged of him to believe her, for it had been remarked, that those who had dared to question their existence, always had some proof given, which obliged them, with grief and heartbreaking, to confess it was true. She detailed to him the traditional appearance of these monsters, and his horror was increased, by hearing a pretty accurate description of Lord Ruthven; he, however, still persisted in persuading her, that there could be no truth in her fears, though at the same time he wondered at the many coincidences which had all tended to excite a belief in the supernatural power of Lord Ruthven.

Aubrey began to attach himself more and more to Ianthe; her innocence, so contrasted with all the affected virtues of the women among whom he had sought for his vision of romance, won his heart; and while he ridiculed the idea of a young man of English habits, marrying an uneducated Greek girl, still he found himself more and more attached to the almost fairy form before him. He would tear himself at times from her, and, forming a plan for some antiquarian research, he would depart, determined not to return until his object was attained; but he always found it impossible to fix his attention upon the ruins around him, whilst in his mind he retained an image that seemed alone the rightful possessor of his thoughts. Ianthe was unconscious of his love, and was ever the same frank infantile being he had first known. She always seemed to part from him with reluctance; but it was because she had no longer any one with whom she could visit her favourite haunts, whilst her guardian was occupied in sketching or uncovering some fragment which had yet escaped the destructive hand of time. She had appealed to her parents on the subject of Vampyres, and they both, with several present, affirmed their existence, pale with horror at the very name. Soon after, Aubrey determined to proceed upon one of his excursions, which was to detain him for a few hours; when they heard the name of the place, they all at once begged of him not to return at night, as he must necessarily pass through a wood, where no Greek would ever remain, after the day had closed, upon any consideration. They described it as the resort of the vampyres in their nocturnal orgies, and denounced the most heavy evils as impending upon him who dared to cross their path. Aubrey made light of their representations, and tried to laugh them out of the idea; but when he saw them shudder at his daring thus to mock a superior, infernal power, the very name of which apparently made their blood freeze, he was silent.

Next morning Aubrey set off upon his excursion unattended; he was surprised to observe the melancholy face of his host, and was concerned to find that his words, mocking the belief of those horrible fiends, had inspired them with such terror. When he was about to depart, Ianthe came to the side of his horse, and earnestly begged of him to return, ere night allowed the power of these beings to be put in action; he promised. He was, however, so occupied in his research, that he did not perceive that daylight would soon end, and that in the horizon there was one of those specks which, in the warmer climates, so rapidly gather into a tremendous mass, and pour all their rage upon the devoted country. He at last, however, mounted his horse, determined to make up by speed for his delay: but it was too late. Twilight, in these southern climates, is almost unknown; immediately the sun sets, night begins: and ere he had advanced far, the power of the storm was above – its echoing thunders had scarcely an interval of rest; its thick heavy rain forced its way through the canopying foliage, whilst the blue forked lightning seemed to fall and radiate at his very feet. Suddenly his horse took fright, and he was carried with dreadful rapidity through the entangled forest. The animal at last, through fatigue, stopped, and he found, by the glare of lightning, that he was in the neighbourhood of a hovel that hardly lifted itself up from the masses of dead leaves and brushwood which surrounded it. Dismounting, he approached, hoping to find some one to guide him to the town, or at least trusting to obtain shelter from the pelting of the storm. As he approached, the thunders, for a moment silent, allowed him to hear the dreadful shrieks of a woman mingling with the stifled, exultant mockery of a laugh, continued in one almost unbroken sound; he was startled: but, roused by the thunder which again rolled over his head, he, with a sudden effort, forced open the door of the hut. He found himself in utter darkness: the sound, however, guided him. He was apparently unperceived; for, though he called, still the sounds continued, and no notice was taken of him. He found himself in contact with some one, whom he immediately seized; when a voice cried, 'Again baffled!' to which a loud laugh succeeded; and he felt himself grappled by one whose strength seemed superhuman: determined to sell his life as dearly as he could, he struggled; but it was in vain: he was lifted from his feet and hurled with enormous force against the ground – his enemy threw himself upon him, and kneeling upon his breast, had placed his hands upon his throat – when the glare of many torches penetrating through the hole that gave light in the day, disturbed him; he instantly rose, and, leaving his prey, rushed through the door, and in a moment the crashing of the branches, as he broke through the wood, was no longer heard. The storm was now still; and Aubrey, incapable of moving, was soon heard by those without. They entered; the light of their torches fell upon the mud walls, and the thatch loaded on every individual straw with heavy flakes of soot. At the desire of Aubrey they searched for her who had attracted him by her cries; he was again left in darkness; but what was his horror, when the light of the torches once more burst upon him, to perceive the airy form of his fair conductress brought in a lifeless corpse. He shut his eyes, hoping that it was but a vision arising from his disturbed imagination; but he again saw the same form, when he unclosed them, stretched by his side. There was no colour upon her cheek, not even upon her lip; yet there was a stillness about her face that seemed almost as attaching as the life that once dwelt there: upon her neck and breast was blood, and upon her throat were the marks of teeth having opened the vein: to this the men pointed, crying, simultaneously struck with horror, 'A Vampyre! a Vampyre!' A litter was quickly formed, and Aubrey was laid by the side of her who had lately been to him the object of so many bright and fairy visions, now fallen with the flower of life that had died within her. He knew not what his thoughts were – his mind was benumbed and seemed to shun reflection, and take refuge in vacancy; he held almost unconsciously in his hand a naked dagger of a particular construction, which had been found in the hut. They were soon met by different parties who had been engaged in the search of her whom a mother had missed. Their lamentable cries, as they approached the city, forewarned the parents of some dreadful catastrophe. To describe their grief would be impossible; but when they ascertained the cause of their child's death, they looked at Aubrey, and pointed to the corpse. They were inconsolable; both died broken-hearted.

Aubrey being put to bed was seized with a most violent fever, and was often delirious; in these intervals he would call upon Lord Ruthven and upon Ianthe – by some unaccountable combination he seemed to beg of his former companion to spare the being he loved. At other times he would imprecate maledictions upon his head, and curse him as her destroyer. Lord Ruthven chanced at this time to arrive at Athens, and, from whatever motive, upon hearing of the state of Aubrey, immediately placed himself in the same house, and became his constant attendant. When the latter recovered from his delirium, he was horrified and startled at the sight of him whose image he had now combined with that of a Vampyre; but Lord Ruthven, by his kind words, implying almost repentance for the fault that had caused their separation, and still more by the attention, anxiety, and care which he showed, soon reconciled him to his presence. His lordship seemed quite changed; he no longer appeared that apathetic being who had so astonished Aubrey; but as soon as his convalescence began to be rapid, he again gradually retired into the same state of mind, and Aubrey perceived no difference from the former man, except that at times he was surprised to meet his gaze fixed intently upon him, with a smile of malicious exultation playing upon his lips: he knew not why, but this smile haunted him. During the last stage of the invalid's recovery, Lord Ruthven was apparently engaged in watching the tideless waves raised by the cooling breeze, or in marking the progress of those orbs, circling, like our world, the moveless sun; indeed, he appeared to wish to avoid the eyes of all.

Aubrey's mind, by this shock, was much weakened, and that elasticity of spirit which had once so distinguished him now seemed to have fled for ever. He was now as much a lover of solitude and silence as Lord Ruthven; but much as he wished for solitude, his mind could not find it in the neighbourhood of Athens; if he sought it amidst the ruins he had formerly frequented, Ianthe's form stood by his side; if he sought it in the woods, her light step would appear wandering amidst the underwood, in quest of the modest violet; then suddenly turning round, would show, to his wild imagination, her pale face and wounded throat, with a meek smile upon her lips. He determined to fly scenes, every feature of which created such bitter associations in his mind. He proposed to Lord Ruthven, to whom he held himself bound by the tender care he had taken of him during his illness, that they should visit those parts of Greece neither had yet seen. They travelled in every direction, and sought every spot to which a recollection could be attached: but though they thus hastened from place to place, yet they seemed not to heed what they gazed upon. They heard much of robbers, but they gradually began to slight these reports, which they imagined were only the invention of individuals, whose interest it was to excite the generosity of those whom they defended from pretended dangers. In consequence of thus neglecting the advice of the inhabitants, on one occasion they travelled with only a few guards, more to serve as guides than as a defence. Upon entering, however, a narrow defile, at the bottom of which was the bed of a torrent, with large masses of rock brought down from the neighbouring precipices, they had reason to repent their negligence; for scarcely were the whole of the party engaged in the narrow pass, when they were startled by the whistling of bullets close to their heads, and by the echoed report of several guns. In an instant their guards had left them, and, placing themselves behind rocks, had begun to fire in the direction whence the report came. Lord Ruthven and Aubrey, imitating their example, retired for a moment behind the sheltering turn of the defile: but ashamed of being thus detained by a foe, who with insulting shouts bade them advance, and being exposed to unresisting slaughter, if any of the robbers should climb above and take them in the rear, they determined at once to rush forward in search of the enemy. Hardly had they lost the shelter of the rock, when Lord Ruthven received a shot in the shoulder, which brought him to the ground. Aubrey hastened to his assistance; and, no longer heeding the contest or his own peril, was soon surprised by seeing the robbers' faces around him – his guards having, upon Lord Ruthven's being wounded, immediately thrown up their arms and surrendered.

By promises of great reward, Aubrey soon induced them to convey his wounded friend to a neighbouring cabin; and having agreed upon a ransom, he was no more disturbed by their presence – they being content merely to guard the entrance till their comrade should return with the promised sum, for which he had an order. Lord Ruthven's strength rapidly decreased; in two days mortification ensued, and death seemed advancing with hasty steps. His conduct and appearance had not changed; he seemed as unconscious of pain as he had been of the objects about him: but towards the close of the last evening, his mind became apparently uneasy, and his eye often fixed upon Aubrey, who was induced to offer his assistance with more than usual earnestness – 'Assist me! you may save me – you may do more than that – I mean not my life, I heed the death of my existence as little as that of the passing day; but you may save my honour, your friend's honour.' – 'How? Tell me how? I would do any thing,' replied Aubrey. – 'I need but little – my life ebbs apace – I cannot explain the whole – but if you would conceal all you know of me, my honour were free from stain in the world's mouth – and if my death were unknown for some time in England – I – I – but life.' – 'It shall not be known.' – 'Swear!' cried the dying man, raising himself with exultant violence, 'Swear by all your soul reveres, by all your nature fears, swear that for a year and a day you will not impart your knowledge of my crimes or death to any living being in any way, whatever may happen, or whatever you may see.' His eyes seemed bursting from their sockets: 'I swear!' said Aubrey; he sunk laughing upon his pillow, and breathed no more.

Aubrey retired to rest, but did not sleep; the many circumstances attending his acquaintance with this man rose upon his mind, and he knew not why; when he remembered his oath a cold shivering came over him, as if from the presentiment of something horrible awaiting him. Rising early in the morning, he was about to enter the hovel in which he had left the corpse, when a robber met him, and informed him that it was no longer there, having been conveyed by himself and comrades, upon his retiring, to the pinnacle of a neighbouring mount, according to a promise they had given his lordship, that it should be exposed to the first cold ray of the moon that rose after his death. Aubrey was astonished, and taking several of the men, determined to go and bury it upon the spot where it lay. But, when he had mounted to the summit he found no trace of either the corpse or the clothes, though the robbers swore they pointed out the identical rock on which they had laid the body. For a time his mind was bewildered in conjectures, but he at last returned, convinced that they had buried the corpse for the sake of the clothes.

Weary of a country in which he had met with such terrible misfortunes, and in which all apparently conspired to heighten that superstitious melancholy that had seized upon his mind, he resolved to leave it, and soon arrived at Smyrna. While waiting for a vessel to convey him to Otranto, or to Naples, he occupied himself in arranging those effects he had with him belonging to Lord Ruthven. Amongst other things there was a case containing several weapons of offence, more or less adapted to ensure the death of the victim. There were several daggers and yagatans. Whilst turning them over, and examining their curious forms, what was his surprise at finding a sheath apparently ornamented in the same style as the dagger discovered in the fatal hut; he shuddered; hastening to gain further proof, he found the weapon, and his horror may be imagined when he discovered that it fitted, though peculiarly shaped, the sheath he held in his hand. His eyes seemed to need no further certainty – they seemed gazing to be bound to the dagger; yet still he wished to disbelieve; but the particular form, the same varying tints upon the haft and sheath were alike in splendour on both, and left no room for doubt; there were also drops of blood on each.

He left Smyrna, and on his way home, at Rome, his first inquiries were concerning the lady he had attempted to snatch from Lord Ruthven's seductive arts. Her parents were in distress, their fortune ruined, and she had not been heard of since the departure of his lordship. Aubrey's mind became almost broken under so many repeated horrors; he was afraid that this lady had fallen a victim to the destroyer of Ianthe. He became morose and silent; and his only occupation consisted in urging the speed of the postilions, as if he were going to save the life of some one he held dear. He arrived at Calais; a breeze, which seemed obedient to his will, soon wafted him to the English shores; and he hastened to the mansion of his fathers, and there, for a moment, appeared to lose, in the embraces and caresses of his sister, all memory of the past. If she before, by her infantine caresses, had gained his affection, now that the woman began to appear, she was still more attaching as a companion.

Miss Aubrey had not that winning grace which gains the gaze and applause of the drawing-room assemblies. There was none of that light brilliancy which only exists in the heated atmosphere of a crowded apartment. Her blue eye was never lit up by the levity of the mind beneath. There was a melancholy charm about it which did not seem to arise from misfortune, but from some feeling within, that appeared to indicate a soul conscious of a brighter realm. Her step was not that light footing, which strays where'er a butterfly or a colour may attract – it was sedate and pensive. When alone, her face was never brightened by the smile of joy; but when her brother breathed to her his affection, and would in her presence forget those griefs she knew destroyed his rest, who would have exchanged her smile for that of the voluptuary? It seemed as if those eyes, that face were then playing in the light of their own native sphere. She was yet only eighteen, and had not been presented to the world, it having been thought by her guardians more fit that her presentation should be delayed until her brother's return from the continent, when he might be her protector. It was now, therefore, resolved that the next drawing-room, which was fast approaching, should be the epoch of her entry into the 'busy scene'. Aubrey would rather have remained in the mansion of his fathers, and fed upon the melancholy which overpowered him. He could not feel interest about the frivolities of fashionable strangers, when his mind had been so torn by the events he had witnessed; but he determined to sacrifice his own comfort to the protection of his sister. They soon arrived in town, and prepared for the next day, which had been announced as a drawing-room.

The crowd was excessive – a drawing-room had not been held for a long time, and all who were anxious to bask in the smile of royalty, hastened thither. Aubrey was there with his sister. While he was standing in a corner by himself, heedless of all around him, engaged in the remembrance that the first time he had seen Lord Ruthven was in that very place – he felt himself suddenly seized by the arm, and a voice he recognized too well, sounded in his ear – 'Remember your oath.' He had hardly courage to turn, fearful of seeing a spectre that would blast him, when he perceived, at a little distance, the same figure which had attracted his notice on this spot upon his first entry into society. He gazed till his limbs almost refusing to bear their weight, he was obliged to take the arm of a friend, and forcing a passage through the crowd, he threw himself into his carriage, and was driven home. He paced the room with hurried steps, and fixed his hands upon his head, as if he were afraid his thoughts were bursting from his brain. Lord Ruthven again before him – circumstances started up in dreadful array – the dagger – his oath. – He roused himself, he could not believe it possible – the dead rise again! – He thought his imagination had conjured up the image his mind was resting upon. It was impossible that it could be real – he determined, therefore, to go again into society; for though he attempted to ask concerning Lord Ruthven, the name hung upon his lips, and he could not succeed in gaining information. He went a few nights after with his sister to the assembly of a near relation. Leaving her under the protection of a matron, he retired into a recess, and there gave himself up to his own devouring thoughts. Perceiving, at last, that many were leaving, he roused himself, and entering another room, found his sister surrounded by several, apparently in earnest conversation; he attempted to pass and get near her, when one, whom he requested to move, turned round, and revealed to him those features he most abhorred. He sprang forward, seized his sister's arm, and, with hurried step, forced her towards the street: at the door he found himself impeded by the crowd of servants who were waiting for their lords; and while he was engaged in passing them, he again heard that voice whisper close to him – 'Remember your oath!' – he did not dare to turn, but, hurrying his sister, soon reached home.

Aubrey became almost distracted. If before his mind had been absorbed by one subject, how much more completely was it engrossed, now that the certainty of the monster's living again pressed up his thoughts. His sister's attentions were now unheeded, and it was in vain that she entreated him to explain to her what had caused his abrupt conduct. He only uttered a few words, and those terrified her. The more he thought, the more he was bewildered. His oath startled him; – was he then to allow this monster to roam, bearing ruin upon his breath, amidst all he held dear, and not avert its progress? His very sister might have been touched by him. But even if he were to break his oath, and disclose his suspicions, who would believe him? He thought of employing his own hand to free the world from such a wretch; but death, he remembered, had been already mocked. For days he remained in this state; shut up in his room, he saw no one, and ate only when his sister came, who, with eyes streaming with tears, besought him, for her sake, to support nature. At last, no longer capable of bearing stillness and solitude, he left his house, roamed from street to street, anxious to fly that image which haunted him. His dress became neglected, and he wandered, as often exposed to the noon-day sun as to the mid-night damps. He was no longer to be recognized; at first he returned with the evening to the house; but at last he laid him down to rest wherever fatigue overtook him. His sister, anxious for his safety, employed people to follow him; but they were soon distanced by him who fled from a pursuer swifter than any – from thought. His conduct, however, suddenly changed. Struck with the idea that he left by his absence the whole of his friends, with a fiend amongst them, of whose presence they were unconscious, he determined to enter again into society, and watch him closely, anxious to forewarn, in spite of his oath, all whom Lord Ruthven approached with intimacy. But when he entered into a room, his haggard and suspicious looks were so striking, his inward shud-derings so visible, that his sister was at last obliged to beg of him to abstain from seeking, for her sake, a society which affected him so strongly. When, however, remonstrance proved unavailing, the guardians thought proper to interpose, and, fearing that his mind was becoming alienated, they thought it high time to resume again that trust which had been before imposed upon them by Aubrey's parents.

Desirous of saving him from the injuries and sufferings he had daily encountered in his wanderings, and of preventing him from exposing to the general eye those marks of what they considered folly, they engaged a physician to reside in the house, and take constant care of him. He hardly appeared to notice it, so completely was his mind absorbed by one terrible subject. His incoherence became at last so great, that he was confined to his chamber. There he would often lie for days, incapable of being roused. He had become emaciated, his eyes had attained a glassy lustre; – the only sign of affection and recollection remaining displayed itself upon the entry of his sister; then he would sometimes start, and seizing her hands, with looks that severely afflicted her, he would desire her not to touch him. 'Oh, do not touch him – if your love for me is aught, do not go near him!' When, how-ever, she inquired to whom he referred, his only answer was 'True! true!' and again he sank into a state, whence not even she could rouse him. This lasted many months: gradually, however, as the year was passing, his incoherences became less frequent, and his mind threw off a portion of its gloom, whilst his guardians observed, that several times in the day he would count upon his fingers a definite number, and then smile.

The time had nearly elapsed, when, upon the last day of the year, one of his guardians entering his room, began to converse with his physician upon the melancholy circumstance of Aubrey's being in so awful a situation, when his sister was going next day to be married. Instantly Aubrey's attention was attracted; he asked anxiously to whom. Glad of this mark of returning intellect, of which they feared he had been deprived, they mentioned the name of the Earl of Marsden. Thinking this was a young Earl whom he had met with in society, Aubrey seemed pleased, and astonished them still more by his expressing his intention to be present at the nuptials, and desiring to see his sister. They answered not, but in a few minutes his sister was with him. He was apparently again capable of being affected by the influence of her lovely smile; for he pressed her to his breast, and kissed her cheek, wet with tears, flowing at the thought of her brother's being once more alive to the feelings of affection. He began to speak with all his wonted warmth, and to congratulate her upon her marriage with a person so distinguished for rank and every accomplishment; when he suddenly perceived a locket upon her breast; opening it, what was his surprise at beholding the features of the monster who had so long influenced his life. He seized the portrait in a paroxysm of rage, and trampled it under foot. Upon her asking him why he thus destroyed the resemblance of her future husband, he looked as if he did not understand her; – then seizing her hands, and gazing on her with a frantic expression of countenance, he bade her swear that she would never wed this monster, for he – But he could not advance – it seemed as if that voice again bade him remember his oath – he turned suddenly round, thinking Lord Ruthven was near him but saw no one. In the meantime the guardians and physician, who had heard the whole, and thought this was but a return of his disorder, entered, and forcing him from Miss Aubrey, desired her to leave him. He fell upon his knees to them, he implored, he begged of them to delay but for one day. They, attributing this to the insanity they imagined had taken possession of his mind, endeavoured to pacify him, and retired.

Lord Ruthven had called the morning after the drawing-room, and had been refused with every one else. When he heard of Aubrey's ill health, he readily understood himself to be the cause of it; but when he learned that he was deemed insane, his exultation and pleasure could hardly be concealed from those among whom he had gained this information. He hastened to the house of his former companion, and, by constant attendance, and the pretence of great affection for the brother and interest in his fate, he gradually won the ear of Miss Aubrey. Who could resist his power? His tongue had dangers and toils to recount – could speak of himself as of an individual having no sympathy with any being on the crowded earth, save with her to whom he addressed himself; – could tell how, since he knew her, his existence had begun to seem worthy of preservation, if it were merely that he might listen to her soothing accents; – in fine, he knew so well how to use the serpent's art, or such was the will of fate, that he gained her affections. The title of the elder branch falling at length to him, he obtained an important embassy, which served as an excuse for hastening the marriage (in spite of her brother's deranged state), which was to take place the very day before his departure for the continent.

Aubrey, when he was left by the physician and his guardians, attempted to bribe the servants, but in vain. He asked for pen and paper; it was given him; he wrote a letter to his sister, conjuring her, as she valued her own happiness, her own honour, and the honour of those now in the grave, who once held her in their arms as their hope and the hope of their house, to delay but for a few hours that marriage, on which he denounced the most heavy curses. The servants promised they would deliver it; but giving it to the physician, he thought it better not to harass any more the mind of Miss Aubrey by, what he considered, the ravings of a maniac. Night passed on without rest to the busy inmates of the house; and Aubrey heard, with a horror that may more easily be conceived than described, the notes of busy preparation. Morning came, and the sound of carriages broke upon his ear. Aubrey grew almost frantic. The curiosity of the servants at last overcame their vigilance, they gradually stole away, leaving him in the custody of an helpless old woman. He seized the opportunity, with one bound was out of the room, and in a moment found himself in the apartment where all were nearly assembled. Lord Ruthven was the first to perceive him: he immediately approached, and, taking his arm by force, hurried him from the room, speechless with rage. When on the staircase, Lord Ruthven whispered in his ear – 'Remember your oath, and know, if not my bride today, your sister is dishonoured. Women are frail!' So saying, he pushed him towards his attendants, who, roused by the old woman, had come in search of him. Aubrey could no longer support himself; his rage not finding vent, had broken a blood-vessel, and he was conveyed to bed. This was not mentioned to his sister, who was not present when he entered, as the physician was afraid of agitating her. The marriage was solemnized, and the bride and bridegroom left London.

Aubrey's weakness increased; the effusion of blood produced symptoms of the near approach of death. He desired his sister's guardians might be called, and when the midnight hour had struck, he related composedly what the reader has perused – he died immediately after.

The guardians hastened to protect Miss Aubrey; but when they arrived, it was too late. Lord Ruthven had disappeared, and Aubrey's sister had glutted the thirst of a VAMPYRE!

FRAGMENT OF A STORY
LORD BYRON

This was originally part of the story that Byron told on 17 June 1816, as his contribution to the ghost-story session. He omitted most of the more 'vampiric' aspects of his original story in this published version, probably in order to highlight the differences between his *Fragment* and Polidori's *Vampyre*. The reason Lord Byron published this *Fragment* at all (as an appendix to his poem *Mazeppa*, in 1819) was almost certainly self-defence – it was rushed out just after the appearance of Polidori's 'version' which had been falsely attributed to Byron himself, partly because of a misunderstanding, partly in order to boost sales.

June 17, 1816

IN THE YEAR 17 –, having for some time determined on a journey through countries not hitherto much frequented by travellers, I set out, accompanied by a friend, whom I shall designate by the name of Augustus Darvell. He was a few years my elder, and a man of considerable fortune and ancient family: advantages which an extensive capacity prevented him alike from undervaluing or overrating. Some peculiar circumstances in his private history had rendered him to me an object of attention, of interest, and even of regard, which neither the reserve of his manners, nor occasional indications of an inquietude at times nearly approaching to alienation of mind, could extinguish.

I was yet young in life, which I had begun early; but my intimacy with him was of a recent date: we had been educated at the same schools and university; but his progress through these had preceded mine, and he had been deeply initiated into what is called the world, while I was yet in my novitiate. While thus engaged, I heard much both of his past and present life; and, although in these accounts there were many and irreconcilable contradictions, I could still gather from the whole that he was a being of no common order, and one who, whatever pains he might take to avoid remark, would still be remarkable. I had cultivated his acquaintance subsequently, and endeavoured to obtain his friendship, but this last appeared to be unattainable; whatever affections he might have possessed seemed now, some to have been extinguished, and others to be concentred: that his feelings were acute, I had sufficient opportunities of observing; for, although he could control, he could not altogether disguise them: still he had a power of giving to one passion the appearance of another, in such a manner that it was difficult to define the nature of what was working within him; and the expressions of his features would vary so rapidly, though slightly, that it was useless to trace them to their sources. It was evident that he was a prey to some cureless disquiet; but whether it arose from ambition, love, remorse, grief, from one or all of these, or merely from a morbid temperament akin to disease, I could not discover: there were circumstances alleged which might have justified the application to each of these causes; but, as I have before said, these were so contradictory and contradicted, that none could be fixed upon with accuracy. Where there is mystery, it is generally supposed that there must also be evil: I know not how this may be, but in him there certainly was the one, though I could not ascertain the extent of the other – and felt loth, as far as regarded himself, to believe in its existence. My advances were received with sufficient coolness: but I was young, and not easily discouraged, and at length succeeded in obtaining, to a certain degree, that common-place intercourse and moderate confidence of common and every-day concerns, created and cemented by similarity of pursuit and frequency of meeting, which is called intimacy, or friendship, according to the ideas of him who uses those words to express them.

Darvell had already travelled extensively; and to him I had applied for information with regard to the conduct of my intended journey. It was my secret wish that he might be prevailed on to accompany me; it was also a probable hope, founded upon the shadowy restlessness which I observed in him, and to which the animation which he appeared to feel on such subjects, and his apparent indifference to all by which he was more immediately surrounded, gave fresh strength. This wish I first hinted, and then expressed: his answer, though I had partly expected it, gave me all the pleasure of surprise – he consented; and, after the requisite arrangement, we commenced our voyages. After journeying through various countries of the south of Europe, our attention was turned towards the East, according to our original destination; and it was in my progress through these regions that the incident occurred upon which will turn what I may have to relate.

The constitution of Darvell, which must from his appearance have been in early life more than usually robust, had been for some time gradually giving away, without the intervention of any apparent disease: he had neither cough nor hectic, yet he became daily more enfeebled; his habits were temperate, and he neither declined nor complained of fatigue; yet he was evidently wasting away: he became more and more silent and sleepless, and at length so seriously altered, that my alarm grew proportionate to what I conceived to be his danger.

We had determined, on our arrival at Smyrna, on an excursion to the ruins of Ephesus and Sardis, from which I endeavoured to dissuade him in his present state of indisposition – but in vain: there appeared to be an oppression on his mind, and a solemnity in his manner, which ill corresponded with his eagerness to proceed on what I regarded as a mere party of pleasure little suited to a valetudinarian; but I opposed him no longer – and in a few days we set off together, accompanied only by a serrugee and a single janizary.

We had passed halfway towards the remains of Ephesus, leaving behind us the more fertile environs of Smyrna, and were entering upon that wild and tenantless tract through the marshes and defiles which lead to the few huts yet lingering over the broken columns of Diana – the roofless walls of expelled Christianity, and the still more recent but complete desolation of abandoned mosques – when the sudden and rapid illness of my companion obliged us to halt at a Turkish cemetery, the turbaned tombstones of which were the sole indication that human life had ever been a sojourner in this wilderness. The only caravanserai we had seen was left some hours behind us, not a vestige of a town or even cottage was within sight or hope, and this 'city of the dead' appeared to be the sole refuge of my unfortunate friend, who seemed on the verge of becoming the last of its inhabitants.

In this situation, I looked round for a place where he might most conveniently repose: contrary to the usual aspect of Mahometan burial-grounds, the cypresses were in this few in number, and these thinly scattered over its extent; the tombstones were mostly fallen, and worn with age: upon one of the most considerable of these, and beneath one of the most spreading trees, Darvell supported himself, in a half-reclining posture, with great difficulty. He asked for water. I had some doubts of our being able to find any, and prepared to go in search of it with hesitating despondency: but he desired me to remain; and turning to Suleiman, our janizary, who stood by us smoking with great tranquillity, he said, 'Suleiman, verban su' (*i.e.* 'bring some water') and went on describing the spot where it was to be found with great minuteness, at a small well for camels, a few hundred yards to the right: the janizary obeyed. I said to Darvell, 'How did you know this?' He replied, 'From our situation; you must perceive that this place was once inhabited, and could not have been so without springs: I have also been here before.'

'You have been here before! How came you never to mention this to me? and what could you be doing in a place where no one would remain a moment longer than they could help it?'

To this question I received no answer. In the mean time Suleiman returned with the water, leaving the serrugee and the horses at the fountain. The quenching of his thirst had the appearance of reviving him for a moment; and I conceived hopes of his being able to proceed, or at least to return, and I urged the attempt. He was silent – and appeared to be collecting his spirits for an effort to speak. He began:

'This is the end of my journey, and of my life; I came here to die; but I have a request to make, a command – for such my last words must be. You will observe it?'

'Most certainly; but I have better hopes.'

'I have no hopes, nor wishes, but this – conceal my death from every human being.'

'I hope there will be no occasion; that you will recover, and –'

'Peace! it must be so: promise this.'

'I do.'

'Swear it, by all that – ' He here dictated an oath of great solemnity.

'There is no occasion for this. I will observe your request; and to doubt me is – '

'It cannot be helped – you must swear.'

I took the oath, it appeared to relieve him. He removed a seal ring from his finger, on which were some Arabic characters, and presented it to me. He proceeded:

'On the ninth day of the month, at noon precisely (what month you please, but this must be the day), you must fling this ring into the salt springs which run into the Bay of Eleusis; the day after, at the same hour, you must repair to the ruins of the temple of Ceres, and wait one hour.'

'Why?'

'You will see.'

'The ninth day of the month, you say?'

'The ninth.'

As I observed that the present was the ninth day of the month, his countenance changed, and he paused. As he sat, evidently becoming more feeble, a stork, with a snake in her beak, perched upon a tombstone near us; and, without devouring her prey, appeared to be steadfastly regarding us. I know not what impelled me to drive it away, but the attempt was useless; she made a few circles in the air, and returned exactly to the same spot. Darvell pointed to it, and smiled – he spoke – I know not whether to himself or to me – but the words were only, ''Tis well!'

'What is well? What do you mean?'

'No matter; you must bury me here this evening, and exactly where that bird is now perched. You know the rest of my injunctions.'

He then proceeded to give me several directions as to the manner in which his death might be best concealed. After these were finished, he exclaimed, 'You perceive that bird?'

'Certainly.'

'And the serpent writhing in her beak?'

'Doubtless: there is nothing uncommon in it; it is her natural prey. But it is odd that she does not devour it.'

He smiled in a ghastly manner, and said faintly, 'It is not yet time!' As he spoke, the stork flew away. My eyes followed it for a moment – it could hardly be longer than ten might be counted. I felt Darvell's weight, as it were, increase upon my shoulder, and, turning to look upon his face, perceived that he was dead!

I was shocked with the sudden certainty which could not be mistaken – his countenace in a few minutes became nearly black. I should have attributed so rapid a change to poison, had I not been aware that he had no opportunity of receiving it unperceived. The day was declining, the body was rapidly altering, and nothing remained but to fulfil his request. With the aid of Suleiman's yagatan and my own sabre, we scooped a shallow grave upon the spot which Darvell had indicated: the earth easily gave way, having already received some Mahometan tenant. We dug as deeply as the time permitted us, and throwing the dry earth upon all that remained of the singular being departed, we cut a few sods of greener turf from the less withered soil around us, and laid them upon his sepulchre.

Between astonishment and grief, I was tearless.

A VISIT TO THE THEATRE

ALEXANDRE DUMAS

Polidori's *Vampyre* was phenomenally successful in Paris, where the public would not accept that it could possibly have been written by anyone except Lord Byron. By February 1820, a full-length novel entitled *Lord Ruthwen ou les Vampires* (dedicated to Lord Byron) had already been concocted – the first vampire novel, in fact. By June 1820, three dramatizations (not counting parodies) were running simultaneously – *Le Vampire* at the Porte-Saint-Martin, *Le Vampire* (another one) at the Vaudeville and *Les Trois Vampires* at the Variétés. The plot of *Les Trois Vampires*, the most original, concerned the adventures of M. Gobetout, a Byron fanatic, who decided to treat the lovers of his two daughters and his maid as if they were vampires: the curtain came down, predictably enough, on a triple marriage.

A more direct adaptation of Polidori's *Vampyre* (by Charles Nodier, the distinguished Romantic writer and collector of weird stories) was revived two years later at the Porte-Saint-Martin theatre, and this was the version Alexandre Dumas went to see, later recalling the evening in his *Memoirs*. Nodier's *Le Vampire* must have made a profound impression on the young Dumas, for he was to rewrite the play twenty-eight years later: Dumas's five-act version of *Le Vampire* (again!), which opened in December 1851, attempted to synthesize *all* the most successful elements of the Lord Ruthven formula. But his interest in vampirism did not stop there: the first section of his multi-volume *Thousand and One Phantoms* (1848), entitled *Une Journée à Fontenay-aux-Roses*, contains a long sub-plot about the activities of an aristocratic vampire; this sub-plot was published separately in England under the title *The Pale-Faced Lady* (as a story in the *Parlour Novelist* volume *In the Moonlight*). *The Pale-Faced Lady* is a strange and over-long marriage of an adventure story (*Corsican Brothers* style) with the Ruthven formula, set in a relatively new location for the genre – the Carpathian Mountains.

This extract from Dumas's Memoirs *brilliantly evokes the atmosphere of a Paris theatre at the height of the* Vampyre *craze, and Dumas manages to intersperse some useful (if not always accurate) comments on more general aspects of vampirism as well, in between acts of the play.*

T HE CURTAIN ROSE. The overture was intended to represent a storm. The scene opened in the cave of Staffa. Malvina slept on a tomb. Oscar sat on another. A third enclosed Lord Ruthven, who was to come out of it at a given moment. The part of Malvina was taken by Madame Dorval; Oscar, or the angel of marriage, by Moessard; Lord Ruthven, or the Vampire, by Philippe.

Alas! who could have known at that moment, when I was looking eagerly beyond the curtain, taking in the whole scene, decorations and characters combined, that I should be present at Philippe's funeral, watch by Madame Dorval's death-bed, and see Moessard crowned?

In the prologue, there was another angel, called Ithuriel, the angel of the moon, talking with the angel of marriage. This was Mademoiselle Denotte. I do not know whether she is now living or dead . . . The narrative was carried on between the angel of marriage and the angel of the moon, two angels who, as they wore the same armour, might have been taken to belong to the same family.

Malvina had lost herself in hunting; the storm terrifying her, she had taken shelter in the cave of Staffa. There, unable to keep awake, she had fallen asleep on a tomb. The angel of marriage was watching over her. The angel of the moon, who had slid down on a ray of the pale goddess, through the cracks of the basaltic roof, asked why the angel of marriage sat there, and, above all, how it came about that there was a young girl in the grotto of Staffa.

The angel of marriage replied that, as Malvina, sister of Lord Aubrey, was to espouse Lord Marsden next day, he had been summoned by the importance of the occasion, and that his looks, when Ithuriel interrupted him in the act of silently gazing upon the beautiful betrothed girl, and the sadness depicted upon his face, sprang from knowledge of the misfortunes in store for the young maiden, who was about to fall from the arms of Love into those of Death. Then Ithuriel began to understand.

'Explain thyself,' said Ithuriel, 'is it true that horrible phantoms *come* [*viennent*] sometimes . . .?'

My neighbour trembled, as though an asp had bitten him in his sleep.

'*Vinssent!* he cried – '*vinssent!!*'

Cries of 'Silence!' burst forth all over the theatre, and I too clamoured loudly for silence, for I was enthralled by this opening.

The angel of the moon, interrupted in the middle of her sentence, threw an angry look across the orchestra, and went on:

'Is it true that horrible phantoms come [*viennent*] under the cloak of the rights of marriage, to suck blood from the throat of a timid maiden?'

'*Vinssent! vinssent! vinssent!*' murmured my neighbour.

Fresh cries of '*Hush!*' drowned his exclamation, which it must be confessed was less bold and less startling this time than the first.

Oscar replied: 'Yes! and these monsters are called vampires. A Power whose inscrutable decrees we are not permitted to call in question, has permitted certain miserable beings, who are tormented by the punishments which their crimes have drawn upon them on this earth, to enjoy a frightful power, which they exercise by preference over the nuptial couch and over the cradle; sometimes their formidable shapes appear clothed in the hideous guise death has bestowed upon them; others, more highly favoured, because their career is more brief and their future more fearful, obtain permission to reclothe themselves with the fleshy vesture lost in the tomb, and reappear before the living in the bodily shapes they formerly possessed.'

'And when do these monsters appear?' asked Ithuriel.

'The first hour of the morning wakes them in their sepulchre,' replied Oscar. 'When the sound of its sonorous stroke has died away among the echoes of the mountains, they fall back motionless in their everlasting tombs. But there is one among them over whom my power is more limited . . . what am I saying? . . . Fate herself can never go back on her decisions! . . . After having carried desolation into twenty different countries, always conquered, ever continuing, the blood which sustains its horrible existence

ever renewing its vitality . . . in thirty-six hours, at one o'clock in the morning, it has at length to submit to annihilation, the lawful punishment of an
infinite succession of crimes, if it cannot, at that time, add yet another crime,
and count one more victim.'

'My God! think of writing a play like that!' murmured my neighbour.

It seemed to me that he was too critical; for I thought this dialogue was
couched in the finest style imaginable. The prologue continued. Several persons
who had heard my neighbour gave vent to various whispered comments on
the presumption of this indefatigable interrupter.

It is unnecessary to point out that the young betrothed asleep on the
tomb was the innocent heroine who was destined to be the bride of the
Vampire, and had the public been in any doubt, all their doubts would have
been dispersed after the last scene of the prologue.

'What do I hear?' said Ithuriel; 'thy conversation has kept me a long
while in these caves.'

As the angel of the moon asks this question, the silvery chime of a distant clock is heard striking one, and the reverberation is repeated in echoes
again and again.

Oscar. 'Stay and see.'

All the tombs open as the hour sounds; pale shades rise half out of their
graves and then fall back under their monumental stones as the sound of
the echoes dies away.

A Spectre, clad in a shroud, escapes from the most conspicuous of these
tombs: his face is exposed; he glides to the place where Miss Aubrey sleeps,
exclaiming –

'Malvina!'

'*Oscar,* 'withdraw.'

Spectre. 'She belongs to me!'

Oscar puts his arms round the sleeping girl. 'She belongs to God, and
thou wilt soon belong to the regions of nothingness.'

The Spectre retires, but repeats threateningly, 'To nothingness.'

Ithuriel crosses the stage in a cloud.

The scene changes and represents an apartment in the house of Sir Aubrey.

'Absurd! absurd!' exclaimed my neighbour.

I did not at all agree with him: I thought the staging magnificent; I had nothing to say about Malvina, for she had not spoken; but Philippe seemed to be exceedingly fine, notwithstanding his paleness, and Moessard very good. Moreover, crude as it was, it was an attempt at Romanticism – a movement almost entirely unknown at that time. This intervention of immaterial and superior beings in human destiny had a fanciful side to it which pleased my imagination. The play began.

Sir Aubrey (the reader will see presently why I underline the word *Sir*) – *Sir* Aubrey met Lord Ruthven, a rich English traveller, at Athens, and they became friends. During their wanderings about the Parthenon and their day-dreams by the seashore, they planned means for tying the bonds of their friendship more firmly, and, subject to Malvina's consent, they decided upon a union between the young girl, who was at home in the castle of Staffa, and the noble traveller, who had become her brother's closest friend. Unfortunately, during an excursion which Aubrey and Ruthven made to the suburbs of Athens, to attend the wedding of a young maiden endowed privately by Lord Ruthven, the two companions were attacked by brigands: a sharp defence put the assassins to flight; but Lord Ruthven was struck down mortally wounded. His last words were a request that his friend would place him on a hillock bathed by the moon's rays. Aubrey carried out this last request, and laid the dying man on the place indicated; then, as his friend's eyes closed and his breathing ceased, Aubrey began to search for his scattered servitors; but when he returned with them, an hour later, the body had disappeared. Aubrey fancied that the assassins must have taken the body away to remove all traces of their crime.

When he returned to Scotland, he broke the news of Lord Ruthven's death to his brother, Lord Marsden, and told him of the close relationship that had united them during their travels. Then Marsden claimed succession to his brother's rights, and proposed to marry Malvina, if Malvina would consent to this substitution. Malvina, who did not know either the one or the other, made no objection to Lord Marsden's claim or to her brother's wishes.

Lord Marsden is announced. Malvina feels that slight embarrassment which, like an early morning mist, always comes over the hearts of young maidens at the approach of their betrothed. Aubrey, overjoyed, rushes to greet him; but when he sees him he utters a cry of surprise. It is not Lord Marsden – that is to say, a person hitherto unknown – who stands before him; it is his friend Lord Ruthven!

Aubrey's astonishment is intense; but all is explained. Ruthven did not die; he only fainted: the coolness of the night air brought him back to consciousness. Aubrey's departure and his return to Scotland had been too prompt for Ruthven to send him word; but when he was well he returned to Ireland, to find his brother dead; he inherited his name and his fortune, and, under that name, with twice the fortune he had before, he offered to spouse Malvina, and rejoiced in anticipation at the joy he would cause his beloved Aubrey, by his reappearance before him. Ruthven is charming: his friend has not overrated him. He and Malvina were both so favourably impressed with one another that, under the pretext of very urgent business, he asked to be allowed to marry her within twenty-four hours. Malvina makes a proper show of resistance before yielding. They return to Marsden's castle. The curtain falls.

Now I had been watching my neighbour almost as much as the play. When the curtain fell, he uttered an exclamation of disdain accompanied by a deep-drawn sigh.

'Pooh!' he said.

I took advantage of this moment to renew our conversation.

'Excuse me, monsieur,' I said, 'but at the conclusion of the prologue you said, "How absurd!"'

'Yes,' said my neighbour, 'I suppose I did say so; or, if I did not say it, I certainly thought it.'

'Do you then condemn the use of supernatural beings in the drama?'

'Not at all; on the contrary, I admire it extremely. All the great masters have made potent use of it: Shakespeare in *Hamlet*, in *Macbeth* and in *Julius Caesar*, Molière in *Le Festin de Pierre*, which he ought rather to have called *Le Convive de Pierre*, for his title to be really significant; Voltaire in *Sémiramis*;

Goethe in *Faust*. No, on the contrary, I highly approve of the use of the supernatural, because I believe in it.'

'What! you have faith in the supernatural?'

'Most certainly.'

'In everyday life?'

'Certainly. We elbow every moment against beings who are unknown to us because they are invisible to us: the air, fire, the earth, are all inhabited. Sylphs, gnomes, water-sprites, hobgoblins, bogies, angels, demons, fly, float, crawl, and leap around us. What are those shooting stars of the night, meteors which astronomers in vain try to explain to us, and of which they can discover neither cause nor end, if they are not angels carrying God's orders from one world to another? Some day we shall see it all.'

'Did you say, we shall see?'

'I am convinced of it.'

Then came the three raps and the curtain rose, revealing the entrance to a farm, a chain of snowy mountains, and a window. The farm represented on the stage was that belonging to Marsden Castle.

While Ruthven's preparations for marrying Malvina were in progress, Edgard, one of his vassals, married Lovette. Lovette made the prettiest, the sweetest and the most graceful betrothed imaginable: she was Jenny Vertpré, at twenty.

Lord Ruthven, who really loved Malvina, would much rather have sucked the blood of another man's wife than that of his own; so, at the request of Edgard, his servant, he willingly acceded to be present at his nuptials. The marriage takes place. Lord Ruthven is seen sitting down: the ballet is just about to begin, when an ancient bard comes forward with his harp; he was a guest at every castle, the poet invited to every marriage. He recognized Ruthven, who did not recognize him, being otherwise employed in ogling poor Lovette.

The first couplet of the bard's song rouses Lord Ruthven's anger, who sees in it a warning addressed to Lovette, and who consequently fears to see his victim snatched away from him. So he turns his bewitching glance from the young girl to glare furiously on the bard, who continues unconcernedly.

A third stanza and Lovette will escape from the Vampire. The bard, who is the angel of marriage in disguise, must not therefore be allowed to sing his third stanza. Lord Ruthven complains that the song brings back unhappy memories, and sends the old man away.

Then, as night draws on, as there is no time to lose, since, unless he can suck the blood of a maiden before one o'clock in the morning, he must die, he seeks an interview with Lovette. Lovette would fain decline; but Edgard is afraid of displeasing his lord and master, who, left alone with Lovette, endeavours to seduce her, swears to her that he loves her, and places a purse full of gold in her hand. Just at that moment the bard's harp is heard and the refrain of the song:

> *Gardez-vous, jeune fiancée,*
> *De l'amour qui donne la mort!*

Then everybody comes on, and the ballet begins. Towards the middle of the ballet, Lovette withdraws, tired; Ruthven, who has not let her go out of sight, follows her. Edgard soon perceives that neither Lovette nor his Lord are present. He goes out in his turn. Cries are heard from the wing; Lovette runs on, terrified; a pistol-shot is heard: Lord Ruthven falls mortally wounded on the stage.

'He tried to dishonour my betrothed!' cried Edgard, who appears, his pistol still smoking in his hand.

Aubrey dashes towards the wounded man. Lord Ruthven still breathes; he asks to be left alone with his friend. Everybody goes off.

'One last promise, Aubrey,' says Lord Ruthven.

'Oh, ask it, take my life! ... it will be unbearable to me without thee,' replies Aubrey.

'My friend, I only ask thee for profound secrecy for twelve hours.'

'For twelve hours?'

'Promise me that Malvina shall not know anything of what has happened – that you will not do anything to avenge my death before the hour of one in the morning has struck ... Swear secrecy by my dying breath! ...'

'I swear it!' says Aubrey, stretching forth his hands. The moon comes out from behind clouds and shines brilliantly during Ruthven's last words.

'Aubrey,' says Ruthven, 'the queen of night casts light upon me for the last time . . . Let me see her and pay my final vows to heaven!'

Ruthven's head falls back at these words. Then Aubrey, helped by Lovette's father, carries the dead man to the rocks in the distance, kisses his hand for the last time, and retires, led away by the old man. At that moment the moonlight completely floods Ruthven's body with its rays and lights up the frozen mountains . . .

The curtain falls, and the whole house applauds enthusiastically, save my neighbour, who still growls under his breath. Such inveterate animosity against a play which appeared to me to be full of interest astonished me, coming from a person who seemed so well disposed as he. He had not merely contented himself with noisy exclamations, as I have indicated, but, still worse, during the whole of the last scene he had played in a disturbing fashion with a key which he several times put to his lips.

'Really, monsieur,' I said, 'I think you are very hard on this piece.'

My neighbour shrugged his shoulders.

'Yes, monsieur, I know it, and the more so because the author considers himself a man of genius, a man of talent, the possessor of a good style; but he deceives himself. I saw the piece when it was played three years ago, and now I have seen it again. Well, what I said then, I repeat: the piece is dull, unimaginative, improbable. Yes, see how he makes vampires act! And then *Sir* Aubrey! People don't talk of *Sir* Aubrey. Aubrey is a family name, and the title of *Sir* is only used before the baptismal name. Ah! the author was wise to preserve his anonymity; he showed his sense in doing that.'

I took advantage of a moment when my neighbour stopped to take breath, and I said –

'Monsieur, you said just now, "Yes, see how he makes vampires act!" Did you not say so? I was not mistaken, was I?'

'No.'

'Well, by employing such language you gave me the impression that you believe they really exist?'

'Of course they exist.'

'Have you ever seen any, by chance?'

'Certainly I have seen them. With my own eyes, as Orgon and Tartuffe.'

'Whereabouts?'

'In Illyria.'

'In Illyria? Ah! Have you been in Illyria?'

'Three years.'

'And you saw vampires there?'

'Illyria, you must know, is the historic ground of vampires, like Hungary, Servia and Poland.'

'No, I did not know . . . I do not know anything. Where were the vampires you saw?'

'At Spalatro. I was lodging with a good man of sixty-two. He died. Three days after his burial, he appeared to his son, in the night, and asked for something to eat: the son gave him all he wanted; he ate it, and then vanished. The next day the son told me what had happened, telling me he felt certain his father would not return once only, and asking me to place myself, the following night, at a window to see him enter and go out. I was very anxious to see a vampire. I stood at the window, but that night he did not come. The son then told me, fearing lest I should be discouraged, that he would probably come on the following night. On the following night I placed myself again at my window, and sure enough, towards midnight, the old man appeared, and I recognized him perfectly. He came from the direction of the cemetery; he walked at a brisk pace, but his steps made no sound. When he reached the door, he knocked; I counted three raps: the knocks sounded hard on the oak, as though it were struck with a bone and not a finger. The son opened the door and the old man entered . . .'

I listened to this story with the greatest attention, and I began to prefer the intervals to the melodrama.

'My curiosity was too highly excited for me to leave my window,' continued my neighbour; 'there I stayed. Half an hour later, the old man came out; he returned whence he had come – that is to say, in the direction of the cemetery. He disappeared round the corner of a wall. At the same moment, almost, my door opened. I turned round quickly and saw the son. He was very pale. "Well,' I said, "so your father came?" "Yes . . . did you see him enter?" "Enter and come out . . . What did he do today?" "He asked me for food and drink, as he did the other day." "And did he eat and drink?" "He ate and drank . . . But that is not all . . . this is what troubles me. He said to me . . ." "Ah! he said something else than a mere request for food and drink?" "Yes, he said to me, 'This is the second time I have come and eaten with thee. It is now thy turn to come and eat with me.'" "The devil! . . ." "I am to expect him the same hour the day after tomorrow." "The deuce you are!" 'Yes, yes, that is just what worries me." The day but one after, he was found dead in bed! The same day two or three other people in the same village who had also seen the old man, and to whom he had spoken, fell ill and died too. It was then recognized that the old man was a vampire. I was questioned; I told all I had seen and heard. Justice demanded an examination of the graveyard. They opened the tombs of all those who had died during the previous six weeks: every corpse was in a state of decomposition. But when they came to Kisilowa's tomb – that was the old man's name – they found him with his eyes open, his lips red, his lungs breathing properly, although he was as rigid as if in death. They drove a stake through his heart; he uttered a loud cry and blood gushed out from his mouth: then they laid him on a stack of wood, reduced him to ashes and scattered the ashes to the four winds . . . I left the country soon after. I never heard if his son turned into a vampire too.'

'Why should he have become a vampire too?' I asked.

'Ah! because it is the custom of those who die from a vampire bite to become vampires.'

'Really, you say this as though it were a known fact.'

'But indeed it is a known, registered and well-established fact! Do you doubt it? . . . Read Dom Calmet's *Traité des apparitions*, vol. ii, pp. 41 *et seq.*; you will find a record signed by the hadnagi Barriavar and the ancient heiduques; further by Battiw, first lieutenant of the regiment of Alexander of Wurtemberg; by Clercktinger, surgeon-major of the Furstenberg regiment; by three other surgeons of the company and by Goltchitz, captain at Slottats, stating that in the year 1730, a month after the death of a certain heiduque, who lived in Medreiga, named Arnold-Paul, who had been crushed by the fall of a hay waggon, four people died suddenly, and, from the nature of their death, according to the traditions of the country, it was evident that they had been the victims of vampirism; they then called to mind that, during his life, this Arnold-Paul had often related how, in the neighbourhood of Cossova, on the Turko-Servian frontier, he had been worried by a Turkish vampire, for they too hold the belief that those who have been passive vampires during their lives become active vampires after their death, but that he had found a cure in the eating of earth from the vampire's grave, and in rubbing himself with its blood – precautions which did not prevent him from becoming a vampire after his death; for, four persons having died, they thought the deed was due to him, and they exhumed his body forty days after his burial: he was quite recognizable, and his body bore the colour of life; his hair, his nails and his beard had grown; his veins were filled with a bloody fluid, which exuded from all parts of his body upon the shroud in which he was wrapped round: the hadnagi, or bailiff of the place, in the presence of those who performed the act of exhumation, and who was a man experienced in cases of vampirism, caused a very sharp stake to be driven through the heart of the said Arnold-Paul, after the usual custom, piercing his body through and through, a frightful cry escaping from his lips, as though he were alive; this act accomplished, they cut off his head, burned him to ashes, and did the same with the corpses of the four or five other victims of vampirism, lest they, in their turn, should cause the deaths of others; but none of these precautions prevented the same wonders from being renewed, five years later, about the year 1735, when seventeen people, belonging to the same village, died from vampirism, some without any previous illness, others after having languished two or three days; among others a young person, named Stranoska, daughter of the heiduque Jeronitzo, went to bed in perfect health, waked up in the middle of the night, trembling all over, uttering fearful shrieks, and saying that the son of the heiduque Millo, who had died nine weeks before, had tried to strangle her during her sleep; she languished from that instant, and died in three days' time: since what she had said of the son of Millo led them to suspect him of being a vampire, they exhumed him, and found him in a state which left no doubt of the fact of vampirism; they discovered, in short, after prolonged investigation, that the defunct Arnold-Paul had not only killed the four persons already referred to, but also many animals, of which fresh vampires, and particularly Millo's son, had eaten; on this evidence, they decided to disinter all who had died since a certain date, and among about forty corpses they discovered seventeen which bore evident signs of vampirism; so they pierced their hearts, cut off their heads, then burnt them and threw their bodies into the river.'

'Does the book which contains this evidence cost much, monsieur?'

'Oh dear no! You will pick it up anywhere, two volumes, in 18mo, of 480 pages each. It will cost you from forty sous to three francs.'

'Thanks, I shall give myself the pleasure of buying a copy.'

'Now will you allow me to depart? . . . Three years ago I thought the third act pretty bad; it will seem worse to me today.'

'If you really must, monsieur . . .'

'Yes, really you must let me go . . .'

I knew it would be impertinent to retain my neighbour any longer. Though his conversation, which had covered a wide range of subjects in a short time, was agreeable and highly edifying to myself, it was evident he could not say the same of mine. I could not teach him anything, save that I was ignorant of everything he knew. So I effaced myself with a sigh, not daring to ask him who he was . . .

I watched him withdraw with regret: a vague presentiment told me that, after having done me so much service, this man would become one of my closest friends. In the meanwhile, he had made the intervals far more interesting than the play.

Happily the bell was ringing for the third act, and so the intervals were at an end.

The only definite feeling I was conscious of, when my neighbour had gone, was one of utter loneliness in that vast building. So I gave my whole attention to the play. Could I judge clearly? No, certainly not as yet: the *Vampire* was one of the first melodramas I had come across.

The third act was but a repetition of what had passed in the first. Ruthven, whom his friend Aubrey believed dead at Marsden's farm, comes to life again, a sepulchral Endymion, under the kisses of the moon. He returns to the castle before Malvina's brother and urges forward his marriage; then Aubrey comes back and finds the bride adorned and the chapel prepared. He approaches his sister to tell her the terrible news of the death of her betrothed, and, seeing him pale and distressed, Malvina exclaims:

'Dear brother, you are in trouble! . . . For heaven's sake, tell me all!'

'Rally your courage, then,' says Aubrey.

'You terrify me!' exclaims Malvina.

Then, turning towards the door –

'Milord is long a-coming,' she says.

'Since I must rend your heart, know that all my plans are broken. A fearful, unlooked-for event has deprived us, me of a friend, you of a husband! . . . The unfortunate Ruthven . . .'

At this juncture Ruthven comes forward, seizes Aubrey by the arm and says to him in a grim voice –

'Think of thy oath!'

At these words, and just as the whole audience burst into applause, a loud whistle sounded from one of the boxes. I turned round, and everybody in the orchestra and the pit did likewise. The hired applauders rose in a body and, climbing on the forms, shouted, 'Put him out!' But the whistler continued to whistle, hidden in his box, sheltered behind the railing as behind an impregnable rampart. I do not know why, but I came to the conclusion that it was my neighbour who was at last gratifying to his heart's content his desire to deride the piece which had disgusted him throughout the night. The play was totally stopped: Philippe, Madame Dorval and Thérigny stood on the stage without being able to utter a syllable; shouts of 'Put him out!' increased and a police officer was sent for. By dint of gazing hard into the box I could see through the bars, and there I discerned, in the dusky interior, the untoward whistler. It was indeed my neighbour. The police officer arrived. In spite of all his protestations, the whistler was expelled from the theatre, and the piece went on in the midst of stampings and bravoes.

The play was drawing to its close. Aubrey, seized by Lord Ruthven's attendants, is carried away from Malvina's side, and she remains unprotected. Ruthven bears her off; a door opens – it is that of the chapel, illuminated for the noctural marriage. Malvina hesitates to contract the marriage without the presence of her brother; but Ruthven becomes more and more urgent; for unless the blood of a young damsel gives him renewed life within a very few minutes, he *will be annihilated*, as the angel of marriage had predicted! Suddenly, Aubrey, who has escaped from his guardians, appears in the chapel; he stops his sister; he implores her not to go on any farther with the proceedings. Ruthven again recalls Aubrey to his oath.

'Yes,' says Aubrey, 'but the hour is just about to strike when I may reveal everything.'

'Wretch!' cries Ruthven, drawing a dagger, 'if you utter one word . . .'

'You shall only take her bathed in my blood!' cries Aubrey, redoubling his resistance.

'Well, then, you shall both perish!' says Ruthven.

He is about to strike Aubrey. One o'clock sounds; Malvina falls fainting in the arms of Bridget; thunder rumbles.

'Annihilation! annihilation!' shrieks Ruthven.

He lets his dagger fall and tries to flee. Shades come up out of the ground and carry him off; the destroying angel appears in a cloud; lightning flashes, and Ruthven is engulfed amidst the shades.

VARNEY THE VAMPYRE

JAMES MALCOLM RYMER

Montague Summers (and other vampirologists from the 1920s onwards) thought that *Varney the Vampyre* was the work of Thomas Preskett Prest – the most prolific writer of the 'Salisbury Square' school of hacks and author of *Sweeney Todd*. But in 1963 Louis James established beyond any doubt that *Varney* was the work of the Scotsman James Malcolm Rymer – the evidence being two of Rymer's own scrapbooks. Rymer (also known as Errym and Merry) was an ex-civil engineer who began working for Lloyd's printing house early in the 1840s. He hoped that this would be a stepping-stone to a more respectable literary career and, in an article on *Popular Writing* (June 1842), poured scorn on penny-dreadful fiction:

> If an author wishes to become popular – that is, to be read by the majority – he should, ere he begins to write, study well the animals for whom he is about to cater . . . But, it may be said, How then are we to account for the taste which maintained for so long for works of terror and blood? Most easily. It is the privilege of the ignorant and the weak to love superstition. The only strong mental sensation they are capable of is *fear* . . . There are millions of minds that have no resource between vapid sentimentality, and the ridiculous spectra of the nursery.

But Rymer was to realize a few years later that he had an unusual talent for writing successful penny-bloods – his two most famous works, *Ada the Betrayed* and *Varney* (both 1845–47), were among Lloyd's best-sellers up to fifteen years after first publication. His cynicism about 'the ignorant and the weak', however, occasionally reveals itself in the way he writes: Louis James has described Rymer as 'an intelligent and versatile writer, who could manipulate the clichés of Gothic melodrama with a detachment that borders on the camp'. This detachment is apparent in the (many) sections of *Varney* where he openly attacks his audience. But Rymer also seems to have 'studied well the animals for whom he was about to cater': at the end of the first part of the story, Sir Francis Varney claims to have been using his supposed 'vampirism' to terrorize the Bannerworth family, in order to steal their buried treasure (this, for sceptical urban readers); in the second half, he discovers, in a chilling moment, that he really *is* a vampire (this, for those who want 'the ridiculous spectra of the nursery').

Seven years before *Varney*, Polidori's *Vampyre* had been reissued by the *Romanticist's and Novelist's Library* in a penny illustrated format. Rymer gleaned most of his plot ideas from this source, but, in the process of keeping a successful idea on the boil (for over 850 pages), he also contributed significant changes to the *Ruthven* formula – changes which were to find their way into Bram Stoker's *Dracula* fifty years later.

The extracts from *Varney* which I have chosen are intended to provide a sample of Rymer's style, to demonstrate the connections with *Dracula* (the 'Clara Crofton' episode perhaps being the origin of Bram Stoker's 'Lucy Westenra' episode – albeit in a characteristically melodramatic style), and to show how Rymer extended the *Ruthven* formula (sometimes by lifting whole scenes from Shakespeare!). One change which Rymer introduced was not taken up by Bram Stoker: the vampire is never destroyed by the forces of good in *Varney*; while the heroes stand by, it is the enraged mob which always performs the ritual. This plot motif was later to become something of a trademark in the horror films made by Universal Studios, Hollywood, in the early 1930s.

THE SOLEMN TONES OF AN OLD CATHEDRAL clock have announced midnight – the air is thick and heavy – a strange, death-like stillness pervades all nature. Like the ominous calm which precedes some more than usually terrific outbreak of the elements, they seem to have paused even in their ordinary fluctuations, to gather a terrific strength for the great effort. A faint peal of thunder now comes from far off. Like a signal gun for the battle of the winds to begin, it appeared to awaken them from their lethargy, and one awful, warring hurricane swept over a whole city, producing more devastation in the four or five minutes it lasted, than would a half century of ordinary phenomena.

It was as if some giant had blown upon some toy town, and scattered many of the buildings before the hot blast of his terrific breath; for as suddenly as that blast of wind had come did it cease, and all was as still and calm as before.

Sleepers awakened, and thought that what they had heard must be the confused chimera of a dream. They trembled and turned to sleep again.

All is still – still as the very grave. Not a sound breaks the magic of repose. What is that – a strange, pattering noise, as of a million of fairy feet? It is hail – yes, a hail-storm has burst over the city. Leaves are dashed from the trees, mingled with small boughs; windows that lie most opposed to the direct fury of the pelting particles of ice are broken, and the rapt repose that before was so remarkable in its intensity, is exchanged for a noise which, in its accumulation, drowns every cry of surprise or consternation which here and there arose from persons who found their houses invaded by the storm.

Now and then, too, there would come a sudden gust of wind that in its strength, as it blew laterally, would, for a moment, hold millions of the hail-stones suspended in mid air, but it was only to dash them with redoubled force in some new direction, where more mischief was to be done.

Oh, how the storm raged! Hail – rain – wind. It was, in very truth, an awful night.

There is an antique chamber in an ancient house. Curious and quaint carvings adorn the walls, and the large chimney-piece is a curiosity of itself. The ceiling is low, and a large bay window, from roof to floor, looks to the west. The window is latticed, and filled with curiously painted glass and rich stained pieces, which send in a strange, yet beautiful light, when sun or moon shines into the apartment. There is but one portrait in that room, although the walls seem panelled for the express purpose of containing a series of pictures. That portrait is of a young man, with a pale face, a stately brow, and a strange expression about the eyes, which no one cared to look on twice.

There is a stately bed in that chamber, of carved walnutwood is it made, rich in design and elaborate in execution; one of those works of art which owe their existence to the Elizabethan era. It is hung with heavy silken and damask furnishing; nodding feathers are at its corners – covered with dust are they, and they lend a funereal aspect to the room. The floor is of polished oak.

God! how the hail dashes on the old bay window! Like an occasional discharge of mimic musketry, it comes clashing, beating, and cracking upon the small panes; but they resist it – their small size saves them; the wind, the hail, the rain, expend their fury in vain.

The bed in that old chamber is occupied. A creature formed in all fashions of loveliness lies in a half sleep upon that ancient couch – a girl young and beautiful as a spring morning. Her long hair has escaped from its confinement and streams over the blackened coverings of the bedstead; she has been restless in her sleep, for the clothing of the bed is in much confusion. One arm is over her head, the other hangs nearly off the side of the bed near to which she lies. A neck and bosom that would have formed a study for the rarest sculptor that ever Providence gave genius to, were half disclosed. She moaned slightly in her sleep, and once or twice the lips moved as if in prayer – at least one might judge so, for the name of Him who suffered for all came once faintly from them.

She has endured much fatigue, and the storm does not awaken her; but it can disturb the slumbers it does not possess the power to destroy entirely. The turmoil of the elements wakes the senses, although it cannot entirely break the repose they have lapsed into.

Oh, what a world of witchery was in that mouth, slightly parted, and exhibiting within the pearly teeth that glistened even in the faint light that came from that bay window. How sweetly the long silken eyelashes lay upon the cheek. Now she moves, and one shoulder is entirely visible – whiter, fairer than the spotless clothing of the bed on which she lies, is the smooth skin of that fair creature, just budding into womanhood, and in that transition state which presents to us all the charms of the girl – almost of the child, with the more matured beauty and gentleness of advancing years.

Was that lightning? Yes – an awful, vivid, terrifying flash – then a roaring peal of thunder, as if a thousand mountains were rolling one over the other in the blue vault of Heaven! Who sleeps now in that ancient city? Not one living soul. The dread trumpet of eternity could not more effectually have awakened anyone.

The hail continues. The wind continues. The uproar of the elements seems at its height. Now she awakens – that beautiful girl on the antique bed; she opens those eyes of celestial blue, and a faint cry of alarm bursts from her lips. At least it is a cry which, amid the noise and turmoil without, sounds but faint and weak. She sits upon the bed and presses her hands upon her eyes. Heavens! what a wild torrent of wind, and rain, and hail! The thunder likewise seems intent upon awakening sufficient echoes to last until the next flash of forked lightning should again produce the wild concussion of the air. She murmurs a prayer – a prayer for those she loves best; the names of those dear to her gentle heart come from her lips; she weeps and prays; she thinks then of what devastation the storm must surely produce, and to the great God of Heaven she prays for all living things. Another flash – a wild, blue, bewildering flash of lightning streams across that bay window, for an instant bringing out every colour in it with terrible distinctness. A shriek bursts from the lips of the young girl, and then, with eyes fixed upon that window, which, in another moment, is all darkness, and with such an expression of terror upon her face as it had never before known, she trembled, and the perspiration of intense fear stood upon her brow.

'What – what was it?' she gasped; 'real, or a delusion? Oh, God, what was it? A figure tall and gaunt, endeavouring from the outside to unclasp the window. I saw it. That flash of lightning revealed it to me. It stood the whole length of the window.'

There was a lull of the wind. The hail was not falling so thickly – moreover, it now fell, what there was of it, straight, and yet a strange clattering sound came upon the glass of that long window. It could not be a delusion – she is awake, and she hears it. What can produce it? Another flash of lightning – another shriek – there could be now no delusion.

A tall figure is standing on the ledge immediately outside the long window. It is its finger-nails upon the glass that produces the sound so like the hail, now that the hail has ceased. Intense fear paralyses the limbs of that beautiful girl. That one shriek is all she can utter – with hands clasped, a face of marble, a heart beating so wildly in her bosom, that each moment it seems as if it would break its confines, eyes distended and fixed upon the window, she waits, frozen with horror. The pattering and clattering of the nails continue. No word is spoken, and now she fancies she can trace the darker form of that figure against the window, and she can see the long arms moving to and fro, feeling for some mode of entrance. What strange light is that which now gradually creeps up into the air? red and terrible – brighter and brighter it grows. The lightning has set fire to a mill, and the reflection of the rapidly consuming building falls upon that long window. There can be no mistake. The figure is there, still feeling for an entrance, and clattering against the glass with its long nails, that appear as if the growth of many years had been untouched. She tries to scream again but a choking sensation comes over her, and she cannot. It is too dreadful – she tries to move – each limb seems weighed down by tons of lead – she can but in a hoarse faint whisper, –

'Help – help – help – help!'

And that one word she repeats like a person in a dream. The red glare of the fire continues. It throws up the tall gaunt figure in hideous relief against the long window. It shows, too, upon the one portrait that is in the chamber, and that portrait appears to fix its eyes upon the attempting intruder, while the flickering light from the fire makes it look fearfully life-like. A small pane of glass is broken, and the form from without introduces a long gaunt hand, which seems utterly destitute of flesh. The fastening is removed, and one-half of the window, which opens like folding doors, is swung wide open upon its hinges.

And yet now she could not scream – she could not move. 'Help – help! – help!' was all she could say. But, oh, that look of terror that sat upon her face, it was dreadful – a look to haunt the memory for a life-time – a look to obtrude itself upon the happiest moments, and turn them to bitterness.

The figure turns half round, and the light falls upon the face. It is perfectly white – perfectly bloodless. The eyes look like polished tin; the lips are drawn back, and the principal feature next to those dreadful eyes is the teeth – the fearful-looking teeth – projecting like those of some wild animal, hideously, glaringly white, and fang-like. It approaches the bed with a strange, gliding movement. It clashes together the long nails that literally appear to hang from the finger ends. No sound comes from its lips. Is she going mad – that young and beautiful girl exposed to so much terror? she has drawn up all her limbs; she cannot even now say help. The power of articulation is gone, but the power of movement has returned to her; she can draw herself slowly along to the other side of the bed from that towards which the hideous appearance is coming.

But her eyes are fascinated. The glance of a serpent could not have produced a greater effect upon her than did the fixed gaze of those awful, metallic-looking eyes that were bent on her face. Crouching down so that the gigantic height was lost, and the horrible, protruding, white face was the most prominent object, came on the figure. What was it? – what did it want there? – what made it look so hideous – so unlike an inhabitant of the earth, and yet to be on it?

Now she has got to the verge of the bed, and the figure pauses. It seemed as if when it paused she lost the power to proceed. The clothing of the bed was now clutched in her hands with unconscious power. She drew her breath short and thick. Her bosom heaves, and her limbs tremble, yet she cannot withdraw her eyes from that marble-looking face. He holds her with his glittering eye.

The storm has ceased – all is still. The winds are hushed; the church clock proclaims the hour of one: a hissing sound comes from the throat of the hideous being, and he raises his long, gaunt arms – the lips move. He advances. The girl places one small foot from the bed on to the floor. She is unconsciously dragging the clothing with her. The door of the room is in that direction – can she reach it? Has she power to walk? – can she withdraw her eyes from the face of the intruder, and so break the hideous charm? God of Heaven! is it real, or some dream so like reality as to nearly overturn the judgment for ever?

The figure has paused again, and half on the bed and half out of it that young girl lies trembling. Her long hair streams across the entire width of the bed. As she has slowly moved along she has left it streaming across the pillows. The pause lasted about a minute – oh, what an age of agony. That minute was, indeed, enough for madness to do its full work in.

With a sudden rush that could not be foreseen – with a strange howling cry that was enough to awaken terror in every breast, the figure seized the long tresses of her hair, and twining them round his bony hands he held her to the bed. Then she screamed – Heaven granted her then power to scream. Shriek followed shriek in rapid succession. The bed-clothes fell in a heap by the side of the bed – she was dragged by her long silken hair completely on to it again. Her beautifully rounded limbs quivered with the agony of her soul. The glassy, horrible eyes of the figure ran over that angelic form with a hideous satisfaction – horrible profanation. He drags her head to the bed's edge. He forces it back by the long hair still entwined in his grasp. With a plunge he seizes her neck in his fang-like teeth – a gush of blood, and a hideous sucking noise follows. *The girl has swooned, and the vampyre is at his hideous repast!*

Young Ringwood – fiancé of the late Clara Crofton – has heard strange tales about nocturnal happenings in the village church. He suspects that his beloved may have become a vampyre through contact with Varney and decides to see for himself . . .

Yes, it was twelve o'clock, that mysterious hour at which it is believed by many that,

> Graves give up their dead,
> And many a ghost in church-yard decay,
> Rise from their cold, cold bed
> To make night horrible with wild vagary.

Twelve, that hour when all that is human feels a sort of irksome dread, as if the spirits of those who have gone from the great world were too near, loading the still night air with the murky vapours of the grave. A chilliness came over Ringwood and he fancied a strange kind of light was in the church, making objects more visible than in their dim and dusty outlines they had been before.

'Why do I tremble?' he said, 'why do I tremble? Clouds pass away from before the moon, that is all. Soon there may be a bright light here, and lo, all is still; I hear nothing but my own breathing; I see nothing but what is common and natural. Thank heaven, all will pass away in quiet. There will be no horror to recount – no terrific sight to chill my blood. Rest Clara, rest in Heaven.'

Ten minutes passed away, and there was no alarm; how wonderfully relieved was Ringwood. Tears came to his eyes, but they were the natural tears of regret, such as he had shed before for her who had gone from him to the tomb, and left no trace behind, but in the hearts of those who loved her.

'Yes,' he said, mournfully, 'she has gone from me, but I love her still. Still does the fond remembrance of all that she was to me, linger at my heart. She is my own, my beautiful Clara, as she ever was, and as, while life remains, to me she ever will be.'

At the moment that he uttered these words a slight noise met his ears.

In an instant he sprung to his feet in the pulpit, and looked anxiously around him.

'What was that?' he said. 'What was that?'

All was still again, and he was upon the point of convincing himself that the noise was either some accidental one, or the creation of his own fancy, when it came again.

He had no doubt this time. It was a perceptible, scraping, strange sort of sound, and he turned his whole attention to the direction from whence it came. With a cold creeping chill through his frame, he saw that that direction was the one where was the family vault of the Croftons, the last home of her whom he held still in remembrance, and whose memory was so dear to him.

He felt the perspiration standing upon his brow, and if the whole world had been the recompense to him for moving away from where he was he could not have done so. All he could do was to gaze with bated breath, and distended eyes upon the aisle of the church from whence the sound came.

That something of a terrific nature was now about to exhibit itself, and that the night would not go off without some terrible and significant adventure

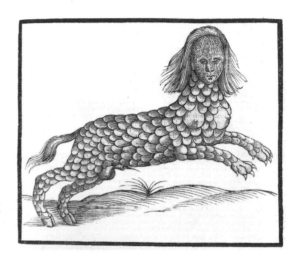

op and above A fearsome Chilean vampire
seizing its prey', as reported by the *Courier*
e l'Europe in October 1784; and the same
mage adapted to suit Marie Antoinette in an
nonymous French Revolutionary engraving
f October 1789. **Above right** A lamia – or
a monster capable of assuming a woman's
orm' – from Edward Topsell's *History of*
our-footed Beasts and Serpents (London, 1658).
ight An Eastern European footsoldier
r *heyduk* brandishing his weapons, from
World Gallery of prints by Christoph Weigel
fter Caspar Luyken (Nuremberg, 1703).

Ein Heyduck.

Top and above Henry Fuseli's painting of *The Nightmare*, first exhibited at the Royal Academy in summer 1782, where it caused a sensation and dominated the reviews; and James Gillray's etching of 1802 *Tales of Wonder*, satirizing three eager and finely dressed consumers of Gothic literature, well past their bedtime.

Top left and right Plate 33 from William Blake's *Jerusalem* (printed *c.* 1820), in which Henry Fuseli's mara or nightmare has morphed into the spectre of a giant bat; and Francisco de Goya's celebrated etching *The Sleep of Reason Produces Monsters* (1799), mainly bats and owls as creatures of the night. **Above** Gustave Doré's illustration of a gigantic, winged Satan in the icy Ninth Circle of Hell, from his version of Dante's *Inferno* (1861).

William Blake's painting of *The Ghost of a Flea* (1819–20) – acorn in one hand, curved spike in the other – which was exhibited in the late nineteenth and early twentieth centuries under the title *A Vampire*.

Clockwise from top left Max Klinger's engraving *Dead Mother* (1898), from his collection *On Death, Part ii*, where Fuseli's mara has become a confused baby; Félicien Rops's *Le Plus Bel Amour de Don Juan* from his series of etchings *Les Diaboliques* (1886); and his earlier print *L'Agonie ou Mors et Vita* (1872), showing a vicious vampire attack – an image he reworked several times up to the late 1890s.

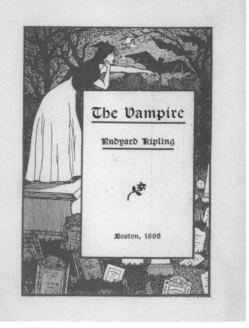

Opposite above and below Illustration by D. M. Friston for Sheridan Le Fanu's lesbian vampire story *Carmilla*, in *The Dark Blue* magazine, Dublin, 1871; and title page of *The Vampire*, poem by Rudyard Kipling, painting by Philip Burne-Jones (often confused with his father Edward), both originally 1897. **Above** Edvard Munch's painting *Vampire* (1893), one of many versions in which she has become flame red haired, cat-like, smothering her supine victim with a kiss.

Edvard Munch's ink and watercolour drawing *Harpy* (1898), where the predator has the body of a bird of prey and the head of a woman, and the prey has become skeletal.

to make it remembered he felt convinced. All he dreaded was to think for a moment what it might be.

His thoughts ran on Clara, and he murmured forth in the most agonizing accents, –

'Anything – any sight but the sight of her. Oh, no, no, no!'

But it was not altogether the sight of her that he dreaded; oh no, it was the fact that the sight of her on such an occasion would bring the horrible conviction with it, that there was some truth in the dreadful apprehension that he had of the new state of things that had ensued regarding the after death condition of that fair girl.

The noise increased each moment, and finally there was a sudden crash.

'She comes! she comes!' gasped Ringwood.

He grasped the front of the pulpit with a frantic violence, and then slowly and solemnly there crossed his excited vision a figure all clothed in white. Yes, white flowing vestments, and he knew by their fashion that they were not worn by the living, and that it was some inhabitant of the tomb that he now looked upon.

He did not see the face. No, that for a time was hidden from him, but his heart told him who it was. Yes, it was his Clara.

It was no dream. It was no vision of a too excited fancy, for until those palpable sounds, and that most fearfully palpable form crossed his sight, he was rather inclined to go the other way, and to fancy what the Sexton had reported was nothing but a delusion of his overwrought brain. Oh, that he could but for one brief moment have found himself deceived.

'Speak!' he gasped; 'speak! speak!'

There was no reply.

'I conjure you, I pray you though the sound of your voice should hurl me to perdition – I implore you, speak.'

All was silent, and the figure in white moved on slowly but surely towards the door of the church, but ere it passed out, it turned for a moment, as if for the very purpose of removing from the mind of Ringwood any lingering doubt as to its identity.

He then saw the face, oh, so well known, yet so pale. It was Clara Crofton!

''Tis she! 'tis she!' was all he could say.

It seemed, too, as if some crevice in the clouds had opened at the moment, in order that he should with an absolute certainty see the countenance of that solemn figure, and then all was more than usually silent again. The door closed, and the figure was gone.

He rose in the pulpit, and clasped his hands. Irresolution seemed for a few moments to sway him to and fro, and then he rushed down into the body of the church.

'I'll follow it,' he cried, 'though it lead me to perdition. Yes, I'll follow it.'

He made his way to the door, and even as he went he shouted:

'Clara! Clara! Clara!'

He reached the threshold of the ancient church; he gazed around him distractedly, for he thought that he had lost all sight of the figure. No – no, even in the darkness and against the night sky, he saw it once again in its sad-looking death raiments. He dashed forward.

The moonbeams at this instant being freed from some dense clouds that had interposed between them and this world, burst forth with resplendant beauty.

There was not a tree, a shrub, nor a flower, but what was made distinct and manifest, and with the church, such was the almost unprecedented lustre of the beautiful planet, that even the inscriptions upon the old tablets and tombs were distinctly visible.

Such a refulgence lasted not many minutes, but while it did, it was most beautiful, and the gloom that followed it seemed doubly black.

'Stay, stay,' he shouted, 'yet a moment, Clara; I swear that what you are that will I be. Take me over to the tomb with you, say but that it is your dwelling-place, and I will make it mine, and declare it a very palace of the affections.'

The figure glided on.

It was in vain that he tried to keep up with it. It threaded the churchyard among the ancient tombs, with a gliding speed that soon distanced him, impeded, as he continually was, by some obstacle or another, owing to looking at the apparition he followed, instead of the ground before him.

Still, on he went, heedless whither he was conveyed, for he might be said to be dragged onward, so much were all his faculties both of mind and body intent upon following the apparition of his beloved.

Once, and once only, the figure paused, and seemed to be aware that it was followed for it flitted round an angle made by one of the walls of the church, and disappeared from his eyes.

In another moment he had turned the same point.

'Clara! Clara!' he shouted. ''Tis I – you know my voice, Clara, Clara.'

She was not to be seen, and then the idea struck him that she must have re-entered the church, and he too, turned, and crossed the threshold. He lingered there for a moment or two, and the whole building echoed to the name of Clara, as with romantic eagerness, he called upon her by name to come forth to him.

Those echoes were the only reply.

Maddened – rendered desperate beyond all endurance, he went some distance into the building in search of her, and again he called.

It was in vain; she had eluded him, and with all the carefulness and all the energy and courage he had brought to bear upon that night's proceedings, he was foiled. Could anything be more agonizing than this to such a man as Ringwood – he who loved her so, that he had not shrunk from her even in death, although she had so shrunk from him.

'I will find her – I will question her,' he cried. 'She shall not escape me; living or dead, she shall be mine. I will wait for her, even in the tomb.'

Before he carried out the intention of going actually into the vault to await her return, he thought he would take one more glance at the churchyard with the hope of seeing her there, as he could observe no indications of her presence in the church.

With this view he proceeded to the door, and emerged into the dim light. He called upon her again by name, and he thought he heard some faint sound in the church behind him. To turn and make a rush into the building was the work of a moment.

He saw something – it was black instead of white – a tall figure – it advanced towards him, and with great force, before he was aware that an attack was at all intended, it felled him to the ground.

The blow was so sudden, so unexpected, and so severe, that it struck him down in a moment before he could be aware of it. To be sure, he had arms with him, but the anxiety and agony of mind he endured that night, since seeing the apparition come from the tomb, had caused him to forget them.

Ringwood recovers. The assailant is, of course, none other than Varney, the Vampyre, protecting his bride. Meanwhile, the villagers – after a 'grand consultation at the ale-house' – have decided to take matters into their own hands . . .

'The vampyre, the vampyre,' cried the blacksmith, 'death to the vampyre – death and destruction to the vampyre.'

'Hurrah!' cried another, 'to the vaults – this way to Sir George Crofton's vault.'

There seemed to be little doubt now, but that this disorderly rabble would execute summary vengeance upon the supposed nocturnal disturber of the peace of the district.

Ever and anon, too, as these shouts of discord, and of threatening vengeance, rose upon the night air, there would come the distant muttering of thunder, for the storm had not yet ceased, although its worst fury had certainly passed away.

Dark and heavy clouds were sweeping up from the horizon, and it seemed to be tolerably evident that some heavy deluge of rain would eventually settle the fury of the elements, and reconcile the discord of wind and electricity.

Several of the rioters were provided with links and matches, so that in a few moments the whole interior of the church was brilliantly illuminated, while at the same time it presented a grotesque appearance, in consequence of the unsteady and wavering flame from the links, throwing myriads of dancing shadows upon the walls.

There would have been no difficulty under any ordinary circumstances in finding the entrance to the vault, where the dead of the Crofton family should have lain in peace, but now since the large flagstone that covered the entrance to that receptacle of the grave was removed, it met their observation at once.

It was strange now to perceive how, for a moment, superstition having led them on so far, the same feeling should induce them to pause, ere they ventured to make their way down these gloomy steps.

It was a critical moment, and probably if any one or two had taken a sudden panic, the whole party might have left the church with precipitation, having done a considerable amount of mischief, and yet as it is so usual with rioters, having left their principal object unaccomplished.

The blacksmith put an end to this state of indecision, for, seizing a link from the man who was nearest to him, he darted down the steps, exclaiming as he did so, –

'Whoever's afraid, need not follow me.'

This was a taunt they were not exactly prepared to submit to, and the consequence was, that in a very few moments the ancient and time-honoured vault of the Crofton's was more full of the living than of the dead.

The blacksmith laid his hand upon Clara's coffin.

'Here it is,' he said, 'I know the very pattern of the cloth, and the fashion of the nails. I saw it at Grigson's the undertaker's before it was taken to the Grange.'

'Is she there – is she there?' cried half a dozen voices at once.

Even the blacksmith hesitated a moment ere he removed the lid from the receptacle of death, but when he did so, and his eyes fell upon the face of the presumed vampyre, he seemed rejoiced to find in the appearances then exhibited some sort of justification for the act of violence of which already he had been the instigator.

'Here you are,' he said, 'look at the bloom upon her lips, why her cheeks are fresher and rosier than ever they were while she was alive; a vampyre my mates, this is a vampyre, or may I never break bread again; and now what's to be done?'

'Burn her, burn her,' cried several.

'Well,' said the blacksmith, 'mind it's as you like. I've brought you here, and shown you what it is, and now you can do what you like, and of course I'll lend you a hand to do it.'

Any one who had been very speculative in this affair, might have detected in these last words of the blacksmith, something like an inclination to creep out of the future consequences of what might next be done, while at the same time shame deterred him from exactly leaving his companions in the lurch.

After some suggestions then, and some argumentation as to the probability or possibility of interruption – the coffin itself, was with its sad and wretched occupant, lifted from the niche where it should have remained until that awful day when the dead shall rise for judgment, and carried up the steps into the church, from thence they passed into the graveyard, but scarcely had they done so, when the surcharged clouds burst over their heads, and the rain came down in perfect torrents.

The deluge was of so frightful, and continuous a character, that they shrank back again beneath the shelter of the church porch, and there waited until its first fury had passed away.

Such an even down storm seldom lasts long in our climate, and the consequence was that in about ten minutes the shower had so far subsided that although a continuous rain was falling it bore but a very distant comparison to what had taken place.

'How are we to burn the body on such a night as this?'

'Aye, how indeed?' said another; 'you could not so much as kindle a fire, and if you did, it would not live many minutes.'

'I'll tell you what to do at once,' said one who had as yet borne but a quiet part in the proceedings; 'I'll tell you what to do at once, for I saw it done myself; a vampyre is quite as secure buried in a cross-road with a stake through its body, as if you burned it in all the fires in the world; come on, the rain won't hinder you doing that.'

This was a suggestion highly approved of, and the more so as there was a cross-road close at hand, so that the deed could be done quick, and the parties dispersed to their respective homes, for already the exertion they had taken, and the rain that had fallen, had had a great effect in sobering them.

And even now the perilous and disgusting operation of destroying the body, by fire or any other way, might have been abandoned, had any one of the party suggested such a course – but the dread of a future imputation of cowardice kept all silent.

Once more the coffin was raised by four of the throng, and carried through the churchyard, which was now running in many little rivulets, in consequence of the rain. The cross-road was not above a quarter of a mile from the spot, and while those who were disengaged from carrying the body, were hurrying away to get spades and mattocks, the others walked through the rain, and finally paused at the place they thought suitable for that ancient superstitious rite, which it was thought would make the vampyre rest in peace.

At last a dozen men now arrived well armed with spades and picks, and they commenced the work of digging a deep, rather than a capacious grave, in silence.

A gloomy and apprehensive spirit seemed to come over the whole assemblage, and the probability is that this was chiefly owing to the fact that they now encountered no opposition, and that they were permitted unimpeded to accomplish a purpose which had never yet been attempted within the memory of any of the inhabitants of the place.

The grave was dug, and about two feet depth of soil was thrown in a huge mound upon the surface; the coffin was lowered, and there lay the corpse within that receptacle of poor humanity, unimprisoned by any lid for that had been left in the vault, and awaiting the doom which they had decreed upon it, but which they now with a shuddering horror shrunk from performing.

A hedge stake with a sharp point had been procured, and those who held it looked around them with terrified countenances, while the few links that had not been extinguished by the rain, shed a strange and lurid glare upon all objects.

'It must be done,' said the blacksmith; 'don't let it be said that we got thus far and then were afraid.'

'Do it then yourself,' said the man that held the stake; 'I dare not.'

'Aye, do,' cried several voices; 'you brought us here, why don't you do it – are you afraid after all your boasting?'

'Afraid – afraid of the dead; I'm not afraid of any of you that are alive, and it's not likely I'm going to be afraid of a dead body; you're a pretty set of cowards. I've no animosity against the girl, but I want that we shall all sleep in peace, and that our wives and children should not be disturbed nocturnally in their blessed repose. I'll do it if none of you'll do it, and then you may thank me afterwards for the act, although I suppose if I get into trouble I shall have you all turn tail upon me.'

'No, we won't – no, we won't.'

'Well, well, here goes, whether you do or not. I – I'll do it directly.'

'He shrinks,' cried one.

'No,' said another; 'he'll do it – now for it, stand aside.'

'Stand aside yourself – do you want to fall into the grave.'

The blacksmith shuddered as he held the stake in an attitude to pierce the body, and even up to that moment it seemed to be a doubtful case, whether he would be able to accomplish his purpose or not; at length, when they all thought he was upon the point of abandoning his design, and casting the stake away, he thrust it with tremendous force through the body and the back of the coffin.

The eyes of the corpse opened wide – the hands were clenched, and a shrill, piercing shriek came from the lips – a shriek that was answered by as many as there were persons present, and then with pallid fear upon their countenances they rushed headlong from the spot.

Epilogue – the final, total destruction of Varney, the Vampyre, and conclusion.

'We extract from the *Algemeine Zeitung* the following most curious story, the accuracy of which of course we cannot vouch for, but still there is a sufficient air of probability about it to induce us to present it to our readers.

'Late in the evening, about four days since, a tall and melancholy-looking stranger arrived, and put up at one of the principal hotels at Naples. He was a most peculiar-looking man, and considered by the persons of the establishment as about the ugliest guest they had ever had within the walls of their place.

'In a short time he summoned the landlord, and the following conversation ensued between him and the strange guest.

'"I want," said the stranger, "to see all the curiosities of Naples, and among the rest Mount Vesuvius. Is there any difficulty?"

'"None," replied the landlord, "with a proper guide."

'A guide was soon secured, who set out with the adventurous Englishman to make the ascent of the burning mountain.

'They went on then until the guide did not think it quite prudent to go any further, as there was a great fissure in the side of the mountain, out of which a stream of lava was slowly issuing and spreading itself in rather an alarming manner.

'The ugly Englishman, however, pointed to a secure mode of getting higher still, and they proceeded until they were very near the edge of the crater itself. The stranger then took his purse from his pocket and flung it to the guide saying, –

'"You can keep that for your pains, and for coming into some danger with me. But the fact was, that I wanted a witness to an act which I have set my mind upon performing."

'The guide says that these words were spoken with so much calmness, that he verily believed the act mentioned as about to be done was some scientific experiment of which he knew that the English were very fond, and he replied,

'"Sir, I am only too proud to serve so generous and so distinguished a gentleman. In what way can I be useful?"

'"You will make what haste you can," said the stranger, "from the mountain, inasmuch as it is covered with sulphurous vapours, inimical to human life, and when you reach the city you will cause to be published an account of my proceedings, and what I say. You will say that you accompanied Varney, the Vampyre to the crater of Mount Vesuvius and that, tired and disgusted with a life of horror, he flung himself in to prevent the possibility of a reanimation of his remains."

'Before, then, the guide could utter anything but a shriek, Varney took one tremendous leap, and disappeared into the burning mouth of the mountain.'

3 THE TEMPESTUOUS
LOVELINESS OF TERROR

MISS JULIE: So you think I can't stand the sight of blood? You think I'm so weak? How I'd love to see your blood, and your brains, on a chopping block! I'd like to see your whole sex swimming in a sea of blood . . . I think I could drink out of your skull, dabble my feet in your chest, and eat your heart roasted whole. You think I'm weak . . .?

from *Miss Julie*, by August Strindberg (1888)

WAKE NOT THE DEAD

ERNST RAUPACH

This story first appeared in English as part of an anthology entitled *Popular Tales and Romances of the Northern Nations* (1823). It was published in Germany the year before. The story came to be wrongly attributed to Johann Ludwig Tieck later in the nineteenth century – and remained so until recently. *Wake Not the Dead* is not really a Folkloric Vampire tale: it is an early example (owing much to Goethe's *Bride of Corinth* and the cult of medievalism) of the Fatal Woman theme, remarkable for the ways in which the author presents his story as a powerful sexual allegory. The relationship between Brunhilda and her 'spell-enthralled' husband Walter, the question of Walter's guilt, the behaviour of Brunhilda as a corpse 'not able of itself to keep up the genial glow of vitality' and, finally, the sheer sexual terror of the story's climax, are all handled in ways which place *Wake Not the Dead* among the finest early examples in prose of the Romantic Agony. For Walter rashly dares to awaken the dead from the sleep of the grave, a 'sleep which dreameth not': and he prefers the dark lady to the fair lady . . . This story is also known as *Let the Dead Rest*.

'WILT THOU FOR EVER SLEEP? Wilt thou never more awake, my beloved, but henceforth repose for ever from thy short pilgrimage on earth? O yet once again return! and bring back with thee the vivifying dawn of hope to one whose existence hath, since thy departure, been obscured by the dunnest shades. What! dumb? for ever dumb? Thy friend lamenteth, and thou heedest him not? He sheds bitter, scalding tears, and thou reposest unregarding his affliction? He is in despair, and thou no longer openest thy arms to him as an asylum from his grief? Say then, doth the paly shroud become thee better than the bridal veil? Is the chamber of the grave a warmer bed than the couch of love? Is the spectre death more welcome to thy arms than thy enamoured consort? Oh! return, my beloved, return once again to this anxious disconsolate bosom.' Such were the lamentations which Walter poured forth for his Brunhilda, the partner of his youthful passionate love: thus did he bewail over her grave at the midnight hour, what time the spirit that presides in the troublous atmosphere, sends his legions of monsters through mid-air; so that their shadows, as they flit beneath the moon and across the earth, dart as wild, agitating thoughts that chase each other o'er the sinner's bosom: thus did he lament under the tall linden trees by her grave, while his head reclined on the cold stone.

Walter was a powerful lord in Burgundy, who, in his earliest youth, had been smitten with the charms of the fair Brunhilda, a beauty far surpassing in loveliness all her rivals; for her tresses, dark as the raven face of night, streaming over her shoulders, set off to the utmost advantage the beaming lustre of her slender form, and the rich dye of a cheek whose tint was deep and brilliant as that of the western heaven: her eyes did not resemble those burning orbs whose pale glow gems the vault of night, and whose immeasurable distance fills the soul with deep thoughts of eternity, but rather as the sober beams which cheer this nether world, and which, while they enlighten, kindle the sons of earth to joy and love. Brunhilda became the wife of Walter, and both being equally enamoured and devoted, they abandoned themselves to the enjoyment of a passion that rendered them reckless of aught besides, while it lulled them in a fascinating dream. Their sole apprehension was lest aught should awaken them from a delirium which they prayed might continue for ever. Yet how vain is the wish that would arrest the decrees of destiny! as well might it seek to divert the circling planets from their eternal course. Short was the duration of this phrenzied passion; not that it gradually decayed and subsided into apathy, but death snatched away his blooming victim, and left Walter to a widowed couch. Impetuous, however, as was his first burst of grief, he was not inconsolable, for ere long another bride became the partner of the youthful nobleman.

Swanhilda also was beautiful; although nature had formed her charms on a very different model from those of Brunhilda. Her golden locks waved bright as the beams of morn: only when excited by some emotion of her soul did a rosy hue tinge the lily paleness of her cheek: her limbs were proportioned in the nicest symmetry, yet did they not possess that luxuriant fullness of animal life: her eye beamed eloquently, but it was with the milder radiance of a star, tranquillizing to tenderness rather than exciting to warmth. Thus formed, it was not possible that she should steep him in his former delirium, although she rendered happy his waking hours – tranquil and serious, yet cheerful, studying in all things her husband's pleasure, she restored order and comfort in his family, where her presence shed a general influence all around. Her mild benevolence tended to restrain the fiery, impetuous disposition of Walter: while at the same time her prudence recalled him in some degree from his vain, turbulent wishes, and his aspirings after unattainable enjoyments, to the duties and pleasures of actual life. Swanhilda bore her husband two children, a son and a daughter; the latter was mild and patient as her mother, well contented with her solitary sports, and even in these recreations displayed the serious turn of her character. The boy possessed his father's fiery, restless disposition, tempered, however, with the solidity of his mother. Attached by his offspring more tenderly towards their mother, Walter now lived for several years very happily: his thoughts would frequently, indeed, recur to Brunhilda, but without their former violence, merely as we dwell upon the memory of a friend of our earlier days, borne from us on the rapid current of time to a region where we know that he is happy.

But clouds dissolve into air, flowers fade, the sands of the hour-glass run imperceptibly away, and even so, do human feelings dissolve, fade, and pass away, and with them too, human happiness. Walter's inconstant breast again sighed for the ecstatic dreams of those days which he had spent with his equally romantic, enamoured Brunhilda – again did she present herself to his ardent fancy in all the glow of her bridal charms, and he began to draw a parallel between the past and the present; nor did imagination, as it is wont, fail to array the former in her brightest hues, while it proportionably obscured the latter; so that he pictured to himself, the one much more rich in enjoyments, and the other, much less so than they really were. This change in her husband did not escape Swanhilda; whereupon, redoubling her attentions towards him, and her cares towards their children, she expected, by this means, to re-unite the knot that was slackened; yet the more she endeavoured to regain his affections, the colder did he grow – the more intolerable did her caresses seem, and the more continually did the image of Brunhilda haunt his thoughts. The children, whose endearments were now become indispensable to him, alone stood between the parents as genii eager to affect a reconciliation; and, beloved by them both, formed a uniting link between them. Yet, as evil can be plucked from the heart of man, only ere its root has yet struck deep, its fangs being afterwards too firm to be eradicated; so was Walter's diseased fancy too far affected to have its disorder stopped, for, in a short time, it completely tyrannized over him. Frequently of a night, instead of retiring to his consort's chamber, he repaired to Brunhilda's grave, where he murmured forth his discontent, saying: 'Wilt thou sleep for ever?'

One night as he was reclining on the turf, indulging in his wonted sorrow, a sorcerer from the neighbouring mountains entered into this field of death for the purpose of gathering, for his mystic spells, such herbs as grow only from the earth wherein the dead repose, and which, as if the last production of mortality, are gifted with a powerful and supernatural influence. The sorcerer perceived the mourner, and approached the spot where he was lying.

'Wherefore, fond wretch, dost thou grieve thus, for what is now a hideous mass of mortality – mere bones, and nerves, and veins? Nations have fallen unlamented; even worlds themselves, long ere this globe of ours was created, have mouldered into nothing; nor hath any one wept over them; why then should'st thou indulge this vain affliction for a child of the dust – a being as frail as thyself, and like thee the creature but of a moment?'

Walter raised himself up: – 'Let yon worlds that shine in the firmament,' replied he, 'lament for each other as they perish. It is true, that I who am myself clay, lament for my fellow-clay: yet is this clay impregnated with a fire, – with an essence, that none of the elements of creation possess – with love: and this divine passion, I felt for her who now sleepeth beneath this sod.' 'Will thy complaints awaken her: or could they do so, would she not soon upbraid thee for having disturbed that repose in which she is now hushed?'

'Avaunt, cold-hearted being: thou knowest not what is love. Oh! that my tears could wash away the earthy covering that conceals her from these eyes;

that my groan of anguish could rouse her from her slumber of death! No, she would not again seek her earthy couch.'

'Insensate that thou art, and couldst thou endure to gaze without shuddering on one disgorged from the jaws of the grave? Art thou too thyself the same from whom she parted; or hath time passed o'er thy brow and left no traces there? Would not thy love rather be converted into hate and disgust?'

'Say rather that the stars would leave yon firmament, that the sun will henceforth refuse to shed his beams through the heavens. Oh! that she stood once more before me; that once again she reposed on this bosom! – how quickly should we then forget that death or time had ever stepped between us.'

'Delusion! mere delusion of the brain, from heated blood, like to that which arises from the fumes of wine. It is not my wish to tempt thee; to restore to thee thy dead; else wouldst thou soon feel that I have spoken truth.'

'How! restore her to me,' exclaimed Walter casting himself at the sorcerer's feet. 'Oh! if thou art indeed able to effect that, grant it to my earnest supplication; if one throb of human feeling vibrates in thy bosom, let my tears prevail with thee: restore to me my beloved; so shalt thou hereafter bless the deed, and see that it was a good work.'

'A good work! a blessed deed!' – returned the sorcerer with a smile of scorn; 'for me there exists nor good nor evil; since my will is always the same. Ye alone know evil, who will that which ye would not. It is indeed in my power to restore her to thee: yet, bethink thee well, whether it will prove thy weal. Consider too, how deep the abyss between life and death; across this, my power can build a bridge, but it can never fill up the frightful chasm.'

Walter would have spoken, and have sought to prevail on this powerful being by fresh entreaties, but the latter prevented him, saying: 'Peace! bethink thee well! and return hither to me tomorrow at midnight. Yet once more do I warn thee, "Wake not the dead."'

Having uttered these words, the mysterious being disappeared. Intoxicated with fresh hope, Walter found no sleep on his couch; for fancy, prodigal of her richest stores, expanded before him the glittering web of futurity; and his eye, moistened with the dew of rapture, glanced from one vision of happiness to another. During the next day he wandered through the woods, lest wonted objects by recalling the memory of later and less happier times, might disturb the blissful idea, that he should again behold her – again fold her in his arms, gaze on her beaming brow by day, repose on her bosom at night: and, as this sole idea filled his imagination, how was it possible that the least doubt should arise: or that the warning of the mysterious old man should recur to his thoughts.

No sooner did the midnight hour approach, than he hastened before the grave-field where the sorcerer was already standing by that of Brunhilda. 'Hast thou maturely considered?' inquired he.

'Oh! restore to me the object of my ardent passion,' exclaimed Walter with impetuous eagerness. 'Delay not thy generous action, lest I die even this night, consumed with disappointed desire; and behold her face no more.'

'Well then,' answered the old man, 'return hither again tomorrow at the same hour. But once more do I give thee this friendly warning, "Wake not the dead."'

All in the despair of impatience, Walter would have prostrated himself at his feet, and supplicated him to fulfil at once a desire now increased to agony; but the sorcerer had already disappeared. Pouring forth his lamentations more wildly and impetuously than ever, he lay upon the grave of his adored one, until the grey dawn streaked the east. During the day, which seemed to him longer than any he had ever experienced, he wandered to and fro, restless and impatient, seemingly without any object, and deeply buried in his own reflections, unquiet as the murderer who meditates his first deed of blood: and the stars of evening found him once more at the appointed spot. At midnight the sorcerer was there also.

'Hast thou yet maturely deliberated?' inquired he, as on the preceding night.

'Oh what should I deliberate?' returned Walter impatiently. 'I need not to deliberate: what I demand of thee, is that which thou hast promised me – that which will prove my bliss. Or dost thou but mock me? If so, hence from my sight, lest I be tempted to lay my hands on thee.'

'Once more do I warn thee,' answered the old man with undisturbed composure, '"Wake not the dead" – let her rest.'

'Aye, but not in the cold grave: she shall rather rest on this bosom which burns with eagerness to clasp her.'

'Reflect, thou mayst not quit her until death, even though aversion and horror should seize thy heart. There would then remain only one horrible means.'

'Dotard!' cried Walter, interrupting him, 'how may I hate that which I love with such intensity of passion? how should I abhor that for which my every drop of blood is boiling?'

'Then be it even as thou wishest,' answered the sorcerer; 'step back.'

The old man now drew a circle round the grave, all the while muttering words of enchantment. Immediately the storm began to bowl among the tops of the trees; owls flapped their wings, and uttered their low voice of omen; the stars hid their mild, beaming aspect, that they might not behold so unholy and impious a spectacle; the stone then rolled from the grave with a hollow sound, leaving a free passage for the inhabitant of that dreadful tenement. The sorcerer scattered into the yawning earth, roots and herbs of most magic power, and of most penetrating odour, so that the worms crawling forth from the earth congregated together, and raised themselves in a fiery column over the grave: while rushing wind burst from the earth, scattering the mould before it, until at length the coffin lay uncovered. The moonbeams fell on it, and the lid burst open with a tremendous sound. Upon this the sorcerer poured upon it some blood from out of a human skull, exclaiming at the same time: 'Drink sleeper, of this warm stream, that thy heart may again beat within thy bosom.' And, after a short pause, shedding on her some other mystic liquid, he cried aloud with the voice of one inspired: 'Yes, thy heart beats once more with the flood of life: thine eye is again opened to sight. Arise, therefore, from the tomb.'

As an island suddenly springs forth from the dark waves of the ocean, raised upwards from the deep by the force of subterraneous fires, so did Brunhilda start from her earthy couch, borne forward by some invisible power. Taking her by the hand, the sorcerer led her towards Walter, who stood at some little distance, rooted to the ground with amazement.

'Receive again,' said he, 'the object of thy passionate sighs: mayest thou never more require my aid; should that, however, happen, so wilt thou find me, during the full of the moon, upon the mountains in that spot and where the three roads meet.'

Instantly did Walter recognize in the form that stood before him, her whom he so ardently loved; and a sudden glow shot through his frame at finding her thus restored to him: yet the night-frost had chilled his limbs and palsied his tongue. For a while he gazed upon her without either motion or speech, and during his pause, all was again become hushed and serene; and the stars shone brightly in the clear heavens.

'Walter!' exclaimed the figure; and at once the well-known sound, thrilling to his heart, broke the spell by which he was bound.

'Is it reality? Is it truth?' cried he, 'or a cheating delusion?'

'No, it is no imposture: I am really living: – conduct me quickly to thy castle in the mountains.'

Walter looked around: the old man had disappeared, but he perceived close by his side, a coal-black steed of fiery eye, ready equipped to conduct him thence; and on his back lay all proper attire for Brunhilda, who lost no time in arraying herself. This being done, she cried; 'Haste, let us away ere the dawn breaks, for my eye is yet too weak to endure the light of day.' Fully recovered from his stupor, Walter leaped into his saddle, and catching up, with a mingled feeling of delight and awe, the beloved being thus mysteriously restored from the power of the grave, he spurred on across the wild, towards the mountains, as furiously as if pursued by the shadows of the dead, hastening to recover from him their sister.

The castle to which Walter conducted his Brunhilda, was situated on a rock between other rocks rising up above it. Here they arrived, unseen by any save one aged domestic, on whom Walter imposed secrecy by the severest threats.

'Here will we tarry,' said Brunhilda, 'until I can endure the light, and until thou canst look upon me without trembling: as if struck with a cold chill.' They accordingly continued to make that place their abode: yet no one knew that Brunhilda existed, save only that aged attendant, who provided their meals. During seven entire days they had no light except that of tapers; during the next seven, the light was admitted through the lofty casements only while the rising or setting-sun faintly illumined the mountain-tops, the valley being still enveloped in shade.

Seldom did Walter quit Brunhilda's side: a nameless spell seemed to attach him to her; even the shudder which he felt in her presence, and which would not permit him to touch her, was not unmixed with pleasure, like that thrilling awful emotion felt when strains of sacred music float under the vault of some temple; he rather sought, therefore, than avoided this feeling. Often too as he had indulged in calling to mind the beauties of Brunhilda, she had never appeared so fair, so fascinating, so admirable when depicted by his imagination, as when now beheld in reality. Never till now had her voice sounded with such tones of sweetness; never before did her language possess such eloquence as it now did, when she conversed with him on the subject of the past. And this was the magic fairy-land towards which her words constantly conducted him. Ever did she dwell upon the days of their first love, those hours of delight which they had participated together when the one derived all enjoyment from the other: and so rapturous, so enchanting, so full of life did she recall to his imagination that blissful season, that he even doubted whether he had ever experienced with her so much felicity, or had been so truly happy. And, while she thus vividly portrayed their hours of past delight, she delineated in still more glowing, more enchanting colours, those hours of approaching bliss which now awaited them, richer in enjoyment than any preceding ones. In this manner did she charm her attentive auditor with enrapturing hopes for the future, and lull him into dreams of more than mortal ecstacy; so that while he listened to her siren strain, he entirely forgot how little blissful was the latter period of their union, when he had often sighed at her imperiousness, and at her harshness both to himself and all his household. Yet even had he recalled this to mind would it have disturbed him in his present delirious trance? Had she not now left behind in the grave all the frailty of mortality? Was not her whole being refined and purified by that long sleep in which neither passion nor sin had approached her even in dreams? How different now was the subject of her discourse! Only when speaking of her affection for him, did she betray anything of earthly feeling: at other times, she uniformly dwelt upon themes relating to the invisible and future world; when in descanting and declaring the mysteries of eternity, a stream of propetic eloquence would burst from her lips.

In this manner had twice seven days elapsed, and, for the first time, Walter beheld the being now dearer to him than ever, in the full light of day. Every trace of the grave had disappeared from her countenance; a roseate tinge like the ruddy streaks of dawn again beamed on her pallid cheek; the faint, mouldering taint of the grave was changed into a delightful violet scent; the only sign of earth that never disappeared. He no longer felt either apprehension or awe, as he gazed upon her in the sunny light of day: it is not until now, that he seemed to have recovered her completely; and, glowing with all his former passion towards her, he would have pressed her to his bosom, but she gently repulsed him, saying? – 'Not yet – spare your caresses until the moon has again filled her horn.'

Spite of his impatience, Walter was obliged to await the lapse of another period of seven days: but, on the night when the moon was arrived at the full, he hastened to Brunhilda, whom he found more lovely than she had ever appeared before. Fearing no obstacles to his transports, he embraced her with all the fervour of a deeply enamoured and successful lover. Brunhilda, however, still refused to yield to his passion. 'What!' exclaimed she, 'is it fitting that I who have been purified by death from the frailty of mortality, should become thy concubine, while a mere daughter of the earth bears the title of thy wife: never shall it be. No, it must be within the walls of thy palace, within that chamber where I once reigned as queen, that thou obtainest the end of thy wishes – and of mine also,' added she, imprinting a glowing kiss on the lips, and immediately disappeared.

Heated with passion, and determined to sacrifice everything to the accomplishment of his desires, Walter hastily quitted the apartment, and shortly after the castle itself. He travelled over mountain and across heath, with the rapidity of a storm, so that the turf was flung up by his horse's hoofs; nor once stopped until he arrived home.

Here, however, neither the affectionate caresses of Swanhilda, or those of his children could touch his heart, or induce him to restrain his furious desires. Alas! is the impetuous torrent to be checked in its devastating course by the beauteous flowers over which it rushes, when they exclaim: – 'Destroyer, commiserate our helpless innocence and beauty, nor lay us waste?' – the stream sweeps over them unregarding, and a single moment annihilates the pride of a whole summer.

Shortly afterwards, did Walter begin to hint to Swanhilda, that they were ill-suited to each other; that he was anxious to taste that wild, tumultuous life, so well according with the spirit of his sex, while she, on the contrary, was satisfied with the monotonous circle of household enjoyments: – that he was eager for whatever promised novelty, while she felt most attached to what was familiarized to her by habit: and lastly, that her cold disposition, bordering upon indifference, but ill assorted with his ardent temperament: it was therefore more prudent that they should seek apart from each other, that happiness which they could not find together. A sigh, and a brief acquiescence in his wishes was all the reply that Swanhilda made: and, on the following morning, upon his presenting her with a paper of separation, informing her that she was at liberty to return home to her father, she received it most submissively: yet, ere she departed, she gave him the following warning: 'Too well do I conjecture to whom I am indebted for this our separation. Often have I seen thee at Brunhilda's grave, and beheld thee there even on that night when the face of the heavens was suddenly enveloped in a veil of clouds. Hast thou rashly dared to tear aside the awful veil that separates the mortality that dreams, from that which dreameth not? Oh! then woe to thee, thou wretched man, for thou hast attached to thyself that which will prove thy destruction.' She ceased: nor did Walter attempt any reply, for the similar admonition uttered by the sorcerer flashed upon his mind, all obscured as it was by passion, just as the lightning glares momentarily through the gloom of night without dispersing the obscurity.

Swanhilda then departed, in order to pronounce to her children, a bitter farewell, for they, according to national custom, belonged to the father; and, having bathed them in her tears, and consecrated them with the holy water of maternal love, she quitted her husband's residence, and departed to the home of her father's.

Thus was the kind and benevolent Swanhilda, driven an exile from those halls, where she had presided with such graces – from halls which were now newly decorated to receive another mistress. The day at length arrived, on which Walter, for the second time, conducted Brunhilda home, as a newly made bride. And he caused it to be reported amongst his domestics, that his new consort had gained his affections by her extraordinary likeness to Brunhilda, their former mistress. How ineffably happy did he deem himself, as he conducted his beloved once more into the chamber which had often witnessed their former joys, and which was now newly gilded and adorned in a most costly style: among the other decorations were figures of angels scattering roses, which served to support the purple draperies, whose ample folds o'ershadowed the nuptial couch. With what impatience did he await the hour that was to put him in possession of those beauties, for which he had already paid so high a price, but, whose enjoyment was to cost him most dearly yet! Unfortunate Walter! revelling in bliss, thou beholdest not the abyss that yawns beneath thy feet, intoxicated with the luscious perfume of the flower thou hast plucked, thou little deemest how deadly is the venom with which it is fraught, although, for a short season, its potent fragrance bestows new energy on all thy feelings.

Happy, however, as Walter now was, his household were far from being equally so. The strange resemblance between their new lady and the deceased Brunhilda, filled them with a secret dismay – an undefinable horror; for there was not a single difference of feature, of tone of voice, or of gesture. To add too to these mysterious circumstances, her female attendants discovered a particular mark on her back, exactly like one which Brunhilda had. A report was now soon circulated, that their lady was no other than Brunhilda herself, who had been recalled to life by the power of necromancy. How truly horrible was the idea of living under the same roof with one who had been an inhabitant of the tomb, and of being obliged to attend upon her, and acknowledge her as mistress! There was also in Brunhilda, much to increase this aversion, and favour their superstition: no ornaments of gold ever decked her person; all that others were wont to wear of this metal, she had formed of silver: no richly coloured and sparkling jewels glittered upon her; pearls alone, lent their pale lustre to adorn her bosom. Most carefully did she always avoid the cheerful light of the sun, and was wont to spend the brightest days in the most retired and gloomy apartments: only during the twilight of the commencing, or declining day did she ever walk abroad, but her favourite hour was, when the phantom light of the moon bestowed on all objects a shadowy appearance, and a sombre hue; always too at the crowing of the cock, an involuntary shudder was observed to seize her limbs. Imperious as before her death, she quickly imposed her iron yoke on every one around her, while she seemed even far more terrible than ever, since a dread of some supernatural power attached to her, and appalled all who approached her. A malignant withering glance seemed to shoot from her eye on the unhappy object of her wrath, as if it would annihilate its victim. In short, those halls which, in the time of Swanhilda were the residence of cheerfulness and mirth, now resembled an extensive desert tomb. With fear imprinted on their pale countenances, the domestics glided through the apartments of the castle; and, in this abode of terror, the crowing of the cock caused the living to tremble, as if they were the spirits of the departed; for the sound always reminded them of their mysterious mistress. There was no one but who shuddered at meeting her in a lonely place, in the dusk of evening, or by the light of the moon, a circumstance that was deemed to be ominous of some evil: so great was the apprehension of her female attendants, they pined in continual disquietude, and, by degrees, all quitted her. In the course of time even others of the domestics fled, for an insupportable horror had seized them.

The art of the sorcerer had indeed bestowed upon Brunhilda an artificial life, and due nourishment had continued to support the restored body; yet, this body was not able of itself to keep up the genial glow of vitality, and to nourish the flame whence springs all the affections and passions, whether of love or hate; for death had for ever destroyed and withered it: all that Brunhilda now possessed was a chilled existence, colder than that of the snake. It was nevertheless necessary that she should love, and return with equal ardour the warm caresses of her spell-enthralled husband, to whose passion alone she was indebted for her renewed existence. It was necessary that a magic draught should animate the dull current in her veins, and awaken her to the glow of life and the flame of love – a potion of abomination – one not even to be named without a curse – human blood, imbibed whilst yet warm, from the veins of youth. This was the hellish drink for which she thirsted: possessing no sympathy with the purer feelings of humanity; deriving no enjoyment from aught that interests in life, and occupies its varied hours; her existence was a mere blank, unless when in the arms of her paramour husband, and therefore was it that she craved incessantly after the horrible draught. It was even with the utmost effort that she could forbear sucking even the blood of Walter himself, as he reclined beside her. Whenever she beheld some innocent child, whose lovely face denoted the exuberance of infantine health and vigour, she would entice it by soothing words and fond caresses into her most secret apartment, where, lulling it to sleep in her arms, she would suck from its bosom the warm, purple tide of life. Nor were youths of either sex safe from her horrid attack: having first breathed upon her unhappy victim, who never failed immediately to sink into a lengthened sleep, she would then in a similar manner drain his veins of the vital juice. Thus children, youths, and maidens quickly faded away, as flowers gnawn by the cankering worm: the fullness of their limbs disappeared; a sallow line succeeded to the rosy freshness of their cheeks, the liquid lustre of the eye was deadened, even as the sparkling stream when arrested by the touch of frost; and their locks became thin and grey, as if already ravaged by the storm of life. Parents beheld with horror this desolating pestilence, devouring their offspring; nor could simple charm, potion or amulet avail aught against it. The grave swallowed up one after the other; or did the miserable victim survive, he became cadaverous and wrinkled even in the very morn of existence. Parents observed with horror, this devastating pestilence snatch away their offspring – a pestilence which, nor herb however potent, nor charm, nor holy taper, nor exorcism could avert. They either beheld their children sink one after the other into the grave, or their youthful forms, withered by the unholy, vampire embrace of Brunhilda, assume the decrepitude of sudden age.

At length strange surmises and reports began to prevail; it was whispered that Brunhilda herself was the cause of all these horrors; although no one could pretend to tell in what manner she destroyed her victims, since no marks of violence were discernible. Yet when young children confessed that she had frequently lulled them asleep in her arms, and elder ones said that a sudden slumber had come upon them whenever she began to converse with them, suspicion became converted into certainty, and those whose offspring had hitherto escaped unharmed, quitted their hearths and home – all their little possessions – the dwellings of their fathers and the inheritance of their children, in order to rescue from so horrible a fate those who were dearer to their simple affections than aught else the world could give.

Thus daily did the castle assume a more desolate appearance; daily did its environs become more deserted; none but a few aged decrepit old women and grey-headed menials were to be seen remaining of the once numerous retinue. Such will in the latter days of the earth, be the last generation of mortals, when child-bearing shall have ceased, when youth shall no more be seen, nor any arise to replace those who shall await their fate in silence.

Walter alone noticed not, or heeded not, the desolation around him; he apprehended not death, lapped as he was in a glowing elysium of love. Far more happy than formerly did he now seem in the possession of Brunhilda. All those caprices and frowns which had been wont to overcloud their former union had now entirely disappeared. She even seemed to doat on him with a warmth of passion that she had never exhibited even during the happy season of bridal love; for the flame of that youthful blood, of which she drained the veins of others, rioted in her own. At night, as soon as he closed his eyes, she would breathe on him till he sank into delicious dreams, from which he awoke only to experience more rapturous enjoyments. By day she would continually discourse with him on the bliss experienced by happy spirits beyond the grave, assuring him that, as his affection had recalled her from the tomb, they were now irrevocably united. Thus fascinated by a continual spell, it was not possible that he should perceive what was taking place around him. Brunhilda, however, foresaw with savage grief that the source of her youthful ardour was daily decreasing, for, in a short time, there remained nothing gifted with youth, save Walter and his children, and these latter she resolved should be her next victims.

On her first return to the castle, she had felt an aversion towards the off-spring of another, and therefore abandoned them entirely to the attendants

appointed by Swanhilda. Now, however, she began to pay considerable attention to them, and caused them to be frequently admitted into her presence.
The aged nurses were filled with dread at perceiving these marks of regard
from her towards their young charges, yet dared they not to oppose the will
of their terrible and imperious mistress. Soon did Brunhilda gain the affection of the children, who were too unsuspecting of guile to apprehend any
danger from her; on the contrary, her caresses won them completely to her.
Instead of ever checking their mirthful gambols, she would rather instruct
them in new sports; often too did she recite to them tales of such strange and
wild interests as to exceed all the stories of their nurses. Were they wearied
either with play or with listening to her narratives, she would take them on
her knees and lull them to slumber. Then did visions of the most surpassing
magnificence attend their dreams: they would fancy themselves in some
garden where flowers of every hue rose in rows one above the other, from
the humble violet to the tall sun-flower, forming a party-coloured broidery
of every hue, sloping upwards towards the golden clouds, where little angels,
whose wings sparkled with azure and gold, descended to bring them delicious
foods, or splendid jewels; or sung to them soothing melodious hymns. So
delightful did these dreams in short time become to the children, that they
longed for nothing so eagerly as to slumber on Brunhilda's lap, for never did
they else enjoy such visions of heavenly forms. Thus were they most anxious
for that which was to prove their destruction: – yet do we not all aspire after
that which conducts us to the grave – after the enjoyment of life? These
innocents stretched out their arms to approaching death, because it assumed
the mask of pleasure; for, while they were lapped in these ecstatic slumbers,
Brunhilda sucked the life-stream from their bosoms. On waking, indeed, they
felt themselves faint and exhausted, yet did no pain, nor any mark betray the
cause. Shortly, however, did their strength entirely fail, even as the summer
brook is gradually dried up; their sports became less and less noisy; their
loud, frolicsome laughter was converted into a faint smile; the full tones of
their voices died away into a mere whisper. Their attendants were filled with
horror and despair; too well did they conjecture the horrible truth, yet dared
not to impart their suspicions to Walter, who was so devotedly attached to

his horrible partner. Death had already smote his prey: the children were but the mere shadows of their former selves, and even this shadow quickly disappeared.

The anguished father deeply bemoaned their loss, for, notwithstanding his apparent neglect, he was strongly attached to them, nor until he had experienced their loss was he aware that his love was so great. His affliction could not fail to excite the displeasure of Brunhilda: 'Why dost thou lament so fondly,' said she, 'for these little ones? What satisfaction could such unformed beings yield to thee, unless thou wert still attached to their mother? Thy heart then is still hers? Or dost thou now regret her and them, because thou art satiated with my fondness, and weary of my endearments? Had these young ones grown up, would they not have attached thee, thy spirit and thy affections more closely to this earth of clay – to this dust, and have alienated thee from that sphere to which I, who have already passed the grave, endeavour to raise thee? Say is thy spirit so heavy, or thy love so weak, or thy faith so hollow, that the hope of being mine for ever is unable to touch thee?' Thus did Brunhilda express her indignation at her consort's grief, and forbade him her presence. The fear of offending her beyond forgiveness, and his anxiety to appease her soon dried up his tears; and he again abandoned himself to his fatal passion, until approaching destruction at length awakened him from his delusion.

Neither maiden, nor youth, was any longer to be seen, either within the dreary walls of the castle, or the adjoining territory: – all had disappeared; for those whom the grave had not swallowed up, had fled from the region of death. Who, therefore, now remained to quench the horrible thirst of the female vampire, save Walter himself? and his death she dared to contemplate unmoved; for that divine sentiment that unites two beings in one joy and one sorrow was unknown to her bosom. Was he in his tomb, so was she free to search out other victims, and glut herself with destruction, until she herself should, at the last day, be consumed with the earth itself, such is the fatal law, to which the dead are subject, when awoke by the arts of necromancy from the sleep of the grave.

She now began to fix her blood-thirsty lips on Walter's breast, when cast into a profound sleep by the odour of her violet breath, he reclined beside her quite unconscious of his impending fate: yet soon did his vital powers begin to decay; and many a grey hair peeped through his raven locks. With his strength, his passion also declined; and he now frequently left her in order to pass the whole day in the sports of the chase, hoping thereby, to regain his wonted vigour. As he was reposing one day in a wood beneath the shade of an oak, he perceived, on the summit of a tree, a bird of strange appearance, and quite unknown to him; but, before he could take aim at it with his bow, it flew away into the clouds; at the same time, letting fall a rose-coloured root which dropped at Walter's feet, who immediately took it up, and, although he was well acquainted with almost every plant, he could not remember to have seen any at all resembling this. Its delightfully odoriferous scent induced him to try its flavour, but ten times more bitter than wormwood, it was even as gall in his mouth; upon which, impatient of the disappointment, he flung it away with violence. Had he, however, been aware of its miraculous quality, and that it acted as a counter charm against the opiate perfume of Brunhilda's breath, he would have blessed it in spite of its bitterness: thus do mortals often blindly cast away in displeasure, the unsavoury remedy that would otherwise work their weal.

When Walter returned home in the evening, and laid him down to repose as usual by Brunhilda's side, the magic power of her breath produced no effect upon him; and for the first time during many months did he close his eyes in a natural slumber. Yet hardly had he fallen asleep, ere a pungent smarting pain disturbed him from his dreams; and, opening his eyes, he discerned, by the gloomy rays of a lamp, that glimmered in the apartment, what for some moments transfixed him quite aghast, for it was Brunhilda, drawing with her lips, the warm blood from his bosom. The wild cry of horror which at length escaped him, terrified Brunhilda, whose mouth was besmeared with the warm blood. 'Monster!' exclaimed he, springing from the couch, 'is it thus that you love me?'

'Aye, even as the dead love,' replied she, with a malignant coldness.

'Creature of blood!' continued Walter, 'the delusion which has so long blinded me is at an end: thou art the fiend who hast destroyed my children

– who hast murdered the offspring of my vassals.' Raising herself upwards and, at the same time, casting on him a glance that froze him to the spot with dread, she replied. 'It is not I who have murdered them; – I was obliged to pamper myself with warm youthful blood, in order that I might satisfy thy furious desires – thou art the murderer!' – These dreadful words summoned, before Walter's terrified conscience, the threatening shades of all those who had thus perished; while despair choked his voice. 'Why,' continued she, in a tone that increased his horror, 'why dost thou make mouths at me like a puppet? Thou who hadst the courage to love the dead – to take into thy bed, one who had been sleeping in the grave, the bed-fellow of the worm – who hast clasped in thy lustful arms, the corruption of the tomb – dost thou, unhallowed as thou art, now raise this hideous cry for the sacrifice of a few lives? – They are but leaves swept from their branches by a storm. – Come, chase these idiot fancies, and taste the bliss thou hast so dearly purchased.' So saying, she extended her arms towards him; but this motion served only to increase his terror, and exclaiming: 'Accursed Being,' – he rushed out of the apartment.

All the horrors of a guilty, upbraiding conscience became his companions, now that he was awakened from the delirium of his unholy pleasures. Frequently did he curse his own obstinate blindness, for having given no heed to the hints and admonitions of his children's nurses, but treating them as vile calumnies. But his sorrow was now too late, for, although repentance may gain pardon for the sinner, it cannot alter the immutable decrees of fate – it cannot recall the murdered from the tomb. No sooner did the first break of dawn appear, than he set out for his lonely castle in the mountains, determined no longer to abide under the same roof with so terrific a being; yet vain was his flight, for, on waking the following morning, he perceived himself in Brunhilda's arms, and quite entangled in her long raven tresses, which seemed to involve him, and bind him in the fetters of his fate; the powerful fascination of her breath held him still more captivated, so that, forgetting all that had passed, he returned her caresses, until awakening as if from a dream he recoiled in unmixed horror from her embrace. During the day he wandered through the solitary wilds of the mountains, as a culprit seeking an asylum from his pursuers; and, at night, retired to the shelter of a cave; fearing less to couch himself within such a dreary place, than to expose himself to the horror of again meeting Brunhilda; but alas! it was in vain that he endeavoured to flee her. Again, when he awoke, he found her the partner of his miserable bed. Nay, had he sought the centre of the earth as his hiding place; had he even imbedded himself beneath rocks, or formed his chamber in the recesses of the ocean, still had he found her his constant companion; for, by calling her again into existence, he had rendered himself inseparably hers; so fatal were the links that united them.

Struggling with the madness that was beginning to seize him, and brooding incessantly on the ghastly visions that presented themselves to his horror-stricken mind, he lay motionless in the gloomiest recesses of the woods, even from the rise of sun till the shades of eve. But, no sooner was the light of day extinguished in the west, and the woods buried in impenetrable darkness, than the apprehension of resigning himself to sleep drove him forth among the mountains. The storm played wildly with the fantastic clouds, and with the rattling leaves, as they were caught up into the air, as if some dread spirit was sporting with these images of transitoriness and decay: it roared among the summits of the oaks as if uttering a voice of fury, while its hollow sound rebounding among the distant hills, seemed as the moans of a departing sinner, or as the faint cry of some wretch expiring under the murderer's hand: the owl too, uttered its ghastly cry as if foreboding the wreck of nature. Walter's hair flew disorderly in the wind, like black snakes wreathing around his temples and shoulders; while each sense was awake to catch fresh horror. In the clouds he seemed to behold the form of the murdered; in the howling wind to hear their laments and groans; in the chilling blast itself he felt the dire kiss of Brunhilda; in the cry of the screeching bird he heard her voice; in the moldering leaves he scented the charnel-bed out of which he had awakened her. 'Murder of thy own off-spring,' exclaimed he in a voice making night, and the conflict of the elements still more hideous, 'paramour of a blood-thirsty vampire, reveller with the corruption of the tomb!' while in his despair he rent the wild locks from his head. Just then the full moon darted from beneath the bursting clouds; and the sight recalled to his remembrance the advice of the sorcerer, when he trembled at the first apparition of Brunhilda rising from her sleep of death; – namely, to seek him, at the season of the full moon, in the mountains, where three roads met. Scarcely had this gleam of hope broke in on his bewildered mind, than he flew to the appointed spot.

On his arrival, Walter found the old man seated there upon a stone, as calmly as though it had been a bright sunny day, and completely regardless of the uproar around. 'Art thou come then?' exclaimed he to the breathless wretch, who, flinging himself at his feet, cried in a tone of anguish: – 'Oh save me – succour me – rescue me from the monster that scattereth death and desolation around her.'

'And wherefore a mysterious warning? why didst thou not perceive how wholesome was the advice – "Wake not the dead"?'

'And wherefore a mysterious warning? why didst thou not rather disclose to me, at once, all the horrors that awaited my sacrilegious profanation of the grave?'

'Wert thou able to listen to any other voice than that of thy impetuous passions? Did not thy eager impatience shut my mouth at the very moment I would have cautioned thee?'

'True, true: – thy reproof is just: but what does it avail now; – I need the promptest aid.'

'Well,' replied the old man, 'there remains even yet a means of rescuing thyself, but it is fraught with horror, and demands all thy resolution.'

'Utter it then, utter it; for what can be more appalling, more hideous than the misery I now endure?'

'Know then,' continued the sorcerer, 'that only on the night of the new moon, does she sleep the sleep of mortals; and then all the supernatural power which she inherits from the grave totally fails her. 'Tis then that thou must murder her.'

'How! murder her!' echoed Walter.

'Aye,' returned the old man calmly, 'pierce her bosom with a sharpened dagger, which I will furnish thee with; at the same time renounce her memory for ever, swearing never to think of her intentionally, and that, if thou dost involuntarily, thou wilt repeat the curse.'

'Most horrible! yet what can be more horrible than she herself is? – I'll do it.'

'Keep then this resolution until the next new moon.'

'What, must I wait until then?' cried Walter, 'alas ere then, either her savage thirst for blood will have forced me into the night of the tomb, or horror will have driven me into the night of madness.'

'Nay,' replied the sorcerer, 'that I can prevent;' and, so saying he conducted him to a cavern further among the mountains. 'Abide here twice seven days,' said he; 'so long can I protect thee against her deadly caresses. Here wilt thou find all due provision for thy wants; but take heed that nothing tempt thee to quit this place. Farewell, when the moon renews itself, then do I repair hither again.' So saying, the sorcerer drew a magic circle around the cave, and then immediately disappeared.

Twice seven days did Walter continue in this solitude, where his companions were his own terrifying thoughts, and his bitter repentance. The present was all desolation and dread; the future presented the image of a horrible deed, which he must perforce commit; while the past was empoisoned by the memory of his guilt. Did he think on his former happy union with Brunhilda, her horrible image presented itself to his imagination with her lips defiled with dripping blood: or, did he call to mind the peaceful days he had passed with Swanhilda, he beheld her sorrowful spirit, with the shadows of her murdered children. Such were the horrors that attended him by day: those of night were still more dreadful, for then he beheld Brunhilda herself, who, wandering round the magic circle which she could not pass, called upon his name, till the cavern re-echoed the horrible sound. 'Walter, my beloved,' cried she, 'wherefore dost thou avoid me? art thou not mine? for ever mine – mine here, and mine hereafter? And dost thou seek to murder me? – ah! commit not a deed which hurls us both to perdition – thyself as well as me.' In this manner did the horrible visitant torment him each night, and, even when she departed, robbed him of all repose.

The night of the new moon at length arrived, dark as the deed it was doomed to bring forth. The sorcerer entered the cavern; 'Come,' said he to Walter, 'let us depart hence, the hour is now arrived;' and he forthwith conducted him in silence from the cave to a coal-black steed, the sight of which recalled to Walter's remembrance the fatal night. He then related to the old man Brunhilda's nocturnal visits, and anxiously inquired whether her apprehensions of eternal perdition would be fulfilled or not. 'Mortal eye,' exclaimed the sorcerer, 'may not pierce the dark secrets of another world, or penetrate the deep abyss that separates earth from heaven.' Walter hesitated to mount the steed. 'Be resolute,' exclaimed his companion, 'but this once is it granted to thee to make the trial, and, should thou fail now, nought can rescue thee from her power.'

'What can be more horrible than she herself? – I am determined;' and he leaped on the horse, the sorcerer mounting also behind him.

Carried with a rapidity equal to that of the storm that sweeps across the plain, they in brief space arrived at Walter's castle. All the doors flew open at the bidding of his companion, and they speedily reached Brunhilda's chamber, and stood beside her couch. Reclining in a tranquil slumber; she reposed in all her native loveliness, every trace of horror had disappeared from her countenance; she looked so pure, meek and innocent that all the sweet hours of their endearments rushed to Walter's memory, like interceding angels pleading in her behalf. His unnerved hand could not take the dagger which the sorcerer presented to him. 'The blow must be struck even now;' said the latter, 'shouldst thou delay but an hour, she will lie at day-break on thy bosom, sucking the warm life drops from thy heart.'

'Horrible! most horrible!' faltered the trembling Water, and turning away his face, he thrust the dagger into her bosom, exclaiming – 'I curse thee for ever!' – and the cold blood gushed upon his hand. Opening her eyes once more, she cast a look of ghastly horror on her husband, and, in a hollow dying accent said – 'Thou too art doomed to perdition.'

'Lay now thy hand upon her corse,' said the sorcerer, 'and swear the oath.' – Walter did as commanded, saying – 'Never will I think of her with love, never recall her to mind intentionally, and, should her image recur to my mind involuntarily, so will I exclaim to it: be thou accursed.'

'Thou has now done everything,' returned the sorcerer; – restore her therefore to the earth, from which thou didst so foolishly recall her; and be sure to recollect thy oath: for, shouldst thou forget it but once, she would return, and thou wouldst be inevitably lost. Adieu – we see each other no more.' Having uttered these words he quitted the apartment, and Walter also fled from this abode of horror, having first given direction that the corse should be speedily interred.

Again did the terrific Brunhilda repose within her grave; but her image continually haunted Walter's imagination, so that his existence was one continued martyrdom, in which he continually struggled, to dismiss from his recollection the hideous phantoms of the past; yet, the stronger his effort to banish them, so much the more frequently and the more vividly did they return; as the nightwanderer, who is enticed by a fire-wisp into quagmire or bog, sinks the deeper into his damp grave the more he struggles to escape. His imagination seemed incapable of admitting any other image than that of Brunhilda: now he fancied he beheld her expiring, the blood streaming from her beautiful bosom: at others he saw the lovely bride of his youth, who reproached him with having disturbed the slumbers of the tomb: and to both he was compelled to utter the dreadful words, 'I curse thee for ever.' The terrible imprecation was constantly passing his lips; yet was he in incessant terror lest he should forget it, or dream of her without being able to repeat it, and then, on awakening, find himself in her arms. Else would he recall her expiring words, and, appalled at their terrific import, imagine that the doom of his perdition was irrecoverably passed. Whence should he fly from himself? or how erase from his brain these images and forms of horror? In the din of combat, in the tumult of war and its incessant pour of victory to defeat; from the cry of anguish to the exultation of victory – in these he hoped to find at least relief of distraction: but here too he was disappointed. The giant fang of apprehension now seized him who had never before known fear; each drop of blood that sprayed upon him seemed the cold blood that had gushed from Brunhilda's wound; each dying wretch that fell beside him looked like her, when expiring, she exclaimed: – 'Thou too art doomed to perdition;' so that the aspect of death seemed more full of dread to him than aught beside, and this unconquerable terror compelled him to abandon the battle-field. At length, after many a weary and fruitless wandering, he returned to his castle. Here all was deserted and silent, as if the sword, or a still more deadly pestilence had laid everything waste: for the few inhabitants that still remained, and even those servants who had once shewn themselves the most attached, now fled from him, as though he had been branded with the mark of Cain. With horror he perceived that, by uniting himself as he had done with the dead, he had cut himself off from the living, who refused to hold any intercourse with him. Often, when he stood on the battlements of his castle, and looked down upon desolate fields, he compared their present solitude with the lively activity they were wont to exhibit, under the strict but benevolent discipline of Swanhilda. He now felt that she alone could reconcile him to life, but durst he hope that one, whom he so deeply aggrieved, could pardon him, and receive him again? Impatience at length got the better of fear; he sought Swanhilda, and, with the deepest contrition, acknowledged his complicated guilt; embracing her knees he beseeched her to pardon him, and to return to his desolate castle, in order that it might again become the abode of contentment and peace. The pale form which she beheld at her feet, the shadow of the lately blooming youth, touched Swanhilda. 'The folly,' said she gently, 'though it has caused me much sorrow, has never excited my resentment or my anger. But say, where are my children?' To this dreadful interrogation the agonized father could for a while frame no reply: at length he was obliged to confess the dreadful truth. 'Then we are sundered for ever,' returned Swanhilda; nor could all his tears or supplications prevail upon her to revoke the sentence she had given.

Stripped of his last earthly hope, bereft of his last consolation, and thereby rendered as poor as mortal can possibly be on this side of the grave, Walter returned homewards; when, as he was riding through the forest in the neighbourhood of his castle, absorbed in his gloomy meditations, the sudden sound of a horn roused him from his reverie. Shortly after he saw appear a female figure clad in black, and mounted on a steed of the same colour: her attire was like that of a huntress, but, instead of a falcon, she bore a raven in her hand; and she was attended by a gay troop of cavaliers and dames. The first salutations being passed, he found that she was proceeding the same road as himself; and, when she found that Walter's castle was close at hand, she requested that he would lodge her for that night, the evening being far

advanced. Most willingly did he comply with this request, since the appearance of the beautiful stranger had struck him greatly; so wonderfully did she
resemble Swanhilda, except that her locks were brown, and her eye dark and
full of fire. With a sumptuous banquet did he entertain his guests, whose
mirth and songs enlivened the lately silent halls. Three days did this revelry
continue, and so exhilarating did it prove to Walter, that he seemed to have
forgotten his sorrows and his fears; nor could he prevail upon himself to
dismiss his visitors, dreading lest, on their departure, the castle would seem
a hundred times more desolate than before, and his grief be proportionately
increased. At his earnest request, the stranger consented to stay seven days,
and again another seven days. Without being requested, she took upon herself
the superintendence of the household, which she regulated as discreetly and
cheerfully as Swanhilda had been wont to do, so that the castle, which had
so lately been the abode of melancholy and horror, became the residence of
pleasure and festivity, and Walter's grief disappeared altogether in the midst
of so much gaiety. Daily did his attachment to the fair unknown increase; he
even made her his confidant; and, one evening as they were walking together
apart from any of her train, he related to her his melancholy and frightful
history. 'My dear friend,' returned she, as soon as he had finished his tale, 'it
ill beseems a man of thy discretion to afflict thyself, on account of all this.
Thou hast awakened the dead from the sleep of the grave, and afterwards
found – what might have been anticipated, that the dead possess no sympathy
with life. What then? thou wilt not commit this error a second time. Thou
hast however murdered the being whom thou hadst thus recalled again to
existence – but it was only in appearance, for thou couldst not deprive that
of life, which properly had none. Thou hast, too, lost a wife and two children:
but, at thy years, such a loss is most easily repaired. There are beauties who
will gladly share thy couch, and make thee again a father. But thou dreadst
the reckoning of hereafter: – go, open the graves and ask the sleepers there
whether that hereafter disturbs them.' In such manner would she frequently
exhort and cheer him, so that, in a short time, his melancholy entirely disappeared. He now ventured to declare to the unknown the passion with which
she had inspired him, nor did she refuse him her hand. Within seven days

afterwards the nuptials were celebrated, and the very foundations of the castle seemed to rock from the wild tumultuous uproar of unrestrained riot. The wine streamed in abundance; the goblets circled incessantly: intemperance reached its utmost bounds, while shouts of laughter, almost resembling madness, burst from the numerous train belonging to the unknown. At length Walter, heated with wine and love, conducted his bride into the nuptial chamber: but, oh horror! scarcely had he clasped her in his arms, ere she transformed herself into a monstrous serpent, which entwining him in its horrid folds, crushed him to death. Flames crackled on every side of the apartment; in a few minutes after, the whole castle was enveloped in a blaze that consumed it entirely: while, as the walls fell in with a tremendous crash, a voice exclaimed aloud – 'Wake not the dead!'

AURELIA

E. T. A. HOFFMANN

This story, written in 1819–20 as one of the twenty-nine tales in his collection *Die Erzählungen der Serapionsbrüder* (*The Serapion Brethren*), is an uncharacteristic example of Hoffmann's work. It is not directly concerned with the themes we normally associate with Hoffmann – the darker side of the human psyche, symbolized by hypnotic states, automata controlled by a demonic power, and the psychological phenomenon of the *Doppelgänger* – and the cynical Lothair (in a critical discussion which introduces the story) associates vampire tales of this type with writers who simply 'blind the eye for a moment with borrowed light'. Serapion was supposed to have been a mad nobleman who cut himself off from society and lived as a hermit, writing tales of fantasy remarkable for their perceptiveness and realism. The Serapion Brethren, according to Hoffmann, would meet periodically to judge each other's efforts by this criterion. The principle of 'Serapionism' (to which all the Brethren were supposed to adhere) involved presenting paranormal phenomena *convincingly*, and the discussion which links all the various tales in Hoffmann's most famous collection normally concerns the strategies by which this can best be achieved: melodramatic vampire tales are thought by Lothair to belong to the more 'obvious' kind of horror story, where the various Gothic trappings (by *showing* everything) tend to obscure 'the *idea* of the thing' – which Hoffmann thought was much more frightening.

Aurelia dates from the most creative part of Hoffmann's life (two years before he died of syphilis) and, in *The Serapion Brethren*, is sandwiched between his best and most famous works. The story may be among those which, according to critic E. F. Bleiler, were 'written hastily, under time pressures, to pay for expensive wines, or to settle tavern bills', but in the context of the challenging discussion which precedes it, *Aurelia* manages to combine stock Gothic trappings with 'Serapionism' (despite Lothair's reservations), and thus deserves a place here. It has long been hard to find in English. This translation comes from a Victorian collection of Hoffmann's *Tales*.

'IT IS REMARKABLE,' SAID SYLVESTER, 'that – unless I mistake – another great writer appeared on the other side of the channel, about the same time as Walter Scott, and has produced works of equal greatness and splendour, but in a different direction. I mean Lord Byron. But his predominant tendency seems to be towards the gloomy, the mysterious and the terrible; and his "Vampire" I have avoided reading, for the bare idea of a vampire makes my blood run cold. So far as I understand the matter, a vampire is an animated corpse which sucks the blood of the living.'

'Ho! ho!' cried Lothair, laughing, 'a writer such as you, my dear friend, Sylvester, must of course have found it necessary to dip more or less deeply into all kinds of accounts concerning magic, witches, sorcery, enchantment, and other such works of the devil, because they are necessary for your work, and part of your stock in trade. And I should suppose you have gone into those subjects yourself with the view of getting some personal experience of them as well. As regards vampirism – that you may see how well read I am in these matters – I will tell you the name of a delightful treatise in which you may study this dark subject. The complete title of this little book is "M. Michael Ranft (Deacon of Nebra), Treatise on the Chewing and Sucking of the Dead in their Coffins; wherein the true nature and description of the Hungarian vampires and bloodsuckers is clearly set forth, and all previous writings on this subject are passed in review and subjected to criticism". This title in itself will convince you of the thoroughness of this treatise, and you will learn from it that a vampire is nothing other that an accursed creature who lets himself be buried as being dead, and then rises out of the grave and sucks people's blood in their sleep. And those people become vampires in their turn. So that, according to the accounts received from Hungary and quoted by this magister, the inhabitants of whole villages become vampires of the most abominable description. To render those vampires harmless they must be dug out of their graves, a stake driven through their hearts, and their bodies burnt to ashes. Those horrible beings very often do not appear in their own proper forms, but *en masque*. A certain officer, I happen to remember, writing from Belgrade to a celebrated doctor in Leipzig for information as to the true nature of vampires, expresses himself thus: "In a village called Kinklina it chanced that two brothers were troubled by a vampire, so that one of them used to sit up by the other at night whilst he slept. The one who was watching used to see something like a dog opening the door, but this dog used to make off when he cried out at it. At last one night they both were asleep at the same time, and the vampire bit and sucked a place under the right ear of one of them, leaving a red mark. The man died of this in three days' time. In conclusion," said the officer, "as the people of this place make all this out to be miraculous, I venture to take the liberty of requesting you to tell me your private opinion as to whether it is caused by the intervention of sympathetic, diabolic, or astral spirits. And I remain, with much respect, &c." Take example by this officer of enquiring mind. As it happens his name occurs to me at this moment. He was an ensign in the Prince Alexander regiment, Sigismund Alexander Friedrich von Kottwitz. The military mind seems to have been considerably exercised on the subject of vampirism about that time. Magister Ranft quotes in his book an offical declaration made by an army surgeon before two of his brother officers concerning the detection and destruction of a vampire. This declaration contains, *inter alia*, the following passage: "Inasmuch as they perceived, from the aforesaid circumstances, that this was unmistakably a vampire, they drove a stake through its heart, upon which it gave vent to a distinct gasp, emitting a considerable quantity of blood." Is that not both interesting and instructive?'

'All this of Magister Ranft's,' said Sylvester, 'may, no doubt, be sufficiently absurd and even rather crack-brained; but, at the same time, if we keep to the subject of vampirism itself, never minding in what particular fashion it may be treated, it certainly is one of the most horrible and terrible notions imaginable. I can conceive nothing more ghastlily repulsive to the mind.'

'Still,' said Cyprian, 'it is capable of providing a material, when dealt with by a writer of imagination possessed of some poetical tact, which has the power of stirring within us that profound sense of awe which is innate in our hearts, and when touched by the electric impulse from an unseen spirit world causes our soul to thrill, not altogether unpleasantly after a fashion. A due amount of poetic tact on the author's part will prevent the horror of the subject from going so far as to be loathsome; for it generally has such an element of the absurd about it that does not impress us so deeply as if that were not the case. Why should not a writer be permitted to make use of the levers of fear, terror, and horror because some feeble soul here and there finds it more than it can bear? Shall there be no strong meat at table because there happen to be some guests there whose stomachs are weak, or who have spoiled their own digestions?'

'My dear, fanciful Cyprian,' Theodore said, 'there was no occasion for your vindication of the horrible. We all know how wonderfully great writers have moved men's hearts to their very depths by means of that lever. We have only to think of Shakespeare. Moreover, who knew better how to use it than our own glorious Tieck in many of his tales? And how finely that author says: "In those imaginary legends the misery cannot reach the world with its rays until they have been broken up into prismatic colours," and I should have supposed that in that condition they would have been endurable by eyes, even not very strong.'

'We have often spoken already,' said Lothair, 'of this most genial writer; the full recognition of whom, in all his grand super-excellence and variety, is reserved for posterity, whilst Wills o' the Wisp rapidly scintillating into our ken and blinding the eye for a moment with borrowed light, go out into darkness just as speedily. On the whole, I believe that the imagination can be moved by very simple means, and that it is often more the *idea* of the thing than the thing itself which causes our fear. Not only could Kleist, for example, "dip" into the aforesaid colour-box, but he could lay the colours *on*, with the power and the genius of the most finished master. He did not need to raise a vampire out of the grave.'

'This discussion about vampirism,' said Cyprian, 'reminds me of a ghastly story which I either heard or read a very long time ago. But I think I heard it, because I seem to remember that the person who told it said that the circumstances had actually happened, and mentioned the name of the family and of their country seat where it took place. But if this story is known to you as being in print, please stop me and prevent my going on with it, because there's nothing more wearisome than to tell people things which they have known for ever so long.'

'I foresee,' said Ottmar, 'that you are going to give us something unusually awful and terrible. But remember Saint Serapion and be as concise as you can, so that Vincenz may have his turn; for I see that he is waiting impatiently to read us that long-promised story of his.'

'Hush! hush!' said Vincenz. 'I could not wish anything better than that Cyprian should hang up a fine dark canvas by way of a background so as to throw out the figures of my tale, which I think are brightly and variedly coloured, and certainly excessively active. So begin, my Cyprianus, and be as gloomy, as frightful, as terrible as the vampirish Lord Byron himself, though I know nothing about him, as I have never read a word of his writings.'

Count Hyppolitus (began Cyprian) had just returned from a long time spent in travelling to take possession of the rich inheritance which his father, recently dead, had left to him. The ancestral home was situated in the most beautiful and charming country imaginable, and the income from the property was amply sufficient to defray the cost of the most extensive improvements. Whatever in the way of architecture and landscape gardening had struck the Count during his travels – particularly in England – as specially delightful and apposite, he was going to reproduce in his own demesne. Architects, landscape gardeners, and labourers of all sorts arrived on the scene as they were wanted, and there commenced at once a complete reconstruction of the place, whilst an extensive park was laid out on the grandest scale, which involved the including within its boundaries of the church, the parsonage, and the burial ground. All those improvements the Count, who possessed the necessary knowledge, superintended himself, devoting himself to this occupation body and soul; so that a year slipped away without its ever having occurred to him to take an old uncle's advice and let the light of his countenance shine in the Residenz before the eyes of the young ladies, so that the most beautiful, the best, and the most nobly born amongst them might fall to his share as wife. One morning, as he was sitting at his draw-ing table sketching the ground-plan of a new building, a certain elderly Baroness – distantly related to his father – was announced as having come to call. When Hyppolitus heard her name he remembered that his father had always spoken of her with the greatest indignation – nay, with absolute abhorrence, and had often warned people who were going to approach her to keep aloof, without explaining what the danger connected with her was. If he was questioned more closely, he said there were certain matters as to which it was better to keep silence. Thus much was certain, that there were rumours current in the Residenz of some most remarkable and unprecedented criminal trial in which the Baroness had been involved, which had led to her separation from her husband, driven her from her home – which was at some considerable distance – and for the suppression of the consequences of which she was indebted to the prince's forbearance. Hyppolitus felt a very painful and disagreeable impression at the coming of a person whom his father had so detested, although the reasons for this detestation were not known to him. But the laws of hospitality, more binding in the country than in town, obliged him to receive this visit.

Never had any one, without being at all ill-favoured in the usual accep-tation of that term, made by her exterior such a disagreeable impression upon the Count as did this Baroness. When she came in she looked him through and through with a glance of fire, and then she cast her eyes down and apologized for her coming in terms which were almost over-humble. She expressed her sorrow that his father, influenced by prejudices against her with which her enemies had impregnated his mind, had formed a mortal hatred to her, and though she was almost starving, in the depths of her pov-erty he had never given her the smallest help or support. As she had now, unexpectedly as she said, come into possession of a small sum of money she had found it possible to leave the Residenz and go to a small country town a short distance off. However, as she was engaged in this journey she had not found it possible to resist the desire to see the son of the man whom, notwithstanding his irreconcilable hatred, she had never ceased to regard with feelings of the highest esteem. The tone in which all this was spoken had the moving accents of sincerity, and the Count was all the more affected by it that, having turned his eyes away from her repulsive face, he had fixed them upon a marvellously charming and beautiful creature who was with her. The Baroness finished her speech. The Count did not seem to be aware that she had done so. He remained silent. She begged him to pardon – attributed it to her embarrassment at being where she was – her having neglected to explain that her companion was her daughter Aurelia. On this the Count found words, and blushing up to the eyes implored the Baroness, with the agitation of a young man overpowered by love, to let him atone in some degree for his father's shortcomings – the result of misunderstandings – and to favour him by paying him a long visit. In warmly enforcing this request he took her hand. But the words and the breath died away on his lips and his blood ran cold. For he felt his hand grasped as if in a vice by fingers cold and stiff as death, and the tall bony form of the Baroness, who was staring at him with eyes evidently deprived of the faculty of sight, seemed to him in its gay many-tinted attire like some bedizened corpse.

'Oh, good heavens! how unfortunate just at this moment,' Aurelia cried out, and went on to lament in a gentle heart-penetrating voice that her mother was now and then suddenly seized by a tetanic spasm, but that it generally passed off very quickly without its being necessary to take any measures with regard to it.

Hyppolitus disengaged himself with some difficulty from the Baroness, and all the glowing life of sweetest love delight came back to him as he took Aurelia's hand and pressed it warmly to his lips. Although he had almost come to man's estate it was the first time that he felt the full force of passion, so that it was impossible for him to hide what he felt, and the manner in which Aurelia received his avowal in a noble, simple, child-like delight, kindled the fairest of hopes within him. The Baroness recovered in a few minutes, and, seemingly quite unaware of what had been happening, expressed her gratitude to the Count for his invitation to pay a visit of some duration at the Castle, saying she would be but too happy to forget the injustice with which his father had treated her.

Thus the Count's household arrangements and domestic position were completely changed, and he could not but believe that some special favour of fortune had brought to him the only woman in all the world who, as a warmly beloved and deeply adored wife, was capable of bestowing upon him the highest conceivable happiness.

The Baroness's manner of conduct underwent little alteration. She continued to be silent, grave, much wrapped up in herself, and when opportunity offered, evinced a gentle disposition, and a heart disposed towards any innocent enjoyment. The Count had become accustomed to the death-like whiteness of her face, to the very remarkable network of wrinkles which covered it, and to the generally spectral appearance which she displayed; but all this he set down to the invalid condition of her health, and also, in some measure, to a disposition which she evinced to gloomy romanticism. The servants told him that she often went out for walks in the night-time, through the park to the churchyard. He was much annoyed that his father's prejudices had influenced him to the extent that they had; and the most earnest recommendations of his uncle that he should conquer the feeling which had taken possession of him, and give up a relationship which must sooner or later drive him to his ruin, had no effect upon him.

In complete certainty of Aurelia's sincere affection, he asked for her hand; and it may be imagined with what joy the Baroness received this proposal, which transferred her into the lap of luxury from a position of the deepest poverty. The pallor and the strange expression, which spoke of some invincible inward pain or trouble, had disappeared from Aurelia's face. The blissfulness of love beamed in her eyes, and shimmered in roses on her cheeks.

On the morning of the wedding-day a terrible event shattered the Count's hopes. The Baroness was found lying on her face dead, not far from the churchyard: and when the Count was looking out of his window on getting up, full of the bliss of the happiness which he had attained, her body was being brought back to the Castle. He supposed she was only in one of her usual attacks; but all efforts to bring her back to life were ineffectual. She was dead. Aurelia, instead of giving way to violent grief, seemed rather to be struck dumb and tearless by this blow, which appeared to have a paralyzing effect on her.

The Count was much distressed for her, and only ventured – most cautiously and most gently – to remind her that her orphaned condition rendered it necessary that conventionalities should be disregarded, and that the most essential matter in the circumstances was to hasten on the marriage as much as possible, notwithstanding the loss of her mother. At this Aurelia fell into the Count's arms, and, whilst a flood of tears ran down her cheeks, cried in a most eager manner, and in a voice which was shrill with urgency:

'Yes, yes! For the love of all the saints. For the sake of my soul's salvation – yes!'

The Count ascribed this burst of emotion to the bitter sense that, in her orphaned condition, she did not know whither to betake herself, seeing that she could not go on staying at the Castle. He took pains to procure a worthy matron as a companion for her, till in a few weeks, the wedding-day again came round. And this time no mischance interfered with it, and it crowned the bliss of Aurelia and Hyppolitus. But Aurelia had all this while been in a curiously strained and excited condition. It was not grief for her mother, but she seemed to be unceasingly, and without cessation, tortured by some inward anxiety. In the midst of the most delicious love-passage she would suddenly clasp the Count in her arms, pale as death, and like a person suddenly seized by some terror – just as if she were trying her very utmost to resist some extraneous power which was threatening to force her to destruction – would cry, 'Oh no – no! Never, never!' Now that she was married, however, it seemed that this strange, overstrained, excited condition in which she had been, abated and left her, and the terrible inward anxiety and disturbance under which she had been labouring seemed to disappear.

The Count could not but suspect the existence of some secret evil mystery by which Aurelia's inner being was tormented, but he very properly thought it would be unkind and unfeeling to ask her about it whilst her excitement lasted, and she herself avoided any explanation on the subject. However, a time came when he thought he might venture to hint gently, that perhaps it would be well if she indicated to him the cause of the strange condition of her mind. She herself at once said it would be a satisfaction to her to open her mind to him, her beloved husband. And great was his amazement to learn that what was at the bottom of the mystery, was the atrociously wicked life which her mother had led, that was so perturbing her mind.

'Can there be anything more terrible,' she said, 'than to have to hate, detest, and abhor one's own mother?'

Thus the prejudices (as they were called) of his father and uncle had not been unfounded, and the Baroness had deceived him in the most deliberate manner. He was obliged to confess to himself – and he made no secret of it – that it was a fortunate circumstance that the Baroness had died on the morning of his wedding-day. But Aurelia declared that as soon as her mother was dead she had been seized by dark and horrible terrors, and could not help thinking that her mother would rise from her grave, and drag her from her husband's arms into perdition.

She said she dimly remembered, one morning when she was a mere child, being awakened by a frightful commotion in the house. Doors opened and shut; strangers' voices cried out in confusion. At last, things becoming quieter, her nurse took her in her arms, and carried her into a large room where there were many people, and the man who had often played with her, and given her sweetmeats, lying stretched on a long table. This man she had always called 'Papa,' and she stretched her hands out to him, and wanted to kiss him. But his lips, always warm before, were cold as ice, and Aurelia broke into violent weeping, without knowing why. The nurse took her to a strange house, where she remained a long while, till at last a lady came and took her away in a carriage. This was her mother, who soon after took her to the Residenz.

When Aurelia got to be about sixteen, a man came to the house whom her mother welcomed joyfully, and treated with much confidentiality, receiving him with much intimacy of friendship, as being a dear old friend. He came more and more frequently, and the Baroness's style of existence was soon greatly altered for the better. Instead of living in an attic, and subsisting on the poorest of fare, and wearing the most wretched old clothes, she took a fine lodging in the most fashionable quarter, wore fine dresses, ate and drank with this stranger of the best and most expensive food and drink daily (he was her daily guest), and took her part in all the public pleasurings which the Residenz had to offer.

Aurelia was the person upon whom this bettering of her mother's circumstances (evidently attributable solely to the stranger) exercised no influence whatever. She remained shut up in her room when her mother went out to enjoy herself in the stranger's company, and was obliged to live just as miserably as before. This man, though about forty, had a very fresh and youthful appearance, a tall, handsome person, and a face by no means devoid of a certain amount of manly good looks. Notwithstanding this, he was repugnant to Aurelia on account of his style of behaviour. He seemed to try to constrain himself, to conduct himself like a gentleman and person of some cultivation, but there was constantly, and most evidently, piercing through this exterior veneer the unmistakable evidence of his really being a totally uncultured person, whose manners and habits were those of the very lowest ranks of the people. And the way in which he began to look at Aurelia filled her with terror – nay, with an abhorrence of which she could not explain the reason to herself.

Up to this point the Baroness had never taken the trouble to say a single word to Aurelia about this stranger. But now she told her his name, adding that this Baron was a man of great wealth, and a distant relation. She lauded his good looks, and his various delightful qualities, and ended by asking Aurelia if she thought she could bring herself to take a liking to him. Aurelia made no secret of the inward detestation which she felt for him. The Baroness darted a glance of lightning at her, which terrified her excessively, and told her she was a foolish, ignorant creature. After this she was kinder to her than she had ever been before. She was provided with grand dresses in the height of the fashion, and taken to share in all the public pleasures. The man now strove to gain her favour in a manner which rendered him more and more abhorrent to her. But her delicate, maidenly instincts were wounded in the most mortal manner, when an unfortunate accident rendered her an unwilling, secret witness of an abominable atrocity between her abandoned and depraved mother and him. When, a few days after this, this man, after having taken a good deal of wine, clasped Aurelia in his arms in a way which left no doubt as to his intention, her desperation gave her strength, and she pushed him from her so that he fell down on his back. She rushed away and bolted herself in her own room. The Baroness told her, very calmly and deliberately, that, inasmuch as the Baron paid all the household expenses, and she had not the slightest intention of going back to the old poverty of their previous life, this was a case in which any absurd coyness would be both ludicrous and inconvenient, and that she would really have to make up her mind to comply with the Baron's wishes, because, if not, he had threatened to part company at once. Instead of being affected by Aurelia's bitter tears and agonized entreaties, the old woman, breaking into the most brazen and shameless laughter, talked in the most depraved manner of a state of matters which would cause Aurelia to bid, for ever, farewell to every feeling of enjoyment of life in such unrestrained and detestable depravity, defying and insulting all sense of ordinary propriety, so that her shame and terror were undescribable at what she was obliged to hear. In fact she gave herself up for lost, and her only means of salvation appeared to her to be immediate flight.

She had managed to possess herself of the key of the hall door, had got together the few little necessaries which she absolutely required, and, just after midnight, was moving softly through the dimly-lighted front hall, at a time when she thought her mother was sure to be fast asleep. She was on the point of stepping quietly out into the street, when the door opened with a clang, and heavy footsteps came noisily up the steps. The Baroness came staggering and stumbling into the hall, right up to Aurelia's feet, nothing upon her but a kind of miserable wrapper all covered with dirt, her breast and her arms naked, her grey hair all hanging down and dishevelled. And close after her came the stranger, who seized her by the hair, and dragged her into the middle of the hall crying out in a yelling voice –

'Wait, you old devil, you witch of hell! I'll serve you up a wedding break-fast.' And with a good thick cudgel which he had in his hand he set to and belaboured and maltreated her in the most shameful manner. She made a terrible screaming and outcry, whilst Aurelia, scarcely knowing what she was about, screamed aloud out of the window for help.

It chanced that there was a patrol of armed police just passing. The men came at once into the house.

'Seize him!' cried the Baroness, writhing in convulsions of rage and pain. 'Seize him – hold him fast! Look at his bare back. He's –'

When the police sergeant heard the Baroness speak the name he shouted out in the greatest delight –

'Hoho! We've got you at last, Devil Alias, have we?' And in spite of his violent resistance, they marched him off.

But notwithstanding all this which had been happening, the Baroness had understood well enough what Aurelia's idea had been. She contented herself with taking her somewhat roughly by the arm, pushing her into her room, and locking her up in it, without saying a word. She went out early the next morning, and did not come back till late in the evening. And during this time Aurelia remained a prisoner in her room, never seeing nor hearing a creature, and having nothing to eat or drink. This went on for several days. The Baroness often glared at her with eyes flashing anger, and seemed to be wrestling with some decision, until, one evening, letters came which seemed to cause her satisfaction.

'Silly creature! all this is your fault. However, it seems to be all coming right now, and all I hope is that the terrible punishment which the Evil Spirit was threatening you with may not come upon you.' This was what the Baroness said to Aurelia, and then she became more kind and friendly, and Aurelia, no longer distressed by the presence of the horrible man, and having given up the idea of escaping, was allowed a little more freedom.

Some time had elapsed, when one day, as Aurelia was sitting alone in her room, she heard a great clamour approaching in the street. The maid came running in, and said that they were taking the hangman's son of — to prison, that he had been branded on the back there for robbery and murder, and had escaped, and was now retaken.

Aurelia, full of anxious presentiment, tottered to the window. Her presentiment was not fallacious. It *was* the stranger (as we have styled him), and he was being brought along, firmly bound upon a tumbril, surrounded by a strong guard. He was being taken back to undergo his sentence. Aurelia, nearly fainting, sank back into her chair, as his frightfully wild look fell upon her, while he shook his clenched fist up at the window with the most threatening gestures.

After this the Baroness was still a great deal away from the house; but she never took Aurelia with her, so that the latter led a sorrowful, miserable existence – occupied in thinking many thoughts as to destiny, and the threatening future which might unexpectedly come upon her.

From the maidservant (who had only come into the house subsequently to the nocturnal adventure which has been described, and who had probably only quite recently heard about the intimacy of the terms in which the Baroness had been living with this criminal), Aurelia learned that the folks in the Residenz were very much grieved at the Baroness's having been so deceived and imposed upon by a scoundrel of this description. But Aurelia knew only too well how differently the matter had really stood; and it seemed to her impossible that, at all events, the men of the police, who had apprehended the fellow in the Baroness's very house, should not have known all about the intimacy of the relations between them, inasmuch as she herself had told them his name, and directed their attention to the brand-marks on his back, as proofs of his identity. Moreover, this loquacious maid sometimes talked in a very ambiguous way about that which people were, here and there, thinking and saying; and, for that matter, would like very much to know better about – as to the courts having been making careful investigations, and having gone so far as to threaten the Baroness with arrest, on account of strange disclosures which the hangman's son had made concerning her.

Aurelia was obliged to admit, in her own mind, that it was another proof of her mother's depraved way of looking at things that, even after this terrible affair, she should have found it possible to go on living in the Residenz. But at last she felt herself constrained to leave the place where she knew she was the object of but too well-founded, shameful suspicion, and fly to a more distant spot. On this journey she came to the Count's Castle, and there ensued what has been related.

Aurelia could not but consider herself marvellously fortunate to have got clear of all these troubles. But how profound was her horror when, speaking to her mother in this blessed sense of the merciful intervention of Heaven in her regard, the latter, with fires of hell in her eyes, cried out in a yelling voice:

'You are my misfortune, horrible creature that you are! But in the midst of your imagined happiness vengeance will overtake you, if I should be carried away by a sudden death. In those tetanic spasms, which your birth cost me, the subtle craft of the devil – '

Here Aurelia suddenly stopped. She threw herself upon her husband's breast, and implored him to spare her the complete recital of what the Baroness had said to her in the delirium of her insanity. She said she felt her inmost heart and soul crushed to pieces at the bare idea of the frightful threatenings – far beyond the wildest imagination's concept of the terrible – uttered to her by her mother, possessed, as she was at the time, by the most diabolical powers.

The Count comforted his bride to the best of his ability, although, he felt himself permeated by the coldest and most deathly shuddering horror. Even when he had regained some calmness, he could not but confess to himself that the profound horribleness of the Baroness, even now that she was dead, cast a deep shadow over his life, sunbright as it otherwise seemed to be.

In a very short time Aurelia began to alter very perceptibly. Whilst the deathly paleness of her face, and the fatigued appearance of her eyes, seemed to point to some bodily ailment, her mental state – confused, variable, restless, as if she were constantly frightened at something – led to the conclusion that there was some fresh mystery perturbing her system. She shunned her husband. She shut herself up in her rooms, sought the most solitary walks in the park. And when she then allowed herself to be seen, her eyes, red with weeping, her contorted features, gave unmistakable evidence of some terrible suffering which she had been undergoing. It was in vain that the Count took every possible pains to discover the cause of this condition of hers, and the only thing which had any effect in bringing him out of the hopeless state into which those remarkable symptoms of his wife's had plunged him, was the deliberate opinion of a celebrated doctor, that this strangely excited condition of the Countess was nothing other than the natural result of a bodily state which indicated the happy result of a fortunate marriage. This doctor, on one occasion when he was at table with the Count and Countess, permitted himself sundry allusions to this presumed state of what the German nation calls 'good hope.' The Countess seemed to listen to all this with indifference for some time. But suddenly her attention became vividly awakened when the doctor spoke of the wonderful longings which women in that condition become possessed by, and which they cannot resist without the most injurious effects supervening upon their own health, and even upon that of the child. The Countess overwhelmed the doctor with questions, and the latter did not weary of quoting the strangest and most entertaining cases of this description from his own practice and experience.

'Moreover,' he said, 'there are cases on record in which women have been led, by these strange, abnormal longings, to commit most terrible crimes. There was a certain blacksmith's wife, who had such an irresistible longing for her husband's flesh that, one night, when he came home the worse for liquor, she set upon him with a large knife, and cut him about so frightfully that he died in a few hours' time.'

Scarcely had the doctor said these words, when the Countess fell back in her chair fainting, and was with much difficulty recovered from the succession of hysterical attacks which supervened. The doctor then saw that he had acted very thoughtlessly in alluding to such a frightful occurrence in the presence of a lady whose nervous system was in such a delicate condition.

However, this crisis seemed to have a beneficial effect upon her, for she became calmer; although, soon afterwards there came upon her a very remarkable condition of rigidity, as of benumbedness. There was a darksome fire in her eyes, and her deathlike pallor increased to such an extent, that the Count was driven into new and most tormenting doubts as to her condition. The most inexplicable thing was that she never took the smallest morsel of anything to eat, evincing the utmost repugnance at the sight of all food, particularly meat. This repugnance was so invincible that she was constantly obliged to get up and leave the table, with the most marked indications of loathing. The doctor's skill was in vain, and the Count's most urgent and affectionate entreaties were powerless to induce her to take even a single drop of medicine of any kind. And, inasmuch as weeks, nay, months, had passed without her having taken so much as a morsel of food, and it had become an unfathomable mystery how she managed to keep alive, the doctor came to the conclusion that there was something in the case which lay beyond the domain of ordinary human science. He made some pretext for leaving the Castle, but the Count saw clearly enough that this doctor, whose skilfulness was well approved, and who had a high reputation to maintain, felt that the Countess's condition was too unintelligible, and in fact, too strangely mysterious, for him to stay on there, witness of an illness impossible to be understood – as to which he felt he had no power to render assistance.

It may be readily imagined into what a state of mind all this put the Count. But there was more to come. Just at this juncture an old, privileged servant took an opportunity, when he found the Count alone, of telling him that the Countess went out every night, and did not come home till daybreak.

The Count's blood ran cold. It struck him, as a matter which he had not quite realized before, that, for a short time back, there had fallen upon him, regularly about midnight, a curiously unnatural sleepiness, which he now believed to be caused by some narcotic administered to him by the Countess, to enable her to get away unobserved. The darkest suspicions and forebodings came into his mind. He thought of the diabolical mother, and that, perhaps, *her* instincts had begun to awake in her daughter. He thought of some possibility of a conjugal infidelity. He remembered the terrible hangman's son.

It was so ordained that the very next night was to explain this terrible mystery to him – that which alone could be the key to the Countess's strange condition.

She herself used, every evening, to make the tea which the Count always took before going to bed. This evening he did not take a drop of it, and when he went to bed he had not the slightest symptom of the sleepiness which generally came upon him as it got towards midnight. However, he lay back on his pillows, and had all the appearance of being fast asleep as usual.

And then the Countess rose up very quietly, with the utmost precautions, came up to his bedside, held a lamp to his eyes, and then, convinced that he was sound asleep, went softly out of the room.

His heart throbbed fast. He got up, put on a cloak, and went after the Countess. It was a fine moonlight night, so that, though Aurelia had got a considerable start of him, he could see her distinctly going along in the distance in her white dress. She went through the park, right on to the burying-ground, and there she disappeared at the wall. The Count ran quickly after her in through the gate of the burying-ground, which he found open. There, in the bright moonlight, he saw a circle of frightful, spectral-looking creatures. Old women, half naked, were cowering down upon the ground, and in the midst of them lay the corpse of a man, which they were tearing at with wolfish appetite.

Aurelia was amongst them.

The Count took flight in the wildest horror, and ran, without any idea where he was going or what he was doing, impelled by the deadliest terror, all about the walks in the park, till he found himself at the door of his own Castle as the day was breaking, bathed in cold perspiration. Involuntarily, without the capability of taking hold of a thought, he dashed up the steps, and went bursting through the passages and into his own bedroom. There lay the Countess, to all appearance in the deepest and sweetest of sleeps. And the Count would fain have persuaded himself that some deceptive dream-image, or (inasmuch as his cloak, wet with dew, was a proof, if any had been needed, that he had really been to the burying-ground in the night) some soul-deceiving phantom had been the cause of his deathly horror. He did not wait for Aurelia's waking, but left the room, dressed, and got on to a horse. His ride, in the exquisite morning, amid sweet-scented trees and shrubs, whence the happy songs of the newly-awakened birds greeted him, drove from his memory for a time the terrible images of the night. He went back to the Castle comforted and gladdened in heart.

But when he and the Countess sat down alone together at table, and, the dishes being brought and handed, she rose to hurry away, with loathing, at the sight of the food as usual, the terrible conviction that what he had seen was true, was reality, impressed itself irresistibly on his mind. In the wildest fury he rose from his seat, crying:

'Accursed misbirth of hell! I understand your hatred of the food of mankind. You get your sustenance out of the burying-ground, damnable creature that you are!'

As soon as those words had passed his lips, the Countess flew at him, uttering a sound between a snarl and a howl, and bit him on the breast with the fury of a hyena. He dashed her from him on to the ground, raving fiercely as she was, and she gave up the ghost in the most terrible convulsions.

The Count became a maniac.

'Well,' said Lothair, after there had been a few minutes of silence amongst the friends, 'you have certainly kept your word, my incomparable Cyprianus, most thoroughly and magnificently. In comparison with this story of yours, vampirism is the merest children's tale – a funny Christmas story, to be laughed at. Oh, truly, everything in it is fearfully interesting, and so highly seasoned with asafoetida that an unnaturally excited palate, which has lost its relish for healthy, natural food, might immensely enjoy it.'

'And yet,' said Theodore, 'our friend has discreetly thrown a veil over a great many things, and has passed so rapidly over others, that his story has merely caused us a passing feeling of the eerie and shuddery – for which we are duly grateful to him. I remember very well having read this story in an old book, where everything was told with the most prolix enumeration of all the details; and the old woman's atrocities in particular were set forth in all their minutiae, truly *con amore*, so that the whole affair produced, and left behind it, a most repulsive impression, which it took a long while to get over. I was delighted when I had forgotten the horrible thing, and Cyprian ought not to have recalled it to my memory; although I must admit that he has acted in accordance with the principles of our patron saint Serapion, and caused us a sufficient thrill of horror, particularly towards the end. It made us all turn pale, particularly the narrator himself!'

WHAT WAS IT?

FITZ-JAMES O'BRIEN

This much-neglected story was first published in *Harper's New Monthly Magazine*, New York, March 1859. Michael Fitz-James O'Brien had emigrated to New York, via England, from his native Limerick, Ireland, in 1852, after an involvement in the riots which followed the great hunger. He started writing regularly for *Harper's* in 1853, and became the self-styled 'Prince of Bohemia' among New York underground authors throughout the 1850s, modelling his life on the recently published *Scènes de la Vie de Bohème*, by Henry Mürger (the basis for the opera *La Bohème*). His particular bugbear was 'the puritanism of the critics'. At the outbreak of the American Civil War he enlisted for the 7th Regiment of the National Guard of New York and, after a short spell as recruiting officer for the McClellan Rifles (during which he was said to have nearly been court-martialled for shooting a member of his own regiment), he was appointed aide de camp to General Lander in West Virginia. During a skirmish with Confederate scavengers (February 1862), O'Brien was shot in the shoulder; just over a month later, he died of lockjaw. In one of his last letters, written when he had just been told he was dying, O'Brien comforted himself with the thought, 'Great Jupiter! I believe in spooks.'

Most of Fitz-James O'Brien's literary output (poems and short stories for *Harper's* and *Putnam's*) was published in the late 1850s. In his best tales of terror, O'Brien (calling himself 'Harry Escott') writes in a matter-of-fact style, full of circumstantial details about the world of the author, which gives all the more impact to the uncanny experiences which ensue – a 'domestic' version of Edgar Allan Poe. *What Was It?*, arguably his masterpiece, is an impressive example of the Invisible Force story (de Maupassant was later to use the idea as the basis for *The Horla*) and represents a literary version of Fuseli's painting *The Nightmare* (the victims being male, this time). What was it? The answer lies in the title of this book.

IT IS, I CONFESS, WITH CONSIDERABLE diffidence that I approach the strange narrative which I am about to relate. The events which I purpose detailing are of so extraordinary a character that I am quite prepared to meet with an unusual amount of incredulity and scorn. I accept all such beforehand. I have, I trust, the literary courage to face unbelief. I have, after mature consideration, resolved to narrate, in as simple and straight-forward a manner as I can compass, some facts that passed under my observation, in the month of July last, and which, in the annals of the mysteries of physical science, are wholly unparalleled.

I live at No. – Twenty-sixth Street, in New York. The house is in some respects a curious one. It has enjoyed for the last two years the reputation of being haunted. It is a large and stately residence, surrounded by what was once a garden, but which is now only a green enclosure used for bleaching clothes. The dry basin of what has been a fountain, and a few fruit trees ragged and unpruned, indicate that this spot in past days was a pleasant, shady retreat, filled with fruits and flowers and the sweet murmur of waters.

The house is very spacious. A hall of noble size leads to a large spiral staircase winding through its centre, while the various apartments are of imposing dimensions. It was built some fifteen or twenty years since by Mr. A –, the well-known New York merchant, who five years ago threw the commercial world into convulsions by a stupendous bank fraud. Mr. A –, as everyone knows, escaped to Europe, and died not long after, of a broken heart. Almost immediately after the news of his decease reached this country and was verified, the report spread in Twenty-sixth Street that No. – was haunted. Legal measures had dispossessed the widow of its former owner, and it was inhabited merely by a caretaker and his wife, placed there by the house agent into whose hands it had passed for purposes of renting or sale. These people declared that they were troubled with unnatural noises. Doors were opened without any visible agency. The remnants of furniture scattered through the various rooms were, during the night, piled one upon the other by unknown hands. Invisible feet passed up and down the stairs in broad daylight, accompanied by the rustle of unseen silk dresses, and the gliding of viewless hands along the massive balusters. The caretaker and his wife declared they would live there no longer. The house agent laughed, dismissed them, and put others in their place. The noises and supernatural manifestations continued. The neighbourhood caught up the story, and the house remained untenanted for three years. Several persons negotiated for it; but, somehow, always before the bargain was closed they heard the unpleasant rumours and declined to treat any further.

It was in this state of things that my landlady, who at the time kept a boarding-house in Bleecker Street, and who wished to move farther up town, conceived the bold idea of renting No. – Twenty-sixth Street. Happening to have in her house rather a plucky and philosophical set of boarders, she laid her scheme before us, stating candidly everything she had heard respecting the ghostly qualities of the establishment to which she wished to remove us. With the exception of two timid persons – a sea-captain and a returned Californian, who immediately gave notice that they would leave – all of Mrs Moffat's guests declared that they would accompany her in her chivalric incursion into the abode of spirits.

Our removal was effected in the month of May, and we were charmed with our new residence. The portion of Twenty-sixth Street where our house is situated, between Seventh and Eighth Avenues, is one of the pleasantest localities in New York. The gardens back of the houses, running down nearly to the Hudson, form, in the summer time, a perfect avenue of verdure. The air is pure and invigorating, sweeping, as it does, straight across the river from the Weehawken heights, and even the ragged garden which surrounded the house, although displaying on washing days rather too much clothes-line, still gave us a piece of greensward to look at, and a cool retreat in the summer evenings, where we smoked our cigars in the dusk, and watched the fireflies flashing their dark lanterns in the long grass.

Of course we had no sooner established ourselves at No. – than we began to expect the ghosts. We absolutely awaited their advent with eagerness. Our dinner conversation was supernatural. One of the boarders, who had purchased Mrs Crowe's *Night Side of Nature* for his own private delectation, was regarded as a public enemy by the entire household for not having bought twenty copies. The man led a life of supreme wretchedness while he was reading this volume. A system of espionage was established, of which he was the victim. If he incautiously laid the book down for an instant and left the room, it was immediately seized and read aloud in secret places to a select few. I found myself a person of immense importance, it having leaked out that I was tolerably well versed in the history of supernaturalism, and had once written a story the foundation of which was a ghost. If a table or a wainscot panel happened to warp when we were assembled in the large drawing-room, there was an instant silence, and everyone was prepared for an immediate clanking of chains and a spectral form.

After a month of psychological excitement, it was with the utmost dissatisfaction that we were forced to acknowledge that nothing in the remotest degree approaching the supernatural had manifested itself. Once the black butler asseverated that his candle had been blown out by some invisible agency while he was undressing himself for the night; but as I had more than once discovered this coloured gentleman in a condition when one candle must have appeared to him like two, I thought it possible that, by going a step farther in his potations, he might have reversed this phenomenon, and seen no candle at all where he ought to have beheld one.

Things were in this state when an incident took place so awful and inexplicable in its character that my reason fairly reels at the bare memory of the occurrence. It was the tenth of July. After dinner was over I repaired, with my friend Dr. Hammond, to the garden to smoke my evening pipe. Independent of certain mental sympathies which existed between the Doctor and myself, we were linked together by a vice. We both smoked opium. We knew each other's secret, and respected it. We enjoyed together that wonderful expansion of thought, that marvellous intensifying of the perceptive faculties, that boundless feeling of existence when we seem to have points of contact with the whole universe – in short, that unimaginable spiritual bliss, which I would not surrender for a throne, and which I hope you, reader, will never – never taste.

Those hours of opium happiness which the Doctor and I spent together in secret were regulated with a scientific accuracy. We did not blindly smoke the drug of paradise, and leave our dreams to chance. While smoking, we carefully steered our conversation through the brightest and calmest channels of thought. We talked of the East, and endeavoured to recall the magical panorama of its glowing scenery. We criticized the most sensuous poets – those who painted life ruddy with health, brimming with passion, happy in the possession of youth and strength and beauty. If we talked of Shakespeare's 'Tempest', we lingered over Ariel, and avoided Caliban. Like the Guebers, we turned our faces to the east, and saw only the sunny side of the world.

The skilful colouring of our train of thought produced in our subsequent visions a corresponding tone. The splendours of Arabian fairyland dyed our dreams. We paced that narrow strip of grass with the tread and port of kings. The song of the *rana arborea*, while he clung to the bark of the ragged plum tree, sounded like the strains of divine musicians. Houses, walls, and streets melted like rain clouds, and vistas of unimaginable glory stretched away before us. It was a rapturous companionship. We enjoyed the vast delight more perfectly because, even in our most ecstatic moments, we were conscious of each other's presence. Our pleasures, while individual, were still twin, vibrating and moving in musical accord.

On the evening in question the tenth of July, the Doctor and myself drifted into an unusually metaphysical mood. We lit our large meerschaums, filled with fine Turkish tobacco, in the core of which burned a little black nut of opium, that, like the nut in the fairy tale, held within its narrow limits wonders beyond the reach of kings; we paced to and fro, conversing. A strange perversity dominated the currents of our thought. They would *not* flow through the sun-lit channels into which we strove to divert them. For some unaccountable reason, they constantly diverged into dark and lonesome beds, where a continual gloom brooded. It was in vain that, after our old fashion, we flung ourselves on the shores of the East, and talked of its gay bazaars, of the splendours of the time of Haroun, of harems and golden palaces. Black afreets continually arose from the depths of our talk, and expanded, like the one the fisherman released from the copper vessel, until they blotted everything bright from our vision. Insensibly, we yielded to the occult force that swayed us, and indulged in gloomy speculation. We had talked some time upon the proneness of the human mind to mysticism, and the almost universal love of the terrible, when Hammond suddenly said to me, 'What do you consider to be the greatest element of terror?'

The question puzzled me. That many things were terrible, I knew. Stumbling over a corpse in the dark; beholding as I once did, a woman floating down a deep and rapid river, with wildly lifted arms, and awful, upturned face, uttering, as she drifted, shrieks that rent one's heart, while we, the spectators, stood frozen at a window which overhung the river at a height of sixty feet, unable to make the slightest effort to save her, but dumbly watching her last supreme agony and her disappearance. A shattered wreck, with no life visible, encountered floating listlessly on the ocean, is a terrible object, for it suggests a huge terror, the proportions of which are veiled. But it now struck me, for the first time, that there must be one great and ruling embodiment of fear – a King of Terrors, to which all others must succumb. What might it be? To what train of circumstances would it owe its existence?

'I confess, Hammond,' I replied to my friend, 'I never considered the subject before. That there must be one Something more terrible than any other thing, I feel. I cannot attempt, however, even the most vague definition.'

'I am somewhat like you, Harry,' he answered. 'I feel my capacity to experience a terror greater than anything yet conceived by the human mind – something combining in fearful and unnatural amalgamation hitherto supposed incompatible elements. The calling of the voices in Brockden Brown's novel of *Wieland* is awful; so is the picture of the Dweller of the Threshold, in Bulwer's *Zanoni*; but,' he added, shaking his head gloomily, 'there is something more horrible still than these.'

'Look here, Hammond,' I rejoined, 'let us drop this kind of talk, for heaven's sake! We shall suffer for it, depend on it.'

'I don't know what's the matter with me to-night,' he replied, 'but my brain is running upon all sorts of weird and awful thoughts. I feel as if I could write a story like Hoffmann, to-night, if I were only master of a literary style.'

'Well, if we are going to be Hoffmannesque in our talk, I'm off to bed. Opium and nightmares should never be brought together. How sultry it is! Good-night, Hammond.'

'Good-night, Harry. Pleasant dreams to you.'

'To you, gloomy wretch, afreets, ghouls, and enchanters.'

We parted, and each sought his respective chamber. I undressed quickly and got into bed, taking with me, according to my usual custom, a book, over which I generally read myself to sleep. I opened the volume as soon as I had laid my head upon the pillow, and instantly flung it to the other side of the room. It was Goudon's *History of Monsters*, a curious French work, which I had lately imported from Paris, but which, in the state of mind I had then reached, was anything but an agreeable companion. I resolved to go to sleep at once; so, turning down my gas until nothing but a little blue point of light glimmered on the top of the tube, I composed myself to rest.

The room was in total darkness. The atom of gas that still remained alight did not illuminate a distance of three inches round the burner. I desperately drew my arm across my eyes, as if to shut out even the darkness, and tried to think of nothing. It was in vain. The confounded themes touched on by Hammond in the garden kept obtruding themselves on my brain. I battled against them. I erected ramparts of would-be blankness of intellect to keep them out. They still crowded upon me. While I was lying still as a corpse, hoping that by a perfect physical inaction I should hasten mental repose, an awful incident occurred. A Something dropped, as it seemed, from the ceiling, plump upon my chest, and the next instant I felt two bony hands encircling my throat, endeavouring to choke me.

I am no coward, and am possessed of considerable strength. The suddenness of the attack, instead of stunning me, strung every nerve to its highest tension. My body acted from instinct, before my brain had time to realize the terrors of my position. In an instant I wound two muscular arms around the creature, and squeezed it, with all the strength of despair, against my chest. In a few seconds the bony hands that had fastened on my throat loosened their hold, and I was free to breath once more. Then commenced a struggle of awful intensity. Immersed in the most profound darkness, totally ignorant of the nature of the Thing by which I was so suddenly attacked, finding my grasp slipping every moment, by reason, it seemed to me, of the entire nakedness of my assailant, bitten with sharp teeth in the shoulder, neck and chest, having every moment to protect my throat against a pair of sinewy, agile hands, which my utmost efforts could not confine – these were a combination of circumstances to combat which required all the strength, skill, and courage that I possessed.

At last, after a silent, deadly, exhausting struggle, I got my assailant under by a series of incredible efforts of strength. Once pinned, with my knee on what I made out to be its chest, I knew that I was victor. I rested for a moment to breathe. I heard the creature beneath me panting in the darkness, and felt the violent throbbing of a heart. It was apparently as exhausted as I was; that was one comfort. At this moment I remembered that I usually placed under my pillow, before going to bed, a large yellow silk pocket handkerchief. I felt for it instantly; it was there. In a few seconds more I had, after a fashion, pinioned the creature's arms.

I now felt tolerably secure. There was nothing more to be done but to turn on the gas, and, having first seen what my midnight assailant was like, arouse the household. I will confess to be actuated by a certain pride in not giving the alarm before; I wished to make the capture alone and unaided.

Never losing my hold for an instant, I slipped from the bed to the floor, dragging my captive with me. I had but a few steps to make to reach the gas burner; these I made with the greatest caution, holding the creature in a grip like a vice. At last I got within arm's length of the tiny speck of blue light which told me where the gas burner lay. Quick as lightning I released my grasp with one hand and let on the full flood of light. Then I turned to look at my captive.

I cannot even attempt to give any definition of my sensations the instant after I turned on the gas. I suppose I must have shrieked with terror, for in less than a minute afterwards my room was crowded with the inmates of the house. I shudder now as I think of that awful moment. *I saw nothing!* Yes; I had one arm firmly clasped round a breathing, panting, corporeal shape, my other hand gripped with all its strength a throat as warm, and apparently fleshly, as my own; and yet, with this living substance in my grasp, with its body pressed against my own, and all in the bright glare of a large jet of gas, I absolutely beheld nothing! Not even an outline – a vapour!

I do not, even at this hour, realize the situation in which I found myself. I cannot recall the astounding incident thoroughly. Imagination in vain tries to compass the awful paradox.

It breathed. I felt its warm breath upon my cheek. It struggled fiercely. It had hands. They clutched me. Its skin was smooth, like my own. There it lay, pressed close up against me, solid as stone – and yet utterly invisible!

I wonder that I did not faint or go mad on the instant. Some wonderful instinct must have sustained me; for, absolutely, in place of loosening my hold on the terrible Enigma, I seemed to gain an additional strength in my moment of horror, and tightened my grasp with such wonderful force that I felt the creature shivering with agony.

Just then Hammond entered my room at the head of the household. As soon as he beheld my face – which, I suppose, must have been an awful sight to look at – he hastened forward, crying, 'Great heaven, Harry! what has happened?'

'Hammond! Hammond!' I cried, 'come here. Oh, this is awful! I have been attacked in bed by something or other, which I have hold of; but I can't see it – I can't see it!'

Hammond, doubtless struck by the unfeigned horror expressed in my countenance, made one or two steps forward with an anxious yet puzzled expression. A very audible titter burst from the remainder of my visitors. This suppressed laughter made me furious. To laugh at a human being in my position! It was the worst species of cruelty. *Now*, I can understand why the appearance of a man struggling violently, as it would seem, with an airy nothing, and calling for assistance against a vision, should have appeared ludicrous. *Then*, so great was my rage against the mocking crowd that had I the power I would have stricken them dead where they stood.

'Hammond! Hammond!' I cried again despairingly, 'for God's sake come to me. I can hold the – the Thing but a short while longer. It is overpowering me. Help me! Help me!'

'Harry,' whispered Hammond, approaching me, 'you have been smoking too much opium.'

'I swear to you, Hammond, that this is no vision,' I answered, in the same low tone. 'Don't you see how it shakes my whole frame with its struggles? If you don't believe me, convince yourself. Feel it – touch it.'

Hammond advanced and laid his hand in the spot I indicated. A wild cry of horror burst from him. He had felt it!

In a moment he had discovered somewhere in my room a long piece of cord, and was the next instant winding it and knotting it about the body of the unseen being that I clasped in my arms.

'Harry,' he said, in a hoarse, agitated voice, for, though he preserved his presence of mind, he was deeply moved, 'Harry, it's all safe now. You may let go, old fellow, if you're tired. The Thing can't move.'

I was utterly exhausted, and I gladly loosed my hold.

Hammond stood holding the ends of the cord that bound the Invisible, twisted round his hand, while before him, self-supporting as it were, he beheld a rope laced and interlaced, and stretching tightly around a vacant space. I never saw a man look so thoroughly stricken with awe. Nevertheless his face expressed all the courage and determination which I knew him to possess. His lips, although white, were set firmly, and one could perceive at a glance that, although stricken with fear he was not daunted.

The confusion that ensued among the guests of the house who were witnesses of this extraordinary scene between Hammond and myself – who beheld the pantomime of binding this struggling Something – who beheld me almost sinking from physical exhaustion when my task of jailer was over – the confusion and terror that took possession of the bystanders, when they saw all this, was beyond description. The weaker ones fled from the apartment. The few who remained clustered near the door and could not be induced to approach Hammond and his Charge. Still incredulity broke out through their terror. They had not the courage to satisfy themselves, and yet they doubted. It was in vain that I begged of some of the men to come near and convince themselves by touch of the existence in that room of a living being which was invisible. They were incredulous, but did not dare to undeceive themselves. How could a solid, living, breathing body be invisible, they asked. My reply was this. I gave a sign to Hammond, and both of us – conquering our fearful repugnance to touch the invisible creature – lifted it from the ground, manacled as it was, and took it to my bed. Its weight was about that of a boy of fourteen.

'Now, my friends,' I said, as Hammond and myself held the creature suspended over the bed, 'I can give you self-evident proof that here is a solid, ponderable body, which, nevertheless, you cannot see. Be good enough to watch the surface of the bed attentively.'

I was astonished at my own courage in treating this strange event so calmly; but I had recovered from my first terror, and felt a sort of scientific pride in the affair, which dominated every other feeling.

The eyes of the bystanders were immediately fixed on my bed. At a given signal Hammond and I let the creature fall. There was the dull sound of a heavy body alighting on a soft mass. The timbers of the bed creaked. A deep impression marked itself distinctly on the pillow, and on the bed itself. The crowd who witnessed this gave a low cry, and rushed from the room. Hammond and I were left alone with our Mystery.

We remained silent for some time, listening to the low, irregular breathing of the creature on the bed, and watching the rustle of the bedclothes as it impotently struggled to free itself from confinement. Then Hammond spoke.

'Harry, this is awful.'

'Ay, awful.'

'But not unaccountable.'

'Not unaccountable! What do you mean? Such a thing has never occurred since the birth of the world. I know not what to think, Hammond. God grant that I am not mad, and that this is not an insane fantasy!'

'Let us reason a little, Harry. Here is a solid body which we touch, but which we cannot see. The fact is so unusual that it strikes us with terror. Is there no parallel, though, for such a phenomenon? Take a piece of pure glass. It is tangible and transparent. A certain chemical coarseness is all that prevents its being so entirely transparent as to be totally invisible. It is not *theoretically impossible*, mind you, to make a glass which shall not reflect a single ray of light – a glass so pure and homogeneous in its atoms that the rays from the sun will pass through it as they do through the air, refracted but not reflected. We do not see the air, and yet we feel it.'

'That's all very well, Hammond, but these are inanimate substances. Glass does not breathe, air does not breathe. *This* thing has a heart that palpitates – a will that moves it – lungs that play and inspire and respire.'

'You forget the phenomena of which we have so often heard of late,' answered the Doctor, gravely. 'At the meetings called "spirit circles," invisible hands have been thrust into the hands of those persons round the table – warm, fleshy hands that seemed to pulsate with mortal life.'

'What? Do you think, then, that this thing is – '

'I don't know what it is,' was the solemn reply; 'but please the gods I will, with your assistance, thoroughly investigate it.'

We watched together, smoking many pipes, all night long, by the bedside of the unearthly being that tossed and panted until it was apparently wearied out. Then we learned by the low, regular breathing that it slept.

The next morning the house was all astir. The boarders congregated on the landing outside my room, and Hammond and myself were lions. We had to answer a thousand questions as to the state of our extraordinary prisoner, for as yet no one person in the house except ourselves could be induced to set foot in the apartment.

The creature was awake. This was evidenced by the convulsive manner in which the bedclothes were moved in its efforts to escape. There was something truly terrible in beholding, as it were, those second-hand indications of the terrible writhings and agonized struggles for liberty which themselves were invisible.

Hammond and myself had racked our brains during the long night to discover some means by which we might realize the shape and general appearance of the Enigma. As well as we could make out by passing our hands over the creature's form, its outlines and lineaments were human. There was a mouth; a round, smooth head without hair; a nose, which, however, was little elevated above the cheeks; and its hands and feet felt like those of a boy. At first we thought of placing the being on a smooth surface and tracing its outline with chalk, as shoemakers trace the outline of the foot. This plan was given up as being of no value. Such an outline would give not the slightest idea of its conformation.

A happy thought struck me. We would take a cast of it in plaster of Paris. This would give us the solid figure, and satisfy all our wishes. But how to do it? The movements of the creature would disturb the setting of the plastic covering, and distort the mould. Another thought. Why not give it chloroform? It had respiratory organs – that was evident by its breathing. Once reduced to a state of insensibility, we could do with it what we would. Doctor X – was sent for; and after the worthy physician had recovered from the first shock of amazement, he proceeded to administer the chloroform. In three minutes afterwards we were enabled to remove the fetters from the creature's body, and a modeller was busily engaged in covering the invisible form with the moist clay. In five minutes more we had a mould, and before evening a rough facsimile of the Mystery. It was shaped like a man – distorted, uncouth, and horrible, but still a man. It was small, not over four feet and some inches in height, and its limbs revealed a muscular development that was unparalleled. Its face surpassed in hideousness anything I had even seen. Gustave Doré, or Callot, or Tony Johannot never conceived anything so horrible. There is a face in one of the latter's illustrations to *Un Voyage où il vous plaira*, which somewhat approaches the countenance of this creature, but does not equal it. It was the physiognomy of what I should fancy a ghoul might be. It looked as if it was capable of feeding on human flesh.

Having satisfied our curiosity, and bound everyone in the house to secrecy, it became a question what was to be done with our Enigma? It was impossible that we should keep such a horror in our house; it was equally impossible that such an awful being should be let loose upon the world. I confess that I would have gladly voted for the creature's destruction. But who would shoulder the responsibility? Who would undertake the execution of this horrible semblance of a human being? Day after day this question was deliberated gravely. The boarders all left the house, Mrs Moffatt was in despair, and threatened Hammond and myself with all sorts of legal penalties if we did not remove the Horror. Our answer was, 'We will go if you like, but we decline taking this creature with us. Remove it yourself if you please. It appeared in your house. On you the responsibility rests.' To this there was, of course, no answer. Mrs Moffatt could not obtain for love or money a person who would even approach the Mystery.

The most singular part of the affair was that we were entirely ignorant of what the creature habitually fed on. Everything in the way of nutriment that we could think of was placed before it, but was never touched. It was awful to stand by, day after day, and see the clothes toss, and hear the hard breathing, and know that it was starving.

Ten, twelve days, a fortnight passed, and it still lived. The pulsations of the heart, however, were daily growing fainter, and had now nearly ceased. It was evident that the creature was dying for want of sustenance. While this terrible life struggle was going on, I felt miserable. I could not sleep. Horrible as the creature was, it was pitiful to think of the pangs it was suffering.

At last it died. Hammond and I found it cold and stiff one morning in the bed. The heart had ceased to beat, the lungs to inspire. We hastened to bury it in the garden. It was a strange funeral, the dropping of that viewless corpse into the damp hole. The cast of its form I gave to Doctor X –, who keeps it in his museum in Tenth Street.

As I am on the eve of a long journey from which I may not return, I have drawn up this narrative of an event the most singular that has ever come to my knowledge.

4 A CREATURE OF FOLKLORE

'Will your ladyships be pleased to buy an amulet against the vampire, which is going like the wolf, I hear, through these woods,' said the mountebank, dropping his hat on the pavement. 'They are dying of it right and left, and here is a charm that never fails; only pinned to the pillow, and you may laugh in his face.'

These charms consisted of oblong strips of vellum, with cabalistic ciphers and diagrams upon them. Carmilla instantly purchased one, and so did I.

He was looking up, and we were smiling down upon him, amused; at least, I can answer for myself. His piercing black eye, as he looked up in our faces, seemed to detect something that fixed for a moment his curiosity . . .

from *Carmilla*, by Sheridan Le Fanu (1872)

THE FAMILY OF THE VOURDALAK

ALEXIS TOLSTOY

Count Alexis Tolstoy, an elder cousin of Count Leo Tolstoy, wrote this story (in French) under the pen-name Krasnorogsky – taken from the name of the Tolstoy family estate Krassny Rog. At the time he wrote it, his favourite reading matter was Gothic horror stories (an unfashionable genre among Russian literati) and the Saint Petersburg journals were sarcastic about what they considered to be his dilettante interest in such things, attributing his work to 'over-indulgence in opium'; but other reviewers were later to see much more in Tolstoy's folkloric tales, and to think that they represented 'an amazingly complex, fantastic design on a canvas of commonplace reality'. This, in essence, was Tolstoy's contribution to the genre: under the influence of *La Guzla* by Prosper Mérimée which masqueraded as a genuine collection of Illyrian folktales, and with a serious interest in the ballads and folktales which had survived in Russia, Tolstoy succeeded in fusing the sexual allegory of vampirism (represented in the story by Sdenka's transformation) with the folklore of peasants who have more 'commonplace' concerns.

The Family of the Vourdalak (part of a cycle of prose works he wrote in the late 1830s and early 1840s) was not published in Russia until 1884 (largely it seems because most of the Saint Petersburg journals had been so dismissive about his earlier attempts in the same genre). As a defender of writers such as Turgenev and Chernyshevsky who had fallen foul of the secret police, Tolstoy was well known in Court circles for his uncompromising views about the role of the artist in society ('I was born not to serve but to sing'), and Tsar Alexander II was later prompted to complain about his behaviour: 'You literary people; one cannot rely on any of you.' There are hints (no more than that) of Tolstoy's political views in this story, although it eventually passed the censors without any trouble; in particular, his association between folklore and nationalism (as against the 'Europeanization' of the superpowers), in the context of Europe after the Congress of Vienna, shows him to have been against the 'Westernizing' party in Russia. Eventually, disillusioned with the Court ('Our entire bureaucracy and government is anathema to art, and that includes the construction of streets and buildings as well as the making of poems'), Tolstoy was granted permission to return to his estates – like Count Leo Tolstoy, he resented 'service' in the capital, when he could be running his estate in the country, and setting up schools for the recently emancipated serfs. He died, bankrupt, in 1875, after taking an overdose of morphine.

The Family of the Vourdalak remains one of the most impressive vampire stories ever written. An atmosphere of primitive terror is sustained from beginning to end, the sexual theme is introduced with a fine sense of construction, and the ending is all the more terrifying because it reads like the last verse of a bizarre peasant ballad. I have translated it from the original French version.

VIENNA. 1815. While the Congress had been in session, the city had attracted all the most distinguished European intellectuals, the fashion leaders of the day, and, of course, members of the highest diplomatic élite. But the Congress of Vienna was no longer in session.

Royalist émigrés were preparing to return to their country châteaux (hoping to stay there this time); Russian soldiers were anxiously awaiting the time when they could return to their abandoned homes; and discontented Poles – still dreaming of liberty – were wondering whether their dreams would come true, back in Cracow, under the protection of the precarious 'independence' that had been arranged for them by the trio of Prince Metternich, Prince Hardenberg and Count Nesselrode.

It was as if a masked ball were coming to an end. Of the assembled 'guests', only a select few had stayed behind and delayed packing their bags in the hope of still finding some amusement, preferably in the company of the charming and glamorous Austrian ladies.

This delightful group of people (of which I was a member) met twice a week in a château belonging to Madame the dowager Princess of Schwarzenberg.

It was a few miles from the city centre, just beyond a little hamlet called Hitzing. The splendid hospitality of our hostess, as well as her amiability and intellectual brilliance, made any stay at her château extremely agreeable.

Our mornings were spent *á la promenade*; we lunched all together either at the château or somewhere in the grounds; and in the evenings, seated around a welcoming fireside, we amused ourselves by gossiping and telling each other stories. A rule of the house was that we should not talk about anything to do with politics. Everyone had had enough of *that* subject. So our tales were based either on legends from our own countries or else on our own experiences.

One evening, when each of us had told a tale and when our spirits were in that tense state which darkness and silence usually create, the Marquis d'Urfé, an elderly émigré we all loved dearly for his childish gaiety and for the piquant way in which he reminisced about his past life and good fortunes, broke the ominous silence by saying, 'Your stories, gentlemen, are all out of the ordinary, of course, but it seems to me that each one lacks an essential ingredient – I mean *authenticity*; for I am pretty sure that none of you has seen with his own eyes the fantastic incidents that he has just narrated, nor can he vouch for the truth of his story on his word of honour as a gentleman.'

We all had to agree with this, so the elderly gentleman continued, after smoothing down his jabot: 'As for me, gentlemen, I know only one story of this kind, but it is at once so strange, so horrible and so *authentic* that it will suffice to strike even the most jaded of imaginations with terror. Having unhappily been both a witness to these strange events and a participant in them, I do not, as a rule, like to remind myself of them – but just this once I will tell the tale, provided, of course, the ladies present will permit me.'

Everyone agreed instantly. I must admit that a few of us glanced furtively at the long shadows which the moonlight was beginning to sketch out on the parquet floor. But soon our little circle huddled closer together and each of us kept silent to hear the Marquis's story. M. d'Urfé took a pinch of snuff, slowly inhaled it and began as follows:

Before I start, mesdames (said d'Urfé), I ask you to forgive me if, in the course of my story, I should find occasion to talk of my *affaires de coeur* more often than might be deemed appropriate for a man of my advanced years. But I assure that they must be mentioned if you are to make full sense of my story. In any case, one can forgive an elderly man for certain lapses of this kind – surrounded as I am by such attractive young ladies, it is no fault of mine that I am tempted to imagine myself a young man again. So, without further apology, I will commence by telling you that in the year 1759 I was madly in love with the beautiful Duchesse de Gramont. This passion, which I then believed was deep and lasting, gave me no respite either by day or by night, and the Duchesse, as young girls often do, enjoyed adding to my torment by her *coquetterie*. So much so that in a moment of spite I determined to solicit and be granted a diplomatic mission to the hospodar of Moldavia, who was then involved in negotiations with Versailles over matters that it would be as tedious as it would be pointless to tell you about.

The day before my departure I called in on the Duchesse. She received me with less mockery than usual and could not hide her emotions as she said, 'D'Urfé, you are behaving like a madman, but I know you well enough to be sure that you will never go back on a decision, once taken. So I will only ask one thing of you. Accept this little cross as a token of my affection and wear it until you return. It is a family relic which we treasure a great deal.'

With *galanterie* that was perhaps misplaced at such a moment I kissed not the relic but the delightful hand which proffered it to me, and I fastened the cross around my neck – you can see it now. Since then, I have never been parted from it.

I will not bore you, mesdames, with the details of my journey nor with the observations that I made on the Hungarians and the Serbians, those poor and ignorant people who, enslaved as they were by the Turks, were brave and honest enough not to have forgotten either their dignity or their time-honoured independence. It's enough for me to tell you that having learned to speak a little Polish during my stay in Warsaw, I soon had a working knowledge of Serbian as well – for these two languages, like Russian and Bohemian, are, as you no doubt know very well, only branches of one and the same root, which is known as Slovonian.

Anyway, I knew enough to make myself understood. One day I arrived in a small village. The name would not interest you very much. I found those who lived in the house where I intended to stay in a state of confusion, which seemed to me all the more strange because it was a Sunday, a day when the Serbian people customarily devote themselves to different pleasures, such as dancing, arquebus shooting, wrestling and so on. I attributed the confusion of my hosts to some very recent misfortune and was about to withdraw when a man of about thirty, tall and impressive to look at, came up to me and shook me by the hand.

'Come in, come in, stranger,' he said. 'Don't let yourself be put off by our sadness; you will understand it well enough when you know the cause.'

He then told me about how his old father (whose name was Gorcha), a man of wild and unmanageable temperament, had got up one morning and had taken down his long Turkish arquebus from a rack on a wall.

'My children,' he had said to his two sons, Georges and Pierre, 'I am going to the mountains to join a band of brave fellows who are hunting that dog Ali Bek.' (That was the name of a Turkish brigand who had been ravaging the countryside for some time.) 'Wait for me patiently for ten days and if I do not return on the tenth, arrange for a funeral mass to be said – for by then I will have been killed. But,' old Gorcha had added, looking very serious indeed, 'if, may God protect you, I should return after the ten days have passed, do not under any circumstances let me come in. I command you, if this should happen, to forget that I was once your father and to pierce me through the heart with an aspen stake, whatever I might say or do, for then I would no longer be human. I would be a cursed *vourdalak*, come to suck your blood.'

It is important at this stage to tell you, mesdames, that the *vourdalaks* (the name given to vampires by Slavic peoples) are, according to local folklore, dead bodies who rise from their graves to suck the blood of the living. In this respect they behave like all types of vampire, but they have one other characteristic which makes them even more terrifying. The *vourdalaks*, mesdames, prefer to suck the blood of their closest relatives and their most intimate friends; once dead, the victims become vampires themselves. People have claimed that entire villages in Bosnia and Hungary have been transformed into *vourdalaks* in this way. The Abbé Augustin Calmet in his strange book on apparitions cites many horrible examples.

Apparently, commissions have been appointed many times by German emperors to study alleged epidemics of vampirism. These commissions collected many eyewitness accounts. They exhumed bodies, which they found to be sated with blood, and ordered them to be burned in the public square after staking them through the heart. Magistrates who witnessed these executions have stated on oath that they heard blood-curdling shrieks coming from these corpses at the moment the executioner hammered his sharpened stake into their hearts. They have formal depositions to this effect and have corroborated them with signatures and with oaths on the Holy Book.

With this information as background, it should be easier for you to understand, mesdames, the effect that old Gorcha's words had on his sons. Both of them went down on their bended knees and begged him to let them go in his place. But instead of replying, he had turned his back on them and had set out for the mountains, singing the refrain of an old ballad. The day I arrived in the village was the very day that Gorcha had fixed for his return, so I had no difficulty understanding why his children were so anxious.

This was a good and honest family. Georges, the older of the two sons, was rugged and weatherbeaten. He seemed to me a serious and decisive man. He was married with two children. His brother Pierre, a handsome youth of about eighteen, looked rather less tough and appeared to be the favourite of a younger sister called Sdenka, who was a genuine Slavic beauty. In addition to the striking beauty of her features, a distant resemblance to the Duchesse de Gramont struck me especially. She had a distinctive line on her forehead which in all my experience I have found only on these two people. This line did not seem particularly attractive at first glance, but became irresistible when you had seen it a few times.

Perhaps I was still very naïve. Perhaps this resemblance, combined with a lively and charmingly simple disposition, was really irresistible. I do not know. But I had not been talking with Sdenka for more than two minutes when I already felt for her an affection so tender that it threatened to become something deeper still if I stayed in the village much longer.

We were all sitting together in front of the house, around a table laden with cheeses and dishes of milk. Sdenka was sewing; her sister-in-law was preparing supper for her children, who were playing in the sand; Pierre, who was doing his best to appear at ease, was whistling as he cleaned a yagatan, or long Turkish knife. Georges was leaning on the table with his head in his hands and looking for signs of movement on the great highway. He was silent.

For my part, I was profoundly affected by the general atmosphere of sadness and, in a fit of melancholy, looked up at the evening clouds which shrouded the dying sun and at the silhouette of a monastery, which was half hidden from my view by a black pine forest.

This monastery, as I subsequently discovered, had been very famous in former times on account of a miraculous icon of the Virgin Mary which, according to legend, had been carried away by the angels and set down on an old oak tree. But at the beginning of the previous century the Turks had invaded this part of the country; they had butchered the monks and pillaged the monastery. Only the walls and a small chapel had survived; an old hermit continued to say Mass there. This hermit showed travellers around the ruins and gave hospitality to pilgrims who, as they walked from one place of devotion to another, liked to rest a while at the Monastery of Our Lady of the Oak. As I have said, I didn't learn all this until much later, for on this particular evening my thoughts were very far from the archaeology of Serbia. As often happens when one allows one's imagination free rein, I was musing on past times – on the good old days of my childhood; on the beauties of France that I had left for a wild and faraway country. I was thinking about the Duchesse de Gramont and – why not admit it? – I was also thinking about several other ladies who lived at the same time as your grandmothers, the memory of whose beauty had quietly entered my thoughts in the train of the beautiful Duchesse. I had soon forgotten all about my hosts and their terrible anxiety.

Suddenly Georges broke the silence. 'Wife,' he said, 'at exactly what time did the old man set out?'

'At eight o'clock. I can clearly remember hearing the monastery bell.'

'Well, that's all right then,' said Georges. 'It cannot be more than half past seven.' And he again looked for signs of movement on the great highway which led to the dark forest.

I have forgotten to tell you, mesdames, that when the Serbians suspect that someone has become a vampire, they avoid mentioning him by name or speaking of him directly, for they think that this would be an invitation for him to leave his tomb. So Georges, when he spoke of his father, now referred to him simply as 'the old man'.

There was a brief silence. Suddenly one of the children started tugging at Sdenka's apron and crying, 'Auntie, when will grandpapa be coming back?'

The only reply he got to this untimely question was a hard slap from Georges. The child began to cry, but his little brother, who by now was surprised and frightened, wanted to know more. 'Father, why are we not allowed to talk about grandpapa?'

Another slap shut him up firmly. Both children now began to howl and the whole family made a sign of the cross. Just at that moment, I heard the sound of the monastery bell. As the first chime of eight was ringing in our ears, we saw a human figure coming out of the darkness of the forest and approaching us.

'It is he, God be praised,' cried Sdenka, her sister-in-law and Pierre all at once.

'May the good God protect us,' said Georges solemnly. 'How are we to know if the ten days have passed or not?'

Everyone looked at him, terror-struck. But the human form came closer and closer. It was a tall old man with a silver moustache and a pale, stern face; he was dragging himself along with the aid of a stick. The closer he got, the more shocked Georges looked. When the new arrival was a short distance from us, he stopped and stared at his family with eyes that seemed not to see – they were dull, glazed, deep sunk in their sockets.

'Well, well,' he said in a dead voice, 'will no one get up to welcome me? What is the meaning of this silence, can't you see I am wounded?'

I saw that the old man's left side was dripping with blood.

'Go and help your father,' I said to Georges. 'And you, Sdenka, offer him some refreshment. Look at him – he is almost collapsing from exhaustion!'

'Father,' said Georges, going up to Gorcha, 'show me your wound. I know all about such things and I can take care of it . . .'

He was just about to take off the old man's coat when Gorcha pushed his son aside roughly and clutched at his body with both hands. 'You are too clumsy,' he said, 'leave me alone . . . Now you have hurt me.'

'You must be wounded in the heart,' cried Georges, turning pale. 'Take off your coat, take it off. You must, I insist.'

The old man pulled himself up to his full height. 'Take care,' he said in a sepulchral voice. 'If you so much as touch me, I shall curse you.'

Pierre rushed between Georges and his father. 'Leave him alone,' he said. 'Can't you see that he's suffering?'

'Do not cross him,' George's wife added. 'You know he has never tolerated that.'

At that precise moment we saw a flock of sheep returning from pasture raising a cloud of dust as it made its way towards the house. Whether the dog which was escorting the flock did not recognize its own master, or whether it had some other reason for acting as it did, as soon as it caught sight of Gorcha it stopped dead, hackles raised, and began to howl as if it had seen a ghost.

'What is wrong with that dog?' said the old man, looking more and more furious. 'What is going on here? Have I become a stranger in my own house? Have ten days spent in the mountains changed me so much that even my own dogs do not recognize me?'

'Did you hear that?' said Georges to his wife.

'What of it?'

'He admits that the ten days *have been spent.*'

'Surely not, for he has come back to us within the appointed time.'

'I know what has to be done.'

The dog continued to howl. 'I want that dog destroyed!' cried Gorcha. 'Well, did you hear me?'

Georges made no move, but Pierre got up with tears in his eyes, and grabbed his father's arquebus; he aimed at the dog, fired, and the creature rolled over in the dust.

Previous page Distinctive yellow cloth cover, with red lettering, of the first edition of *Dracula*, published in June 1897, priced at six shillings. **Top left and right** Exterior view of Whitby Museum, Subscription Library and Warm Bathing Establishment, photographed by Frank Meadow Sutcliffe in the late 1880s; Bram Stoker read diplomat William Wilkinson's book in the library on 19 August 1890 and took copious notes. **Above** Sutcliffe's photograph of the Russian schooner *Dmitry*, wrecked and beached during a storm in October 1885 – the original of the *Demeter* which transports Dracula to Whitby. **Opposite** Three manuscript pages of Bram Stoker's earliest working notes for *Dracula*, probably dating from March 1890: a list of vampire characteristics, chapter headings, and 'characters of the story' – including 'Count Wampyr', later amended by Stoker, on this sheet, to 'Count Dracula'; and photo-portrait of Bram Stoker, 1890s, as usual not smiling.

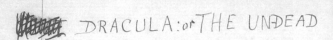

Above Manuscript of the opening of Bram Stoker's 'dramatization' of *Dracula*, performed 18 May 1897 as a legal device – the sole public performance of any adaptation in Stoker's lifetime. Opposite above left Henry Irving as Mephistopheles in the Lyceum Theatre's spectacular 1885 production of *Faust*. Opposite above right Printed cover of the programme for the one-off scissors-and-paste 'dramatization' of *Dracula* at the Lyceum.
Opposite below Top-hatted Henry Irving, followed – a couple of paces behind – by his 'faithful servitor' Bram Stoker, outside the stage door of the Lyceum, October 1902.

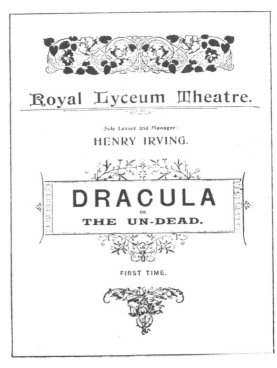

DRACULA

2/- Net.   BRAM STOKER   2/- Net.

Opposite Dustwrapper of a William Rider and Son popular edition of *Dracula*, London, 1916.
Above Dustwrapper by Handfurth for the first edition of the posthumously published collection of Stoker short stories headed by *Dracula's Guest*, April 1914.

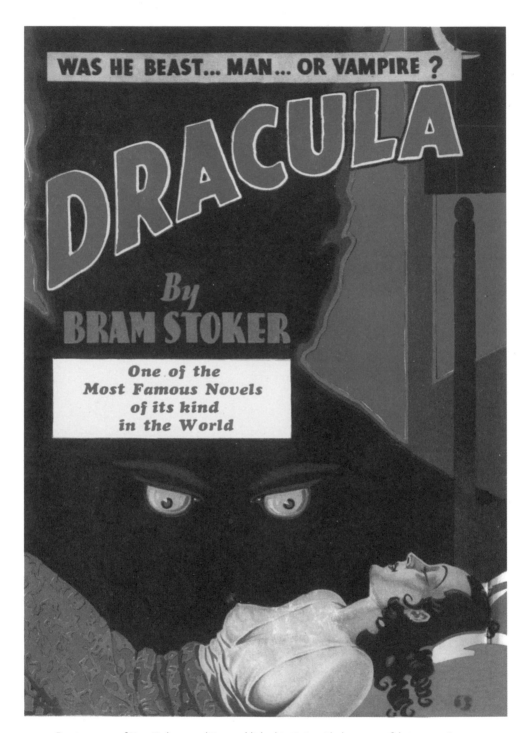

WAS HE BEAST... MAN... OR VAMPIRE?

DRACULA

By
BRAM STOKER

One of the
Most Famous Novels
of its kind
in the World

Dustwrapper of New York 1927 edition, published to tie in with the successful stage version of *Dracula*.

'That was my favourite dog,' he said sulkily. 'I don't know why father wanted it to be destroyed.'

'Because it deserved to be,' bellowed Gorcha. 'Come on now, it's cold and I want to go inside.'

While all this was going on outside, Sdenka had been preparing a cordial for the old man consisting of pears, honey and raisins, laced with *eau de vie*, but her father pushed it aside with disgust. He seemed equally disgusted by the plate of mutton with rice that Georges offered him. Gorcha shuffled over to the fireplace, muttering gibberish from behind clenched teeth.

A pine-log fire crackled in the grate and its flickering light seemed to give life to the pale, emaciated features of the old man. Without the fire's glow, his features could have been taken for those of a corpse.

Sdenka sat down beside him. 'Father,' she said, 'you do not wish to eat anything, you do not wish to rest; perhaps you feel up to telling us about your adventures in the mountains.'

By suggesting that, the young girl knew that she was touching her father's most sensitive spot, for the old man loved to talk of wars and adventures. The trace of a smile creased his colourless lips, although his eyes showed no animation, and as he began to stroke his daughter's beautiful blonde hair, he said: 'Yes, my daughter, yes, Sdenka, I would like to tell you all about my adventures in the mountains – but that must wait for another time, for I am too tired today. I can tell you, though, that Ali Bek is dead and that he perished by my hand. If anyone doubts my word,' continued the old man, looking hard at his two sons, 'here is the proof.'

He undid a kind of sack which was slung behind his back, and pulled out a foul, bloody head which looked about as pale as his own! We all recoiled in horror, but Gorcha gave it to Pierre.

'Take it,' he said, 'and nail it above the door, to show all who pass by that Ali Bek is dead and that the roads are free of brigands – except, of course, for the Sultan's janissaries!'

Pierre was disgusted. But he obeyed. 'Now I understand why that poor dog was howling,' he said. 'He could smell dead flesh!'

'Yes, he could smell dead flesh,' murmured Georges; he had gone out of the room without anyone noticing him and had returned at that moment with something in his hand which he placed carefully against a wall. It looked to me like a sharpened stake.

'Georges,' said his wife, almost in a whisper, 'I hope you do not intend to . . .'

'My brother,' Sdenka added anxiously, 'what do you mean to do? No, no – surely you're not going to . . .'

'Leave me alone,' replied Georges, 'I know what I have to do and I will only do what is absolutely necessary.'

While all this had been going on, night had fallen, and the family went to bed in a part of the house which was separated from my room only by a narrow partition. I must admit that what I had seen that evening had made an impression on my imagination. My candle was out; the moonlight shone through a little window near my bed and cast blurred shadows on the floor and walls, rather like those we see now, mesdames, in this room. I wanted to go to sleep but I could not. I thought this was because the moonlight was so clear; but when I looked for something to curtain the window, I could find nothing suitable. Then I overheard confused voices from the other side of the partition. I tried to make out what was being said.

'Go to sleep, wife,' said Georges. 'And you, Pierre, and you, Sdenka. Do not worry, I will watch over you.'

'But Georges,' replied his wife, 'it is I who should keep watch over you – you worked all last night and you must be tired. In any case, I ought to be staying awake to watch over our eldest boy. You know he has not been well since yesterday!'

'Be quiet and go to sleep,' said Georges. 'I will keep watch for both of us.'

'Brother,' put in Sdenka in her sweetest voice, 'there is no need to keep watch at all. Father is already asleep – he seems calm and peaceful enough.'

'Neither of you understands what is going on,' said Georges in a voice which allowed for no argument. 'Go to sleep, I tell you, and let me keep watch.'

There followed a long silence. Soon my eyelids grew heavy and sleep began to take possession of my senses.

I thought I saw the door of my room opening slowly, and old Gorcha standing in the doorway. Actually, I did not so much see as *feel* his presence, as there was only darkness behind him. I felt his dead eyes trying to penetrate my deepest thoughts as they watched the movement of my breathing. One step forward, then another. Then, with extreme care, he began to walk towards me, with a wolf-like motion. Finally he leapt forward. Now he was right beside my bed. I was absolutely terrified, but somehow managed not to move. The old man leaned over me and his waxen face was so close to mine that I could feel his corpselike breath. Then, with a superhuman effort, I managed to wake up, soaked in perspiration.

There was nobody in my room, but as I looked towards the window I could distinctly see old Gorcha's face pressed against the glass from outside, staring at me with his sunken eyes. By sheer willpower I stopped myself from crying out and I had the presence of mind to stay lying down, just as if I had seen nothing out of the ordinary. Luckily, the old man was only making sure that I was asleep, for he made no attempt to come in, and after staring at me long enough to satisfy himself, he moved away from the window and I could hear his footsteps in the neighbouring room. Georges was sound asleep and snoring loudly enough to wake the dead.

At that moment the child coughed, and I could make out Gorcha's voice. 'You are not asleep little one?'

'No, grandpapa,' replied the child, 'And I would so like to talk with you.'

'So, you would like to talk with me, would you? And what would we talk about?'

'We would talk about how you fought the Turks. I would love to fight the Turks!'

'I thought you might, child, and I brought back a little yagatan for you. I'll give it to you tomorrow.'

'Grandpapa, grandpapa, give it to me now.'

'But, little one, why didn't you talk to me about this when it was daytime?'

'Because papa would not let me.'

'He is careful, your papa . . . So you really would like to have your little yagatan?'

'Oh yes, I would love that, but not here, for papa might wake up.'

'Where then?'

'If we go outside, I promise to be good and not to make any noise at all.'

I thought I could hear Gorcha chuckle as the child got out of bed. I didn't believe in vampires, but the nightmare had preyed on my nerves, and just in case I should have to reproach myself in the morning I got up and banged my fist against the partition. It was enough to wake up the 'seven sleepers', but there was no sign of life from the family. I threw myself against the door, determined to save the child – but it was locked from the outside and I couldn't shift the bolts. While I was trying to force it open, I saw the old man pass by my window with the little child in his arms.

'Wake up! Wake up!' I cried at the top of my voice, as I shook the partition. Even then only Georges showed any sign of movement.

'Where is the old man?' he murmured blearily.

'Quick,' I yelled, 'he's just taken away your child.'

With one kick, Georges broke down the door of his room – which like mine had been locked from the outside – and he sprinted in the direction of the dark forest. At last I succeeded in waking Pierre, his sister-in-law and Sdenka. We all assembled in front of the house and after a few minutes of anxious waiting we saw Georges return from the dark forest with his son. The child had apparently passed out on the highway, but he was soon revived and didn't seem to be any more ill than before. After questioning him we discovered that his grandpapa had not, in fact, done him any harm; they had apparently gone out together to talk undisturbed, but once outside the child had lost consciousness without remembering why. Gorcha himself had disappeared.

As you can imagine, no one could sleep for the rest of that night. The next day, I learned that the River Danube, which cut across the highway about a quarter of a league from the village, had begun to freeze over; drift ice now blocked my route. This often happens in these parts some time between the end of autumn and the beginning of spring. Since the highway was expected to be blocked for some days, I could not think of leaving. In any case, even if I could have left, curiosity – as well as a more powerful emotion – would have held me back. The more I saw Sdenka, the more I felt I was falling in love with her.

I am not among those, mesdames, who believe in love at first sight of the kind which novelists so often write about; but I do believe that there are occasions when love develops more quickly than is usual. Sdenka's strange beauty, her singular resemblance to the Duchesse de Gramont – the lady from whom I had fled in Paris, and who I saw again in this remote setting, dressed in a rustic costume and speaking in a musical foreign tongue – the fascinating line on her forehead, like that for which I had been prepared to kill myself at least twenty times in France: all this, combined with the incredible, mysterious situation in which I found myself . . . everything helped to nurture in me a passion which, in other circumstances, would perhaps have proved itself to be more vague and passing.

During the course of the day I overheard Sdenka talking to her younger brother. 'What do you think of all this?' she asked. 'Do you also suspect our father?'

'I dare not suspect him,' replied Pierre, 'especially since the child insists that he came to no harm. And as for father's disappearance, you know that he never used to explain his comings and goings.'

'I know,' said Sdenka. 'All the more reason why we must think about saving him, for you know that Georges . . .'

'Yes, yes, I know. It would be useless to talk him out of it. We can at least hide the stake. He certainly won't go out looking for another one, since there is not a single aspen tree this side of the mountains.'

'Yes, let's hide the stake – but don't mention it to the children, for they might chatter about it with Georges listening.'

'We must take care not to let that happen,' said Pierre. And they went their separate ways.

At nightfall we had still discovered nothing about old Gorcha. As on the previous night I was lying on my bed, and the moonlight again stopped me from going to sleep. When at last sleep began to confuse my thoughts, I again felt, as if by instinct, that the old man was coming towards me. I opened my eyes and saw his waxen face pressed against my window.

This time I wanted to get up but could not. All my limbs seemed to be paralysed. After taking a good long look at me, the old man disappeared. I heard him wandering around the house and tapping gently on the window of George's room. The child turned over on his bed and moaned as he dreamed. After several minutes silence the tapping on the window resumed. Then the child groaned once again and woke up. 'Is that you, grandpapa?' he asked.

'It is me,' replied a dead voice, 'and I have brought you your little yagatan.'

'But I dare not go outside. Papa has forbidden it.'

'There is no need to go outside; just open the window and embrace me!'

The child got up and I could hear him opening the window. Then somehow finding the strength, I leaped to the foot of my bed and ran over to the partition. I struck it hard with my fist. In a few seconds Georges was on his feet. I heard him mutter an oath. His wife screamed. In no time at all the whole household had gathered around the lifeless child. Just as on the previous occasion, there was no sign of Gorcha. We tried carefully to revive the child, but he was very weak and breathed with difficulty. The poor little chap had no idea why he had passed out. His mother and Sdenka thought it was because of the shock of being caught talking with his grandpapa. I said nothing. However, by now the child seemed to be more calm and everybody except Georges went back to bed.

At daybreak, I overheard Georges waking his wife and whispering with her. Sdenka joined them and I could hear both the women sobbing. The child was dead.

Of the family's despair, the less said the better. Strangely enough no one blamed the child's death on old Gorcha – at least, not openly. Georges sat in silence, but his expression, always gloomy, now became terrible to behold. Two days passed and there was still no sign of the old man. On the night of the third day (the day of the child's burial) I thought I heard footsteps all around the house and an old man's voice which called out the name of the dead child's brother. For a split second I also thought I saw Gorcha's face pressed against my window, but I couldn't be sure if I was imagining it or not, for the moon was veiled by cloud that night. Nevertheless I considered it my duty to mention this apparition to Georges. He questioned the child, who replied that he *had* in fact heard grandpapa calling and had also seen him looking in through the window. Georges strictly charged his son to wake him up if the old man should appear again.

All these happenings did not prevent my passion for Sdenka from developing more and more each day. In the daytime, I couldn't talk to her alone. At night, the mere thought that I would shortly have to leave broke my heart. Sdenka's room was separated from mine only by a kind of corridor which led to the road on one side and a courtyard on the other. When the whole family had gone to bed, I decided to go for a short walk in the fields to ease my mind. As I walked along the corridor I saw that Sdenka's door was slightly open. Instinctively, I stopped and listened. The rustling of her dress, a sound I knew well, made my heart pound against my chest. Then I heard her singing softly. She was singing about a Serbian king who was saying farewell to his lady before going to war.

'Oh my young Poplar,' said the old king, 'I am going to the war and you will forget me.

'The trees which grow beneath the mountain are slender and pliant, but they are nothing beside your young body!

'The berries of the rowan tree which sway in the wind are red, but your lips are more red than the berries of the rowan tree!

'And I am like an old oak stripped of leaves, and my beard is whiter than the foam of the Danube!

'And you will forget me, oh my soul, and I will die of grief, for the enemy will not dare to kill the old King!'

The beautiful lady replied: 'I swear to be faithful to you and never to forget you. If I should break my oath, come to me after your death and drink all my heart's blood!'

And the old king said: 'So be it!'

And he set off for the war. Soon the beautiful lady forgot him . . .!

At this point Sdenka paused, as if she was frightened to finish the ballad. I could restrain myself no longer. That voice – so sweet, so expressive – was the voice of the Duchesse de Gramont . . . Without pausing to think, I pushed open the door and went in. Sdenka had just taken off her knitted jacket (of a kind often worn by women in those regions). All she was wearing was a nightgown of red silk, embroidered with gold, held tight against her body by a simple, brightly coloured belt. Her fine blonde hair hung loose over her shoulders. She looked more beautiful than ever. She did not seem upset by my sudden entry, but she was confused and blushed slightly.

'Oh,' she said, 'why have you come? What will the family think of me if we are discovered?'

'Sdenka, my soul, do not be frightened! Everyone is asleep. Only the cricket in the grass and the mayfly in the air can hear what I have to say to you.'

'Oh my friend, leave me, leave me! If my brother should discover us I am lost!'

'Sdenka, I will not leave you until you have promised to love me for ever, as the beautiful lady promised the king in your ballad. Soon I will have to leave ... Who knows when we will see each other again? Sdenka, I love you more than my soul, more than my salvation ... my life's blood is yours ... may I not be granted one hour with you in return?'

'Many things can happen in an hour,' said Sdenka calmly. But she did let her hand slip into mine.

'You do not know my brother,' she continued, beginning to tremble. 'I fear he will discover us.'

'Calm yourself, my darling Sdenka. Your brother is exhausted from watching late into the night; he has been lulled to sleep by the wind rustling in the trees; heavy is his sleep, long is the night and I only ask to be granted one hour – then, farewell, perhaps for ever!'

'Oh no, no, not for ever!' cried Sdenka; then she recoiled, as if frightened by the sound of her own voice.

'Oh Sdenka, I see only you, I hear only you; I am no longer master of my own destiny; a superior strength commands my obedience. Forgive me, Sdenka!' Like a madman I clutched her to my heart.

'You are no friend to me,' she cried, tearing herself from my embrace and rushing to another part of the room. I do not know what I said to her then, for I was as alarmed as she was by my own forwardness, not because such boldness had failed me in the past – far from it – but because in spite of my passion, I could not help having a sincere respect for Sdenka's innocence. It is true that I had used the language of *galanterie* with this girl at first (a language which did not seem to displease the society ladies of the time), but I was now ashamed of these empty phrases and renounced them when I saw that the young girl was too naïve to comprehend fully what I meant by them – what you, mesdames, to judge by your suggestive smiles, have understood immediately. I stood before her, at a loss as to what to say, when suddenly she began to tremble and look towards the window, terrorstruck. I followed her gaze and clearly saw the corpse-like face of Gorcha, staring at us from outside.

At precisely that moment, I felt a heavy hand on my shoulder.

I froze. It was Georges. 'What are you doing here!' he snapped.

Embarrassed by his tone of voice, I simply pointed towards his father, who was still staring at us through the window – but he disappeared the moment Georges turned to look at him.

'I heard the old man and came to warn your sister,' I stammered.

Georges looked me straight in the eye, as if trying to read my innermost thoughts. Then he took me by the arm, led me to my room and left, without a single word.

The next day the family had gathered in front of the house, around a table laden with jugs of milk and cakes.

'Where is the child?' said Georges.

'In the courtyard,' replied his wife. 'He is playing his favourite game, imagining that he is fighting the Turks single-handed.'

No sooner had she said these words, than to our amazement we saw the tall figure of Gorcha walking slowly towards us from out of the dark forest. He sat at the table just as he had done the day I arrived.

'Father, we welcome you,' murmured George's wife in a hoarse voice.

'We welcome you, father,' whispered Sdenka and Pierre in unison.

'My father,' said Georges firmly, turning pale, 'we are waiting for you to say Grace!'

The old man glared at him and turned away.

'Yes ... Grace – say it now!' repeated Georges, crossing himself. 'Say it this instant, or by St George ...'

Sdenka and her sister-in-law threw themselves at the old man's feet and begged him to say Grace.

'No, no, no,' said the old man. 'He has no right to speak to me in that way, and if he continues, I will curse him!'

Georges got up and rushed into the house. He returned almost immediately, looking furious. 'Where is that stake?' he yelled. 'Where have you hidden it?'

Sdenka and Pierre looked at each other.

'Corpse!' Georges shouted at the old man. 'What have you done with my elder boy? Why have you killed my little child? Give me back my son, you creature of the grave!'

As he said this, he became more and more pale and his eyes began to burn with fury. The old man simply glared at him.

'The stake, the stake,' yelled Georges. 'Whoever has hidden it must answer for all the evils which will befall us!'

At this moment we heard the excited laughter of the younger child. We saw him galloping towards us on a wooden horse, or rather on a long aspen stake, shrieking the Serbian battle cry at the top of his voice. Georges's eyes lit up as he realized what was happening. He grabbed the stake from the child and threw himself at his father. The old man let out a fearful groan and began to sprint towards the dark forest as if possessed by demons. Georges raced after him across the fields, and soon they were both out of sight.

It was after sunset when Georges returned to the house. He was as pale as death; his hair stood on end. He sat down by the fireside, and I could hear his teeth chattering. No one could pluck up the courage to question him. By about the time the family normally went to bed he seemed to be more his usual self and, taking me to one side, said to me quite calmly: 'My dear guest, I have been to the river. The ice has gone, the road is clear – nothing now prevents you from leaving. There is no need,' he added, glancing at Sdenka, 'to take your leave of my family. Through me, the family wishes you all the happiness you could desire and I hope that you will have some happy memories of the time you have spent with us. Tomorrow at daybreak, you will find your horse saddled and your guide ready to escort you. Farewell. Think about your host from time to time, and forgive him if your stay here has not been as carefree as he would have liked.'

As he said this, even Georges's rough features looked almost friendly. He led me to my room and shook my hand for one last time. Then he began to tremble and his teeth chattered as if he were suffering from the cold.

Now I was alone, I had no thoughts of going to sleep – as you can imagine. Other things were on my mind. I had loved many times in my life, and had experienced the whole range of passions – tenderness, jealousy, fury – but never, not even when I left the Duchesse de Gramont, had I felt anything like the sadness that I felt in my heart at that moment. Before sunrise, I changed into my travelling clothes, hoping to have a few words with Sdenka before I departed. But Georges was waiting for me in the hall. There was no chance of my seeing her again.

I leaped into the saddle and spurred on my horse. I made a resolution to return from Jassy via this village, and although that might be some time hence, the thought made me feel easier in my mind. It was some consolation for me to imagine in advance all the details of my return. But this pleasant reverie was soon shattered. My horse shied away from something and nearly had me out of the saddle. The animal stopped dead, dug in its forelegs and began to snort wildly, as if some danger was nearby. I looked around anxiously and saw something moving about a hundred paces away. It was a wolf digging in the ground. Sensing my presence, the wolf ran away; digging my spurs into the horse's flanks, I managed with difficulty to get him to move forward. It was then that I realized that on the spot where the wolf had been standing, there was a freshly dug grave. I seem to remember also that the end of a stake protruded a few inches out of the ground where the wolf had been digging. However, I do not swear to this, for I rode away from that place as fast as I could.

At this point the Marquis paused and took a pinch of snuff.

'Is that the end of the story?' the ladies asked.

'I'm afraid not,' replied M. d'Urfé. 'What remains to be told is a very unhappy memory for me, and I would give much to cast it from my mind.'

My reasons for going to Jassy (he continued) kept me there for much longer than I had expected – well over six months, in fact. What can I say to justify my conduct during that time? It is a sad fact, but a fact nonetheless, that there are very few emotions in this life which can stand the test of time. The success of my negotiations, which were very well received in Versailles – politics, in a word, vile politics, a subject which has become so boring to us in recent times – preoccupied my thoughts and dimmed the memory of Sdenka. In addition, from the moment I arrived, the wife of the hospodar, a very beautiful lady who spoke fluent French, did me the honour of receiving my attentions, singling me out from among all the other young foreigners who were staying in Jassy. Like me, she had been brought up to believe in the principles of French *galanterie*; the mere thought that I should rebuff the advances of such a beautiful lady stirred up my Gallic blood. So I received her advances with courtesy, and since I was there to represent the interests and rights of France, I made a start by representing those of her husband the hospodar as well.

When I was recalled home, I left by the same road I had ridden to Jassy. I no longer even thought about Sdenka or her family, but one evening when I was riding in the countryside, I heard a bell ringing the eight o'clock chime. I seemed to recognize that sound and my guide told me that it came from a nearby monastery. I asked him the name: it was the monastery of Our Lady of the Oak. I galloped ahead and in no time at all we had reached the monastery gate. The old hermit welcomed us and led us to his hostel.

The number of pilgrims staying there put me off the idea of spending the night at the hostel, and I asked if there was any accommodation available in the village.

'You can stay where you like in the village,' replied the old hermit with a gloomy sigh. 'Thanks to that devil Gorcha, there are plenty of empty houses!'

'What on earth do you mean?' I asked. 'Is old Gorcha still alive?'

'Oh no, he's well and truly buried with a stake through his heart! But he rose from the grave to suck the blood of Georges's little son. The child returned one night and knocked on the door, crying that he was cold and wanted to come home. His foolish mother, although she herself had been present at his burial, did not have the strength of mind to send him back to the cemetery, so she opened the door. He threw himself at her throat and sucked away her life's blood. After she had been buried, she in turn rose from the grave to suck the blood of her second son, then the blood of her husband, then the blood of her brother-in-law. They all went the same way.'

'And Sdenka?'

'Oh, she went mad with grief; poor, poor child, do not speak to me of her!'

The old hermit had not really answered my question, but I did not have the heart to repeat it. He crossed himself. 'Vampirism is contagious,' he said after a pause. 'Many families in the village have been afflicted by it, many families have been completely destroyed, and if you take my advice you will stay in my hostel tonight; for even if the *vourdalaks* of the village do not attack you, they will terrify you so much that your hair will have turned white before I ring the bells for morning mass.

'I am only a poor and simple monk,' he continued, 'but the generosity of passing travellers gives me enough to provide for their needs. I can offer you fresh country cheese and sweet plums which will make your mouth water; I also have some flagons of Tokay wine which are every bit as good as those which grace the cellars of His Holiness the Patriarch!'

The old hermit seemed to be behaving more like an inn-keeper than a poor and simple monk. I reckoned he had told me some old wives' tales about the village in order to make me feel grateful enough for his hospitality to show my appreciation in the usual way, by giving the holy man enough to provide for the needs of passing travellers. In any case, the word terror has always had the effect on me that a battle cry has on a war horse. I would have been thoroughly ashamed of myself if I had not set out immediately to see for myself. But my guide, who was less enthusiastic about the idea, asked my permission to stay in the hostel. This I willingly granted.

It took me about half an hour to reach the village. Deserted. No lights shone through the windows, no songs were being sung. I rode past many houses that I knew, all as silent as the grave. Finally I reached Georges's. Whether I was being sentimental or just rash, I don't know, but it was there I decided to spend the night. I got off my horse, and banged on the gate. Still no sign of life. I pushed the gate and the hinges creaked eerily as it slowly opened. Then I crept into the courtyard. In one of the outhouses I found enough oats to last the night, so I left my horse tethered there, still saddled, and strode towards the main house. Although all the rooms were deserted, no doors were locked. Sdenka's room had been occupied only a few hours before. Some of her clothes were draped carelessly over the bed. A few pieces of jewellery that I had given her, including a small enamel cross from Budapest, lay on her table sparkling in the moonlight. Even though my love for her was a thing of the past, I must admit that my heart was heavy. Nevertheless, I wrapped myself up in my cloak and stretched out on her bed. Soon I was asleep. I cannot recall everything, but I do remember that I dreamed of Sdenka, as beautiful, as simple and as loving as she had been when first I met her. I remember also feeling ashamed of my selfishness and my inconstancy. How could I have abandoned that poor child who loved me; how could I have forgotten her? Then her image became confused with that of the Duchesse de Gramont and I saw only one person. I threw myself at Sdenka's feet and begged her forgiveness. From the depths of my being, from the depths of my soul came an indescribable feeling of melancholy and of joy.

I lay there dreaming, until I was almost awakened by a gentle musical sound, like the rustling of a cornfield in a light breeze. I heard the sweet rustling of the corn and the music of singing birds, the rushing of a waterfall and the whispering of trees. Then I realized that all these sounds were merely the swishing of a woman's dress and I opened my eyes. There was Sdenka standing beside my bed. The moon was shining so brightly that I could distinguish every single feature which had been so dear to me and which my dream made me love again as if for the first time. Sdenka seemed more beautiful, and somehow more mature. She was dressed as she had been when last I saw her alone: a simple nightgown of red silk, gold embroidered, and a coloured belt, clinging tightly above her hips.

'Sdenka!' I cried, sitting up. 'Is it really you, Sdenka?'

'Yes, it is me,' she replied in a sweet, sad voice. 'It is that same Sdenka you have forgotten. Why did you not return sooner? Everything is finished now; you must leave; a moment longer and you are lost! Farewell my friend, farewell for ever!'

'Sdenka, you have seen so much unhappiness they say! Come, let us talk, let us ease your pain!'

'Oh, my friend, you must not believe everything they say about us; but leave me, leave me now, for if you stay a moment longer you are doomed.'

'Sdenka, what are you afraid of? Can you not grant me an hour, just one hour to talk with you?'

Sdenka began to tremble and her whole being seemed to undergo a strange transformation. 'Yes,' she said, 'one hour, just one hour, the same hour you begged of me when you came into this room and heard me singing the ballad of the old king. Is that what you mean? So be it, I will grant you one hour! But no, no!' she cried, as if fighting her inclinations, 'leave me, go away! – leave now, I tell you, fly! Fly, while you still have the chance!'

Her features were possessed with a savage strength. I could not understand why she should be saying these things, but she was so beautiful that I determined to stay, whatever she said. At last she surrendered, sat down beside me, and spoke to me of the past; she blushed as she admitted that she had fallen in love with me the moment she set eyes on me. But little by little I began to notice that Sdenka was not as I had remembered her. Her former timidity had given way to a strange wantonness of manner. She seemed more forward, more knowing. It dawned on me that her behaviour was no longer that of the naïve young girl I recalled in my dream. Is it possible, I mused, that Sdenka was never the pure and innocent maiden that I imagined her to be? Did she simply put on an act to please her brother? Was I gulled by an affected virtue? If so, why insist that I leave? Was this perhaps a refinement of *coquetterie*? And I thought I knew her! What did it matter? If Sdenka was not a Diana, as I thought, she began to resemble another goddess at least as attractive – perhaps more so. By God! I preferred the role of Adonis to that of Actaeon.

If this classical style that I adopted seems a little out of place, mesdames, remember that I have the honour to be telling you of incidents which occurred in the year of grace 1758. At that time mythology was *very* fashionable, and I am trying to keep my story in period. Things have changed a lot since then, and it was not so long ago that the Revolution, having overthrown both the traces of paganism and the Christian religion, erected the goddess Reason in their place. This goddess, mesdames, has never been my patron saint, least of all when I am in the presence of other goddesses, and, at the time I am referring to, I was less disposed than ever to worship at her shrine.

I abandoned myself passionately to Sdenka, and willingly outdid even her in the provocative game she was playing. Some time passed in sweet intimacy, until, as Sdenka was amusing me by trying on various pieces of jewellery, I thought it would be a good idea to place the little enamel cross around her neck. But as I tried to do this, Sdenka recoiled sharply.

'Enough of these childish games, my dearest,' she said. 'Let us talk about you and what is on your mind!'

This sudden change in Sdenka's behaviour made me pause a moment and think. Looking at her more closely I noticed that she no longer wore around her neck the cluster of tiny icons, holy relics and charms filled with incense which Serbians are usually given as children, to wear for the rest of their lives.

'Sdenka,' I asked, 'where are those things you used to wear around your neck?'

'I have lost them,' she replied impatiently, and hastily changed the subject.

I do not know exactly why, but at that moment I began to feel a strong sense of foreboding. I wanted to leave, but Sdenka held me back. 'What is this?' she said. 'You asked to be granted an hour, and here you are trying to leave after only a few minutes!'

'Sdenka, you were right when you tried to persuade me to leave; I think I hear a noise and I fear we will be discovered!'

'Calm yourself, my love, everyone is asleep; only the cricket in the grass and the mayfly in the air can hear what I have to say!'

'No, no, Sdenka, I must leave now . . .!'

'Stay, stay,' she implored, 'I love you more than my soul, more than my salvation. You once told me that your life's blood belonged to me . . .!'

'But your brother – your brother, Sdenka – I have a feeling he will discover us!'

'Calm yourself, my soul; my brother has been lulled to sleep by the wind rustling in the trees; heavy is his sleep, long is the night and I ask only to be granted one hour!'

As she said this, Sdenka looked so ravishing that my vague sense of foreboding turned into a strong desire to remain near her. A strange, almost sensual feeling, part fear, part excitement, filled my whole being. As I began to weaken, Sdenka became more tender, and I resolved to surrender, hoping to keep up my guard. However, as I told you at the beginning, I have always overestimated my own strength of mind, and when Sdenka, who had noticed that I was holding back, suggested that we chase away the chill of the night by drinking a few glasses of the good hermit's full-blooded wine, I agreed with a readiness which made her smile. The wine had its desired effect. By the second glass, I had forgotten all about the incident of the cross and the holy relics; Sdenka, with her beautiful blonde hair falling loose over her shoulders, with her jewels sparkling in the moonlight, was quite irresistible. Abandoning all restraint, I held her tight in my arms.

Then, mesdames, a strange thing happened. One of those mysterious revelations that I can never hope to explain. If you had asked me then, I would have denied such things could happen, but now I know better. As I held Sdenka tightly against my body, one of the points of the cross which the Duchesse de Gramont gave me before I left stuck sharply into my chest. The stab of pain that I felt affected me like a ray of light passing right through my body. Looking up at Sdenka I saw for the first time that her features, though still beautiful, were those of a corpse; that her eyes did not see; and that her smile was the distorted grimace of a decaying skull. At the same time, I sensed in that room the putrid smell of the charnel-house. The fearful truth was revealed to me in all its ugliness, and I remembered too late what the old hermit had said to me. I realized what a fearsome predicament I was in. Everything depended on my courage and my self-control.

I turned away from Sdenka to hide the horror which was written on my face. It is then that I looked out of the window and saw the satanic figure of

Gorcha, leaning on a bloody stake and staring at me with the eyes of a hyena. Pressed against the other window were the waxen features of Georges, who at that moment looked as terrifying as his father. Both were watching my every movement, and I knew that they would pounce on me the moment I tried to escape. So I pretended not to know they were there, and, with incredible self-control, continued – yes, mesdames, I actually continued – passionately to embrace Sdenka, just as I had done before my horrifying discovery. Meanwhile, I desperately racked my brains for some means of escape. I noticed that Gorcha and Georges were exchanging knowing glances with Sdenka and that they were showing signs of losing patience. Then, from somewhere outside, I heard a woman's shriek and the sound of children crying, like the howling of wild cats; these noises set my nerves on edge.

Time to make for home, I said to myself, *and the sooner the better!*

Turning to Sdenka, I raised my voice so that her hideous family would be sure to hear me: 'I am tired, my dear child; I must go to bed and sleep for a few hours. But first I must go and see whether my horse needs feeding. I beg you to stay where you are and to wait for me to come back.' I then pressed my mouth against her cold, dead lips and left the room.

I found my horse in a panic, covered with lather and crashing his hooves against the outhouse wall. He had not touched the oats, and the fearful noise he made when he saw me coming gave me gooseflesh, for I feared he would give the game away. But the vampires, who had almost certainly overheard my conversation with Sdenka, did not appear to think that anything suspicious was happening. After making sure that the main gate was open, I vaulted into the saddle and dug my spurs into the horse's flanks.

As I rode out of the gates I just had time to glimpse a whole crowd gathered around the house, many of them with their faces pressed against the windows. I think it was my sudden departure which first confused them, but I cannot be sure: the only sound I could hear at that moment was the regular beat of my horse's hooves which echoed in the night. I was just about to congratulate myself on my cunning, when all of a sudden I heard a fearful noise behind me, like the sound of a hurricane roaring through the mountains. A thousand discordant voices shrieked, moaned and contended with one another. Then complete silence, as if by common assent. And I heard a rhythmic stamping, like a troop of foot soldiers advancing in double-quick time.

I spurred on my horse until I tore into his flanks. A burning fever coursed through my veins. I was making one last effort to preserve my sanity, when I heard a voice behind me which cried out: 'Stop, don't leave me, my dearest! I love you more than my soul, I love you more than my salvation! Turn back, turn back, your life's blood is mine!'

A cold breath brushed my ear and I sensed that Sdenka had leaped on to my horse from behind. 'My heart, my soul!' she cried, 'I see only you, hear only you! I am not mistress of my own destiny – a superior force commands my obedience. Forgive me, my dearest, forgive me!'

Twisting her arms around me she tried to sink her teeth into my neck and to wrench me from my horse. There was a terrible struggle. For some time I had difficulty even defending myself, but eventually I managed to grab hold of Sdenka by curling one arm around her waist and knotting the other hand in her hair. Standing bolt upright in my stirrups, I threw her to the ground!

Then my strength gave out completely and I became delirious. Frenzied shapes pursued me – mad, grimacing faces. Georges and his brother Pierre ran beside the road and tried to block my way. They did not succeed, but just as I was about to give thanks, I looked over my shoulder and caught sight of old Gorcha, who was using his stake to propel himself forward as the Tyrolean mountain men do when they leap over Alpine chasms. But Gorcha did not manage to catch up with me. Then his daughter-in-law, dragging her children behind her, threw one of them to him; he caught the child on the sharpened point of his stake. Using the stake as a catapult, he slung the creature towards me with all his might. I fended off the blow, but with the true terrier instinct the little brat sunk his teeth into my horse's neck, and I had some difficulty tearing him away. The other child was propelled towards me in the same way, but he landed beyond the horse and was crushed to pulp. I do not know what happened after that, but when I regained consciousness it was daylight, and I found myself lying near the road next to my dying horse.

So ended, mesdames, a love affair which should perhaps have cured me for ever of the desire to become involved in any others. Some contemporaries of your grandmothers could tell you whether I had learned my lesson or not. But, joking aside, I still shudder at the thought that if I had given in to my enemies, I would myself have become a vampire. As it was, Heaven did not allow things to come to that, and so far from wishing to suck your blood, mesdames, I only ask – old as I am – to be granted the privilege of shedding my own blood in your service!

THE FATE OF MADAME CABANEL

ELIZA LYNN LINTON

In recent decades the term 'female Gothic' has been applied – especially by American literary scholars – to works of literature written by women in the nineteenth century which use the imagery and the characters of the Gothic novel in order to tell stories which are *really* about hidden aspects of female sexuality. Mary Shelley, with her cybernetic creation of a motherless child in *Frankenstein*, has come to be treated as the key example. *The Fate of Madame Cabanel*, which first appeared some fifty-five years after *Frankenstein*, in 1872, is a short story concerned with precisely this process of transformation. An Englishwoman settles down in a Brittany village, and her 'strangeness' is judged by some of the villagers – especially a peasant woman who is suffering from an acute attack of sexual jealousy – to be an example of vampirism. On this occasion, the vampire-as-metaphor leads to some very real manifestations of mob mania and physical violence, but, strange to say, the story was not written by an active supporter of women's rights. On the contrary, Eliza Lynn Linton (1822–98), who had begun her career as a journalist and writer of fiction with a series of pieces about the sad and frustrating lot of the middle-class Victorian woman, began from the mid-1860s onwards to publish articles (which she republished in book form) attacking the work and ideas of the early feminists. Indeed, her later novels invariably *criticized* the so-called 'girl of the period' (or the New Woman); one of them was even dedicated to 'the sweet girls still left among us'. So *The Fate of Madame Cabanel*, which was published some fourteen years after Linton's most outspoken anti-feminist articles in the *Saturday Review*, is clearly not intended to be read (as may at first sight appear to be the case) as a fable about a misunderstood 'new woman' who expects too much from life. But it remains a rare example of a vampire story which understands and recognizes the metaphorical, or symbolic, meaning of the myth – where female sexuality is concerned – and which uses the form to reflect on its continuing resonance in contemporary society. This makes *Madame Cabanel*, despite its typically late Victorian attitude towards a French rural community, an unusually frightening story, even by today's standards.

PROGRESS HAD NOT INVADED, science had not enlightened, the little hamlet of Pieuvrot, in Brittany. They were a simple, ignorant, superstitious set who lived there, and the luxuries of civilization were known to them as little as its learning. They toiled hard all the week on the ungrateful soil that yielded them but a bare subsistence in return; they went regularly to mass in the little rock-set chapel on Sundays and saints' days; believed implicitly all that monsieur le curé said to them, and many things which he did not say; and they took all the unknown, not as magnificent, but as diabolical.

The sole link between them and the outside world of mind and progress was Monsieur Jules Cabanel, the proprietor, par excellence, of the place; *maire, juge de paix*, and all the public functionaries rolled into one. And he sometimes went to Paris whence he returned with a cargo of novelties that excited envy, admiration, or fear, according to the degree of intelligence in those who beheld them.

Monsieur Jules Cabanel was not the most charming man of his class in appearance, but he was generally held to be a good fellow at bottom. A short, thickset, low-browed man, with blue-black hair cropped close like a mat, as was his blue-black beard, inclined to obesity and fond of good living, he had need have some virtues behind the bush to compensate for his want of personal charms. He was not bad, however; he was only common and unlovely.

Up to fifty years of age he had remained the unmarried prize of the surrounding country; but hitherto he had resisted all the overtures made by maternal fowlers, and had kept his liberty and his bachelor-hood intact. Perhaps his handsome housekeeper, Adèle, had something to do with his persistent celibacy. They said she had, under their breath as it were, down at *la Veuve Prieur's*; but no one dared to so much as hint the like to herself. She was a proud, reserved kind of woman; and had strange notions of her own dignity which no one cared to disturb. So, whatever the underhand gossip of the place might be, neither she nor her master got wind of it.

Presently and quite suddenly, Jules Cabanel, who had been for a longer time than usual in Paris, came home with a wife. Adèle had only twenty-four hours' notice to prepare for this strange home-coming; and the task seemed heavy. But she got through it in her old way of silent determination; arranged the rooms as she knew her master would wish them to be arranged; and even supplemented the usual nice adornments by a voluntary bunch of flowers on the salon table.

'Strange flowers for a bride,' said to herself little Jeannette, the goose-girl who was sometimes brought into the house to work, as she noticed heliotrope – called in France *la fleur des veuves* – scarlet poppies, a bunch of belladonna, another of aconite – scarcely, as even ignorant little Jeannette said, flowers of bridal welcome or bridal significance. Nevertheless, they stood where Adèle had placed them; and if Monsieur Cabanel meant anything by the passionate expression of disgust with which he ordered them out of his sight, madame seemed to understand nothing, as she smiled with that vague, half-deprecating look of a person who is assisting at a scene of which the true bearing is not understood.

Madame Cabanel was a foreigner, and an Englishwoman; young, pretty and fair as an angel.

'*La beauté du diable*,' said the Pieuvrotines, with something between a sneer and a shudder; for the words meant with them more than they mean in ordinary use. Swarthy, ill-nourished, low of stature and meagre in frame as they were themselves, they could not understand the plump form, tall figure and fresh complexion of the Englishwoman. Unlike their own experience, it was therefore more likely to be evil than good. The feeling which had sprung up against her at first sight deepened when it was observed that, although she went to mass with praiseworthy punctuality, she did not know her missal and signed herself *à travers*. *La beauté du diable*, in faith!

'*Pouf!*' said Martin Briolic, the old gravedigger of the little cemetery; 'with those red lips of hers, her rose cheeks and her plump shoulders, she looks like a vampire and as if she lived on blood.'

He said this one evening down at *la Veuve Prieur*'s; and he said it with an air of conviction that had its weight. For Martin Briolic was reputed the wisest man of the district; not even excepting Monsieur le curé who was wise in his own way, which was not Martin's – nor Monsieur Cabanel who was wise in his, which was neither Martins's nor the curé's. He knew all about the weather and the stars, the wild herbs that grew on the plains and the wild shy beasts that eat them; and he had the power of divination and could find where the hidden springs of water lay far down in the earth when he held the baguette in his hand. He knew too, where treasures could be had on Christmas Eve if only you were quick and brave enough to enter the cleft in the rock at the right moment and come out again before too late; and he had seen with his own eyes the White Ladies dancing in the moonlight; and the little imps, the Infins, playing their prankish gambols by the pit at the edge of the wood. And he had a shrewd suspicion as to who, among those black-hearted men of La Crèche-en-bois – the rival hamlet – was a loup-garou, if ever there was one on the face of the earth and no one had doubted that! He had other powers of a yet more mystic kind; so that Martin Briolic's bad word went for something, if, with the illogical injustice of ill-nature his good went for nothing.

Fanny Campbell, or, as she was now Madame Cabanel, would have excited no special attention in England, or indeed anywhere but at such a dead-alive, ignorant, and consequently gossiping place as Pieuvrot. She had no romantic secret as her background; and what history she had was commonplace enough, if sorrowful too in its own way. She was simply an orphan and a governess; very young and very poor; whose employers had quarrelled with her and left her stranded in Paris, alone and almost moneyless; and who had married Monsieur Jules Cabanel as the best thing she could do for herself. Loving no one else, she was not difficult to be won by the first man who showed her kindness in her hour of trouble and destitution; and she accepted her middle-aged suitor, who was fitter to be her father than her husband, with a clear conscience and a determination to do her duty cheerfully and faithfully – all without considering herself as a martyr or an interesting victim sacrificed to the cruelty of circumstances. She did not know, however, of the handsome housekeeper Adèle, nor of the housekeeper's little nephew – to whom the master was so kind that he allowed him to live at the Maison Cabanel and had him well taught by the curé. Perhaps if she had she would have thought twice before she put herself under the same roof with a woman who for a bridal bouquet offered her poppies, heliotrope and poison-flowers.

If one had to name the predominant characteristic of Madame Cabanel it would be easiness of temper. You saw it in the round, soft, indolent lines of her face and figure; in her mild blue eyes and placid, unvarying smile; which irritated the more petulant French temperament and especially disgusted Adèle. It seemed impossible to make madame angry or even to make her understand when she was insulted, the housekeeper used to say with profound disdain; and, to do the woman justice, she did not spare her endeavours to enlighten her. But madame accepted all Adèle's haughty reticence and defiant continuance of mistress-hood with unwearied sweetness; indeed, she expressed herself gratified that so much trouble was taken off her hands, and that Adèle so kindly took her duties on herself.

The consequences of this placid lazy life, where all her faculties were in a manner asleep, and where she was enjoying the reaction from her late years of privation and anxiety, was, as might be expected, an increase in physical beauty that made her freshness and good condition still more remarkable. Her lips were redder, her cheeks rosier, her shoulders plumper than ever; but as she waxed, the health of the little hamlet waned, and not the oldest inhabitant remembered so sickly a season, or so many deaths. The master too, suffered slightly; the little Adolphe desperately.

This failure of general health in undrained hamlets is not uncommon in France or in England; neither is the steady and pitiable decline of French children; but Adèle treated it as something out of all the lines of normal experience; and, breaking her habits of reticence spoke to every one quite fiercely of the strange sickliness that had fallen on Pieuvrot and the Maison Cabanel; and how she believed it was something more than common; while as to her little nephew, she could give neither a name nor find a remedy for the mysterious disease that had attacked him. There were strange things among them, she used to say; and Pieuvrot had never done well since the old times were changed. Jeannette used to notice how she would sit gazing at the English lady, with such a deadly look on her handsome face when she turned from the foreigner's fresh complexion and grand physique to the pale face of the stunted, meagre, fading child. It was a look, she said afterwards, that used to make her flesh get like ice and creep like worms.

One night Adèle, as if she could bear it no longer, dashed down to where old Martin Briolic lived, to ask him to tell her how it had all come about – and the remedy.

'Hold, Ma'am Adèle,' said Martin, as he shuffled his greasy tarot cards and laid them out in triplets on the table; 'there is more in this than one sees. One sees only a poor little child become suddenly sick; that may be, is it not so? and no harm done by man? God sends sickness to us all and makes my trade profitable to me. But the little Adolphe has not been touched by the Good God. I see the will of a wicked woman in this. Hein!' Here he shuffled the cards and laid them out with a kind of eager distraction of manner, his withered hands trembling and his mouth uttering words that Adèle could not catch. 'Saint Joseph and all the saints protect us!' he cried; 'the foreigner – the Englishwoman – she whom they call Madame Cabanel – no rightful madame she! – Ah, misery!'

'Speak, Father Martin! What do you mean!' cried Adèle, grasping his arm. Her black eyes were wild; her arched nostrils dilated; her lips, thin, sinuous, flexible, were pressed tight over her small square teeth.

'Tell me in plain words what you would say!'

'Broucolaque!' said Martin in a low voice.

'It is what I believed!' cried Adèle. 'It is what I knew. Ah, my Adolphe! woe on the day when the master brought that fair-skinned devil home!'

'Those red lips don't come by nothing, Ma'am Adèle,' cried Martin nodding his head. 'Look at them – they glisten with blood! I said so from the beginning; and the cards, they said so too. I drew "blood" and a "bad fair woman" on the evening when the master brought her home, and I said to myself, "Ha, ha, Martin! you are on the track, my boy – on the track. Martin!" – and, Ma'am Adèle, I have never left it! Broucolaque! that's what the cards say, Ma'am Adèle. Vampire. Watch and see; watch and see; and you'll find that the cards have spoken true.'

'And when we have found, Martin?' said Adèle in a hoarse whisper.

The old man shuffled his cards again. 'When we have found, Ma'am Adèle?' he said slowly. 'You know the old pit out there by the forest? – the old pit where the lutins run in and out, and where the White Ladies wring the necks of those who come upon them in the moonlight? Perhaps the White Ladies will do as much for the English wife of Monsieir Cabanel; who knows?'

'They may,' said Adèle, gloomily.

'Courage, brave woman!' said Martin. 'They will.'

The only really pretty place about Pieuvrot was the cemetery. To be sure there was the dark gloomy forest which was grand in its own mysterious way; and there was the broad wide plain where you might wander for a long summer's day and not come to the end of it; but these were scarcely places where a young woman would care to go by herself; and for the rest, the miserable little patches of cultivated ground, which the peasants had snatched from the surrounding waste and where they had raised poor crops, were not very lovely. So Madame Cabanel, who, for all the soft indolence that had invaded her, had the Englishwoman's inborn love for walking and fresh air, haunted the pretty little graveyard a good deal. She had no sentiment connected with it. Of all the dead who laid there in their narrow coffins, she knew none and cared for none; but she liked to see the pretty little flower-beds and the wreaths of immortelles, and the like; the distance too, from her own home was just enough for her; and the view over the plain to the dark belt of forest and the mountains beyond, was fine.

The Pieuvrotines did not understand this. It was inexplicable to them that any one, not out of her mind, should go continually to the cemetery – not on the day of the dead and not to adorn the grave of one she loved – only to sit there and wander among the tombs, looking out on to the plain and the mountains beyond when she was tired.

'It was just like – ' The speaker, one Lesouëf, had got so far as this, when he stopped for a word.

He said this down at *la Veuve Prieur*'s where the hamlet collected nightly to discuss the day's small doings, and where the main theme, ever since she had come among them, three months ago now, had been Madame Cabanel and her foreign ways and her wicked ignorance of her mass-book and her wrong-doings of a mysterious kind generally, interspersed with jesting queries, banded from one to the other, of how Ma'am Adèle liked it? – and what would become of le petit Adolphe when the rightful heir appeared? – some adding that monsieur was a brave man to shut up two wild cats under the same roof together; and what would become of it in the end? Mischief of a surety.

'Wander about the tombs just like what, Jean Lesouëf?' said Martin Briolic. Rising, he added in a low but distinct voice, every word falling clear and clean: 'I will tell you like what, Lesouëf – like a vampire! La femme Cabanel has red lips and red cheeks; and Ma'am Adèle's little nephew is perishing before your eyes. La femme Cabanel has red lips and red cheeks; and she sits for hours among the tombs. Can you read the riddle, my friends? For me it is as clear as the blessed sun.'

'Ha, Father Martin, you have found the word – like a vampire!' said Lesouëf with a shudder.

'Like a vampire!' they all echoed with a groan.

'And I said vampire the first,' said Martin Briolic. 'Call to mind I said it from the first.'

'Faith! and you did,' they answered; 'and you said true.'

So now the unfriendly feeling that had met and accompanied the young Englishwoman ever since she came to Pieuvrot had drawn to a focus. The seed which Martin and Adèle had dropped so sedulously had at last taken root; and the Pieuvrotines would have been ready to accuse of atheism and immorality any one who had doubted their decision, and had declared that pretty Madame Cabanel was only a young woman with nothing special to do, a naturally fair complexion, superb health – and no vampire at all, sucking the blood of a living child or living among the tombs to make the newly buried her prey.

The little Adolphe grew paler and paler, thinner and thinner; the fierce summer sun told on the half-starved dwellers within those foul mud-huts surrounded by undrained marshes; and Monsieur Jules Cabanel's former solid health followed the law of the rest. The doctor, who lived at Crèche-en-bois, shook his head at the look of things; and said it was grave. When Adèle pressed him to tell her what was the matter with the child and with monsieur, he evaded the question; or gave her a word which she neither understood nor could pronounce. The truth was, he was a credulous and intensely suspicious man; a viewy man who made theories and then gave himself to the task of finding them true. He had made the theory that Fanny was secretly poisoning both her husband and the child; and though he would not give Adèle a hint of this, he would not set her mind at rest by a definite answer that went on any other line.

As for Monsieur Cabanel, he was a man without imagination and without suspicion; a man to take life easily and not distress himself too much for the fear of wounding others; a selfish man but not a cruel one; a man whose own pleasure was his supreme law and who could not imagine, still less brook, opposition or the want of love and respect for himself. Still, he loved his wife as he had never loved a woman before. Coarsely moulded, common-natured as he was, he loved her with what strength and passion of poetry nature had given him; and if the quantity was small, the quality was sincere. But that quality was sorely tried when – now Adèle, now the doctor – hinted mysteriously, the one at diabolical influences, the other at underhand proceedings of which it behoved him to be careful, especially careful what he eat and drank and how it was prepared and by whom; Adèle adding hints about the perfidiousness of English women and the share which the devil had in fair hair and brilliant complexions. Love his young wife as he might, this constant dropping of poison was not without some effect. It told much for his steadfastness and loyalty that it should have had only so small effect.

One evening, however, when Adèle, in an agony, was kneeling at his feet – madame had gone out for her usual walk – crying: 'Why did you leave me for such as she is? – I, who loved you, who was faithful to you, and she, who walks among the graves, who sucks your blood and our child's – she who has only the devil's beauty for her portion and who loves you not?' – something seemed suddenly to touch him with electric force.

'Miserable fool that I was!' he said, resting his head on Adèle's shoulders and weeping. Her heart leapt with joy. Was her reign to be renewed? Was her rival to be dispossessed?

From that evening Monsieur Cabanel's manner changed to his young wife but she was too easy-tempered and unsuspicious to notice anything, or if she did, there was too little depth in her own love for him – it was so much a matter of untroubled friendliness only – that she did not fret but accepted the coldness and brusqueness that had crept into his manner as good-naturedly as she accepted all things. It would have been wiser if she had cried and made a scene and come to an open fracas with Monsieur Cabanel. They would have understood each other better; and Frenchmen like the excitement of a quarrel and a reconciliation.

Naturally kind hearted, Madame Cabanel went much about the village, offering help of various kinds to the sick. But no one among them all, not the very poorest – indeed, the very poorest the least – received her civilly or accepted her aid. If she attempted to touch one of the dying children, the mother, shuddering, withdrew it hastily to her own arms; if she spoke to the adult sick, the wan eyes would look at her with a strange horror and the feeble voice would mutter words in a patois she could not understand. But always came the same word, 'broucolaque!'

'How these people hate the English!' she used to think as she turned away, perhaps just a little depressed, but too phlegmatic to let herself be uncomfortable or troubled deeply.

It was the same at home. If she wanted to do any little act of kindness to the child, Adèle passionately refused her. Once she snatched him rudely from her arms, saying as she did so: 'Infamous broucolaque! before my very eyes?' And once, when Fanny was troubled about her husband and proposed to make him a cup of beef-tea à l'Anglaise, the doctor looked at her as if he would have looked through her; and Adèle upset the saucepan; saying insolently – but yet hot tears were in her eyes – 'Is it not fast enough for you, madame? Not faster, unless you kill me first!'

To all of which Fanny replied nothing; thinking only that the doctor was very rude to stare so fixedly at her and that Adèle was horribly cross; and what an ill-tempered creature she was; and how unlike an English housekeeper!

But Monsieur Cabanel, when he was told of the little scene, called Fanny to him and said in a more caressing voice than he had used to her of late: 'Thou wouldst not hurt me, little wife? It was love and kindness, not wrong, that thou wouldst do?'

'Wrong? What wrong could I do?' answered Fanny, opening her blue eyes wide. 'What wrong should I do to my best and only friend?'

'And I am thy friend? thy lover? thy husband? Thou lovest me dear?' said Monsier Cabanel.

'Dear Jules, who is so dear; who so near?' she said kissing him, while he said fervently:

'God bless thee!'

The next day Monsieur Cabanel was called away on urgent business. He might be absent for two days, he said, but he would try to lessen the time; and the young wife was left alone in the midst of her enemies, without even such slight guard as his presence might prove.

Adèle was out. It was a dark, hot summer's night, and the little Adolphe had been more feverish and restless than usual all the day. Towards evening he grew worse; and though Jeannette, the goose-girl, had strict commands not to allow madame to touch him, she grew frightened at the condition of the boy; and when madame came into the small parlour to offer her assistance, Jeannette gladly abandoned a charge that was too heavy for her and let the lady take him from her arms.

Sitting there with the child in her lap, cooing to him, soothing him by a low, soft nursery song, the paroxysm of his pain seemed to her to pass and it was as if he slept. But in that paroxysm he had bitten both his lip and tongue; and the blood was now oozing from his mouth. He was a pretty boy; and his mortal sickness made him at this moment pathetically lovely. Fanny bent her head and kissed the pale still face – and the blood that was on his lips was transferred to hers.

While she still bent over him – her woman's heart touched with a mysterious force and prevision of her own future motherhood – Adèle, followed by old Martin and some others of the village, rushed into the room.

'Behold her!' she cried, seizing Fanny by the arm and forcing her face upwards by the chin – behold her in the act! Friends, look at my child – dead, dead in her arms; and she with his blood on her lips! Do you want more proofs? Vampire that she is, can you deny the evidence of your own senses?'

'No! no!' roared the crowd hoarsely. 'She is a vampire – a creature cursed by God and the enemy of man; away with her to the pit. She must die as she has made others to die!'

'Die, as she has made my boy to die!' said Adèle; and more than one who had lost a relative or child during the epidemic echoed her words, 'Die, as she has made mine to die!'

'What is the meaning of all this?' said Madame Cabanel, rising and facing the crowd with the true courage of an Englishwoman. 'What harm have I done to any of you that you should come about me, in the absence of my husband, with these angry looks and insolent words?'

'What harm hast thou done?' cried old Martin, coming close to her. 'Sorceress as thou art, thou hast bewitched our good master; and vampire as thou art, thou nourishest thyself on our blood! Have we not proof of that at this very moment? Look at thy mouth – cursed broucolaque; and here lies thy victim, who accuses thee in his death!'

Fanny laughed scornfully, 'I cannot condescend to answer such folly,' she said lifting her head. 'Are you men or children?'

'We are men, madame,' said Legros the miller; 'and being men we must protect our weak ones. We have all had our doubts – and who more cause that I, with three little ones taken to heaven before their time – and now we are convinced.'

'Because I have nursed a dying child and done my best to soothe him!' said Madame Cabanel with unconscious pathos.

'No more words!' cried Adèle, dragging her by the arm from which she had never loosed her hold. 'To the pit with her, my friends, if you would not see all your children die as mine has died – as our good Legros's have died!'

A kind of shudder shook the crowd; and a groan that sounded in itself a curse burst from them.

'To the pit!' they cried. 'Let the demons take their own!'

Quick as thought Adèle pinioned the strong white arms whose shape and beauty had so often maddened her with jealous pain; and before the poor girl could utter more than one cry Legros had placed his brawny hand over her mouth. Though this destruction of a monster was not the murder of a human being in his mind, or in the mind of any there, still they did not care to have their nerves disturbed by cries that sounded so human as Madame Cabanel's. Silent then, and gloomy, that dreadful cortège took its way to the forest, carrying its living load; gagged and helpless as if it had been a corpse among them. Save with Adèle and old Martin, it was not so much personal animosity as the instinctive self-defence of fear that animated them. They were executioners, not enemies; and the executioners of a more righteous law than that allowed by the national code. But one by one they all dropped off till their numbers were reduced to six; of whom Legros was one, and Lesouëf, who had lost his only sister, was also one.

The pit was not more than an English mile from the Maison Cabanel. It was a dark and lonesome spot, where not the bravest man of all that assembly would have dared to go alone after nightfall, not even if the curé had been with him; but a multitude gives courage, said old Martin Briolic; and half a dozen stalwart men, led by such a woman as Adèle, were not afraid of even lutins or the White Ladies.

As swiftly as they could for the burden they bore, and all in utter silence, the cortège strode over the moor; one or two of them carrying rude torches; for the night was black and the way was not without its physical dangers. Nearer and nearer they came to the fatal bourn; and heavier grew the weight of their victim. She had long ceased to struggle; and now lay as if dead in the hands of her bearers. But no one spoke of this or of aught else. Not a word was exchanged between them; and more than one, even of those left, began to doubt whether they had done wisely, and whether they had not better have trusted to the law. Adèle and Martin alone remained firm to the task they had undertaken; and Legros too was sure; but he was weakly and humanly sorrowful for the thing he felt obliged to do. As for Adèle, the woman's jealousy, the mother's anguish and the terror of superstition, had all wrought in her so that she would not have raised a finger to have lightened her victim of one of her pains, or have found her a woman like herself and no vampire after all.

The way got darker; the distance between them and their place of execution shorter; and at last they reached the border of the pit where this fearful monster, this vampire – poor innocent Fanny Cabanel – was to be thrown. As they lowered her, the light of their torches fell on her face.

'Grand Dieu!' cried Legros, taking off his cap; 'she is dead!'

'A vampire cannot die,' said Adèle, 'it is only an appearance. Ask Father Martin.'

'A vampire cannot die unless the evil spirits take her, or she is buried with a stake thrust through her body,' said Martin Briolic sententiously.

'I don't like the look of it,' said Legros; and so said some others.

They had taken the bandage from the mouth of the poor girl; and as she lay in the flickering light, her blue eyes half open; and her pale face white with the whiteness of death, a little return of human feeling among them shook them as if the wind had passed over them.

Suddenly they heard the sound of horses' hoofs thundering across the plain. They counted two, four, six; and they were now only four unarmed men, with Martin and Adèle to make up the number. Between the vengeance of man and the power and malice of the wood-demons, their courage faded and their presence of mind deserted them. Legros rushed frantically into the vague darkness of the forest; Lesouëf followed him; the other two fled over the plain while the horsemen came nearer and nearer. Only Adèle held the torch high above her head, to show more clearly both herself in her swarthy passion and revenge and the dead body of her victim. She wanted no concealment; she had done her work, and she gloried in it. Then the horsemen came plunging to them – Jules Cabanel the first, followed by the doctor and four gardes champêtres.

'Wretches! murderers!' was all he said, as he flung himself from his horse and raised the pale face to his lips.

'Master,' said Adèle, 'she deserved to die. She is a vampire and she has killed our child.'

'Fool!' cried Jules Cabanel, flinging off her hand. 'Oh, my loved wife!

thou who did no harm to man or beast, to be murdered now by men who are worse than beasts!'

'She was killing thee,' said Adèle. 'Ask monsieur le docteur. What ailed the master, monsieur?'

'Do not bring me into this infamy,' said the doctor looking up from the dead. 'Whatever ailed monsieur, she ought not to be here. You have made yourself her judge and executioner, Adèle, and you must answer for it to the law.'

'You say this too, master?' said Adèle.

'I say so too,' returned Monsieur Cabanel. 'To the law you must answer for the innocent life you have so cruelly taken – you and all the fools and murderers you have joined to you.'

'And is there to be no vengeance for our child?'

'Would you revenge yourself on God, woman?' said Monsieur Cabanel sternly.

'And our past years of love, master?'

'Are memories of hate, Adèle,' said Monsieur Cabanel, as he turned again to the pale face of his dead wife.

'Then my place is vacant,' said Adèle, with a bitter cry. 'Ah, my little Adolphe, it is well you went before!'

'Hold, Ma'am Adèle!' cried Martin.

But before a hand could be stretched out, with one bound, one shriek, she had flung herself into the pit where she had hoped to bury Madame Cabanel; and they heard her body strike the water at the bottom with a dull splash, as of something falling from a great distance.

'They can prove nothing against me, Jean,' said old Martin to the garde who held him. 'I neither bandaged her mouth nor carried her on my shoulders. I am the gravedigger of Pieuvrot, and, *ma foi*, you would all do badly, you poor creatures, when you die, without me! I shall have the honour of digging madame's grave, never doubt it; and, Jean,' he whispered, 'they may talk as they like, those rich aristos who know nothing. She is a vampire, and she shall have a slatte through her body yet! Who knows better than I? If we do not tie her down like this, she will come out of her grave and suck our blood; it is a way these vampires have.'

'Silence there!' said the garde, commanding the little escort. 'To prison with the assassins; and keep their tongues from wagging.'

'To prison with martyrs and the public benefactors,' retorted old Martin. 'So the world rewards its best!'

And in this faith he lived and died, as a forçat at Toulon, maintaining to the last that he had done the world a good service by ridding it of a monster who else would not have left one man in Pieuvrot to perpetuate his name and race. But Legros and also Lesouëf, his companion, doubted gravely of the righteousness of that act of theirs on that dark summer's night in the forest; and though they always maintained that they should not have been punished, because of their good motives, yet they grew in time to disbelieve old Martin Briolic and his wisdom, and to wish that they had let the law take its own course unhelped by them – reserving their strength for the grinding of the hamlet's flour and the mending of the hamlet's sabots – and the leading of a good life according to the teaching of monsieur le curé and the exhortations of their own wives.

5 THE GENESIS OF DRACULA

Having some time at my disposal when in London, I had visited the British Museum, and made search among the books and maps of the library regarding Transylvania; it had struck me that some foreknowledge of the country could hardly fail to have some importance in dealing with a noble of that country . . . I shall enter here some of my notes, as they may refresh my memory when I talk over my travels with Mina.

'Jonathan Harker's Journal', from Chapter I of *Dracula*,
by Bram Stoker (1897)

'THIS MAN BELONGS TO ME'

When Oxford University Press announced in 1983 that it was about to reissue Bram Stoker's *Dracula* as the hundredth title in the *World's Classics* series, it did so as if looking down from the great height of some ivory tower; authors from the acknowledged great tradition, the press said, would 'no doubt turn in their graves' if they knew that they would in future be sharing the library shelves with Bram Stoker. And when the novelist and biographer A. N. Wilson deigned to write an Introduction for OUP, he proved to be even more apologetic:

> *Dracula*, is, patently . . . not a great work of literature. The writing is of a powerful, workaday sensationalist kind. No one in their right mind would think of Stoker as 'a great writer'. How can someone who is *not* a great writer be said to have written a classic? . . . [By making] your hair stand on end. And that, from the first page to the last, is what *Dracula* is meant to do.

Apart from anything else, adds Wilson, Stoker hadn't even taken the trouble to do much background reading before cobbling together his *magnum opus*. At least if he had been a *scholar*, it is implied, he might have earned his place at the high table on that ticket:

> Stoker was obviously well-enough versed in the better-known sensational-ist vampire literature – *Varney, the Vampire, Carmilla* and so on. It would seem likely that he did some – but very little – research for his fantasy and that, like Jonathan Harker, he 'had visited the British Museum, and made search among the books and maps in the Library regarding Transylvania' . . . [Stoker's] imagination was not a uniquely original one. Vampires from *Varney* and Le Fanu; a setting and a personage hastily 'got up' from a few hours in the British Museum. What is there left to say of Bram Stoker's originality or achievement?

The answer is: a great deal. Evidently, A. N. Wilson had done *some* research for his anaemic contribution – but very little. For, over a decade before his Introduction was published, and sixty years after they were originally sold (probably to a Liverpool bookseller) at Sotheby's, London, Bram Stoker's 'original Foundation Notes and Data for his *Dracula*' were acquired by the Rosenbach Foundation in Philadelphia in 1970. One of the first published references to them was in the journal *Notes and Queries* of January-February 1977, where Joseph S. Bierman had written:

> The Stoker material in the Collection consists of handwritten and typewritten notes, dated and undated, about numerous subjects of central or tangential interest to a writer who was thinking of settings, characters, and plot for a story of the supernatural; descriptions of topography, landscape and customs from the work of contemporary travellers in Danubian countries; notes on a theory of dreams; transcriptions of tombstone inscriptions; accounts of conversations with old sailors and coastguardsmen; and notes for the novel itself.

Bierman could have added: notes on books about necromancy and natural history; a bibliography of general works about the existence – and analysis – of myth and superstition; material concerning injuries to the head and the removal of blood-clots (authenticated by Bram's elder brother, William, who was proudly referred to as 'Sir William Thornley Stoker' following his knighthood in 1895); a reference to the vampires of Malaysia; a railway timetable; and manuals about the weather.

These 'Foundation Notes', which amount to some eighty manuscript or typescript pages (collected into three quarto volumes), prove conclusively that, however one may rate his talents as a writer of English prose, Bram Stoker did a great deal of research when he was preparing his masterpiece. The first dated notes were written on 14 March 1890 (that is, eight months *before* he published his first full-length adventure novel, *The Snake's Pass*), and the last were written on 5 April 1896 (that is, *after* he had published two more novels, *The Watter's Mou* and *The Shoulder of Shasta*, as well as seven short stories). So the book which was to become *Dracula* was on his mind for at least six years, and then for a further fourteen months, until final publication in May 1897.

From the evidence of the 'Notes', Stoker's part-time research – which took place during precious days or weeks off from his demanding duties at the Lyceum Theatre – involved a number of different locations: Whitby, Yorkshire (where in summer 1890 he noted eighty-seven names on tombstones in the cliff-top churchyard, including one 'Ann Swales, 6 Feb 1795, aet 100' whose name was later used for the elderly sailor 'Mr Swales', and transcribed various conversations with real-life old salts); possibly Regent's Park Zoo (where he speculated about the effect his vampire might have on the caged animals); his office at the Lyceum; and, indeed, 'the British Museum . . . in the Library'. It is likely, also, that the Munich incidents which were originally to open Jonathan Harker's shorthand journal were based on memories of Stoker's fact-finding mission to southern Germany, on behalf of Henry Irving, in the mid-1880s, when he was preparing for their barnstorming Lyceum adaptation of *Faust*. And we know that Stoker's visits to Port Erroll (now Cruden Bay) in northwest Scotland, on the Buchan coastline, just north of Aberdeen, for several summers from 1893 onwards provided a suitably romantic setting for much of the actual drafting of the novel. Some have even suggested that there may be a Scots folkloric basis for *Dracula* – with nearby Slains Castle, home of the Earls of Erroll, as 'Castle Dracula' – but there is very little evidence for this. Just Florence Stoker's comment in 1927: 'It was up on a lonely part of the east coast of Scotland, and he seemed to get obsessed by the spirit of the thing. There he would sit for hours, like a great bat, perched on the rocks of the shore . . . thinking it out'. Needless to say, Bram Stoker never visited the land beyond the forest.

Discovery of the 'Notes' has helped to shed light on some of the confusions surrounding the genesis of *Dracula*. In brief, they reveal that:

1   Stoker started planning the book in 1890 (rather than 1895 or 1896 as asserted by his earliest biographers).

2   The book was intended to be set in the year 1893 (Stoker the ex-civil servant was as meticulous – even obsessed – about dates as he was about

train timetables and weather conditions, and he made several efforts to make the timescale 'fit').

3 It was from the beginning to be presented in the epistolary form recently made popular by Wilkie Collins.

4 The Count was originally Count –, then somewhat prosaically 'Count Wampyr'; the first direct reference to 'Count Dracula' occurs on 29 February 1892, following Stoker's discovery of the name in William Wilkinson's book, in summer 1890 (see page 111).

5 The novel was originally (1890) to be set in Austrian Styria; only later (by 1892) did Stoker decide to move it eastwards to Transylvania, after reading various mid-Victorian travellers' tales about the region that is now called Romania.

6 From its earliest stages until perhaps several years later, the story was to begin with a series of letters from lawyers, and from the Count to these lawyers, about the proposed purchase of a property in England (Stoker, who himself qualified to be called to the Bar in 1890, seems to have been fascinated by the details of house conveyancing, as well as what he calls the 'conveyance of bodies', and his hero in the finished novel learns – just before he sets out for Transylvania – that he has passed his examinations and become 'a full-blown solicitor').

7 The story was then to involve the newly qualified solicitor Jonathan Harker in a series of adventures in Munich, *en route* for the Count's castle: an incident in the Munich 'Dead House', where Harker first catches sight of the Count (although he doesn't realize this until much later in the story); an 'adventure snowstorm and wolf' (a revised version of which was later to be turned into the short story *Dracula's Guest*, published 1914); and visits to the Old Pinakothek Museum (where one imagines Harker was very struck by Rubens's *Two Satyrs*) and the Opera to see – what else? – Wagner's *Flying Dutchman*. All of these would appear to have remained in the novel right up until the final draft stage.

The typesetter's version of the full text, which came to light in 1977 and is now in a private collection, suggests that the first three chapters were excised at the last minute.

8   Stoker's revised 'rules' for vampire behaviour – or, to put it another way, his extensions to the genre – were invented early on, although there is, in fact, no *explicit* reference to vampirism in the very first notes.

9   The basic structure of the book – Eastern Europe, to Whitby, to London and environs, eastern Europe – was established from the outset: a structure which looks suspiciously like the 'synopsis of scenery' page in a Lyceum programme – four acts, each with seven scenes, many supplied with ready-made curtain lines.

10 The final title of the book (an important contributory factor in its popular success) was settled *very* late in the day. Stoker was unsure in his 'Notes' about whether to call it *The Undead* or *The Dead Undead*, and we know that his contract to the publishers Constable and Company – signed and dated 20 May 1897 – mentions only the title *The Un-Dead*. This remains a mystery, since the book was published that very month (so both parties knew of the title *Dracula* and the subtitle *or The Un-Dead*, before the contract was signed).

Above all, the 'Notes' in the Rosenbach Foundation confirm that the dream (was it *really* a nightmare?) from which the novel eventually emerged was there from the very beginning.

In March 1890 Bram Stoker wrote on a piece of scrap paper, in hand-writing which he always called 'an extremely bad hand': 'Young man goes out – sees girls one tries – to kiss him not on the lips but throat. Old Count interferes – rage and fury diabolical . . . This man belongs to me I want him.' Six days later, he reiterated: 'Loneliness, the Kiss "this man belongs to me"'. Again, in February 1892, in one of the many 'structures' he scribbled down: 'Bistritz – Borgo Pass – Castle – Sortes Virgil – Belongs to me'. And in shorthand, again and again, over the next few years: '& the visitors – is it a dream – women stoop to kiss him. terror of death. Suddenly Count turns

her away – "this man belongs to me" '; 'May 15 Monday Women kissing';
'Book I Ch 8 Belongs to me'.

Whatever the changes that happened between 1890 and 1897 to the
novel's beginning, its characters, its villain, its locations and its length, one
incident and one alone remained constant right up to publication day, the
incident which occurs when, as Jonathan Harker recalls in his Journal entry
for 15 May, 'I suppose I must have fallen asleep; I hope so, but I fear . . . I
cannot in the least believe that it was all sleep.'

Bram's son Noel Thornley Stoker always claimed that his father had told
him that the story owed its origin to a powerful nightmare – a fact which
subsequently led his early biographers Harry Ludlam (1962) and Daniel
Farson (1975) to speculate, from little or no evidence, about 'a too generous
helping of dressed crab at supper' followed by something about 'a vampire
King rising from the tomb'.

The 'Notes' certainly seem to confirm the nightmare story, for the very
first time, but it isn't as simple, or as tacky, as this green-lit nightmare straight
out of a Victorian melodrama. It involves three sexually active women whose
'kisses' (as Stoker euphemistically calls them) are intended to penetrate a
less sexually active man, while the man experiences 'some longing and . . .
some deadly fear', and is a nightmare which comes to an abrupt end when
the demon Count hisses 'this man belongs to me!' In the novel, he then
says to the three vampire women that 'I too can love', just after 'looking at
[Harker's] face attentively'. The recently qualified – albeit unimaginative –
lawyer doesn't know what to make of this at all. The best he can come up
with is that Dracula 'certainly left me under the impression that he would
have made a wonderful solicitor'! In March 1890, while trying to exorcize the
same (or a similar) nightmare, Bram Stoker started planning *The Un-Dead*.
A timely reminder – as we examine his 'Foundation Notes and Data' – that
the novel isn't just a pile of pieces of information about the author (as it has
tended to be treated by commentators in recent years); it is also a *structure*
held together well below the surface of the text. Maybe this was what, to
get back to A. N. Wilson's Introduction, eventually promoted Bram Stoker
from the third to the first eleven with the resulting book, *Dracula*.

BRAM STOKER'S WORKING
PAPERS FOR *DRACULA*

Most of these are included in Volume One of the Rosenbach Stoker
Collection, with some at the beginning of Volume Two. They consist of story
outlines, chapter headings, lists of characters, contents pages, timescales, and
various notes about the behaviour and characteristics of vampires. In the
Collection no attempt has been made to arrange these papers in chronological
order; the order is, presumably, the same as when the lot was auctioned by
Sotheby's on Monday 7 July 1913, fourteen months after Stoker's death, for
the papers in Volume One are numbered consecutively from one to thirty-six.

I have rearranged the sequence of Stoker's notes to present them – as
far as possible from the available evidence – in chronological order. And I
have concentrated on the genesis of Chapters I–III of the published novel,
the first three chapters of Jonathan Harker's journal, from his arrival in
Bistritz on 3 May to the nocturnal visit by the 'three young women' on the
night of 15–16 May. Not only are these by far the best-known chapters of
Dracula – they reappear in all the major screen adaptations – but they are
also the chapters for which Bram Stoker did some of the most interesting
research. This presentation of the papers – paraphrased from the original
manuscripts – is intended to enable the reader to follow the various 'stages'
through which the opening chapters of *Dracula* went, as Stoker himself
shaped and reshaped them, from March 1890 to April 1896.

The first notes are dated '8/3/90' and consist of a brief outline of the opening section of the novel. At that early stage, the novel was to begin with a
letter from 'Count –' to a solicitor, followed by much legal correspondence
involving the President of the Law Society, the solicitor named Abraham
Aaronson, and another letter from the Count, in Styria, asking Aaronson

to come in person or send a trustworthy agent who, he stipulates, is not able to speak the German language.*

Then there were to be letters from the trustworthy agent to his Principal, and to his girlfriend, describing the journey to the castle in Styria, including a visit to the Munich Dead House, followed by a train journey to Styria, where he is met by a coachman (who is really the Count) at the station.†

The letters would then describe the arrival at an ancient castle, the first appearance of the Count (as himself), with his devil-dark eyes, and the atmosphere in the castle where the old Count *seems* alone but clearly is not. There followed the incident with the girls who try to kiss him not on the lips but on the throat, culminating in the Count saying, 'This man belongs to me I want him.' After that, the young lawyer describes becoming a prisoner in the castle and, to pass the time, consulting his law directory for the *Sortes Virgilianae*: he has been instructed to buy a large property for the Count, with a consecrated church in the grounds, situated near a river.‡

The next notes are, in effect, an early cast list for the novel. The cast (in

---

*Abraham Aaronson was to become Peter Hawkins, solicitor of Exeter, and the published novel dealt with the Count's business transaction – the purchase of the estate at Purfleet – in flashback, during Chapter II of Harker's journal (entries for 5 and 7 May). The only legal document to survive the transition from notes to finished text was a nine-line extract from Peter Hawkins's sealed letter, which the Count hands to Harker. Otherwise, the details all emerge from two conversations between Dracula and his guest. In these notes of March 1890, the Count evidently lives in Styria (where Le Fanu's *Carmilla* was set). Since Styria was largely German-speaking, the stipulation that the agent does not speak German was presumably to protect the Count from gossiping peasants. As historian Clive Leatherdale has pointed out, in Stoker's short story *Dracula's Guest* Jonathan Harker cannot speak German – 'it was difficult to argue with a man', writes Harker, 'when I did not know his language' – whereas in the final version of *Dracula* we are told on the first page that he has a 'smattering of German . . . indeed, I don't know how I should be able to get on without it'.

†This Munich incident is developed by Stoker in subsequent notes. It involves Harker catching his first glimpse of the Count near a mortuary; only when Harker is safely back in England, and the Count has come to look exactly as he did in Munich, does the young solicitor realize the connection. The incident survived the change of locale from Styria to Translyvania.

‡This is the earliest example of Bram Stoker extending the 'rules' of the vampire genre: the Count, it seems, has to rest in consecrated earth. There will be many more such extensions. Stoker's speciality was blending folklore with vampire lore – plus his own imagination.

March 1890) includes Abraham Aaronson; the lawyer's clerk who goes to Styria; a mad doctor; a mad patient who has 'a theory of perpetual life'; a 'Philosophic Historian'; a German professor of history; a detective inspector; an undertaker; a girl who dies; another girl who is the young lawyer's bright and sceptical sister; and the Count's two servants in London (a silent man and a dumb woman), who are said to be controlled by the evil powers of the Count.*

Then comes a full chapter outline, written on Lyceum Theatre notepaper and dated '14/3/90'. The outline consists of four 'Books', headed *Styria to London, Tragedy, Discovery* and *Punishment*, each broken up into seven chapters. It reads like the synopsis page of a theatre programme.

Book I begins with the lawyer's correspondence, and the clerk's visit to Styria, via Munich (where he encounters 'wolves' and 'blue flame and c'). After arriving at the castle, he experiences 'Loneliness, the Kiss "this man belongs to me"'. Then Dr Seward's diary takes over, with details of the old chapel and the Sortes Virgilianae ('notes in letter'), and of someone called the fly patient who, the notes add, is in love with death.†

Book II begins at Whitby, Yorkshire, with arguments concerning uncanny happenings, a storm, the arrival of a ship and Lucy walking in her sleep. Then Mina's wedding takes place in London, followed by a night of

---

* In this cast list the character who was to become the Dutch Professor Abraham Van Helsing was no less than *three* separate characters: historian, German professor of history and detective inspector. In the event, Van Helsing was to become philosophic historian, philosopher, priest, detective and scientist. The detective-story element of the story was evidently to be stronger during the early stages: there are references in subsequent notes to 'tracing the criminal' and to the conundrum caused to the Count's trackers because they are 'in want of a clue to whereabouts'. Also in this list the Count has two strange servants in London, whereas in *Dracula* one of Stoker's more atmospheric touches was to have the Count a shabby genteel aristocrat, without servants – he does all the domestic chores himself. Although the Count apologizes to Harker, 'My people are not available', the young solicitor realizes that the Count has no 'people' in his employ when he discovers his host making the bed and laying the dinner table. The Mina Harker character was at this stage to be the young lawyer's 'shrewd, sceptical sister.'

† The name 'Styria' was written first by Stoker and then, at some later date, deleted to make way for 'Transylvania'. The names Seward, Lucy, Mina and Harker were all written first time round. This may mean that between 8 March and 14 March 1890 Bram Stoker settled on these proper names. The Van Helsing character (or characters) does not appear at all in this outline.

terror ('wolf missing') and Count Dracula's visit to the lunatic asylum. It ends with the death of Lucy (the 'tragedy' of the Book's title), the opening of the vault and a vow.*

Book III opens with Harker's diary, various suspicions and inquiries, and 'The Dinner'. Mina begins to suspect the Count, and the Texan goes on a visit to Transylvania, where he finds himself 'on the track'. The Count's house is searched for clues, and a 'blood-red room' is discovered. The Count disappears, but at the end of the Book he is sighted by Harker.†

Book IV opens on another dinner party and a vigilante committee. The net closes on the Count ('remaining earth') and the scene shifts back to Styria. The last chapter, entitled 'A Tourist's Tale', includes 'one killed by a wolf (wehr?)', and finishes on the *aide-mémoire* 'Bring in the Texan'.

There follows another cast list, this time headed *Historiae Personae*, which includes some characters who were to appear in the finished novel: Dr Seward, the 'Girl engaged to him', Lucy Westenra, the lawyer Peter

---

*The phrase 'Count Dracula' was evidently added later, between Chapters 5 and 6 of Book II, as must have been another reference to 'Dracula' in Book III, Chapter 3. Before that, he was 'Count Wampyr'.

†Bram Stoker originally had the idea of including a dinner-party scene (at Dr Seward's), in Book III, where each of the thirteen diners would be given a number and would be asked to narrate something strange, the 'order of numbers' making the story complete. The punch-line would be that the Count would enter the room. This strange variation on Lord Byron's 'we will each write a ghost story' (at the end of which, in a sense, *The Vampyre* walked in) also, perhaps, relates to one of Stoker's odder performances, which was serialized on 30 January 1892 in the *Gentlewoman* magazine. It was Chapter 10 of *The Fate of Fenella*, the other nine chapters being written by 'well-known writer(s) of Fiction, without consulting his or her collaborateurs, the result being a ... literary curiosity'; they included Arthur Conan Doyle and F. Anstey. *The Fate of Fenella* was published, complete, later in the year. Stoker eventually junked the idea of the 'dinner of thirteen'. Later in Book III, the (as yet unnamed) Texan was to visit Transylvania on his own, and possibly be killed by a were-wolf. In the final version of *Dracula*, Quincey P. Morris falls victim to the 'knives of the gypsies', but he has such a tangential relationship to the rest of the plot that some commentators have even suggested he is secretly in league with the Count himself (in a kind of American-Transylvanian unholy alliance). Morris (at first named 'Brutus') was also originally, to have been 'an ... inventor from Texas', a 'Tourist' and a walking example of Yankee know-how who arms himself with the latest Maxim Gun for the final assault on the Castle. Stoker's reference to 'a vigilante committee' and 'a necktie party' suggest that the novel had more Western connections in the author's mind at one stage, in common with his novel *The Shoulder of Shasta*, published in October 1895.

Hawkins from Exeter, his clerk Jonathan Harker, Harker's fianceé, the pupil teacher Wilhelmina Murray, known as Mina, a Mad Patient with 'theory of getting life', and a Texan named 'Brutus Morris'. It includes even more characters who were *not* to survive the drafting process: two lawyers called Arthur Abbott and Wm. Young, a friend and schoolfellow of Mina called Kate Reed, the Count's two English servants, a detective named Cotford, a psychical research agent named Alfred Singleton, an American inventor from Texas (unnamed), a German professor named Max Windshoeffel and a painter named Francis Aytoun. At this early stage, the Count was still to be called 'Count Wampyr'.*

The next document, again written on Lyceum Theatre notepaper, consists of three short checklists of the 'characteristics of Count Wampyr'. According to Stoker's notes, the Count:

goes through fog entirely by instinct;

must cross running water at the exact flood or slack of the tide;

has an influence over rats, and over the animals in the zoological gardens
  ('wolves, hyenas cowed – rage of eagle and Lion');

absolutely despises death and the dead;

loves creating evil thoughts in others, and banishing good ones – thus
  destroying their will;

can see in the dark, and can even get through the thickest of London fogs
  by instinct;

is insensible to the beauties of music;

has 'white teeth', and the magic power of making himself large or small;

must be brought or helped, or in some way welcomed over the threshold;

---

*In this cast list the Van Helsing character was still to be divided into three – only this time it was as a detective, a psychical research agent and a German professor, and each of these characters had been given a name: Cotford, Alfred Singleton and Max Windshoeffel. Perhaps Professor Windshoeffel was based upon the other German professor called Max in Bram Stoker's life at the time – Professor Max Müller of Oxford. The appearance of the fine artist 'Francis Aytoun' may relate to the next two documents. Wilhelmina gets her full name for the first time, as does Lucy, and Mina's friend and confidante Kate Reed (later to be jettisoned) makes her first appearance. The phrase 'Count Wampyr' was changed by Stoker to 'Count Dracula' on this sheet at a later date.

is enormously strong, even though he never – apparently – eats or drinks;

has an ambivalent attitude towards the icons of religion: he can be moved
only by relics older than his own *real* date or century (that is, when he
actually lived) – more recent relics leave him unmoved;

always uses for money his stores of old gold, which are eventually 'traced
to Salzburg banking house';

'Immortality – Gladstone' . . .

Where the Count's image is concerned:

painters can't make a likeness of him – however hard the artist tries, the
subject always ends up looking like someone else;

equally, it is impossible to photograph (or 'Codak') him – the resulting
print always makes him appear 'black or like skeleton corpse';

and there are no looking glasses in the Count's house – because he has no
reflection and casts no shadow; the lights in his house must therefore be
specially arranged 'to give no shadow'.

As to the Count's folkloric background:

a long thorny branch of a wild rose must be placed in his coffin, to prevent
him leaving it;

a swallow – or 'galinele lui Dieu' – is considered lucky, as the fowl of the
Lord;

crow, unlucky, notably when it flies over a person's head;

St George's Day is on 24 April ('our May 6'), and the night before is, by
tradition, a Witches' Sabbat.*

---

*These three checklists of Count Wampyr's 'characteristics' (rather than those of vampires in
general) include some predictable entries as well as some surprises. In addition to the 'characteristics' of the Folkloric Vampire, they incorporate some plot elements (the Count at London
Zoo; the influence over rats and 'lower' life forms; the London fog; the Count's favoured
currency of old gold) which relate only to the story of *Dracula*. Other 'characteristics', which
Stoker did not in the end use, seem to belong to the world of *The Yellow Book* and have more
to do with Oscar Wilde than folklore: the *fin-de-siècle* vampire is insensible to the beauties
of music, he *loves* to create evil thoughts and 'painters cannot paint him – their likenesses
[are] always like some one else'. This latter 'characteristic' suggests a close family resemblance
to Wilde's *The Picture of Dorian Gray* (which, in 1891, had just been published) and may also

Also appended to the document is a series of short notes concerning the visit of the lawyer's clerk to Munich, en route for the Castle. As he is walking past the Dead House in Munich, the young man is to see a waxen face among the funeral flowers. At first he thinks it is a corpse, but it turns out to be the face of a living man. Long afterwards, when the Count is in London – and when his 'white moustache' has grown – Harker will recognize the Count's face as the one he saw among the flowers in Munich. Evidently, the face presented by the Count when he is in his castle is appreciably different – perhaps younger.*

There follows later a brief contents page, dated 29/2/92, outlining the structure of the beginning of the novel. Harker's diary, with its Munich

---

connect with the character 'A Painter – Francis Aytoun' in the previous cast list. Stoker was, of course, an acquaintance of Wilde, and a friend of his neighbour in Cheyne Walk, Chelsea, James McNeill Whistler. Wilde's play *Salomé* was written in Paris in 1891. He decided to cast Sarah Bernhardt in the title role during a party at Henry Irving's (with Stoker probably present), and when *Salomé* was published in February 1893, Wilde immediately sent a signed copy of it to Florence Stoker (this Salomé, especially in Beardsley's famous illustration, is a seductive little vampire, part-vampire and part vamp). The idea that vampires could be moved only by relics older than their own *real* date sounds ancient and folkloric, but appears to have been invented by Stoker. The more up-to-date idea that you cannot photograph (or 'Codak') a vampire because he will come out looking like a corpse is logical – if that is the correct word in the circumstances – but also new. In *Dracula* Harker does use his 'Kodak' to photograph the house at Purfleet (or rather 'views of it from various points') but sadly, he never tries this relatively new process out on the Count himself. The references to the swallow as the fowl of the Lord, the crow as unlucky and the dates of St George's Day are all taken verbatim from Emily Gerard's *Transylvanian Superstitions* (see pages 355–62). The 'Salzburg banking house' reference would suggest that these lists date from the time when the book was still to be set in Austrian Styria – that is, before February 1892; in the finished text Dracula's bankers are Herren Klopstock and Billreuth of Buda-Pesth. The bizarre line, 'Immortality – Gladstone', unless it refers to the bag of that name, remains a puzzle, whatever the date. There is no mention of the fact that vampires are nocturnal creatures. That may be because Stoker chose to ignore this particular 'rule'; Dracula can function in the daytime, although he is not at his best. When Stoker notes that the Count never eats or drinks, he must presumably be referring to solid food and vintage wine; in the novel itself, the Count does have a preferred beverage, but it has to be served at body temperature. After noting that he has never *seen* the Count eat or drink, Harker sensibly observes, 'He must be a very peculiar man.'

*In the published novel the Count has a 'great white moustache', or a 'heavy moustache' – as befits a retired military commander – when Harker first meets him at the Castle. There is the suggestion that Dracula gets *younger* (rather than more ancient) as the story progresses.

interlude, still forms Chapter 2. Chapter 1 consists of correspondence about 'Purchase of Estate'. Chapter 3 continues the Munich story (so it remains an extensive section of the narrative) and takes us to 'Bistritz – Borgo Pass – Castle'. What happens there, as Stoker cryptically adds, is 'Sortes Virgil. Belongs to Me'.*

Another memo represents a slight refinement of the outline structure of February 1892. It still opens on lawyers' letters about 'Purchase of Estate' but is more explicit about 'Harker's diary – Munich – Wolf' and 'Harker's diary – Munich – Death House', and cross-cuts between Harker's journey from 'Bistritz to Castle Dracula' and Dr Seward's diary entries concerning the 'Fly man', so that the 'Fly man' (who was later to become Renfield) heralds Harker's arrival at the Castle rather than, as in the published version, the Count's arrival at his English residence. Also, the 'Belongs to Me' incident appears to be cross-cut with events in Whitby. The most significant aspect of this memo is that it explicitly mentions 'Castle Dracula' for the very first time.

One of the next documents is a fully worked-out structure, letter by letter, of Book I. It begins with a letter from Sir Robert Parton, President of the Law Society, to Peter Hawkins of Cathedral Place, Exeter, stating that he has been contacted by one 'Count Wampyr'. Peter Hawkins, we learn from another letter, has gout (like Stoker) and decides to let Harker handle the conveyancing of an estate to the Count which he finds at Purfleet. Letter 6 is from Kate Reed to Lucy Westenra, telling Lucy about Harker's visit to a school to see pupil-teacher Mina Murray; there is a postscript in which Kate tells of 'how she thought after writing it would be well to ask Mina's permission before telling her story'. She continues this theme: 'she knows it's all over long ago, and that she goes to stay with her on summer holidays

---

*This revised structure is particularly significant for its references to 'Bistritz – Borgo Pass'. By the end of February 1892 Stoker had decided to shift the location from Styria to Bistrita in Transylvania. Since his knowledge of the Borgo Pass (and of how to spell Romanian place-names) came from Charles Boner's *Transylvania* (see pages 362–67), and of local folklore from Gerard, it appears that he had read these two books by this date. He would also have known about the name 'Dracula' as early as summer 1890. So by 1892 all the key pieces of the jigsaw were already in place – *five years* before publication.

at Whitby'. Letter 8 is a telegram from 'Dracula to Hawkins', asking that Harker set out for Munich.*

The structure then changes from the letter form to 'journal in shorthand of Jonathan Harker on his first journey abroad'. Since this journal is being written especially to show Mina on Harker's return, all business matters have been deliberately omitted. Chapter 2 begins with the directions which have been sent by the Count, to go by the direct service to Munich and then to 'stop at (Hotel Marienbad) Quatre Saisons and await instructions'. On his first day, Harker visits the Pinakothek Museum, and also the Dead House. There he catches sight of 'old man on bier' – among some flowers – who seems at first to be a corpse but in fact isn't. He goes back to the Quatre Saisons hotel. The following morning he receives a wire from 'Transylvania. Bistritz', giving him details of the next leg of his journey. Chapter 3 (still in journal form) describes the journey to Bistritz, where Harker checks into his hotel. The Count's name is well known there, for it was the hoteliers who sent on the telegram; but when they hear of the young man's destination, they become 'all very sad and mysterious'. There are some strange gifts for him ('see xix century'). [These 'gifts' are an explicit reference to Gerard's article in the *Nineteenth Century* magazine.] Harker is deposited at the Borgo Pass by the Diligence, where he is met by a 'driver man muffled' on a carriage. The journey from the Borgo Pass to the Castle is eventful: some wolves surround the carriage, some blue flames are sighted, until, amid the howlings of wolves and dogs, thunder and other 'weird sounds' – they eventually

---

*Strangely, although the name 'Count Wampyr' appears in Letters 1–5, later crossed out by Bram Stoker and superseded by the new name 'Count Dracula', from Letter 8 onwards the name 'Dracula' was written first time round – and continues that way throughout Stoker's summary. Perhaps the early chapters were being copied from a previous (but post-'Abraham Aaronson') version. Peter Hawkins's attack of gout, mentioned here for the first time, is still there in the finished novel. 'An attack of gout,' he writes in Chapter II, 'from which malady I am a constant sufferer, forbids absolutely any travelling on my part.'

The two letters from confidante Kate Reed seem to imply, first, that she has some 'story' which is of interest to Mina and, second, that it is 'all over long ago', so they can remain friends. Could it possibly have been a romance with Jonathan? In the published version, he is *very* correct on such matters.

arrive at the Castle at midnight. At this juncture, 'enter Count-supper-to bed-describe room, &c'.*

Chapter 4 continues Harker's account in his journal of his stay in the Castle. Although Harker is left all alone in the daytime, he feels he is a prisoner: 'the books – sortes Virgilianae – the visitors – is it a dream – woman stoops to kiss him – terror of death – suddenly Count turns her away – "This man belongs to me".'†

Bram Stoker's finalized outline of the early part of the novel is evidently an attempt to sort out the timescale of his story. It is written on a printed, all-purpose diary with no dates on it – just the headings *189 – Monday – Sunday, Morning, Evening* and *Remarks.*

The outline begins on 16 March with Count Dracula's letter to Peter Hawkins (dated, Stoker adds, 4 March old style), then continues on 21 March with Sir Robert Parton's letter to Hawkins – the President of the Law Society to a senior solicitor. Hawkins's letter to the Count is written on Thursday, 23 March, and the reply from Dracula a week later (18 March old style). Jonathan Harker visits Purfleet on 12 April and starts his house-deeds search on Thursday, 13 April – the same day as Count Dracula writes to the *maître d'hôtel* of the Quatre Saisons in Munich. Two days later, Harker writes to Hawkins, and on Sunday, 16 April, he visits Mina at the school where she teaches.‡

The following day, Kate writes to Lucy, and on Wednesday, 19 April, Hawkins writes another letter to Dracula.

Following a telegram from Dracula dispatched on Monday, 24 April, Harker leaves London on the night of the 25th at 8.05 p.m., arrives in Paris early the following morning, leaves Paris at 8.25 a.m. and arrives in Munich at 8.35 p.m. Having checked into the Quatre Saisons late on Wednesday,

---

* Stoker's shorthand 'enter Count' reads like a stage direction for Henry Irving!

† Later in this structure, at Book III, Chapter 7, Jonathan Harker 'sees the Count – met him going into the Munich Death-House': clearly, for some reason, by then the Count's appearance has become the same as in Book I, Chapter 2. The 'dinner of revenge' is also still there.

‡ Either Stoker wasn't concentrating, or Mina taught at a boarding-school. Otherwise, why should she be visited at school on a Sunday?

26 April, Harker has his 'adventure snow storm and wolf' on the following day, gets back to the Hotel early on the morning of the 28th and spends all 29 April recovering ('home all day'). On the evening of Sunday, 30 April, he goes to the opera to see Wagner's *Flying Dutchman*. Monday, 1 May, is the day of the Dead House incident, and is also Walpurgis Night. Harker leaves Munich by train at 8.35 that evening. His destination is Vienna, via Salzburg.*

Tuesday, 2 May, is spent travelling: a change of trains at Vienna in the morning (arrive 6.45 a.m., depart 8.25 a.m.), another at Buda-Pesth over lunchtime (arrive 1.30 p.m., depart 2.00 p.m.), followed by arrival at Klausenburg at 10.34 p.m. After an overnight stay at Klausenburg (2–3 May), Harker leaves by the 8 a.m. train and arrives in Bistritz twelve hours later. After another overnight stay, he leaves Bistritz at 2 p.m. – by coach – and reaches the Borgo Pass seven hours later at 9.00 p.m. (or one hour earlier than the scheduled eight hours). Harker finally reaches the Castle, driven by the muffled and disguised coachman, in the early hours of Friday, 5 May. It takes him two days to realize that the Castle is in fact 'a prison', and on Tuesday, 9 May, he tries to write home about his experiences so far ('Castle – letters home'). On the Wednesday, he sees the Count crawling out of his window and down the wall of the Castle (the first mention of this sight in

---

*This Wagnerian curtain-raiser to the events in Transylvania provides a nice link with the world of Henry Irving (who performed W. G. Wills's version of the legend of the Flying Dutchman, *Vanderdecken*, from June 1878 onwards) and with Bram Stoker's personal interests. *Vanderdecken* was reviewed by Stoker: 'the chief actor is not quick but dead . . . and in the last act . . . answers the question "where are we?": "Between the living and the dead".' In *Recollections*, he wrote that '[Irving] gave one a wonderful impression of a dead man, fictitiously alive'. Irving was to add the suggestion that the Dutchman was cast on the shore, and restored to life by the waves. After the opening night, Stoker helped Irving to 'cut and alter the play', and in 1891–92 was involved in discussions with Irving and Hall Caine about a new version of the story – which were to come to nothing because in Irving's view Caine had made the character of the Captain 'too brutal at the start'. Stoker was a great fan of Wagner's operatic music, and especially of Hans Richter's interpretations. In the 1890s, according to the *Personal Reminiscences*, 'with my wife I attended the Wagner Cycle at Bayreuth . . . and heard Wagner's *Meistersinger* in all its magnificent perfection'. Stoker was also to discuss the lighting effects in *The Flying Dutchman*, with Richter, over lunch on 24 October 1900. The events in Munich, according to this late timescale by Stoker, occur in an unexpected order. First, the adventure of the 'snow storm and wolf', then the visit to the opera, then Walpurgis Nacht, then the Dead House incident. On the first line of *Dracula* as published, all of this is reduced to 'Left Munich at 8.35 p.m.'; only the time of departure survives from the drafting stage.

the *Notes*), and on Thursday, 11 May, he sees 'the women-kissing'. Friday is spent in bed, 'told to write letters'. To judge by the crossings-out, Stoker then changed his mind about the dating of the incidents in the Castle. He substituted the night of Friday, 12 May, for the window incident, and Monday, 15 May, for 'women kissing'.*

Appended to the timescale was a timetable of train arrivals and departures from London to Paris, Paris to Munich, Munich to Vienna via Salzburg, Vienna to Budapest, Budapest to Klausenburg, Klausenburg to Bistritz and of the coach journey from Bistritz to the Borgo Pass. Stoker simply transposed this timetable (probably from Baedeker's) into his own order of events. There followed some lists of these places and arrival and departure dates.†

* On the manuscript of this timescale, Stoker wrote – just before the entry for Thursday, 11 May – 'Jonathan's Diary' as a heading. This would suggest that all the previous incidents were to be communicated in the form of a collection of documents: the legal letters, Kate's letter, Dracula's telegram, then letters home from the Castle. Stoker also wrote 'Seward's Diary' against the dates Wednesday, 3 May, and Saturday, 6 May, so at one stage the account of the journey from Vienna to Transylvania *may* have been compiled from Harker's reminiscences to Dr Seward; or he may still have intended to cross-cut between the journey and Seward's simultaneous experiences. If 'Jonathan's Diary' *was* to begin on Thursday, 11 May, then its first page would have described 'the women kissing' incident, which would, of course, have given it even more prominence in the story. The date he finally settled on for this incident, Monday, 15 May, was the same as in the published novel.

The whole of this detailed breakdown of the story outline into dates and times, in a printed diary, was evidently written *after* Stoker had made up his mind about the details of the story itself. It suggests that the initial legal correspondence was present until the final stages of drafting the novel, as was Kate Reed's correspondence with Lucy. Also Jonathan Harker's five-day stopover in Munich (why five days?) survived until a very late stage. These dates and days correspond with the year 1893. It is quite possible that Stoker was already sorting out the timescale of *Dracula* in that same year, perhaps on holiday in Scotland, for we know that he wanted the events to seem 'exactly contemporary'.

† He was evidently keen to establish an aura of 'authenticity' around his story, by getting all the dates and timetables right, so that, as he put it in his opening words to *Dracula*, his history 'may stand forth as simple fact'. It was a passion shared by Count Dracula himself, who owns 'such books of reference as the London Directory, the "Red" and "Blue" books, Whitaker's Almanack, the Army and Navy Lists, and ... the Law List'. Later, Jonathan Harker discovers the Count 'lying on the sofa, reading, of all things in the world, an English Bradshaw's Guide'. As Henry Irving's manager, Stoker would have had to look after the complex logistics of his national and international tours, involving constant reference to Bradshaw's and, for overseas, Baedeker's guides.

BRAM STOKER'S RESEARCH PAPERS
FOR *DRACULA*

Most of these are included in Volumes Two and Three of the Rosenbach Stoker Collection. They consist of notes, transcribed passages, personal memos, page references, raw data or bibliographies from the books and articles Stoker was reading as he prepared for his novel. Many of these research papers were typed – either as an *aide mémoire* or, perhaps later, in preparation for their sale. Some were both typed and handwritten. Altogether, there are notes from or references to nearly forty books and articles, plus transcribed conversations and personal descriptions of places. Again, they do not appear to be in any particular order and the pages of Volumes Two and Three are unnumbered.

In reconstructing the progress of Bram Stoker's research for the first three chapters of *Dracula*, I have presented key passages from books or articles he was reading – the ones he chose to isolate in his own notes – and (as with the working papers) have rearranged the extracts as far as possible in chronological order. Sometimes the working papers provide clues as to when these books and articles were read; sometimes the research papers help us to date Stoker's own notes. Together, they provide an unusually detailed insight into the way Bram Stoker worked and, indeed, into the way his mind worked.

'Account of the Principalities of Wallachia and Moldavia, etc., Wm Wilkinson late consul of Bukorest, Longmans, 1820 (Whitby Library 0.1097)'*

... the population increased, and a great number of small towns and villages were built in the country [of Wallachia]. Frequent hostilities against

---

*Amazingly, Bram Stoker first came across the name DRACULA while reading a memoir by the 'Late British Consul Resident at Bukorest' in the library of the Literary and Philosophical Society at Whitby, Yorkshire. He even noted down the class-mark! Since we know that Stoker

the Hungarians, arising from the claims of sovereignty of the latter, accustomed the Wallachians to war; and in 1391 the Voïvode Mirtza [*voïvode* was a Slavonic title, equivalent to that of Commanding Prince] collected a numerous force, and attached the neighbouring possessions of the Turks with the view of rescuing them from their hands. The Sultan Bajazet being at that moment employed in Asia in a troublesome war with the Prince of Castomona, had left his conquests near the Danube without the means of defence. But when the news of their invasion reached him, he suspended his operations in Asia, and returned to Adrianople, from whence he sent a numerous army to Wallachia. The Voïvode marched to meet the Turks; and, after a bloody battle, he was defeated, and compelled to become tributary to the Sultan. The annual amount of the tribute was fixed at three thousand piasters [a piaster and a half is equal to an English shilling].

Wallachia continued to pay it until the year 1444; when Ladislas King of Hungary, preparing to make war against the Turks, engaged the Voïvode DRACULA to form an alliance with him. The Hungarian troops marched through the principality and were joined by four thousand Wallachians under the command of DRACULA's son.

The Hungarians being defeated at the celebrated battle of Varna, Hunniades their general, and regent of the Kingdom during Ladislas's minority, returned in haste to make new preparations for carrying on the war. But the Voïvode, fearful of the Sultan's vengeance, arrested and kept him prisoner during a year, pretending thereby to show to the Turks that he treated him

was holidaying there, between late July and the end of August 1890 (when he scribbled his notes for Chapters VI–VIII of *Dracula*, the ones which describe events in Whitby between 24 July and 18 August), it seems certain he discovered Dracula that same summer, some four or five months *after* he started thinking about the book. The other passages he copied from Wilkinson primarily concerned a) the tendency of the Boyar class to claim that 'none in Europe can boast of more genuine nobility', b) the ornate carriages – or *calèches* – used by the now impoverished Boyars, 'ornamented in the most gaudy manner . . . and driven by a gypsy in rags', c) the most common form of public transport, 'a kind of vehicle . . . which is not unlike a very small crate for earthenware', and d) the state of the roads in the Carpathian Mountains. The passage from Wilkinson's book reprinted here contains the one and only reference to the historical Dracula, Vlad the Impaler, in all of Stoker's research papers. Whole books of speculation have been written on the basis of this reference.

as an enemy. The moment Hunniades reached Hungary, he assembled an army and placed himself at the head of it, returned to Wallachia, attacked and defeated the Voïvodate, and caused him to be beheaded in his presence; after which he raised to the Voïvodate one of the primates of the country, of the name of *Dan*.

The Wallachians under this Voïvode joined again the Hungarians in 1448, and made war on Turkey; but being totally defeated at the battle of Cossova, in Bulgaria, and finding it no longer possible to make any stand against the Turks, they submitted again to the annual tribute, which they paid until the year 1460, when the Sultan Mahomet II, being occupied in completing the conquest of the islands in the Archipelago, afforded them a new opportunity of shaking off the yoke. Their Voïvode, also named DRACULA,* did not remain satisfied with mere prudent measures of defence: with an army he crossed the Danube and attacked the few Turkish troops that were stationed in his neighbourhood; but this attempt, like those of his predecessors, was only attended with momentary success.† Mahomet, having turned his arms against him, drove him back to Wallachia, whither he pursued and defeated him. The Voïvode escaped into Hungary, and the Sultan caused his brother Bladus to be named in his place. He made a treaty with Bladus, by which he bound the Wallachians to perpetual tribute; and laid the foundations of that slavery, from which no efforts have yet had the power of extricating them with any lasting efficacy.

*Wilkinson's footnote – the reference: 'DRACULA in the Wallachian language means Devil. The Wallachians were, at that time, as they are at present, used to give this as a surname to any person who rendered himself conspicuous either by courage, cruel actions, or cunning'. (W. W.)

†In his research notes Stoker compressed this sentence to read 'Their Voïvode [DRACULA] crossed Danube and attacked Turkish troops. Only momentary success'. By omitting the words 'also named', he implied a confusion between the two Draculas, *père* and *fils*. It was Stoker who wrote the name in capital letters.

'Transylvanian Superstitions, Mme E. de Laszowska Gerard. XIX Century, Vol. XVIII, July 1885, pp. 130–50*'

Transylvania might well be termed the land of superstition, for nowhere else does this curious crooked plant of delusion flourish as persistently and in such bewildering variety. It would almost seem as though the whole species of demons, pixies, witches, and hobgoblins, driven from the rest of Europe by the wand of science, had taken refuge within this mountain rampart, well aware that here they would find secure lurking-places, whence they might defy their persecutors yet awhile . . .

The spirit of evil (or, not to put too fine a point upon it, the devil) plays a conspicuous part in the Roumenian code of superstition, and such designa-tions as the Gregynia Drakuluj (devil's garden), the Gania Drakuluj (devil's mountain), Yadu Drakuluj (devil's hell or abyss), &c. &c., which we frequently find attached to rocks, caverns, or heights, attest the fact that these people believe themselves to be surrounded on all sides by a whole legion of evil spirits.

The devils are furthermore assisted by witches and dragons, and to all of these dangerous beings are ascribed peculiar powers on particular days and at certain places . . .

*One of the main reasons why Bram Stoker changed the location for Chapters I–III of *Dracula* from Styria to Transylvania was that he had read about 'the whole species of demons, pixies, witches, and hobgoblins, driven from the rest of Europe by the wand of science, [who] had taken refuge within this mountain rampart'. And he had read about them (between 14 March 1890 and 29 February 1892) in Gerard's colourful article on *Transylvanian Superstitions*, which she later revised for *The Land Beyond the Forest*. Emily Gerard was married to a commander in the Austro-Hungarian cavalry who had been briefly posted to Transylvania. Unlike the writers of Stoker's other research sources, she had little or no interest in politics and society, but was evidently fascinated in a superior kind of way by strange folktales, the stranger the better. Several of them found their way – almost word for word – into *Dracula*: the significance of the eve of St George's, the legend of the blue flames, the buried treasure, the Scholomance or Devil's School, the evil power of the *nosferatu* and its first cousin the were-wolf. Others found their way into Stoker's working notes – in particular, into his first list of vampire characteristics and into the Bistritz section of his revised plot structure ('see XIX century', he wrote). After the publication of *Dracula*, Bram Stoker was himself to contribute four articles to *The Nineteenth Century and After* (as it was by then known). It was Gerard who invented the word '*nosferatu*' as a synonym for 'vampire' – apparently based on a mis-hearing of the Romanian 'necuratul', meaning The Evil One.

To different hours of the day are likewise ascribed different influences, favourable or the reverse. Thus it is always considered unlucky to look at oneself in the glass after sunset; also it is not wise to sweep the dust over the threshold in the evening, or to give back a sieve or a whip which has been borrowed of a neighbour.

The exact hour of noon is precarious on account of the evil spirit *Pripolniza*, and so is midnight because of the *miase nópte* (night spirit), and it is safer to remain within doors at these hours. If, however, some misguided peasant does happen to leave his home at midnight, and espies (as very likely he may) a flaming dragon in the sky, he need not necessarily give himself up as lost, for if he have the presence of mind to stick a fork into the ground alongside of him, the fiery monster will thereby be prevented from carrying him off.

The finger which ventures to point at a rainbow will be straightway seized by a gnawing disease, and a rainbow appearing in December is always considered to bode misfortune.

The Greek Church, to which the Roumenians exclusively belong, has an abnormal number of feast-days, to almost each of which peculiar customs and superstitions are attached. I will here only attempt to mention a few of the principal ones ...

In the night preceding Easter Sunday witches and demons are abroad, and hidden treasures are said to betray their site by a glowing flame. No God-fearing peasant will, however, allow himself to be tempted by the hopes of such riches, which he cannot on that day appropriate without sin. On no account should he presume to absent himself from the midnight church service, and his devotion will be rewarded by the mystic qualities attached to the wax candle he has carried in his hand, and which when lighted hereafter during a thunderstorm will infallibly keep the lightning from striking his house.

The greatest luck which can befall a mortal is to be born on Easter Sunday while the bells are ringing, but it is not lucky to die on that day. The spoon with which the Easter eggs have been removed from the boiling pot is carefully treasured up, and worn in the belt by the shepherd; it gives him the power to distinguish the witches who seek to molest his flock.

Perhaps the most important day in the year is St. George's, the 23rd of

April (corresponds to our 6th of May), the eve of which is still frequently kept by occult meetings taking place at night in lonely caverns or within ruined walls, and where all the ceremonies usual to the celebration of a witches' Sabbath are put into practice.

The feast itself is the great day to beware of witches, to counteract whose influence square-cut blocks of green turf are placed in front of each door and window. This is supposed effectually to bar their entrance to the house or stables, but for still greater safety it is usual here for the peasants to keep watch all night by the sleeping cattle.

This same night is the best for finding treasures, and many people spend it in wandering about the hills trying to probe the earth for the gold it contains. Vain and futile as such researches usually are, yet they have in this country a somewhat greater semblance of reason than in most other parts, for perhaps nowhere else have so many successive nations been forced to secrete their riches in flying from an enemy, to say nothing of the numerous veins of undiscovered gold and silver which must be seaming the country in all directions. Not a year passes without bringing to light some earthern jar containing old Dacian coins, or golden ornaments of Roman origin, and all such discoveries serve to feed and keep up the national superstition.

In the night of St. George's Day (so say the legends) all these treasures begin to burn, or, to speak in mystic language, to 'bloom' in the bosom of the earth, and the light they give forth, described as a bluish flame resembling the colour of lighted spirits of wine, serves to guide favoured mortals to their place of concealment. The conditions to the successful raising of such a treasure are manifold, and difficult of accomplishment. In the first place, it is by no means easy for a common mortal who has not been born on a Sunday nor at midday when the bells are ringing, to hit upon a treasure at all. If he does, however, catch sight of a flame such as I have described, he must quickly stick a knife through the swaddling rags of his right foot, and then throw the knife in the direction of the flame he has seen. If two people are together during this discovery they must not on any account break silence till the treasure is removed, neither is it allowed to fill up the hole from which anything has been taken, for that would induce a speedy death. Another important feature to be noted is that the lights seen before midnight on St. George's Day, denote treasures kept by benevolent spirits, while those which appear at a later hour are unquestionably of a pernicious nature ...

The feast of St. Elias, the 20th of July (August 1st) is a very unlucky day, on which the lightning may be expected to strike. If a house struck by lightning begins to burn, it is not allowed to put out the flames, because God has lit the fire and it would be presumption if man were to dare to meddle. In some places it is believed that a fire lit by lightning can only be put out with milk.

An approved method for averting the danger of the dwelling being struck by lightning is to form a top by sticking a knife through a piece of bread, and spin it on the floor of the loft during the whole time the storm lasts. The ringing of bells is likewise very efficacious, provided, however, that the bell in question has been cast under a perfectly cloudless sky.

As I am on the subject of thunderstorms, I may as well here mention the *Scholomance*, or school supposed to exist somewhere in the heart of the mountains, and where all the secrets of nature, the language of animals, and all imaginable magic spells and charms are taught by the devil in person. Only ten scholars are admitted at a time, and when the course of learning has expired and nine of them are released to return to their homes, the tenth scholar is detained by the devil as payment, and mounted upon an *Ismeju* (dragon) he becomes henceforward the devil's aide-de-camp, and assists him in 'making the weather,' that is to say, preparing the thunderbolts.

A small lake, immeasurably deep, lying high up among the mountains to the south of Hermanstadt, is supposed to be the cauldron where is brewed the thunder, and in fair weather the dragon sleeps beneath the waters. Roumenian peasants anxiously warn the traveller to beware of throwing a stone into this lake lest it should wake the dragon and provoke a thunderstorm. It is, however, no mere superstition that in summer there occur almost daily thunderstorms at this spot, about the hour of midday, and numerous cairns of stones round the shores attest the fact that many people have here found their death by lightning. On this account the place is shunned, and no Roumenians will venture to rest here at the hour of noon ...

Of the household animals, the sheep is the most highly prized by the

Roumenian, who makes of it his companion and frequently his counsellor, and by its bearing it is supposed often to give warning when danger is near.

The swallow is here, as elsewhere, a luck-bringing bird, and goes by the name of *galinele lui Dieu* (fowls of the Lord). There is always a treasure to be found near the place where the first swallow has been espied.

The crow, on the contrary, is a bird of evil omen, and is particularly ominous when it flies straight over the head of any man.

The magpie perched upon a roof gives notice of the approach of guests, but a shrieking magpie meeting or accompanying a traveller denotes death.

The cuckoo is an oracle to be consulted in manifold contingencies. This bird plays a great part in Roumenian poetry, and is frequently supposed to be the spirit of an unfortunate lover.

It is never permissible to kill a spider, as that would entail misfortune.

A toad taking up its residence in a cow-byre is assuredly in the service of a witch, and has been sent there to purloin the milk. It should therefore be stoned to death; but the same liberty must not be taken with the equally pernicious weasel, and if these animals be found to inhabit a barn or stable, the peasant must endeavour to render them harmless by diverting their thoughts into a safer channel. To this end a tiny threshing-flail must be prepared for the male weasel, and a distaff for his female partner, and laid at a place the animals are known to frequent.

The skull of a horse placed over the gate of the courtyard, or the bones of fallen animals, buried under the doorstep, are preservatives against ghosts.

The place where a horse has rolled on the ground is unwholesome, and the man who steps upon it will be speedily attacked by eruptions, boils or other skin diseases.

Black fowls are always viewed with suspicion, as possibly standing in the service of a witch, and the Brahmaputra fowl is curiously enough considered to be the offspring of the devil with a Jewish girl . . .

It is bad luck if your path be traversed by a hare, but a fox or wolf crossing your road is a good omen.

Likewise, it is lucky to meet a woman with a jug full of water, while an empty jug is unlucky; therefore, the Roumenian maiden who meets you on the way back from the well will, smiling, display her brimming pitcher as she passes, with a pleased consciousness of bringing good luck; while the girl whose pitcher is empty will slink past shamefacedly, as though she had a crime to conceal.

Every orthodox Roumenian woman is careful to do homage to the water-spirit, the *wodna zena* or *zona*, which resides in each spring, by spilling a few drops on the ground, after she has emptied her jug. She will never venture to draw the water against the current, for that would strike the spirit home and provoke her anger.

The Roumenian in general avoids the neighbourhood of deep pools of water, especially whirlpools, for here resides the dreadful *balaur*, or the *wodna muz*, the cruel waterman who lies in wait for human victims.

Each forest has likewise its own particular spirit, its *mama padura*, or forest mother. This fairy is in general supposed to be good-natured, especially towards children who have lost their way in the wood. Less to be trusted is *Panusch* (surely a corruption of the Greek god Pan?), who haunts the forest glades and lies in wait for helpless maidens.

Ravaging diseases, like the pest, cholera, &c., are attributed to a spirit called the *dschuma*, to whom is sometimes given the shape of a fierce virgin, sometimes that of a toothless old hag. This spectre can only be driven away if a red shirt, which must be spun, woven, and sewed all in one night by seven old women, is hung out at the entrance of the afflicted village . . .

Pomanas, or funeral feasts, are repeated [by the Roumenians] after a fortnight, six weeks, and on each anniversary for the next seven years; also, whenever the defunct has appeared in dream to any member of the family, this likewise calls for another *Pomana*; and when these conditions are not exactly complied with, the soul thus neglected is apt to wander complaining about the earth, and cannot find rest. These restless spirits, called *Strigoi*, are not malicious, but their appearance bodes no good, and may be regarded as omens of sickness or misfortune.

More decidedly evil, however, is the vampire, or *nosferatu*, in whom every Roumenian peasant believes as firmly as he does in heaven or hell. There are two sorts of vampires – living and dead. The living vampire is in general the illegitimate offspring of two illegitimate persons, but even a flawless pedigree will not ensure anyone against the intrusion of a vampire into his family vault, since every person killed by a *nosferatu* becomes likewise a vampire after death, and will continue to suck the blood of other innocent people till the spirit has been exorcised, either by opening the grave of the person suspected and driving a stake through the corpse, or firing a pistol shot into the coffin. In very obstinate cases it is further recommended to cut off the head and replace it in the coffin with the mouth filled with garlic, or to extract the heart and burn it, strewing the ashes over the grave.

That such remedies are often resorted to, even in our enlightened days, is a well-attested fact, and there are probably few Roumenian villages where such has not taken place within the memory of the inhabitants.

First cousin to the vampire, the long exploded were-wolf of the Germans is here to be found, lingering yet under the name of the *Prikolitsch*. Sometimes it is a dog instead of a wolf, whose form a man has taken either voluntarily or as penance for his sins. In one of the villages a story is still told (and believed) of such a man, who driving home from church on Sunday with his wife, suddenly felt that the time for his transformation had come. He therefore gave over the reins to her, and stepped aside into the bushes, where, murmuring the mystic formula, he turned three somersaults over a ditch. Soon after this the woman, waiting in vain for her husband, was attacked by a furious dog, which rushed, barking, out of the bushes and succeeded in biting her severely, as well as tearing her dress. When, an hour later, this woman reached home alone she was met by her husband, who advanced smiling to meet her, but between his teeth she caught sight of the shreds of her dress which had been bitten out by the dog, and the horror of the discovery caused her to faint away . . .

We do not require to go far for the explanation of the extraordinary tenacity of life of the were-wolf legend in a country like Transylvania, where real wolves still abound. Every winter here brings fresh proof of the boldness and cunning of these terrible animals, whose attacks on flocks and farms are often conducted with a skill which would do honour to a human intellect. Sometimes a whole village is kept in trepidation for weeks together by some particularly audacious leader of a flock of wolves, to whom the peasants not unnaturally attribute a more than animal nature, and one may safely prophesy that so long as the real wolf continues to haunt the Transylvanian forests, so long will his spectre brother survive in the minds of the inhabitants.

Many ancient Roumenian legends tell us that every new church or otherwise important building became a human grave, as it was thought indispensable to its stability to wall in a living man or woman, whose spirit henceforward haunts the place. In later times people having become less cruel, or more probably, because murder is now attended with greater inconvenience to the actors, this custom underwent some modifications, and it became usual in place of a living man to wall in his shadow instead. This is done by measuring the shadow of a person with a long piece of cord, or a ribbon made of strips of reed, and interring this measure instead of the person himself, who, unconscious victim of the spell thrown upon him, will pine away and die within forty days. It is an indispensable condition to the success of this proceeding that the chosen victim be ignorant of the part he is playing, therefore careless passers-by near a building place may often hear the warning cry 'Beware, lest they take thy shadow!' So deeply engrained is this superstition that not long ago there were still professional shadow-traders, who made it their business to provide architects with the necessary victims for securing their walls. 'Of course the man whose shadow is thus interred must die,' argues the Roumenian, 'but as he is unaware of his doom he does not feel any pain or anxiety, so it is less cruel than walling in a living man . . .'

'*Transylvania*, Charles Boner, Longmans, 1865'*

THE LAND BEYOND THE FOREST

. . . I went at once to an inn, whose exterior with neatly-painted green blinds seemed to promise decent accommodation. But what dirt and disorder! It

---

*If Emily Gerard first introduced Bram Stoker to Transylvanian folktales (or, as she preferred to call them, 'Superstitions'), Charles Boner first introduced Stoker to the history and geography of the region he was in the process of choosing as the main location for his novel, in a book called *Transylvania: Its Products and Its People*. Since Boner was also the author of *Chamois* required good practice to breakfast in such a place; however, I was not unused to similar trials, and the meal was soon well over.* And now for a conveyance to Hátzeg! My man is already at the door with a little four-wheeled waggon crammed full of hay, with carpets spread on the top on which I was to enthrone myself. But those miserable rats of ponies! Why, they will never get to Hátzeg by the evening! 'Won't they, though?' said my blackguard-looking Jew driver; 'they are in prime condition,' (they were skin and bone, I beg to observe,) 'and you'll see how they can run.'

And away we go, – I on my hay throne, and my little shaggy team springing along at a good gallop. For awhile we passed a whole population all streaming into town. There were troops of women and cart-loads of peasants and young girls in holiday attire, nearly all in snow-white shifts with broad stripes of embroidery, red or blue, over the shoulders and round the sleeves; and large silver medals hanging from their necks over their bosom. Some wore around their head a large white kerchief, but so full and long that it fell over them like a veil and flowed low down behind. There is something very graceful and feminine in this spotless head-gear, with its many and waving folds. Others had brighter-hued kerchiefs, but purple seemed to be the favourite colour. Anon came a chattering company in brand-new jackets of sheepskin without sleeves, all embroidered with red and green and blue leather, and having a

---

Hunting in the Mountains of Bavaria, the 'Products' he described were often of the fur-coated variety. From the chapters 'The Land Beyond the Forest', 'Ferae', 'To Bistritz' and 'Law and Lawlessness', Stoker also read descriptions of village life in the Carpathians, of the remote mountain castle of Terzburg south of Kronstadt ('it might have been the abode of some robber knight, or of Blue Beard, [looking] from the windows high up over the perpendicular rock') and of the town of Bistritz ('1836–50', he duly noted, 'five conflagrations, by which three hundred and twenty-five houses were destroyed'). The excellent pull-out maps of the region would have helped to orient him. Boner's attitudes towards the 'locals' he encountered were, if anything, even more patronising than those of the author of *Dracula*. One of the typescript notes Stoker took was to prove particularly important: 'p. 417 BORGO PRUND. To E. of Bistritz.' He later crossed this out, having made use of the information.

*Boner's footnote: All the rooms being engaged, I was allowed to go into the bedchamber of the landlord and landlady to make my morning toilette. But filthy and untidy as the place was, there was still a long coil of steel hoop hanging up there to make a crinoline for mine hostess. The charms of crinoline seem to be everywhere irresistible.

very holiday air. Then others with a sort of scarlet fez upon their heads; and some with a covering having two horn-like corners rising in front, reminding you of Aaron's budding ornament. Now a gipsy passed, dark as a Hindoo; and though most of the wayfarers were clean and in their Sunday clothes, there were some who, it was evident, had no thought of merry-making, and everything about their persons was blackened, coarse, and dirty. Pleasing and picturesque as the simple clothing of these women is when fresh and tidy, in the contrary state it has an air of perfectly savage life. The 'obrescha,' being then almost black with dirt, and torn and entangled, looks like horsehair hanging and flying about, and has a most strange, uncomely appearance.* Now in the distance a whole bevy of young girls come stepping on, with shifts and head-gear white as the daisies of the field, and as they breast the morning breeze, the bright red 'obrescha' streaming and fluttering in the wind, might almost make you think a flock of flamingoes was moving over the plain. Most of them had distaffs stuck in their girdle, and one with arms distended was winding off red yarn; the sun, too, was shining, and lighted up the bright figures, which quite illumined the sober-coloured autumn landscape. It is astonishing how they can spin as they walk, for they advance at a brisk rate, and their feet and merry tongue keep pace with each other.

What busts you see here, where stays are unknown, and there is nothing to cramp the full development of the figure! The linen covering does not conceal the beautiful outline of the bosom, but rather serves to define it; marking now an oval bud and now a full-rounded form. And the drapery falls over this loveliest feminine feature in a sharp angular line, as though beneath were firmest marble; and marble it is, but glowing with passionate life.

On our road my driver pointed out to me a point in the mountains where one evening he had seen 'a gold fire.' – 'And what is that?' I asked. "Tis a light which hovers over the spot where gold is buried.' – 'Of course you went and

---

*Boner's footnote: The 'obrescha' is the girdle worn by the women over the shift, and consists of a broad band of plaited twine-like cord, from which, before and behind, hangs a fringe reaching nearly to the ankle. It is much the same thing as that which savage tribes wear as their sole covering. It is of a bright red, and contrasts greatly with the white linen beneath.

took possession of it,' I said, laughing. 'Yes, but being so far I could not find the exact spot, and therefore got nothing.'

His two horses, which still went along bravely, had, he told me, cost him forty florins. We met a peasant who had bought a cow and her calf and was now driving them home. For both he had paid only eight florins; such was the effect of the dearth and drought in Hungary.

The road was even all the way, with wooded hills at a little distance on either side. The villages were neatly built, the houses good and solid-looking, and, if I remember rightly, often standing separate. They stood in a row far back from the roadside, so that an immense breadth was thus given to the street. Owing to this mode of building, a village spread to a considerable length. The neatness and regularity all gave evidence of former military supervision, and the road, too, was broad and smooth as a billiard-table.

'You'll see the difference when we get to Transylvania,' said my man to me; 'directly we get there, all is bad, – roads, bridges, everything.' I observed here, as well as later elsewhere, that the people of a military frontier always piqued themselves on their superior condition, seeming to appreciate their orderly state after they had been once broken in and got accustomed to it. We stopped at a hovel which the driver called an inn, – a wretched place, with dirt, dirt, dirt in abundance. Wallachian peasants were lying asleep on benches, and the whole place looked miserable and broken down. Like Dr. Johnson in a similar predicament, I had recourse to eggs, superintending the frying of them myself. The people were Germans; they said that all the innkeepers along the road were so. And even here in this miserable hole there were two crinolines hanging on the wall of the dirty room; the second being a miniature one, for a little child. This produce of civilization was a droll contrast to a group of gipsies a little further on. A boy was leaping about perfectly naked. One little girl among them had a cape fastened at the neck just covering the shoulders; but for this she was – to use a penny-a-liner term – as 'nude' as her companion. They were like little savages, and so were those other children who had a few rags on.

We are so accustomed to see the place where our dead repose protected and tended with evident care, and the graves marked by what, however humble, has some pretension to artistic skill, that it produced quite a strange and jarring sensation to observe a churchyard fenced in by hurdles, and opposite it, close to the roadside, another unenclosed, the mounds which were in it marked with mere sticks from the hedge.

Presently my little Jew, pointing to a broken bridge with an air of satisfaction, exclaimed, 'Here is Transylvania! Look how bad the road is!' which I felt in all my limbs was true enough. 'You see the difference between this and the frontier.' This road leading on to Hátzeg was not a high-road, however; for in Transylvania also these are excellently kept.

We were now approaching the Eiserne Thor Pass. On the right were dense woods, on the left, hills without any forest. Gradually the ridges before you sink down, and you see a dip where you can pass through. Just this spot is the Pass. You now descend somewhat, and presently the whole Hátzeg valley is outspread before you.

This vale is the pride of the Transylvanians. The question if I had seen it was always put to me when it was known I was travelling through the country. The road passes over a fertile plain covered with maize-fields, and on your right are mountains, whose peaks were just catching the last rays of the sun as we hastened onwards.

On the slopes of the hillsides stand villages, with their simple churches; and in all directions, from the foot of the mountains up towards their summits, are rustic dwellings dotting the grand declivity. It is very like the valley of the Inn between Innsbruck and Kufstein, except that here the vale itself is very much broader . . .

What makes the wolf so formidable an enemy to the farmer is, his habit of tearing in pieces more animals than he can devour. He destroys for the sake of destroying, and not merely to satisfy his hunger. They are timid brutes, and travel so quickly that it is difficult to get at them. Tonight they ravage a flock, but by the morning they are in a thicket miles away; so that when the district, up in arms, proceeds to scour the country in pursuit, not a wolf is to be found . . . In winter they come into the villages during the night, to get what they can – a pig or fowl or goose, it is indifferent what. The peasantry lose much stock in this way by their depradations; but it is only when very cold that the animals venture thus close to human habitations. I once met one on returning home late from a party, close to the last houses of the town of Bistritz. It was moonlight; the thermometer 27° Réaum below freezing-point. I was walking in the middle of the road, where it was light as day; the houses on my right were all in shade, and close to the walls I thought I saw a large dog skulking. The animal sneaked stealthily on, to avoid me and my companion, then crossed the road, when at once I saw by its peculiar gait that it was a wolf. 'Why, look that's a wolf!' I exclaimed, astonished. 'Yes,' said the other very calmly, and walked on. Passing the road, it went away over the fields.

In 1614 there were so many wolves, and of such unusual size, around Kronstadt, attacking not only cattle but men, 'that', relates the historian, 'at last we thought they must be lions'. The magistrate of Schässburg paid one florin reward for seven wolves killed. Bears, too, roamed about, and some of the inhabitants of the mountains were as wild as they . . .

The weather was beautiful, and I hardly think a Canadian winter could be more bright. To the east of Bistritz lies Borgó Prund,* and thither I drove to see and to purchase some of the manufactures of the Roumain women. The country thereabouts reminded me at once of the scenery in the Valley of the Inn. Here, too, is the so-called 'Mittel Land', a ridge of low hills rising in the vale between the higher mountains. Even now their bold forms and gentle slopes were most attractive; and in summer, when the woods on the upland are in full leaf, and the pastures green and enlivened with flocks and herds, the scene must be most lovely . . . Still further on, towards the pass into Moldavia, the scenery increases in picturesqueness and nothing can be better than the road thither.

*Evidently, this information was new to Stoker.

'A.F. Crosse
Round About the Carpathians, London, Blackwoods, 1878'*

The more civilisation closes around one, the more enjoyable is an occasional 'try back' into barbarism. This feeling made the mere fact of camping out seem delightful. Our first care was to select a suitable spot; we found a clearing that promised well, and here we made a halt. We deposited our *batterie de cuisine*, arranged our plaids, and then proceeded to make a fire with a great lot of dried sticks and logs of wood. The fire was soon crackling and blazing away in grand style, throwing out mighty tongues of flame, which lit up the dark recesses of the forest.

Now came the supper, which consisted of robber-steak and tea. I always stuck to my tea as the most refreshing beverage after a long walk or ride. I like coffee in the morning before starting – good coffee, mind; but in the evening there is nothing like tea. The robber-steak is capital, and deserves an 'honourable mention' at least: it is composed of small bits of beef, bacon, and onion strung alternately on a piece of stick; it is seasoned with pinches of *paprika* and salt, and then roasted over the fire, the lower end of the stick being rolled backwards and forwards between your two palms as you hold it over the hot embers. It makes a delicious relish with a hunch of bread . . .

A useful cart-horse could be bought, I found, for about six or seven pounds. I daresay I could have picked out a few from the lot fit for riding, but of course they were rough animals, mere peasant horses. Some of the

---

*Bram Stoker gleaned further details of Transylvanian life from Andrew F. Crosse's memoir. Crosse, a self-styled 'Fellow of the Chemical Society', describes in hearty style how he travelled around the wild Carpathians – armed only with a bowie knife, a revolver and a double-barrelled shotgun – and managed to bump into an old schoolfriend from Westminster in the process. Most of the recipes in *Dracula*, some of the phrases (such as 'the vast Carpathian horsehose'), aspects of the topography and the description of golden Mediasch wine ('it produces an agreeable pricking on the tongue') or Tokay wine (about which Stoker noted 'Sometimes Tokay (wine) gets sick in Spring – the time when the sap rises in living plants. Memo: guess cause!') all came from Crosse. The bowie knife references may have been the source of Quincey Morris's preferred weapon, the 'great bowie knife' in the novel. And it is possible that Crosse's own 'persona' helped to shape the character of Jonathan Harker (in early drafts of *Dracula*). This was, for him, an important source of information about Transylvania.

colts, brought in a string fresh from the mountains, were wild, untamed-looking creatures; but hardly as wild as the Wallacks who led them, dressed in sheepskin, and followed each by his savage wolf-like dog. The dogs are very formidable in Hungary. It is never safe to take a walk, even in the environs of a town, without a revolver, on account of these savage brutes, who, faithful to their masters, are liable to make the most ferocious attacks on strangers. This special kind of dog is in fact most useful – to the shepherd on the lonely *puszta*, to the keeper of the vineyard through the night-watches, when the wild boar threatens his ravages – and in short he acts the part of rural police generally . . .

The *leiterwagen* has no counterpart in England, and the literal rendering of a ladder-waggon hardly conveys the proper notion of the thing itself. This long cart, it is needless to say, is without springs; but it has the faculty of accommodating itself to the inequalities of the road in a marvellous manner. It has, moreover, a snake-like vertebrae, and even twists itself when necessary . . .

The pace was so slow that I confess it made me impatient, but our path through the forest was too narrow and too steep to do more than walk our horses in single file. The character of the vegetation visibly changed as we ascended. We left the oak and beech, and came upon a forest of pine-trees, and I thought of the lines –

'This is the forest primeval. The murmuring pines and the hemlocks. Bearded with moss, and in garments green, indistinct in the twilight.'

The grey moss which hangs in such abundant festoons from the fir-trees has a most singular effect, almost weird at times. These ancients of the forest with their long grey beards and hoary tresses, look very solemn indeed in the gloaming.

What unheeded wealth in these majestic trees, which grow but to decay! Enormous trunks lay on every side: some had passed into the rottenness which gives new life; and here fungi of bright and varied hues, grey lichen, and green moss preserved together the contour of the gigantic stem, which, prostrate and decayed now, had once held its head high amongst the lordlings of the forest.

. . . There are a great many 'settled gipsies' in Transylvania. Of course they are legally free, but they attach themselves peculiarly to the Magyars, from a profound respect they have for everything that is aristocratic; and in Transylvania the name Magyar holds almost as a distinctive term for class as well as race. The gipsies do not assimilate with the thrifty Saxon, but prefer to be hangers-on at the castle of the Hungarian noble:* they call themselves by his name, and profess to hold the same faith, be it Catholic or Protestant. Notwithstanding that, the gipsy has an incurable habit of pilfering here as elsewhere; yet they can be trusted as messengers and carriers – indeed I do not know what people would do without them, for they are as good as a general 'parcels-delivery company' any day; and certainly they are ubiquitous, for never is a door left unlocked but a gipsy will steal in, to your cost . . .

Before wrapping my plaid round me for the night, I threw some fresh wood on the fire, which, crushing down upon the hot embers, sent up a scintillating shower of sparks that ran a mad race in and out of the greenery. I saw that the horses were all right, I put my gun handy, and then I gave myself up to sleep.

I do not know how long I had slept, but I was conscious of being bothered, and could not rouse myself at once. I dreamed that a bear was sniffing at me, but instead of being the least surprised or frightened, I said to myself in my dream, as if it was quite a common occurrence, 'That's the bear again, he always comes when I am asleep.' The next moment, however, I was very effectually awakened by a tug that half lifted me off the ground. I must mention that I had tied my horse's halter to my waist-belt in case of any alarm in the night, for I sleep so soundly always that no ordinary noise or movement ever wakes me. I sprang up of course, calling the Wallack at the same time. Something had frightened the horses, and they had attempted to bolt. We found them trembling from head to foot, but we could not discover the cause of their fright.† I fired off my revolver twice, the Wallack in the

---

*The gypsies who 'prefer to be hangers-on at the castle of the Hungarian noble' evidently gave Stoker the idea for his 'Szgany . . . [who] attach themselves as a rule to some great noble or *boyar*, and call themselves by his name', and who are thus in league with Dracula.

†Stoker wrote himself a memo about this passage: 'Mem. Horses to be disturbed at approach of Count Dracula and smell blood'. So the incident of Crosse's frightened horses eventually

meantime had lighted a bundle of resinous fir branches as a torch. He had carefully arranged it before he slept; it is a capital thing, as it gives a good light on an emergency.

After making an examination of the place all round, and finding nothing, we made up a bright fire, and again laid ourselves down to rest. I had my saddle for a pillow, and it was not half bad. Before giving myself over to sleep I listened and listened again, but I heard nothing except the hooting of the owls answering each other in the distance. The night had grown very cold, and a heavy dew was falling, but notwithstanding these discomforts I had another good nap . . .

There is a diligence service twice daily, occupying fourteen hours or thereabouts, dependent, of course, on the state of the roads, which can be very bad – inconceivably bad. For the sake of the excursion I took a place in the *postwagen* one day as far as Sinia, where there is a modern hotel and very tolerable quarters. The scenery of the pass is very romantic. In places the road winds round the face of the precipice, and far below is a deep sunless glen, through which the mountain torrent rushes noisily over its rocky bed; at other times you skirt the stream with its green margin of meadow – a pastoral oasis amidst the wild grandeur of bare limestone peaks and snowy summits. The autumnal colouring on the hanging woods of oak and beech was something more brilliant than I ever remember to have seen; the effect of being oneself in shadow and seeing the glory of the sunlight on the foliage of the other side of the defile, was most striking. Above this ruby mountain rose other heights with a girdle of dark fir, and higher still were visible yet loftier peaks, clothed in the dazzling whiteness of fresh-fallen snow. In the Southern Carpathians there is no region of perpetual snow, but the higher summits are generally snow-clad late in the spring and very early in the autumn. I was told there is good bear-hunting in this district . . .

In all parts of the country where travellers are possible, the invariable reply to a demand for something to eat is the query, 'Would the gentleman

turned into the famous meeting with Dracula (as coachman) in the Borgo Pass, and the reaction of the horses as they approach Castle Dracula at the end of the story.

like *paprika handl?*' and he had better like it, for his chances are small of getting anything else. While I was seeing after my horse, the woman of the inn caught a miserable chicken, which I am sure could have had nothing to regret in this life; and in a marvellously short time the bird was stewed in red pepper, and called *paprika handl* ...

I fancy [my host] Count M – was much amused at the fact of an English gentleman travelling about alone on horseback, without any servants or other impedimenta. I remember a friend of mine telling me that once in Italy, when he declined to hire a carriage from a peasant at a perfectly exorbitant price, and said he preferred walking, the fellow called after him, saying, 'We all know you English are mad enough for anything!'

I don't know whether the Hungarian Count drew the same conclusion in my case, but I could see he was very much amused; I don't think any other people understand the Englishman's love of adventure.*

'Major E.C. Johnson
On the Track of the Crescent, Hurst & Blackett, 1885'†

DINNER AT PESTH

In the evening the 'gentlemanly' old guide of the hotel – who looked like the inevitable 'retired major' of an English boarding-house – took me to the Restaurant Karl, in the Jozsef-ter, and ordered for me a real Hungarian dinner.

---

*This sentiment reappears, almost verbatim, at the end of *Dracula's Guest*, and may have formed part of an early draft of *Dracula*. The Count writes (of his guest) to the maître d'hôtel of the Quatre Saisons in Munich, 'He is English and therefore adventurous.'

†To judge by his many comparisons between Wallachian peasants and 'our friend Paddy', between their dwellings and 'a cluster of cabins in the Emerald Isle', Major E. C. Johnson, intrepid and self-opinionated author of *On the Track of the Crescent: Erratic Notes from the Piraeus to Pesth*, must once have served in Ireland, as well as on the Nepalese frontier. Whether or not this endeared him to Bram Stoker, and whether or not Stoker shared the Major's clubland approach to storytelling, he certainly derived much 'Roumanian' background from Johnson's book. In addition to the longer extracts he annotated, this background included the costumes (as Stoker duly wrote, 'coloured apron called a CATRINTSA'; 'a broad belt or girdle called an OBRENSKA'; 'Chemisette open at neck – no stays'), the language (Johnson 'managed to get on pretty well with French and German'), and the role of the Szekelys in the history of

The Magyar bill of fare is rather elaborate and, besides various mysterious fishes dressed in oil and fat, red deer, wild boar, bustards, and frogs, when in season, of course includes the eternal 'bif-stek' for the Angolok. After a good deal of whispering between my guide and the waiter, and the usual dismal wait, which was relieved by a little playing with various *hors-d'œuvres*, something like the Smörgåsbord of the Swedes, a fish, which seemed a sort of trout, was brought in, accompanied by a hot rich sauce. This was 'fogas' (*perca lucio perca*), pronounced 'fogush', a fish only found in the Balaton lake, near the famous watering-place, Füred . . .

The fogas was followed by my old Spanish friend, a spatch cock, covered with red pepper. This condiment, my 'old gentleman' explained, was the national Paprika – a form of cayenne, and used in almost all Hungarian dishes. As to its mildness I subsequently had some doubts, for my throat next morning was a 'caution'. I next partook of another national dish, *Töltött Káposzta* – a cabbage filled with rice, meat, and spices – a most delicious, but slightly dyspeptic, dish, requiring a little carbonate of soda after it. I wound up with the indispensable water-melon, green outside and red inside, with black pips, and washed all down with a bottle of Neszmélyi – a kind of cross between Hock and Chablis. This, with a variety of sweets, completed a repast, to the general excellence of which the Hungarian wine largely contributed . . .

ANOTHER DINNER

We had dinner soon after my arrival, the Count R – 's two stewards and his secretary sitting down with us. I was sorry to learn, in the course of conversation, that the Countess was a great sufferer from rheumatism. This did not, however, surprise me afterwards, for a damp mist rose from the marshes morning and evening [with the hazy line of the Carpathians in the distance] and rain was the order of the day and night. At dinner the chief dish was, as is usual in Hungary, *Paprikás csirke*. This is prepared by giving some ancient chanticleer the 'happy despatch,' cutting his remains into small

Hungary and Transylvania. Stoker took seven pages of typescript notes on this book – more than any other on the subject – and later crossed out the references as he used them.

pieces, and putting them into water, in company with flour, cream, butter, and a great deal of *paprika*, or red pepper. This is a dish to dream of, though at first dreaming is out of the question, for the 'griff', after his first taste of the delicious condiment, is usually kept awake by a throat compared with which a lime-kiln in full blast would be coolness itself. Such was my experience, and the Count had a hearty laugh next morning when I recounted it. He insisted on my having a 'hair of the dog that bit me'; and, in short, I soon became 'paprika-ised'. . .

One morning I accompanied the Countess, and her daughter and her husband, to see the old church of St. Demeter. We found the churchyard filled with villagers – some kneeling and smiting their breasts, others standing, and throwing their arms aloft, and all groaning and wailing. It seemed that one of their little ones had just been consigned to its earthy cradle, and all the kindly villagers had turned out to join in the mourning. The Catholic priest came forward and welcomed the 'distinguished party.' He was a fine, portly, and close-shaven man, and very gentlemanly in his manner. He told us that this was the fourth funeral which he had attended since the previous morning, and that two of the deaths were from diphtheria, which was then very prevalent in the village. Under his guidance, we inspected the church, which had no particularly interesting features, except a very fine organ, and some extremely gaudy and grotesque images of saints and virgins – the latter contrasting very strangely with the bare unornamented walls. The building was, however, prettily situated on a little hill, from which there was a very extensive view down the valley of the Maros. Near the church are the ruins of a nunnery, little besides a tower remaining. These ruins are said to be haunted by their former occupants, who, on a certain night of the year, 'revisit the glimpses of the moon,' and, in company with an equal number of departed monks, have a ball. A Prussian officer, who once stayed with Count R –, declared that he had seen this uncanny revelry, but he admitted that he had previously seen a bottle of schnaps.

> 'The warder looks down from the tower at night
> On the churchyard asleep in the moon's pale light . . .

Ha! can it be real? the graves open all,

And the skeletons come to their midnight ball;

Bone clatters to bone, legs find their own feet,

And balls with their sockets all readily meet.

For dancing the shrouds are too lengthy and wide,

So, to make tripping easy and steady,

On tombstones and graves they are all cast aside,

And now for the ball we are ready.' – GOETHE.

Leaving the somnolent town [of Szász Régen] we took a northerly direction, the river Maros being on our right, while the Carpathians, towering to the clouds came into view. The road now rose rapidly, and it became clear that we were approaching a higher region. We passed many families tightly packed into leiterwagens, all the men taking off their hats and bowing. I observed, however, that these courtesies came only from the Wallachs, the Saxons taking no notice of us whatever – to show, I suppose, their Teutonic, and independent nature. We met several women on horseback, riding *en cavalier*, and in some instances having the mouth covered – a survival, no doubt, of the Turkish occupation. They looked funny, ungainly bundles, with their voluminous head-dresses, stuffed jackets, and big boots.

A large cross, with a coarsely carved figure of our Saviour, was a prominent object by the roadside, and to it all the Wallachs paid the greatest reverence, some kneeling before it for some minutes. The Saxons, however, took no more notice of it than they did of us. These crosses in the Tyrol generally mark the spot where some deed of blood has been perpetrated, and, I dare say, have the same sad signification in Transylvania. Generally, these crucifixes have, in addition to a figure of the Saviour, one of the Virgin Mary; and in this the heart is exposed, and a dagger or arrows are sticking in it.

Soon after we had passed this cross, the grand old castle for which we were bound came into view. Perched up on a height, its frowning battlements and grim old towers presented a perfect picture of a mediæval stronghold, while the cottages which constituted the village of Vécs were clustered round the base, like chickens round the parent hen. The approach to the castle wound round the hill on which the latter stood, and, after passing this, we crossed the drawbridge which spanned the moat, and drew up before the hall-door, in front of which was a charming terrace, planted with trees and flowers. From here there was a lovely view down the road by which we had come, and up the valley to the mountains.

We were very kindly received by the Baron and his charming wife, who was a B – ffy, and, under their hospitable guidance, we straightway commenced an exploration of their beautiful home. The part of the castle in which the family resided had evidently been added in modern times. It was in the form of a tower, to harmonise with the original building, and had a marble staircase, of spiral shape, which led up to the various rooms. On the walls hung war and hunting trophies without number. Stags' heads, with immense antlers, glared at us with their glassy eyes, while the stuffed heads of shaggy Bruins grinned a ghastly welcome from the centre of stars, made of glittering and deadly blades. These latter had, no doubt, been wielded by many a doughty ancestor of the Baron, for the Keménys made their mark in the sanguinary field of war in days gone by, as the living representative of the family does in the more peaceful, but hardly less exciting, field of politics at the present day.

The top of the spiral staircase opened on to a lovely veranda, in every corner of which were flowers that loaded the air with sweetness; while marble dolphins, upheld by cupids, poured forth, with a soothing murmur, refreshing streams which were most delightful after our hot drive. From the veranda we passed through large, open windows, into the great drawing-room, which was furnished and ornamented in the most luxurious manner. On the walls hung magnificent Gobelin tapestry, or beautiful glass cases full of old coins, medals, and military orders; inlaid cabinets, mosaic tables, and escritoires, barred our progress over the Turkey carpet, in whose thick folds our footsteps were hushed; while handsome chandeliers of varied coloured glass hung from the ceiling. Nor were the fine arts neglected, for, on a tall easel, in one corner of the room, was an unfinished water-colour landscape, and in another a grand piano.

The Baroness now proposed a walk through the grounds, so we descended another staircase, also spiral, and entered a long picture-gallery, wherein

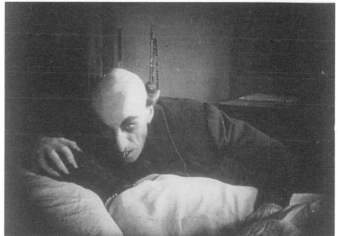

Count Orlok
(Max Schreck) has his
feast disturbed by the
crowing of the cock in
F. W. Murnau's *Nosferatu:
A Symphony of Horror*
(1922), the first major
vampire film.

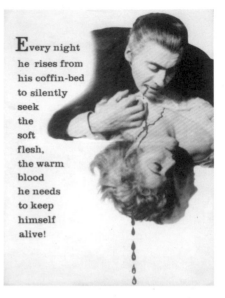

Every night
he rises from
his coffin-bed
to silently
seek
the
soft
flesh,
the warm
blood
he needs
to keep
himself
alive!

Previous spread The vampire's victim Léone (Sybille Schmitz) in Carl Dreyer's strange, ritualized *Vampyr* (1932), very loosely based on Le Fanu's *Carmilla*. **Top left** Publicity photo of Bela Lugosi (the Count), in evening dress on the wide steps of his castle, in Tod Browning's *Dracula* (1931). **Top right** Poster for Hammer's first *Dracula* (aka *Horror of Dracula*, 1958), showing Christopher Lee as the Count biting Melissa Stribling as Mina. **Above** Tod Browning directs Bela Lugosi and Carol Borland (Luna) on the set of *Mark of the Vampire* (1935), a remake of *London After Midnight* (1927) in which the vampires are explained away.

Two versions of Le Fanu's story. **Top** Carmilla (Annette Vadim), transposed to Italy, seduces Georgia Monteverdi (Elsa Martinelli) in Roger Vadim's *Blood and Roses* (1960). **Above** Carmilla Karnstein (Ingrid Pitt) seduces Emma Morton (Madeline Smith) in Roy Ward Baker's *The Vampire Lovers* (1970).

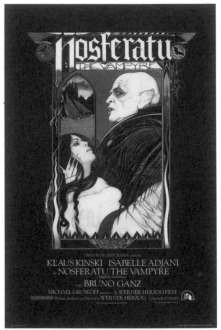

Top left The severed head of Gorcha (Boris Karloff), on the poster for Mario Bava's *Black Sabbath* (1963), the third segment based on Alexis Tolstoy's *The Family of the Vourdalak*.
Top right Retro-style poster for Werner Herzog's elaborate remake of *Nosferatu the Vampyre* (1979), this time with Klaus Kinski as the Count, and much melancholy Romanticism.
Above Vampirized Lucy Westenra (Sadie Frost), in a bizarre wedding dress inspired by the Australian frilled lizard, cornered in her crypt in Francis Ford Coppola's stylish *Bram Stoker's Dracula* (1992).

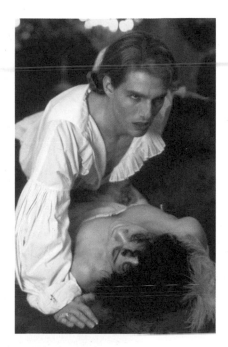

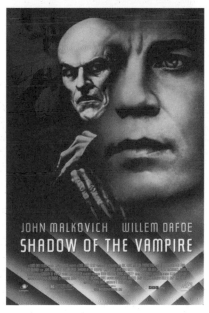

Clockwise from top left Tom Cruise as Lestat de Lioncourt in Neil Jordan's *Interview with the Vampire* (1994), adapted by Anne Rice from her novel; Sarah Michelle Gellar as Buffy Summers of Sunnydale High in the first season (of seven) of television's *Buffy the Vampire Slayer* (1997); poster for E. Elias Merhige's *Shadow of the Vampire* (2000), an imagined version of the making of Murnau's *Nosferatu* – in which Max Schreck really is a vampire; and English-language poster for Tomas Alfredson's critically acclaimed *Let the Right One In* (2008), featuring Lina Leandersson as the pallid vampire Eli, set in a suburb of Stockholm.

Poster for Catherine Hardwicke's *Twilight* (2008), with Robert Pattinson as fang-free Edward Cullen and Kristen Stewart as smitten Bella Swan – will they or won't they?

hung the portraits of many a grim-looking Magyar, in gorgeous attire, and with fierce moustaches whose up-curled points seemed to endanger their eyesight. Leaving these warriors, we came out upon a grand walk, bordered with rose-trees. This led along an old, moss-covered, balustraded wall – a continuation of the wall of the terrace in front of the castle; and from here, as from the front, there was a beautiful view up the valley of the Maros. The grey, weather-beaten walls of the old castle bordered the path for some distance, and formed a marked contrast to the long, straight, red-tiled roof of the modern addition to the building.

Immediately above us frowned an old tower, in which was a long slit rather than a window. This, the Baron informed me, had been the torture-chamber, whence the wretched prisoners, having been racked and otherwise tortured, were cast through a trap in the floor into a deep pit below, to writhe out the brief remnant of their existence. Openings of a similar kind in the other towers showed where the prisoners' dungeons had been, and even below the level of the moat human beings had passed weary years in damp and darkness, without a ray of light, or of hope. To complete the respectable antiquity of this tower, I need scarcely say that, of course, it is haunted. That monsters, capable of inflicting such fiendish cruelties on their fellow-men had lived, was already known to me, from having seen similar proofs in the castle of Nuremberg and elsewhere, and there is no doubt that in the Middle Ages such horrible practices were pretty general. This dismal thought, however, was dissipated by the reflection that they are no longer possible, and by the lovely scene before me. The bright, warm sunshine, the soft, well-kept lawn, the sweet-smelling flowers, the air teeming with every kind of insect life, from the brilliant and ubiquitous butterfly to the humming bee: all these rapidly asserted their power of charm, and I thoroughly enjoyed the scene.

Passing through the gardens, we now entered a wood, a path through which led to a shady nook which commanded a view of the whole valley. Here a convenient seat invited us to rest – an invitation which we accepted. The forest covered the side of the hill on which the castle was built, right down to the valley below, the white road here and there peeping through the trees as it gradually ascended. Along this road a herd of buffaloes was being driven in a cloud of dust. They looked like black-beetles, and their drivers mere specks. The hill on which the castle stood was so steep towards the Gallician frontier that it formed a very strong military position, which, if cleared for the use of modern artillery, would be impregnable by a *coup-de-main*. In front of us, as far as the eye could reach, was an interminable stretch of forest, right up to the base of the mountain range, brilliant in numberless shades of green, blue, and brown, and melting into a dusky purple as it became more stunted, and was lost in the haze surrounding the rocky crags. These towered range above range till they were crowned by the mighty 'Isten-Szék' (God's Seat),* the abode of eternal snow. This view reminded me strongly of my first sight of the Himalayan range from the Nepaulese frontier, and caused that awe-inspired feeling of the littleness of man, when face to face with the stupendous grandeur of nature, which I always experience when in the presence of mountains, and brought to my recollection Kant's grand idea, that the sublime effect of vast physical objects excites a consciousness of a moral power stronger than all nature, and I felt how right was this great analyser of psychological phenomena.

The Carpathians, towering aloft in their savage grandeur, are a spectacle not readily to be forgotten. They are almost inaccessible, and their steep and rocky sides are cut by numerous chasms, through which descend the waters which fertilise Transylvania. Immense mineral wealth is contained in these mountains, but it has not, as yet, been developed as it might, and should, be . . .

My repast over [I was shown] the equipage which was to take me on to Kolozsvár. Ye gods! my horror! A heavy old Berlin, hermetically closed against the entrance of any air, and in which it was only possible to sit bolt upright; glass in front and at the sides, so as to ensure the occupant being

---

*Stoker noted 'Many crosses by roadside', and 'Torture tower – narrow windows'. This important passage may well have suggested the internal geography, and even the location, of Castle Dracula. For, in the novel as published, Jonathan Harker hears a fellow passenger say, 'Look! Isten szek! - God's seat!', and observes that 'by the roadside were many crosses'. The Castle is reached by 'always ascending' and it is located 'on the very edge of a terrible precipice . . . it is a veritable prison'.

thoroughly cooked, when the sun had had full play for an hour or two; and finally springs (or what there was of them), all in the wrong places.*

To draw this antediluvian go-cart, there had been dug up, from somewhere, two old broken-kneed bags of bones, which could not be classified under any species of the genus *equus* known to Western Europe, and round their necks had been hung some 'jingles' – to deceive them, I suppose, into the idea that they were skittish young colts. The harness which completed this equipage was, in many places, much more indebted for its continuity to the ropemaker than to the saddler. There is a delicious irony in the name which the Germans of Transylvania have given to these awful equipages. They call them *Gelegenheiten* (opportunities). This opportunity was not, however, the phantom goddess of success, but a very substantial failure.

'Book of Were-wolves, S. Baring-Gould, Smith Elder, 1865'†

Among the Bulgarians and Slovakians the were-wolf is called *vrkolak*, a name resembling that given it by the modern Greeks βρύκόλακας. The

---

*Like Count Dracula's *calèche*, perhaps.

†'Listen to them – the children of the night. What music they make!', says Count Dracula, when he hears the howling of many wolves. And the children of the night – from the wolves of Transylvania, to the immense dog which leaps ashore at Whitby, to the Norwegian grey wolf named Bersicker at London Zoo – play an important part in *Dracula*, as creatures and as metaphors (of 'man into wolf'). The Reverend Sabine Baring-Gould, author of well over 100 books and a vampire story *Margery of Quether* (1884), as well as a guide to the folktales of Dartmoor and 'Onward, Christian Soldiers', provided Stoker with much of his were-wolf lore. He described the exhaustion which follows 'the berserkr rage', for a Scandinavian were-wolf; he unearthed a strange dance of the were-wolves at which 'each had in his or her hand a green taper with a blue flame' (to which Stoker added 'mem. Green taper with blue flame in Count's house'); and he stimulated the idea (subsequently abandoned) that Quincey Morris should die of a were-wolf's bite – perhaps to 'rise again' at some future time. Bram Stoker was mainly interested in the chapter 'folk-lore relating to were-wolves'. In the following chapter, 'natural causes of lycanthropy', he *could* have read a three-page account of the life and crimes of Elizabeth Báthory, the 'bloody Hungarian Countess' who bathed in the blood of countless virgins for her own cosmetic purposes, but there is no evidence that he did. He took two manuscript pages of notes from *The Book of Were-wolves*, but none from that chapter. Stoker transcribed the word 'werewolf' as 'wehrwolf', 'were wolf' or just 'w.w.'.

Greek were-wolf is closely related to the vampire. The lycanthropist falls into a cataleptic trance, during which his soul leaves his body, enters that of a wolf and ravens for blood. On the return of the soul, the body is exhausted and aches as though it had been put through violent exercise. After death lycanthropists become vampires. They are believed to frequent battlefields in wolf or hyæna shapes, and to suck the breath from dying soldiers, or to enter houses and steal the infants from their cradles. Modern Greeks call any savage-looking man, with dark complexion, and with distorted, misshapen limbs, a βρύκσλακας, and suppose him to be invested with the power of running in wolf-form.

The Serbs connect the vampire and the were-wolf together, and call them by one name *vlkoslak*. These rage chiefly in the depths of winter: they hold their annual gatherings, and at them divest themselves of their wolf-skins, which they hang on the trees around them. If any one succeeds in obtaining the skin and burning it, the *vlkoslak* is thenceforth disenchanted.

The power to become a were-wolf is obtained by drinking the water which settles in a foot-print left in clay by a wolf.

Among the White Russians the *wawkalak* is a man who has incurred the wrath of the devil, and the evil one punishes him by transforming him into a wolf and sending him among his relations, who recognize him and feed him well. He is a most amiably disposed were-wolf, for he does no mischief, and testifies his affection for his kindred by licking their hands. He cannot, however, remain long in any place, but is driven from house to house, and from hamlet to hamlet, by an irresistible passion for change of scene. This is an ugly superstition, for it sets a premium on standing well with the evil one.

The Slovakians merrily term a drunkard a *vlkodlak*, because, forsooth, he makes a beast of himself . . .

[The were-wolf's appearance] was peculiar. His hair was of a tawny red and thickly matted, falling over his shoulders and completely covering his narrow brow. His small pale-grey eyes twinkled with an expression of horrible ferocity and cunning, from deep sunken hollows. The complexion was of a dark olive colour; the teeth were strong and white, and the canine teeth protruded over the lower lip when the mouth was closed. The hands were large and powerful, the nails black and pointed like bird's talons ...

A were-wolf may easily be detected, even when devoid of his skin; for his hands are broad, and his fingers short, and there are always some hairs in the hollow of his hand ... By day the were-wolf has the human form, though he may be known by the meeting of his eyebrows above the nose ... It is only when another person tells him that he is a were-wolf, or reproaches him with being such, that a man can be freed from the ban ...*

Baedeker's Southern Germany and Austria, Including Hungary and Transylvania, 1880†

MUNICH

Hotels Four Seasons, Maximilians-Strasse, near the Hof-Theater ... Marienbad, Barer-Str 4, with a large garden and baths.

---

*These two passages *may* have provided Bram Stoker with what he needed for the physical description of Count Dracula: 'His eyebrows were very massive, almost meeting over the nose, and with bushy hair that seemed to curl in its own profusion. The mouth ... was rather cruel-looking, with peculiarly sharp white teeth; these protruded over the lips ... the backs of his hands ... were rather coarse – broad, with squat fingers. Strange to say, there were hairs in the centre of his palm. The nails ... cut to a sharp point'. The Count has another characteristic in common with were-wolves: on account of his unbalanced diet, his breath smells 'rank'.

†Baedeker's would have been the handiest source of information on overseas travel for Bram Stoker. Although the timetable he drew up for Jonathan Harker was not footnoted, it is most likely that this was the source. Harker's odyssey could have been undertaken by any tourist from late Victorian Britain; the only mystery is why he planned to take the train from Munich to Salzburg to Vienna, when the most direct route was via Linz (without a change!). The hotels mentioned in the first few pages of *Dracula* (the Hôtel Royale in Klausenburg and the Golden Krone in Bistritz) did not, in fact, exist, but there was a König Matthias in Klausenburg and a Golden Krone in *Salzburg* (where Harker may originally have been heading, when the story was to be set in Styria). There was also a Krone Hotel in Oravicza, Transylvania, according to A. F. Crosse. One missed opportunity: the 'portraits of celebrities ... of historical value only', in the Ambras Collection, just outside Vienna, included an oil painting of Vlad the Impaler, the original Dracula. Stoker evidently didn't know about this. He was meticulous in his notes about train times, connections and routes.

Theatres   Hof- and Nationaltheater, on the E. side of the Max-Josephs-Platz, the largest in Germany, accommodating 2,500 spectators ... where operas are generally performed on Sundays, Mondays, Thursdays and Fridays (closed in July) ...

Collections, etc.   Pinakothek, Old (i.e. 'Repository of Pictures', from the Greek) daily (except Sat.) 9–3 (in Winter 9–2) ... it contains upwards of 1,400 pictures ... Munich offers the traveller the best opportunity of becoming acquainted with the versatility of *Rubens*.

MUNICH TO SALZBURG

Railway in 5¼ to 6¾ hours ... with 'a distant view of the Alps', on a journey which 'then skirts wooded and grassy hills'.

SALZBURG

Hotels   Goldne Krone (opposite the house where Mozart was born).

SALZBURG TO LINZ/LINZ TO VIENNA

Railway in 7½ hours.

VIENNA (THE OUTER DISTRICTS)

Ambras Collection of ancient armour and curiosities, founded at the Château of Ambras near Innsbruck by Archduke Ferdinand of the Tyrol (d. 1696) and transferred to Vienna in 1806. *Room 1* Equestrian armour ... of Stephen Báthory, Prince of Transylvania and King of Poland (d. 1586) in steel and gold ... *Room IV.* On the walls are portraits of celebrities (141 in number) of the 15th–16th century, chiefly of the House of Hapsburg, and of historical value only.

VIENNA TO PEST

Railway in 7–9 hours; views of the Danube ... and the Carpathian Mountains gradually become more prominent. The line traverses innumerable vineyards, at a considerable height above the river.

At Pest, the railway station is at the N. extremity of the long Waitzner-Strasse ... the trains for Transylvania also start from this station.

PEST TO KLAUSENBURG

Railway in 12–15 hours. In the distance appear the spurs of the Transylvanian Carpathians ... then the line ascends in long curves, affording charming views of the mountains.

Plan of Tour of Transylvania ... The two principal approaches to the country are afforded by the ... railway by Klausenburg to Kronstadt ... and the railway by Arad and Hermannstadt to Kronstadt (for those coming from Pest) ... In districts to which neither trains nor diligences have as yet penetrated, very fair carriages may be hired at the rate of 6–7 fl. a day. Where the roads are impractical for these vehicles, ox-carts and riding horses are used. The saddles are generally very poor, and require the aid of shawls or rugs to make them comfortable. Guides are necessary for trips among the mountains, and may be obtained in the neighbouring villages ... The official language is Hungarian ... German, however, is understood by almost everyone with whom the tourist is likely to come in contact.

KLAUSENBURG TO BISTRITZ

Klausenburg (Hotels Europa; National; Pannonia; König Matthias; Biasini). Diligence (comfortable, for 12 pers), daily in 12–13 hours ... Among the hills, a little way to the left, are the picturesque ruins ... and magnificent views.

Bistritz (Town Hotel), a royal free town ... the walls and towers, with which it is still surrounded, give the town a quaint and medieval air, but it possesses no other attractions ... in consequence of repeated conflagrations.

Bistritz to Suczawa in the Bukovina, diligence in 23 hours. The road crosses the *Borgo Pass* to Suczawa Itzkani, which is a station on the Bucharest railway. [Borgo Pass, therefore, in 7–8 hrs].

Books in Bram Stoker's library,
relevant to the writing of *Dracula**

Anon., *Faustus, His Life, Death and Descent into Hell*, translated from the German (1825).

Robert Blair, *The Grave, a Poem*, illustrated by William Blake (1813).

Austin Brereton, *Henry Irving, a biographical Sketch* (1884).

E.A. Wallis Budge, *The Mummy: Chapters in Egyptian Funereal Archeology* (1893).

Lord Byron, *Childe Harold's Pilgrimage*, Cantos I–II (1812).

Edward Dowden, *Life of P. B. Shelley*, 2 vols (1886).

E.T.A. Hoffmann, *Weird Tales*, translated by J. T. Bealby, 2 vols (1885).

J.C. Lavater, *Essays on Physiognomy*, translated by Henry Hunter, 5 vols (1789).

R.K. Leather and Ricd le Gallienne, *The Student and the Body Snatcher* (1890).

D. MacRitchie, *Fians, Fairies and Picts* (1893).

F.D. Millet, *The Danube, from the Black Forest to the Black Sea* (1893).

William Shakespeare, *Works – Reduced Facsimile of First Folio* (1876). – *Works – The Henry Irving Edition*, 8 vols. (1888–90).

M. Shelley, *Frankenstein, the Modern Man-Demon* (nd).

P.B. Shelley, *Poetical Works*, with a Memoir by Leigh Hunt, 4 vols (nd). – *Queen Mab* (1821).

J. Sheridan Le Fanu, *The Watcher and Other Weird Stories* (1894).

W. Sikes, *British Goblins: Welsh Folk-Lore, Fairy Mythology, etc.* (1880).

Adam Smith, *Inquiry into the Nature & Causes of the Wealth of Nations* (1778).

---

*When Stoker's 'Original Notes and Data for His Dracula' were auctioned at Sotheby's (7 July 1913), 'the Library of the late Bram Stoker, Esq.' was also sold. I have included in this list all the most relevant books from that library which were published before the spring of 1896 – that is, when Stoker was still in the process of planning *Dracula*. We can never, of course, be certain that these books had actually been added to his personal library by that time, but it is gratifying to see that William Blake, Lord Byron, Percy and Mary Shelley, E. T. A. Hoffmann, two books about *Faust*, Sheridan Le Fanu, Robert Louis Stevenson and *The Yellow Book* were all on Bram Stoker's shelves. He also wrote a short booklist among his manuscript notes – mainly about 'primitive superstitions', 'sea monsters', 'credulities', and Mayo's *Letters on the Truths Contained in Popular Superstitions*.

R.L. Stevenson, *Works*, 30 vols (1894 onwards).

- *The Body Snatcher* (from the *Pall Mall Gazette*, 31st January 1895).

A. Tennyson, *Maud and Other Poems* (1855).

W.S. Walsh, *Faust, the Legend and the Poem* (1888).

The Yellow Book (various issues from 1890s).

6 COUNT DRACULA

'... I seek not gaiety nor mirth, not the bright voluptuousness of much sunshine and sparkling waters which please the young and gay. I am no longer young. And my heart, through heavy years of mourning over the dead, is not attuned to mirth. Moreover the walls of my castle are broken; the shadows are many, and the wind breathes cold through the broken battlements and casements. I love the shade and the shadow, and would be alone with my thoughts when I may.'

Somehow his words and his looks did not seem to accord, or else it was that his cast of face made his smile look malignant and saturnine ...

from *Dracula*, by Bram Stoker (1897)

DRACULA'S GUEST

BRAM STOKER

The short story *Dracula's Guest* was first published in April 1914 – two years after Bram Stoker's death and about a year after his private papers had been sold at Sotheby's – as part of the collection *Dracula's Guest and Other Weird Stories*. In her introduction Florence Stoker revealed that her late husband had been planning to republish some of his short stories dating 'mainly from the earlier years of his strenuous life', but that she had added to his original list of stories 'an hitherto unpublished episode from *Dracula*. It was originally excised owing to the length of the book, and may prove of interest to the many readers of what is considered my husband's most remarkable work.' More recently, commentators have speculated that Stoker may have deleted it not only for reasons of 'length' but also because the story of Jonathan Harker's adventures in Munich too closely resembled Sheridan Le Fanu's vampire tale *Carmilla*. For A. N. Wilson, 'the fact that Stoker had this tale and its Styrian Countess in mind is proved by the cancelled chapter from *Dracula* . . .'

Yet *Dracula's Guest*, at least as it was published in Florence Stoker's collection, cannot possibly have been a cancelled chapter from *Dracula*. As Clive Leatherdale has noted, Harker's character in the short story is much more positive, even aggressive, than the Harker of *Dracula*, the story does not appear to have been written in journal form (unless it had been significantly restructured as a short story) and there are other inconsistencies between story and novel, such as the young solicitor's linguistic abilities. *Dracula's Guest* clearly bears a close relationship with Stoker's working notes for *Dracula*, but it was not simply cancelled from the novel, at the publisher's request, and included verbatim in Florence's collection.

As the notes show, Bram Stoker originally intended to include various incidents during Harker's stay in Munich; these remained in the various drafts of what was to become *Dracula* until quite a late stage. In his notes '8/3/90', there are references to the Munich Dead House, and in his chapter outline of '14/3/90' these are supplemented by a reference to 'wolves' and 'blue flame and c'. Then, as part of his list of 'characteristics of Count Wampyr', Stoker again refers to an incident where Harker is walking past the Dead House and catches sight of an old man's waxen face (which at first he thinks is that of a corpse). Some notes of '29/2/92' refer to 'Harker's Diary – Munich', and subsequent notes add 'Harker's Diary – Munich – wolf'. In the more thorough structure and timescale which Stoker probably compiled in 1893, Dracula orders Harker – by telegram – to travel via Munich, to stay in the Quatre Saisons (originally Stoker's preferred hotel was the Marienbad) and to await instructions. In the note-form structure, Harker spends one day in Munich visiting the Pinakothek Museum and the Dead House (where he sees 'old man on bier'). Then, on the following morning, he receives a telegram from Bistritz letting him know about the next leg of his journey. Harker spends no less than five days in Munich before leaving on the 8.35 p.m. train: on day one, he experiences 'adventure snowstorm and wolf', on days two and three he recovers at the Quatre Saisons, on day four he sees Wagner's *Flying Dutchman* at the Hof-theater in Max-Josephs-Platz, and on day five – which also happens to come after Walpurgis Night – he visits the Dead House.

The short story *Dracula's Guest* evidently concerns the wolf and snowstorm incident, which Stoker had first conceived as early as 1890. Jonathan Harker is staying at the Quatre Saisons, and his adventure (rather than the Dead House incident) takes place on Walpurgis Night, or, according to Stoker's timescale, on Sunday, 30 April/Monday, 1 May 1893. Incidentally, the name of the *maître d'hôtel* at the Quatre Saisons in 1893 was in fact Schimon (rather than Delbrück); the hotel had been in the Schimon family for the past forty years. The quotation 'the dead travel fast' (from Bürger's poem *Lenore*) was at some stage removed from the Munich section of the novel to be spoken by one of Harker's travelling companions in the Borgo Pass, during the opening section of *Dracula*; so was the appearance of the 'blue flame'. But what happened to the Dead House incident, and the visits to the Pinakothek and the Hof-theater? We simply don't know. The most likely explanation of the relationship between *Dracula's Guest* and *Dracula* is that the short story was written, or re-written, as a freestanding story, based upon Bram Stoker's manuscript notes. Whether Stoker did this himself remains a mystery. If he knew he had another money-spinner on his hands, then why didn't he publish *Dracula's Guest* in his own lifetime? And why did *he* not intend to include it in his own collection of short stories?

Whatever the solution to this mystery, and whatever its provenance, *Dracula's Guest* remains a classic. Florence Stoker was right to call it a 'weird story'.

WHEN WE STARTED OUR DRIVE THE SUN was shining brightly on Munich, and the air was full of the joyousness of early summer. Just as we were about to depart, Herr Delbrück (the maître d'hôtel of the Quatre Saisons, where I was staying) came down, bareheaded, to the carriage and, after wishing me a pleasant drive, said to the coachman, still holding his hand on the handle of the carriage door:

'Remember you are back by nightfall. The sky looks bright but there is a shiver in the north wind that says there may be a sudden storm. But I am sure you will not be late.' Here he smiled, and added, 'for you know what night it is.'

Johann answered with an emphatic, 'Ja, mein Herr,' and, touching his hat, drove off quickly. When we had cleared the town, I said, after signalling to him to stop:

'Tell me, Johann, what is to-night?'

He crossed himself, as he answered laconically: 'Walpurgisnacht.' Then he took out his watch, a great, old-fashioned German silver thing as big as a turnip, and looked at it, with his eyebrows gathered together and a little impatient shrug of his shoulders. I realised that this was his way of respect-fully protesting against the unnecessary delay, and sank back in the carriage, merely motioning him to proceed. He started off rapidly, as if to make up for lost time. Every now and then the horses seemed to throw up their heads and sniffed the air suspiciously. On such occasions I often looked round in alarm. The road was pretty bleak, for we were traversing a sort of high, wind-swept plateau. As we drove, I saw a road that looked but little used, and which seemed to dip through a little, winding valley. It looked so inviting that even at the risk of offending him, I called Johann to stop – and when he had pulled up, I told him I would like to drive down that road. He made all sorts of excuses, and frequently crossed himself as he spoke. This somewhat piqued my curiosity, so I asked him various questions. He answered fencingly, and repeatedly looked at his watch in protest. Finally I said:

'Well, Johann, I want to go down this road. I shall not ask you to come unless you like; but tell me why you do not like to go, that is all I ask.' For answer he seemed to throw himself off the box, so quickly did he reach the ground. Then he stretched out his hands appealingly to me, and implored me not to go. There was just enough of English mixed with the German for me to understand the drift of his talk. He seemed always just about to tell me something – the very idea of which evidently frightened him; but each time he pulled himself up, saying as he crossed himself:

'Walpurgisnacht!'

I tried to argue with him, but it was difficult to argue with a man when I did not know his language. The advantage certainly rested with him, for although he began to speak in English, of a very crude and broken kind, he always got excited and broke into his native tongue – and every time he did so, he looked at his watch. Then the horses became restless and sniffed the air. At this he grew very pale, and, looking around in a frightened way, he suddenly jumped forward, took them by the bridles and led them on some twenty feet. I followed, and asked why he had done this. For answer he crossed himself, pointed to the spot we had left and drew his carriage in the direction of the other road, indicating a cross, and said, first in German, then in English: 'Buried him – him what killed themselves.'

I remembered the old custom of burying suicides at cross-roads: 'Ah! I see, a suicide. How interesting!' But for the life of me I could not make out why the horses were frightened.

Whilst we were talking, we heard a sort of sound between a yelp and a bark. It was far away; but the horses got very restless, and it took Johann all his time to quiet them. He was pale, and said: 'It sounds like a wolf – but yet there are no wolves here now.'

'No?' I said, questioning him; 'isn't it long since the wolves were so near the city?'

'Long, long,' he answered, 'in the spring and summer; but with the snow the wolves have been here not so long.'

Whilst he was petting the horses and trying to quiet them, dark clouds drifted rapidly across the sky. The sunshine passed away, and a breath of cold wind seemed to drift past us. It was only a breath, however, and more in the nature of a warning than a fact, for the sun came out brightly again. Johann looked under his lifted hand at the horizon and said:

'The storm of snow, he comes before long time.' Then he looked at his watch again, and, straightway holding his reins firmly – for the horses were still pawing the ground restlessly and shaking their heads – he climbed to his box as though the time had come for proceeding on our journey.

I felt a little obstinate and did not at once get into the carriage.

'Tell me,' I said, 'about this place where the road leads,' and I pointed down.

Again he crossed himself and mumbled a prayer, before he answered: 'It is unholy.'

'What is unholy?' I enquired.

'The village.'

'Then there is a village?'

'No, no. No one lives there hundreds of years.' My curiosity was piqued: 'But you said there was a village.'

'There was.'

'Where is it now?'

Whereupon he burst out into a long story in German and English, so mixed up that I could not quite understand exactly what he said, but roughly I gathered that long ago, hundreds of years, men had died there and been buried in their graves; and sounds were heard under the clay, and when the graves were opened, men and women were found rosy with life, and their mouths red with blood. And so, in haste to save their lives (aye, and their souls! – and here he crossed himself) those who were left fled away to other places, where the living lived, and the dead were dead and not – not something. He was evidently afraid to speak the last words. As he proceeded with his narration, he grew more and more excited. It seemed as if his imagination had got hold of him, and he ended in a perfect paroxysm of fear – white-faced, perspiring, trembling and looking round him, as if expecting that some dreadful presence would manifest itself there in the bright sunshine on the open plain. Finally, in an agony of desperation, he cried:

'Walpurgisnacht!' and pointed to the carriage for me to get in. All my English blood rose at this, and, standing back, I said:

'You are afraid, Johann – you are afraid. Go home, I shall return alone; the walk will do me good.' The carriage door was open. I took from the seat my oak walking-stick – which I always carry on my holiday excursions – and closed the door, pointing back to Munich, and said, 'Go home, Johann – Walpurgisnacht doesn't concern Englishmen.'

The horses were now more restive than ever, and Johann was trying to hold them in, while excitedly imploring me not to do anything so foolish. I pitied the poor fellow, he was so deeply in earnest; but all the same I could not help laughing. His English was quite gone now. In his anxiety he had forgotten that his only means of making me understand was to talk my language, so he jabbered away in his native German. It began to be a little tedious. After giving the direction, 'Home!' I turned to go down the cross-road into the valley.

With a despairing gesture, Johann turned his horses towards Munich. I leaned on my stick and looked after him. He went slowly along the road for a while: then there came over the crest of the hill a man tall and thin. I could see so much in the distance. When he drew near the horses, they began to jump and kick about, then to scream with terror. Johann could not hold them in; they bolted down the road, running away madly. I watched them out of sight, then looked for the stranger, but I found that he, too, was gone.

With a light heart I turned down the side road through the deepening valley to which Johann had objected. There was not the slightest reason, that I could see, for his objection; and I daresay I tramped for a couple of hours without thinking of time or distance, and certainly without seeing a person or a house. So far as the place was concerned, it was desolation itself. But I did not notice this particularly till, on turning a bend in the road, I came upon a scattered fringe of wood; then I recognised that I had been impressed unconsciously by the desolation of the region through which I had passed.

I sat down to rest myself, and began to look around. It struck me that it was considerably colder than it had been at the commencement of my walk – a sort of sighing sound seemed to be around me, with, now and then, high overhead, a sort of muffled roar. Looking upwards I noticed that great thick clouds were drifting rapidly across the sky from North to South at a great height. There were signs of coming storm in some lofty stratum of the air. I was a little chilly, and, thinking that it was the sitting still after the exercise of walking, I resumed my journey.

The ground I passed over was now much more picturesque. There were no striking objects that the eye might single out; but in all there was a charm of beauty. I took little heed of time and it was only when the deepening twilight forced itself upon me that I began to think of how I should find my way home. The brightness of the day had gone. The air was cold, and the drifting of clouds high overhead was more marked. They were accompanied by a sort of far-away rushing sound, through which seemed to come at intervals that mysterious cry which the driver had said came from a wolf. For a while I hesitated. I had said I would see the deserted village, so on I went, and presently came on a wide stretch of open country, shut in by hills all around. Their sides were covered with trees which spread down to the plain, dotting, in clumps, the gentler slopes and hollows which showed here and there. I followed with my eye the winding of the road, and saw that it curved close to one of the densest of these clumps and was lost behind it.

As I looked there came a cold shiver in the air, and the snow began to fall. I thought of the miles and miles of bleak country I had passed, and then hurried on to seek the shelter of the wood in front. Darker and darker grew the sky, and faster and heavier fell the snow, till the earth before and around me was a glistening white carpet the further edge of which was lost in misty vagueness. The road was here but crude, and when on the level its boundaries were not so marked, as when it passed through the cuttings; and in a little while I found that I must have strayed from it, for I missed underfoot the hard surface, and my feet sank deeper in the grass and moss. Then the wind grew stronger and blew with ever increasing force, till I was fain to run before it. The air became icy-cold, and in spite of my exercise I began to suffer. The snow was now falling so thickly and whirling around me in such rapid eddies that I could hardly keep my eyes open. Every now and then the heavens were torn asunder by vivid lightning, and in the flashes I could see ahead of me a great mass of trees, chiefly yew and cypress all heavily coated with snow.

I was soon amongst the shelter of the trees, and there, in comparative silence, I could hear the rush of the wind high overhead. Presently the blackness of the storm had become merged in the darkness of the night. By-and-by the storm seemed to be passing away: it now only came in fierce puffs or blasts. At such moments the weird sound of the wolf appeared to be echoed by many similar sounds around me.

Now and again, through the black mass of drifting cloud, came a straggling ray of moonlight, which lit up the expanse, and showed me that I was at the edge of a dense mass of cypress and yew trees. As the snow had ceased to fall, I walked out from the shelter and began to investigate more closely. It appeared to me that, amongst so many old foundations as I had passed, there might be still standing a house in which, though in ruins, I could find some sort of shelter for a while. As I skirted the edge of the copse, I found that a low wall encircled it, and following this I presently found an opening. Here the cypresses formed an alley leading up to a square mass of some kind of building. Just as I caught sight of this, however, the drifting clouds obscured the moon, and I passed up the path in darkness. The wind must have grown colder, for I felt myself shiver as I walked; but there was hope of shelter, and I groped my way blindly on.

I stopped, for there was a sudden stillness. The storm had passed; and, perhaps in sympathy with nature's silence, my heart seemed to cease to beat. But this was only momentarily; for suddenly the moonlight broke through the clouds, showing me that I was in a graveyard, and that the square object before me was a great massive tomb of marble, as white as the snow that lay on and all around it. With the moonlight there came a fierce sigh of the storm, which appeared to resume its course with a long, low howl, as of many dogs or wolves. I was awed and shocked, and felt the cold perceptibly grow upon me till it seemed to grip me by the heart. Then while the flood of moonlight still fell on the marble tomb, the storm gave further evidence of renewing, as though it was returning on its track. Impelled by some sort of fascination, I approached the sepulchre to see what it was, and why such a thing stood alone in such a place. I walked around it, and read, over the Doric door, in German –

COUNTESS DOLINGEN OF GRATZ IN STYRIA
SOUGHT AND FOUND DEATH, 1801.

On the top of the tomb, seemingly driven through the solid marble – for the structure was composed of a few vast blocks of stone – was a great iron spike or stake. On going to the back I saw, graven in great Russian letters:

THE DEAD TRAVEL FAST

There was something so weird and uncanny about the whole thing that it gave me a turn and made me feel quite faint. I began to wish, for the first time, that I had taken Johann's advice. Here a thought struck me, which came under almost mysterious circumstances and with a terrible shock. This was Walpurgis Night!

Walpurgis Night, when, according to the belief of millions of people, the devil was abroad – when the graves were opened and the dead came forth and walked. When all evil things of earth and air and water held revel. This very place the driver had specially shunned. This was the depopulated village of centuries ago. This was where the suicide lay; and this was the place where I was alone – unmanned, shivering with cold in a shroud of snow with a wild storm gathering again upon me! It took all my philosophy, all the religion I had been taught, all my courage, not to collapse in a paroxysm of fright.

And now a perfect tornado burst upon me. The ground shook as though thousands of horses thundered across it; and this time the storm bore on its icy wings, not snow, but great hailstones which drove with such violence that they might have come from the thongs of Balearic slingers – hailstones that beat down leaf and branch and made the shelter of the cypresses of no more avail than though their stems were standing corn. At the first I had rushed to the nearest tree; but I was soon fain to leave it and seek the only spot that seemed to afford refuge, the deep Doric doorway of the marble tomb. There, crouching against the massive bronze door, I gained a certain amount of protection from the beating of the hailstones, for now they only drove against me as they ricocheted from the ground and the side of the marble.

As I leaned against the door, it moved slightly and opened inwards. The shelter of even a tomb was welcome in that pitiless tempest, and I was about to enter it when there came a flash of forked-lightning that lit up the whole expanse of the heavens. In the instant, as I am a living man, I saw, as my eyes were turned into the darkness of the tomb, a beautiful woman, with rounded cheeks and red lips, seemingly sleeping on a bier. As the thunder broke overhead, I was grasped as by the hand of a giant and hurled out into the storm. The whole thing was so sudden that, before I could realise the shock, moral as well as physical, I found the hailstones beating me down. At the same time I had a strange, dominating feeling that I was not alone. I looked towards the tomb. Just then there came another blinding flash, which seemed to strike the iron stake that surmounted the tomb and to pour through to the earth, blasting and crumbling the marble, as in a burst of flame. The dead woman rose for a moment of agony, while she was lapped in the flame, and her bitter scream of pain was drowned in the thundercrash. The last thing I heard was this mingling of dreadful sound, as again I was seized in the giant grasp and dragged away, while the hailstones beat on me, and the air around seemed reverberant with the howling of wolves. The last sight that I remembered was a vague, white, moving mass, as if all the graves around me had sent out the phantoms of their sheeted dead, and that they were closing in on me through the white cloudiness of the driving hail.

Gradually there came a sort of vague beginning of consciousness; then a sense of weariness that was dreadful. For a time I remembered nothing, but slowly my senses returned. My feet seemed positively racked with pain, yet I could not move them. They seemed to be numbed. There was an icy feeling at the back of my neck and all down my spine, and my ears, like my feet, were dead, yet in torment; but there was in my breast a sense of warmth which was, by comparison, delicious. It was as a nightmare – a physical nightmare, if one may use such an expression; for some heavy weight on my chest made it difficult for me to breathe.

This period of semi-lethargy seemed to remain a long time, and as it faded away I must have slept or swooned. Then came a sort of loathing, like the first stage of sea-sickness, and a wild desire to be free from something – I knew not what. A vast stillness enveloped me, as though all the world were asleep or dead – only broken by the low panting as of some animal close to me. I felt a warm rasping at my throat, then came a consciousness of the awful truth, which chilled me to the heart and sent the blood surging up through my brain. Some great animal was lying on me and now licking my throat. I feared to stir, for some instinct of prudence bade me lie still; but the brute seemed to realise that there was now some change in me, for it raised its head. Through my eyelashes I saw above me the two great flaming eyes of a gigantic wolf. Its sharp white teeth gleamed in the gaping red mouth, and I could feel its hot breath fierce and acrid upon me.

For another spell of time I remembered no more. Then I became conscious of a low growl, followed by a yelp, renewed again and again. Then, seemingly very far away, I heard a 'Holloa! holloa! as of many voices in unison. Cautiously I raised my head and looked in the direction whence the sound came; but the cemetery blocked my view. The wolf still continued to yelp in a strange way, and a red glare began to move round the grove of cypresses, as though following the sound. As the voices drew closer, the wolf yelped faster and louder. I feared to make either sound or motion. Nearer came the red glow, over the white pall which stretched into the darkness around me. Then all at once from beyond the trees there came at a trot a troop of horsemen bearing torches. The wolf rose from my breast and made for the cemetery. I saw one of the horsemen (soldiers by their caps and their long military cloaks) raise his carbine and take aim. A companion knocked up his arm, and I heard the ball whizz over my head. He had evidently taken my body for that of the wolf. Another sighted the animal as it slunk away, and a shot followed. Then, at a gallop, the troop rode forward – some towards me, others following the wolf as it disappeared amongst the snow-clad cypresses.

As they drew nearer I tried to move, but was powerless, although I could see and hear all that went on around me. Two or three of the soldiers jumped from their horses and knelt beside me. One of them raised my head, and placed his hand over my heart.

'Good news, comrades!' he cried. 'His heart still beats!'

Then some brandy was poured down my throat; it put vigour into me, and I was able to open my eyes fully and look around. Lights and shadows were moving among the trees, and I heard men call to one another. They drew together, uttering frightened exclamations; and the lights flashed as the others came pouring out of the cemetery pell-mell, like men possessed. When the further ones came close to us, those who were around me asked them eagerly:

'Well, have you found him?'

The reply rang our hurriedly:

'No! no! Come away quick – quick! This is no place to stay, and on this of all nights!'

'What was it?' was the question, asked in all manner of keys. The answer came variously and all indefinitely as though the men were moved by some common impulse to speak, yet were restrained by some common fear from giving their thoughts.

'It – it – indeed!' gibbered one, whose wits had plainly given out for the moment.

'A wolf – and yet not a wolf!' another put in shudderingly.

'No use trying for him without the sacred bullet,' a third remarked in a more ordinary manner.

'Serve us right for coming out on this night! Truly we have earned our thousand marks!' were the ejaculations of a fourth.

'There was blood on the broken marble,' another said after a pause – 'the lightning never brought that there. And for him – is he safe? Look at his throat! See, comrades, the wolf has been lying on him and keeping his blood warm.'

The officer looked at my throat and replied:

'He is all right; the skin is not pierced. What does it all mean? We should never have found him but for the yelping of the wolf.'

'What became of it?' asked the man who was holding up my head, and who seemed the least panic-stricken of the party, for his hands were steady and without tremor. On his sleeve was the chevron of a petty officer.

'It went to its home,' answered the man, whose long face was pallid, and who actually shook with terror as he glanced around him fearfully. 'There are graves enough there in which it may lie. Come, comrades – come quickly! Let us leave this cursed spot.'

The officer raised me to a sitting posture, as he uttered a word of command; then several men placed me upon a horse. He sprang to the saddle behind me, took me in his arms, gave the word to advance; and, turning our faces away from the cypresses, we rode away in swift, military order.

As yet my tongue refused its office, and I was perforce silent. I must have fallen asleep; for the next thing I remembered was finding myself standing up, supported by a soldier on each side of me. It was almost broad daylight, and to the north a red streak of sunlight was reflected, like a path of blood, over the waste of snow. The officer was telling the men to say nothing of what they had seen, except that they found an English stranger, guarded by a large dog.

'Dog! that was no dog,' cut in the man who had exhibited such fear. 'I think I know a wolf when I see one.'

The young officer answered calmly: 'I said a dog.'

'Dog!' reiterated the other ironically. It was evident that his courage was rising with the sun; and, pointing to me, he said, 'Look at his throat. Is that the work of a dog, master?'

Instinctively I raised my hand to my throat, and as I touched it I cried out in pain. The men crowded round to look, some stooping down from their saddles; and again there came the calm voice of the young officer:

'A dog, as I said. If aught else were said we should only be laughed at.'

I was then mounted behind a trooper, and we rode on into the suburbs of Munich. Here we came across a stray carriage, into which I was lifted, and it was driven off to the Quatre Saisons – the young officer accompanying me, whilst a trooper followed with his horse, and the others rode off to their barracks.

When we arrived, Herr Delbrück rushed so quickly down the steps to meet me, that it was apparent he had been watching within. Taking me by both hands he solicitously led me in. The officer saluted me and was turning to withdraw, when I recognised his purpose, and insisted that he should come to my rooms. Over a glass of wine I warmly thanked him and his brave comrades for saving me. He replied simply that he was more than glad, and that Herr Delbrück had at the first taken steps to make all the searching party pleased; at which ambiguous utterance the maître d'hôtel smiled, while the officer pleaded duty and withdrew.

'But Herr Delbrück,' I enquired, 'how and why was it that the soldiers searched for me?'

He shrugged his shoulders, as if in depreciation of his own deed, as he replied:

'I was so fortunate as to obtain leave from the commander of the regiment on which I served, to ask for volunteers.'

'But how did you know I was lost?' I asked.

'The driver came hither with the remains of his carriage, which had been upset when the horses ran away.'

'But surely you would not send a search-party of soldiers merely on this account?'

'Oh, no!' he answered; 'but even before the coachman arrived, I had this telegram from the Boyar whose guest you are,' and he took from his pocket a telegram which he handed to me, and I read:

BISTRITZ.

Be careful of my guest – his safety is most precious to me. Should aught happen to him, or if he be missed, spare nothing to find him and ensure his safety. He is English and therefore adventurous. There are often dangers from snow and wolves and night. Lose not a moment if you suspect harm to him. I answer your zeal with my fortune. – Dracula.

As I held the telegram in my hand, the room seemed to whirl around me; and, if the attentive maître d'hôtel had not caught me, I think I should have fallen. There was something so strange in all this, something so weird and impossible to imagine, that there grew on me a sense of my being in some way the sport of opposite forces – the mere vague idea of which seemed in a way to paralyse me. I was certainly under some form of mysterious protection. From a distant country had come, in the very nick of time, a message that took me out of the danger of the snow-sleep and the jaws of the wolf.

DRACULA

BRAM STOKER

The first extract is from Chapter I of the novel, where Jonathan Harker describes in his shorthand journal the journey from Munich (which he leaves on the evening of Monday, 1 May 1893), via Klausenburg and Bistritz, to the Borgo Pass and Castle Dracula (where he arrives, in the early hours of Friday, 5 May 1893). It is the section of the novel into which Bram Stoker distilled much of his research concerning the history, topography, geography and folklore of Transylvania; sometimes he transcribed his sources almost word for word. It is also the best-known and best-loved section of the entire book. The second extract is from Chapter III – again, part of Harker's journal. It describes the young solicitor's experiences on the nights of Friday, 12/Saturday, 13 May, and Monday, 15/Tuesday, 16 May, experiences that are almost certainly part of the horrifying nightmare which stimulated the novel in the first place. Or was it a nightmare? Jonathan Harker isn't quite sure – and nor, it seems, was Bram Stoker himself. The only certain thing is that the incident of the brides of Dracula makes the victim's – and the reader's – skin 'tingle as one's flesh does when the hand that is to tickle it approaches nearer – nearer . . .'

Jonathan Harker's Journal
(*Kept in shorthand.*)

3 May. Bistritz. – Left Munich at 8.35 p.m., on 1st May, arriving at Vienna early next morning; should have arrived at 6.46, but train was an hour late. Buda-Pesth seems a wonderful place, from the glimpse which I got of it from the train and the little I could walk through the streets. I feared to go very far from the station, as we had arrived late and would start as near the correct time as possible. The impression I had was that we were leaving the West and entering the East; the most western of splendid bridges over the

Danube, which is here of noble width and depth, took us among the traditions of Turkish rule.

We left in pretty good time, and came after nightfall to Klausenburgh. Here I stopped for the night at the Hotel Royale. I had for dinner, or rather supper, a chicken done up some way with red pepper, which was very good but thirsty. (*Mem.*, get recipe for Mina.) I asked the waiter, and he said it was called 'paprika hendl,' and that, as it was a national dish, I should be able to get it anywhere along the Carpathians. I found my smattering of German very useful here; indeed, I don't know how I should be able to get on without it.

Having had some time at my disposal when in London, I had visited the British Museum, and made search among the books and maps in the library regarding Transylvania; it had struck me that some foreknowledge of the country could hardly fail to have some importance in dealing with a nobleman of that country. I find that the district he named is in the extreme east of the country, just on the borders of three states, Transylvania, Moldavia and Bukovina, in the midst of the Carpathian mountains; one of the wildest and least known portions of Europe. I was not able to light on any map or work giving the exact locality of the Castle Dracula, as there are no maps of this country as yet to compare with our own Ordnance Survey maps; but I found that Bistritz, the post town named by Count Dracula, is a fairly well-known place. I shall enter here some of my notes, as they may refresh my memory when I talk over my travels with Mina.

In the population of Transylvania there are four distinct nationalities: Saxons in the South, and mixed with them the Wallachs, who are the descendants of the Dacians; Magyars in the West, and Szekelys in the East and North. I am going among the latter, who claim to be descended from Attila and the Huns. This may be so, for when the Magyars conquered the country in the eleventh century they found the Huns settled in it. I read that every known superstition in the world is gathered into the horseshoe of the Carpathians, as if it were the centre of some sort of imaginative whirlpool; if so my stay may be very interesting. (*Mem.*, I must ask the Count all about them.)

I did not sleep well, though my bed was comfortable enough, for I had all sorts of queer dreams. There was a dog howling all night under my window, which may have had something to do with it; or it may have been the paprika, for I had to drink up all the water in my carafe, and was still thirsty. Towards morning I slept and was awakened by the continuous knocking at my door, so I guess I must have been sleeping soundly then. I had for breakfast more paprika, and a sort of porridge of maize flour which they said was 'mamaliga,' and egg-plant stuffed with forcemeat, a very excellent dish, which they call 'impletata.' (*Mem.*, get recipe for this also.) I had to hurry breakfast, for the train started a little before eight, or rather it ought to have done so, for after rushing to the station at 7:30 I had to sit in the carriage for more than an hour before we began to move. It seems to me that the further east you go the more unpunctual are the trains. What ought they to be in China?

All day long we seemed to dawdle through a country which was full of beauty of every kind. Sometimes we saw little towns or castles on the top of steep hills such as we see in old missals; sometimes we ran by rivers and streams which seemed from the wide stony margin on each side of them to be subject to great floods. It takes a lot of water, and running strong, to sweep the outside edge of a river clear. At every station there were groups of people, sometimes crowds, and in all sorts of attire. Some of them were just like the peasants at home or those I saw coming through France and Germany, with short jackets and round hats and home-made trousers; but others were very picturesque. The women looked pretty, except when you got near them, but they were very clumsy about the waist. They had all full white sleeves of some kind or other, and most of them had big belts with a lot of strips of something fluttering from them like the dresses in a ballet, but of course there were petticoats under them. The strangest figures we saw were the Slovaks, who were more barbarian than the rest, with their big cow-boy hats, great baggy dirty-white trousers, white linen shirts, and enormous heavy leather belts, nearly a foot wide, all studded over with brass nails. They wore high boots, with their trousers tucked into them, and had long black hair and heavy black moustaches. They are very picturesque, but do not look prepossessing. On the stage they would be set down at once as some old Oriental band of brigands. They are, however, I am told, very harmless and rather wanting in natural self-assertion.

It was on the dark side of twilight when we got to Bistritz, which is a very interesting old place. Being practically on the frontier – for the Borgo Pass leads from it into Bukovina – it has had a very stormy existence, and it certainly shows marks of it. Fifty years ago a series of great fires took place, which made terrible havoc on five separate occasions. At the very beginning of the seventeenth century it underwent a siege of three weeks and lost 13,000 people, the casualties of war proper being assisted by famine and disease.

Count Dracula had directed me to go to the Golden Krone Hotel, which I found, to my great delight, to be thoroughly old-fashioned, for of course I wanted to see all I could of the ways of the country. I was evidently expected, for when I got near the door I faced a cheery-looking elderly woman in the usual peasant dress – white undergarment with long double apron, front, and back, of coloured stuff fitting almost too tight for modesty. When I came close she bowed and said, 'The Herr Englishman?' 'Yes,' I said, 'Jonathan Harker.' She smiled, and gave some message to an elderly man in white shirt-sleeves, who had followed her to the door. He went, but immediately returned with a letter: –

> My Friend. – Welcome to the Carpathians. I am anxiously expecting you.
> Sleep well to-night. At three to-morrow the diligence will start for Bukovina;
> a place on it is kept for you. At the Borgo Pass my carriage will await you
> and will bring you to me. I trust that your journey from London has been
> a happy one, and that you will enjoy your stay in my beautiful land.
>
> Your friend,
>
> DRACULA.

4 May. – I found that my landlord had got a letter from the Count, directing him to secure the best place on the coach for me; but on making inquiries as to details he seemed somewhat reticent, and pretended that he could not understand my German. This could not be true, because up to then he had understood it perfectly; at least, he answered my questions exactly as if he did. He and his wife, the old lady who had received me, looked at each other in a frightened sort of way. He mumbled out that the money had been sent in a letter, and that was all he knew. When I asked him if he knew Count

Dracula, and could tell me anything of his castle, both he and his wife crossed themselves, and, saying that they knew nothing at all, simply refused to speak further. It was so near the time of starting that I had no time to ask any one else, for it was all very mysterious and not by any means comforting.

Just before I was leaving, the old lady came up to my room and said in a very hysterical way:

'Must you go? Oh! young Herr, must you go?' She was in such an excited state that she seemed to have lost her grip of what German she knew, and mixed it all up with some other language which I did not know at all. I was just able to follow her by asking many questions. When I told her that I must go at once, and that I was engaged on important business, she asked again:

'Do you know what day it is?' I answered that it was the fourth of May. She shook her head as she said again:

'Oh, yes! I know that! I know that, but do you know what day it is?' On my saying that I did not understand, she went on:

'It is the eve of St. George's Day. Do you know that tonight, when the clock strikes midnight, all the evil things in the world will have full sway? Do you know where you are going, and what you are going to?' She was in such evident distress that I tried to comfort her, but without effect. Finally she went down on her knees and implored me not to go; at least to wait a day or two before starting. It was all very ridiculous but I did not feel comfortable. However, there was business to be done, and I could allow nothing to interfere with it. I therefore tried to raise her up, and said, as gravely as I could, that I thanked her, but my duty was imperative, and that I must go. She then rose and dried her eyes, and taking a crucifix from her neck offered it to me. I did not know what to do, for, as an English Churchman, I have been taught to regard such things as in some measure idolatrous, and yet it seemed so ungracious to refuse an old lady meaning so well and in such a state of mind. She saw, I suppose, the doubt in my face, for she put the rosary round my neck, and said, 'For your mother's sake,' and went out of the room. I am writing up this part of the diary whilst I am waiting for the coach, which is, of course late; and the crucifix is still round my neck. Whether it is the old lady's fear, or the many ghostly traditions of this place, or the crucifix itself, I do not know, but I am not feeling nearly as easy in my mind as usual. If this book should ever reach Mina before I do, let it bring my good-bye. Here comes the coach!

5 May. The Castle. – The grey of the morning has passed, and the sun is high over the distant horizon, which seems jagged, whether with trees or hills I know not, for it is so far off that big things and little are mixed. I am not sleepy, and, as I am not to be called till I awake, naturally I write till sleep comes. There are many odd things to put down, and, lest who reads them may fancy that I dined too well before I left Bistritz, let me put down my dinner exactly. I dined on what they called 'robber steak' – bits of bacon, onion, and beef, seasoned with red pepper, and strung on sticks and roasted over the fire, in the simple style of the London cat's meat! The wine was Golden Mediasch, which produces a queer sting on the tongue, which is, however, not disagreeable. I had only a couple of glasses of this, and nothing else.

When I got on the coach the driver had not taken his seat, and I saw him talking with the landlady. They were evidently talking of me, for every now and then they looked at me, and some of the people who were sitting on the bench outside the door – which they call by a name meaning 'word-bearer' – came and listened, and then looked at me, most of them pityingly. I could hear a lot of words often repeated, queer words, for there were many nationalities in the crowd; so I quietly got my polyglot dictionary from my bag and looked them out. I must say they were not cheering to me, for amongst them were 'Ordog' – Satan, 'polok' – hell, 'stregoica' – witch, 'vrolok' and 'vlkoslak' – both of which mean the same thing, one being Slovak and the other Servian for something that is either were-wolf or vampire. (*Mem.*, I must ask the Count about these superstitions.)

When we started, the crowd round the inn door, which had by this time swelled to a considerable size, all made the sign of the cross and pointed two fingers towards me. With some difficulty I got a fellow-passenger to tell me what they meant; he would not answer at first, but on learning that I was English, he explained that it was a charm or guard against the evil eye. This was not very pleasant for me, just starting for an unknown place to meet an unknown man; but every one seemed so kindhearted, and so sorrowful, and so sympathetic that I could not but be touched. I shall never forget the last glimpse which I had of the inn-yard and its crowd of picturesque figures, all crossing themselves, as they stood round the wide archway, with its background of rich foliage of oleander and orange trees in green tubs clustered in the centre of the yard. Then our driver, whose wide linen drawers covered the whole front of the box-seat – 'gotza' they call them – cracked his big whip over his four small horses, which ran abreast, and we set off on our journey.

I soon lost sight and recollection of ghostly fears in the beauty of the scene as we drove along, although had I known the language or rather languages, which my fellow-passengers were speaking, I might not have been able to throw them off so easily. Before us lay a green sloping land full of forests and woods, with here and there steep hills, crowned with clumps of trees or with farmhouses, the blank gable end to the road. There was everywhere a bewildering mass of fruit blossom – apple, plum, pear, cherry; and as we drove by I could see the green grass under the trees spangled with the fallen petals. In and out amongst these green hills of what they call here the 'Mittel Land' ran the road, losing itself as it swept round the grassy curve, or was shut out by the straggling ends of pine woods, which here and there ran down the hillsides like tongues of flame. The road was rugged, but still we seemed to fly over it with a feverish haste. I could not understand then what the haste meant, but the driver was evidently bent on losing no time in reaching Borgo Prund. I was told that this road is in summertime excellent, but that it had not yet been put in order after the winter snows. In this respect it is different from the general run of roads in the Carpathians, for it is an old tradition that they are not to be kept in too good order. Of old the Hospadars would not repair them, lest the Turk should think that they were preparing to bring in foreign troops, and so hasten the war which was always really at loading point.

Beyond the green swelling hills of the Mittel Land rose mighty slopes of forest up to the lofty steeps of the Carpathians themselves. Right and left of us they towered, with the afternoon sun falling full upon them and bringing out all the glorious colours of this beautiful range, deep blue and purple in the shadows of the peaks, green and brown where grass and rock mingled, and an endless perspective of jagged rock and pointed crags, till these were themselves lost in the distance, where the snowy peaks rose grandly. Here and there seemed mighty rifts in the mountains, through which, as the sun began to sink, we saw now and again the white gleam of falling water. One of my companions touched my arm as we swept round the base of a hill and opened up the lofty, snow-covered peak of a mountain, which seemed, as we wound on our serpentine way, to be right before us: –

'Look! Isten szek!' – 'God's seat!' – and he crossed himself reverently.

As we wound on our endless way, and the sun sank lower and lower behind us, the shadows of the evening began to creep round us. This was emphasised by the fact that the snowy mountain-top still held the sunset, and seemed to glow out with a delicate cool pink. Here and there we passed Cszeks and Slovaks, all in picturesque attire, but I noticed that goitre was painfully prevalent. By the roadside were many crosses, and as we swept by, my companions all crossed themselves. Here and there was a peasant man or woman kneeling before a shrine, who did not even turn round as we approached, but seemed in the self-surrender of devotion to have neither eyes nor ears for the outer world. There were many things new to me: for instance, hay-ricks in the trees, and here and there very beautiful masses of weeping birch, their white stems shining like silver through the delicate green of the leaves. Now and again we passed a leiter-wagon – the ordinary peasant's cart – with its long snake-like vertebra, calculated to suit the inequalities of the road. On this were sure to be seated quite a group of home-coming peasants, the Cszeks with their white, and the Slovaks with their coloured, sheepskins, the latter carrying lance-fashion their long staves, with axe at end. As the evening fell it began to get very cold, and the growing twilight seemed to merge into one dark mistiness the gloom of the trees, oak, beech, and pine, though in the valleys which ran deep between the spurs of the hills, as we ascended through the Pass, the dark firs stood out here and there against the background of late-lying snow. Sometimes, as the road was cut through the pine woods that seemed in the darkness to be closing down upon us, great masses of greyness, which here and there bestrewed the trees, produced a peculiarly weird and solemn effect, which carried on the thoughts and grim fancies engendered earlier in the evening, when the falling sunset threw into strange relief the ghost-like clouds which amongst the Carpathians seem to wind ceaselessly through the valleys. Sometimes the hills were so steep that, despite our driver's haste, the horses could only go slowly. I wished to get down and walk up them, as we do at home, but the driver would not hear of it. 'No, no,' he said; 'you must not walk here; the dogs are too fierce'; and then he added, with what he evidently meant for grim pleasantry – for he looked round to catch the approving smile of the rest – 'and you may have enough of such matters before you go to sleep.' The only stop he would make was a moment's pause to light his lamps.

When it grew dark there seemed to be some excitement amongst the passengers, and they kept speaking to him, one after the other, as though urging him to further speed. He lashed the horses unmercifully with his long whip, and with wild cries of encouragement urged them on to further exertions. Then through the darkness I could see a sort of patch of grey light ahead of us, as though there were a cleft in the hills. The excitement of the passengers grew greater; the crazy coach rocked on its great leather springs, and swayed like a boat tossed on a stormy sea. I had to hold on. The road grew more level, and we appeared to fly along. Then the mountains seemed to come nearer to us on each side and to frown down upon us; we were entering on the Borgo Pass. One by one several of the passengers offered me gifts, which they pressed upon me with an earnestness which would take no denial; these were certainly of an odd and varied kind, but each was given in simple good faith, with a kindly word, and a blessing, and that strange mixture of fear-meaning movements which I had seen outside the hotel at Bistritz – the sign of the cross and the guard against the evil eye. Then, as we flew along, the driver leaned forward, and on each side the passengers, craning over the edge of the coach, peered eagerly into the darkness. It was evident that something very exciting was either happening or expected, but though I asked each passenger, no one would give me the slightest explanation. This state of excitement kept on for some little time; and at last we saw before us the Pass opening out on the eastern side. There were dark, rolling clouds overhead, and in the air the heavy, oppressive sense of thunder. It seemed as though the mountain range had separated two atmospheres, and that now we had gone into the thunderous one. I was now myself looking out for the conveyance which was to take me to the Count. Each moment I expected to see the glare of lamps through the blackness; but all was dark. The only light was the flickering rays of our own lamps, in which the steam from our hard-driven horses rose in a white cloud. We could see now the sandy road lying white before us, but there was on it no sign of a vehicle. The passengers drew back with a sigh of gladness, which seemed to mock my own disappointment. I was already thinking what I had best do, when the driver, looking at his watch, said to the others something which I could hardly hear, it was spoken so quietly and in so low a tone; I thought it was 'An hour less than the time.' Then turning to me, he said in German worse than my own: –

'There is no carriage here. The Herr is not expected after all. He will now come on to Bukovina, and return to-morrow or the next day; better the next day.' Whilst he was speaking the horses began to neigh and snort and plunge wildly, so that the driver had to hold them up. Then, amongst a chorus of screams from the peasants and a universal crossing of themselves, a calèche, with four horses, drove up behind us, overtook us, and drew up beside the coach. I could see from the flash of our lamps, as the rays fell on them, that the horses were coal-black and splendid animals. They were driven by a tall man, with a long brown beard and a great black hat, which seemed to hide his face from us. I could only see the gleam of a pair of very bright eyes, which seemed red in the lamplight, as he turned to us. He said to the driver: –

'You are early to-night, my friend.' The man stammered in reply: –

'The English Herr was in a hurry,' to which the stranger replied: –

'That is why, I suppose, you wished him to go on to Bukovina. You cannot deceive me, my friend, I know too much, and my horses are swift.' As he spoke he smiled, and the lamplight fell on a hard-looking mouth, with very red lips and sharp-looking teeth, as white as ivory. One of my companions whispered to another the line from Burger's 'Lenore': –

Denn die Todten reiten schnell –
(For the dead travel fast.)

The strange driver evidently heard the words, for he looked up with a gleam-
ing smile. The passenger turned his face away, at the same time putting out
his two fingers, and crossing himself. 'Give me the Herr's luggage,' said the
driver; and with exceeding alacrity my bags were handed out and put in the
calèche. Then I descended from the side of the coach, as the calèche was
close alongside, the driver helping me with a hand which caught my arm in
a grip of steel; his strength must have been prodigious. Without a word he
shook the reins, the horses turned, and we swept into the darkness of the
Pass. As I looked back I saw the steam from the horses of the coach by the
light of the lamps, and projected against it the figures of my late companions crossing themselves. Then the driver cracked his whip and called to his
horses, and off they swept on their way to Bukovina. As they sank into the
darkness I felt a strange chill, and a lonely feeling came over me; but a cloak
was thrown over my shoulders, and a rug across my knees, and the driver
said in excellent German: –

'The night is chill, mein Herr, and my master the Count bade me take
all care of you. There is a flask of slivovitz (the plum brandy of the country)
underneath the seat, if you should require it.' I did not take any, but it was a
comfort to know it was there all the same. I felt a little strangely, and not a
little frightened. I think had there been any alternative I should have taken
it, instead of prosecuting that unknown night journey. The carriage went at
a hard pace straight along, then we made a complete turn and went along
another straight road. It seemed to me that we were simply going over and
over the same ground again; and so I took note of some salient point, and
found that this was so. I would have liked to have asked the driver what this
all meant, but I really feared to do so, for I thought that, placed as I was,
any protest would have had no effect in case there had been an intention to
delay. By-and-by, however, as I was curious to know how time was passing,
I struck a match, and by its flame looked at my watch; it was within a few
minutes of midnight. This gave me a sort of shock, for I suppose the general

superstition about midnight was increased by my recent experiences. I waited with a sick feeling of suspense.

Then a dog began to howl somewhere in a farmhouse far down the road – a long, agonised wailing, as if from fear. The sound was taken up by another dog, and then another and another, till, borne on the wind which now sighed softly through the Pass, a wild howling began, which seemed to come from all over the gloom of the night. At the first howl the horses began to strain and rear, but the driver spoke to them soothingly, and they quieted down, but shivered and sweated as though after a run-away from sudden fright. Then, far off in the distance, from the mountains on each side of us began a louder and a sharper howling – that of wolves – which affected both the horses and myself in the same way – for I was minded to jump from the calèche and run, whilst they reared again and plunged madly, so that the driver had to use all his great strength to keep them from bolting. In a few minutes, however, my own ears got accustomed to the sound, and the horses so far became quiet that the driver was able to descend and to stand before them. He petted and soothed them, and whispered something in their ears, as I have heard of horse-tamers doing, and with extraordinary effect, for under his caresses they became quite manageable again, though they still trembled. The driver again took his seat, and shaking his reins, started off at a great pace. This time, after going to the far side of the Pass, he suddenly turned down a narrow roadway which ran sharply to the right.

Soon we were hemmed in with trees, which in places arched right over the roadway till we passed as through a tunnel; and again great frowning rocks guarded us boldly on either side. Though we were in shelter, we could hear the rising wind, for it moaned and whistled through the rocks, and the branches of the trees crashed together as we swept along. It grew colder and colder still, and fine, powdery snow began to fall, so that soon we and all around us were covered with a white blanket. The keen wind still carried the howling of the dogs, though this grew fainter as we went on our way. The baying of the wolves sounded nearer and nearer, as though they were closing round on us from every side. I grew dreadfully afraid, and the horses shared my fear. The driver, however, was not in the least disturbed;

he kept turning his head to left and right, but I could not see anything through the darkness.

Suddenly, away on our left, I saw a faint flickering blue flame. The driver saw it at the same moment; he at once checked the horses, and, jumping to the ground, disappeared into the darkness. I did not know what to do, the less as the howling of the wolves grew closer; but while I wondered the driver suddenly appeared again, and without a word took his seat, and we resumed our journey. I think I must have fallen asleep and kept dreaming of the incident, for it seemed to be repeated endlessly, and now looking back, it is like a sort of awful nightmare. Once the flame appeared so near the road, that even in the darkness around us I could watch the driver's motions. He went rapidly to where the blue flame arose – it must have been very faint, for it did not seem to illumine the place around it at all – and gathering a few stones, formed them into some device. Once there appeared a strange optical effect: when he stood between me and the flame he did not obstruct it, for I could see its ghostly flicker all the same. This startled me, but as the effect was only momentary, I took it that my eyes deceived me straining through the darkness. Then for a time there were no blue flames, and we sped onwards through the gloom, with the howling of the wolves around us, as though they were following in a moving circle.

At last there came a time when the driver went further afield than he had yet gone, and during his absence, the horses began to tremble worse than ever and to snort and scream with fright. I could not see any cause for it, for the howling of the wolves had ceased altogether; but just then the moon, sailing through the black clouds, appeared behind the jagged crest of a beetling, pine-clad rock, and by its light I saw around us a ring of wolves, with white teeth and lolling red tongues, with long, sinewy limbs and shaggy hair. They were a hundred times more terrible in the grim silence which held them than even when they howled. For myself, I felt a sort of paralysis of fear. It is only when a man feels himself face to face with such horrors that he can understand their true import.

All at once the wolves began to howl as though the moonlight had had some peculiar effect on them. The horses jumped about and reared, and looked helplessly round with eyes that rolled in a way painful to see; but the living ring of terror encompassed them on every side; and they had perforce to remain within it. I called to the coachman to come, for it seemed to me that our only chance was to try to break out through the ring and to aid his approach. I shouted and beat the side of the calèche, hoping by the noise to scare the wolves from that side, so as to give him a chance of reaching the trap. How he came there, I know not, but I heard his voice raised in a tone of imperious command, and looking towards the sound, saw him stand in the roadway. As he swept his long arms, as though brushing aside some impalpable obstacle, the wolves fell back and back further still. Just then a heavy cloud passed across the face of the moon, so that we were again in darkness.

When I could see again the driver was climbing into the calèche, and the wolves had disappeared. This was all so strange and uncanny that a dreadful fear came upon me, and I was afraid to speak or move. The time seemed interminable as we swept on our way, now in almost complete darkness, for the rolling clouds obscured the moon. We kept on ascending, with occasional periods of quick descent, but in the main always ascending. Suddenly, I became conscious of the fact that the driver was in the act of pulling up the horses in the courtyard of a vast ruined castle, from whose tall black windows came no ray of light, and whose broken battlements showed a jagged line against the moonlit sky . . .

The second extract from Jonathan Harker's journal is dated 12 May, a week later.

'I TRUST YOU WILL FORGIVE ME,' said the Count, 'but I have much work to do in private this evening. You will, I hope, find all things as you wish.' At the door he turned, and after a moment's pause said: –

'Let me advise you, my dear young friend – nay, let me warn you with all seriousness, that should you leave these rooms you will not by any chance go to sleep in any other part of the castle. It is old, and has many memories, and there are bad dreams for those who sleep unwisely. Be warned! Should sleep now or ever overcome you, or be like to do, then haste to your own chamber or to these rooms, for your rest will then be safe. But if you be not careful in this respect, then' – He finished his speech in a gruesome way, for he motioned with his hands as if he were washing them. I quite understood; my only doubt was as to whether any dream could be more terrible than the unnatural, horrible net of gloom and mystery which seemed closing around me.

Later. – I endorse the last words written, but this time there is no doubt in question. I shall not fear to sleep in any place where he is not. I have placed the crucifix over the head of my bed – I imagine that my rest is thus freer from dreams; and there it shall remain.

When he left me I went to my room. After a little while, not hearing any sound, I came out and went up the stone stair to where I could look out towards the South. There was some sense of freedom in the vast expanse, inaccessible though it was to me, as compared with the narrow darkness of the courtyard. Looking out on this, I felt that I was indeed in prison, and I seemed to want a breath of fresh air, though it were of the night. I am beginning to feel this nocturnal existence tell on me. It is destroying my nerve. I start at my own shadow, and am full of all sorts of horrible imaginings. God knows that there is ground for my terrible fear in this accursed place! I looked out over the beautiful expanse, bathed in soft yellow moonlight till it was almost as light as day. In the soft light the distant hills became melted, and the shadows in the valleys and gorges of velvety blackness. The mere beauty seemed to cheer me; there was peace and comfort in every breath I drew. As I leaned from the window my eye was caught by something moving a storey below me, and somewhat to my left, where I imagined, from the order of the rooms, that the windows of the Count's own room would look out. The window at which I stood was tall and deep, stone-mullioned, and though weatherworn, was still complete; but it was evidently many a day since the case had been there. I drew back behind the stonework, and looked carefully out.

What I saw was the Count's head coming out from the window. I did not see the face, but I knew the man by the neck and the movement of his back and arms. In any case I could not mistake the hands which I had had so many opportunities of studying. I was at first interested and somewhat amused, for it is wonderful how small a matter will interest and amuse a man when he is a prisoner. But my very feelings changed to repulsion and terror when I saw the whole man slowly emerge from the window and begin to crawl down the castle wall over that dreadful abyss, *face down* with his cloak spreading out around him like great wings. At first I could not believe my eyes. I thought it was some trick of the moonlight, some weird effect of shadow; but I kept looking, and it could be no delusion. I saw the fingers and toes grasp the corners of the stones, worn clear of the mortar by the stress of years, and by thus using every projection and inequality move downwards with considerable speed, just as a lizard moves along a wall.

What manner of man is this, or what manner of creature is it in the semblance of man? I feel the dread of this horrible place overpowering me; I am in fear – in awful fear – and there is no escape for me; I am encompassed about with terrors that I dare not think of . . .

15 May. – Once more have I seen the Count go out in his lizard fashion. He moved downwards in a sidelong way, some hundred feet down, and a good deal to the left. He vanished into some hole or window. When his head had disappeared, I leaned out to try and see more, but without avail – the distance was too great to allow a proper angle of sight. I knew he had left the castle now, and thought to use the opportunity to explore more than I had dared to do as yet. I went back to the room, and taking a lamp, tried all the doors. They were all locked, as I had expected, and the locks were comparatively new; but I went down the stone stairs to the hall where I had entered originally. I found I could pull back the bolts easily enough and unhook the great chains; but the door was locked, and the key was gone. That key must be in the Count's room; I must watch should his door be unlocked, so that I may get in and escape. I went on to make a thorough examination of the various stairs and passages, and to try the doors that opened from them. One or two small rooms near the hall were open, but there was nothing to see in them except old furniture, dusty with age and moth-eaten. At last, however, I found one door at the top of the stairway which, though it seemed to be locked, gave a little under pressure. I tried it harder, and found that it was not really locked, but that the resistance came from the fact that the hinges had fallen somewhat, and the heavy door rested on the floor. Here was an opportunity which I might not have again, so I exerted myself, and with many efforts forced it back so that I could enter. I was now in a wing of the castle further to the right than the rooms I knew and a storey lower down. From the windows I could see that the suite of rooms lay along to the south of the castle, the windows of the end room looking out both west and south. On the latter side, as well as to the former, there was a great precipice. The castle was built on the corner of a great rock, so that on three sides it was quite impregnable, and great windows were placed here where sling, or bow, or culverin could not reach, and consequently light and comfort, impossible to a position which had to be guarded, were secured. To the west was a great valley, and then, rising far away, great jagged mountain fastnesses, rising peak on peak, the sheer rock studded with mountain ash and thorn, whose roots clung in cracks and crevices and crannies of the stone. This was evidently the portion of the castle occupied by the ladies in bygone days, for the furniture had more air of comfort than any I had seen. The windows were curtainless, and the yellow moonlight, flooding in through the diamond panes, enabled one to see even colours, whilst it softened the wealth of dust which lay over all and disguised in some measure the ravages of time and the moth. My lamp seemed to be of little effect in the brilliant moonlight, but I was glad to have it with me, for there was a dread of loneliness in the place which chilled my heart and made my nerves tremble. Still, it was better than living alone in the rooms which I had come to hate from the presence of the Count, and after trying a little to school my nerves, I found a soft quietude come over me. Here I am, sitting at a little oak table where in old times possibly some fair lady sat to pen, with much thought and many blushes, her illspelt love-letter, and writing in my diary in shorthand all that has happened since I closed it last. It is nineteenth century up-to-date with a vengeance. And yet, unless my senses deceive me, the old centuries had, and have, powers of their own which mere 'modernity' cannot kill.

Later: the Morning of 16 May. – God preserve my sanity, for to this I am reduced. Safety and the assurance of safety are things of the past. Whilst I live on here there is but one thing to hope for, that I may not go mad, if, indeed, I be not mad already. If I be sane, then surely it is maddening to think that of all the foul things that lurk in this hateful place the Count is the least dreadful to me; that to him alone I can look for safety, even though this be only whilst I can serve his purpose. Great God! merciful God! Let me be calm, for out of that way lies madness indeed. I begin to get new lights on certain things which have puzzled me. Up to now I never quite knew what Shakespeare meant when he made Hamlet say: –

> 'My tablets! quick, my tablets!
> 'Tis meet that I put it down,' etc.,

for now, feeling as though my own brain were unhinged or as if the shock had come which must end in its undoing, I turn to my diary for repose. The habit of entering accurately must help to soothe me.

The Count's mysterious warning frightened me at the time; it frightens me more now when I think of it, for in future he has a fearful hold upon me. I shall fear to doubt what he may say!

When I had written in my diary and had fortunately replaced the book and pen in my pocket I felt sleepy. The Count's warning came into my mind, but I took a pleasure in disobeying it. The sense of sleep was upon me, and with it the obstinacy which sleep brings as outrider. The soft moonlight soothed, and the wide expanse without gave a sense of freedom which refreshed me. I determined not to return to-night to the gloom-haunted rooms, but to sleep here, where, of old, ladies had sat and sung and lived sweet lives whilst their gentle breasts were sad for their menfolk away in the midst of remorseless wars. I drew a great couch out of its place near the corner, so that as I lay, I could look at the lovely view to east and south, and unthinking of and uncaring for the dust, composed myself for sleep. I suppose I must have fallen asleep; I hope so, but I fear, for all that followed was startlingly real – so real that now sitting here in the broad, full sunlight of the morning, I cannot in the least believe that it was all sleep.

I was not alone. The room was the same, unchanged in any way since I came into it; I could see along the floor, in the brilliant moonlight, my own footsteps marked where I had disturbed the long accumulation of dust. In the moonlight opposite me were three young women, ladies by their dress and manner. I thought at the time that I must be dreaming when I saw them, for, though the moonlight was behind them, they threw no shadow on the floor. They came close to me, and looked at me for some time, and then whispered together. Two were dark, and had high aquiline noses, like the Count, and great dark, piercing eyes that seemed to be almost red when contrasted with the pale yellow moon. The other was fair, as fair as can be, with great wavy masses of golden hair and eyes like pale sapphires. I seemed somehow to know her face, and to know it in connection with some dreamy fear, but I could not recollect at the moment how or where. All three had brilliant white teeth that shone like pearls against the ruby of their voluptuous lips. There was something about them that made me uneasy, some longing and at the same time some deadly fear. I felt in my heart a wicked, burning desire that they would kiss me with those red lips. It is not good to note this down, lest some day it should meet Mina's eyes and cause her pain; but it is the truth. They whispered together, and then they all three laughed – such a silvery, musical laugh, but as hard as though the sound never could have come through the softness of human lips. It was like the intolerable, tingling sweetness of water-glasses when played on by a cunning hand. The fair girl shook her head coquettishly, and the other two urged her on. One said: –

'Go on! You are first, and we shall follow; yours is the right to begin.' The other added: –

'He is young and strong; there are kisses for us all.' I lay quiet, looking out under my eyelashes in an agony of delightful anticipation. The fair girl advanced and bent over me till I could feel the movement of her breath upon me. Sweet it was in one sense, honey-sweet, and sent the same tingling through the nerves as her voice, but with a bitter underlying the sweet, a bitter offensiveness, as one smells in blood.

I was afraid to raise my eyelids, but looked out and saw perfectly under the lashes. The girl went on her knees, and bent over me, simply gloating. There was a deliberate voluptuousness which was both thrilling and repulsive, and as she arched her neck she actually licked her lips like an animal, till I could see in the moonlight the moisture shining on the scarlet lips and on the red tongue as it lapped the white sharp teeth. Lower and lower went her head as the lips went below the range of my mouth and chin and seemed about to fasten on my throat. Then she paused, and I could hear the churning sound of her tongue as it licked her teeth and lips, and could feel the hot breath on my neck. Then the skin of my throat began to tingle as one's flesh does when the hand that is to tickle it approaches nearer – nearer. I could feel the soft, shivering touch of the lips on the super-sensitive skin of my throat, and the hard dents of two sharp teeth, just touching and pausing there. I closed my eyes in a languorous ecstasy and waited – waited with beating heart.

But at that instant, another sensation swept through me as quick as lightning. I was conscious of the presence of the Count, and of his being as if lapped in a storm of fury. As my eyes opened involuntarily I saw his strong hand grasp the slender neck of the fair woman and with giant's power draw it back, the blue eyes transformed with fury, the white teeth champing with rage, and the fair cheeks blazing red with passion. But the Count! Never did I imagine such wrath and fury, even to the demons of the pit. His eyes were positively blazing. The red light in them was lurid, as if the flames of hell-fire blazed behind them. His face was deathly pale, and the lines of it were hard like drawn wires; the thick eyebrows that met over the nose now seemed like a heaving bar of white-hot metal. With a fierce sweep of his arm, he hurled the woman from him, and then motioned to the others, as though he were beating them back; it was the same imperious gesture that I had seen used to the wolves. In a voice which, though low and almost in a whisper seemed to cut through the air and then ring round the room he said: –

'How dare you touch him, any of you? How dare you cast eyes on him when I had forbidden it? Back, I tell you all! This man belongs to me! Beware how you meddle with him, or you'll have to deal with me.' The fair girl, with a laugh of ribald coquetry, turned to answer him: –

'You yourself never loved; you never love!' On this the other women joined, and such a mirthless, hard, soulless laughter rang through the room that it almost made me faint to hear; it seemed like the pleasure of fiends. Then the Count turned, after looking at my face attentively, and said in a soft whisper: –

'Yes, I too can love; you yourselves can tell it from the past. Is it not so? Well, now I promise you that when I am done with him you shall kiss him at your will. Now go! go! I must awaken him, for there is work to be done.'

'Are we to have nothing tonight?' said one of them, with a low laugh, as she pointed to the bag which he had thrown upon the floor, and which moved as though there were some living thing within it. For answer he nodded his head. One of the women jumped forward and opened it. If my ears did not deceive me there was a gasp and a low wail, as of a half-smothered child. The women closed round, whilst I was aghast with horror; but as I looked they disappeared, and with them the dreadful bag. There was no door near them, and they could not have passed me without my noticing. They simply seemed to fade into the rays of the moonlight and pass out through the window, for I could see outside the dim, shadowy forms for a moment before they entirely faded away.

Then horror overcame me, and I sank down unconscious.

I awoke in my own bed. If it be that I had not dreamt, the Count must have carried me here. I tried to satisfy myself on the subject, but could not arrive at any unquestionable result. To be sure, there were certain small evidences, such as that my clothes were folded and laid by in a manner which was not my habit. My watch was still unwound, and I am rigorously accustomed to wind it the last thing before going to bed, and many such details. But these things are no proof, for they may have been evidences that my mind was not as usual, and, from some cause or another, I had certainly been much upset. I must watch for proof. Of one thing I am glad: if it was that the Count carried me here and undressed me, he must have been hurried in his task, for my pockets are intact. I am sure this diary would have been a mystery to him which he would not have brooked. He would have taken or destroyed it. As I look round this room, although it has been to me so full of fear, it is now a sort of sanctuary, for nothing can be more dreadful than those awful women, who were – who *are* – waiting to suck my blood.

THE MODERNIST VAMPIRE

The poet W. B. Yeats had read about vampires, during his occult phase, in volume two of Joseph Ennemoser's *The History of Magic* (translated from the German in 1852). In *The Land of Heart's Desire* (1894), Yeats's first performed play – set in rural Sligo in the eighteenth century – a faery-child, or demon, is invited over the threshold of a cottage and 'is about to dance but suddenly sees the crucifix and shrieks and covers her eyes'. 'What is that ugly thing?' she asks. 'Take it away!' Mary/Maive, the daughter-in-law of the house, desperately wants the faeries to spirit her away from a dull, too godly atmosphere. Father Hart disagrees, and calls them 'the children of the fiend . . .', the elf-children. In the dream-like play *The Shadowy Waters* (1904), a sailor refers to 'Some place of shining women that cast no shadow, having lived before the making of the earth' – who, on a ghost-ship near the world's end, are assisted by undead sailors in the shape of man-headed birds. As Roy Foster has pointed out in his essay on *Protestant Magic*, 'For those who have accompanied Jonathan Harker through Dracula's castle, none of this is new.' Yeats in fact knew Bram Stoker, and signed a copy of his *The Countess Cathleen* for him in 1892, while Stoker was working on *Dracula*. Ennemoser had included long extracts from d'Argens's *Lettres Juives* and Calmet's *The Phantom World*, with generous quotations from the official reports on the 'epidemics' in Kisilova (1725–30) and Medvegia (1731–32) – and had concluded with the mid-eighteenth-century thought 'Thanks be to God, we are by no means credulous . . . Nevertheless, we cannot refuse to believe that to be true which is juridically attested . . .'

From *Stone Cottage – Pound, Yeats and Modernism*, by James Langenbach (Oxford, 1988, pp. 108–9)

At the outbreak of the First World War Yeats wondered if citizens of rival nations would ever visit one another again. This worry was a personal one, for both he and Ezra Pound were unable to travel to the continent. Pound lamented his cultural isolation in *Three Cantos* (1917), asserting his ability to travel mentally if not physically: 'I walk Verona. (I am here in England) / I can see Can Grande. (Can see whom you will)'. Yeats also settled for imagined journeys. He had planned to travel to Austria in August 1914 but the trip was cancelled when the war was declared. A few months later he wrote to [lawyer and generous patron] John Quinn that he had been awake much of the night reading Bram Stoker's *Dracula* – not because he valued the work highly; indeed it interested him no more than any other sensational story. Yeats read the book because his cancelled trip to Austria [in August 1914] would have featured a night in the real Dracula castle, which had been haunted for generations. On the way to the castle Yeats was to have visited another haunted house, but its present owner was fighting, perhaps killed, and now, Yeats told Quinn, the house's 'priceless imp has no one to haunt'. Yeats mentioned to Quinn that his evening of reading had strained his eyes and given him a headache as if he had drunk too much claret . . .

From *Ulysses*, by James Joyce (1914–22)

Across the sands of all the world, followed by the sun's flaming sword, to the west, trekking to evening lands. She trudges, schlepps, trains, drags, trascines for load. A tide westering, moondrawn, in her wake. Tides, myriad islanded, within her, blood not mine, *oinopa ponton*, a winedark sea. Behold the handmaid of the moon. In sleep the wet sign calls her hour, bids her rise. Bridebed, childbed, bed of death, ghost-candled. *Omnis caro ad te veniet.* He comes, pale vampire, through storm his eyes, his bat sails bloodying the sea, mouth to her mouth's kiss. Here. Put a pin in that chap, will you? My tablets. Mouth to her kiss. No. Must be two of em. Glue em well. Mouth to her mouth's kiss.

from *The Waste Land*, by T. S. Eliot (1922)

A woman drew her long black hair out tight
And fiddled whisper music on those strings
And bats with baby faces in the violet light
Whistled, and beat their wings
And crawled head downward down a blackened wall
And upside down in air were towers
Tolling reminiscent bells, that kept the hours
And voices singing out of empty cisterns and exhausted wells.

POSTSCRIPT

THE LADY OF THE HOUSE OF LOVE
FROM *THE BLOODY CHAMBER*

ANGELA CARTER

In 1974, I went on a research trip from Bath to the Carpathian Mountains in Romania – in the footsteps of Jonathan Harker – to collect background material for the *Dracula* sections of the first version of this book. Not on a bicycle but in a hired car, a Dacia 13 better known as a Renault 12, with notebook and camera on the back seat. At precisely the same time, my good friend Angela Carter was thinking about her first BBC radio play *Vampirella*, which would turn into the short story *The Lady of the House of Love* – the starting-point of her collection *The Bloody Chamber*. We had been to see *Nosferatu* together in Bristol – she particularly loved the intertitle 'And when he crossed over the bridge, the phantoms came to meet him' – and we both read assorted books from my collection about vampires, including those by Montague Summers, Mario Praz, Gabriel Ronay, and a bizarre French picture-book compilation called *La Musée des Vampires*. We would talk about these, and haemosexuality in general, until the very witching hour of night. As both the radio play and the story evolved, the hero became a dashing young chap out of *The Boy's Own Paper c.* 1914, who goes for a cycling tour of the land beyond the forest. Angela was much amused, and intrigued, by my own tour. The hero of *The Lady of the House of Love* is rather naive and boyishly enthusiastic; has studied the good old English tradition of literature at university and absorbed the 'eat your broccoli' school of criticism; looks as though he has 'the head of a lion'; and still believes that demons can be redeemed with the innocence of a kiss. He has all sorts of exotic adventures in the Carpathians, which was a nice thought. At least he *almost* does. When confronted by the cloistered vampire Countess in her dark glasses in her glittering castle, the hero keeps dark thoughts at bay by clinging onto the world of *facts*; by repressing his imagination as he has been brought up to do. So he doesn't realize what is happening to him. I like to think that

Angela was exercising her poetic imagination here . . . Then his regiment leaves for France . . .

So the origins of Angela Carter's story, and of this book, are closely intertwined. Angela wrote that 'fairy tales, folk tales, tales from the oral tradition . . . are all of them the most vital connection we have to the imagination of the ordinary men and women whose labour created our world'. She also said that fairy tales and folktales were the sorts of stories in which one king drops in on another king to borrow a cup of sugar. Her own stories would shift gear from artful sensuality to bawdy jokes with no warning at all. So although she took the clichés of the traditional vampire story – which we often discussed – magnified them and turned them into elaborately wrought artifice, she was also fascinated by the deep roots of Gothic fantasy in everyday life. In this sense, *The Lady* is a bridge between the classic vampire story, its postmodern variations, and the worlds of *Buffy the Vampire Slayer* (1997–2003), *True Blood* (2008–14) and *Twilight* (2005–8), where the relationship between Bella Swan and Edward Cullen is one of chaste yearning or erotic abstinence – leaving the reader to fantasize about what might happen next. Stephenie Meyer has recalled that the idea for *Twilight* originally came to her in a dream, when she was twenty-nine years old, about an ordinary teenage girl and a 'fantastically beautiful' young man having a deep conversation: the twist was that the mysterious young man happened to be a vampire, albeit a benign one. That dream again. The vampire has travelled from European castles and forests to a woodland glade – or an American high school . . . or a town in Louisiana . . . or to Forks in Washington State. Critics have written that Angela Carter's story must have been influenced by Anne Rice's novel *Interview with the Vampire* (1976) – with its emphasis on the inner life of the vampire, its psyche, and the creature's move from bogeyman to narrator. In fact, *Interview* was not published when she was working on *Vampirella* and *The Lady of the House of Love*. But all the stories in this book *were* published – and they were the crucible out of which her now-classic tale emerged. Which makes it a very suitable finale.

AT LAST THE REVENANTS BECAME so troublesome the peasants abandoned the village and it fell solely into the possession of subtle and vindictive inhabitants who manifest their presences by shadows that fall almost imperceptibly awry, too many shadows, even at midday, shadows that have no source in anything visible; by the sound, sometimes, of sobbing in a derelict bedroom where a cracked mirror suspended from a wall does not reflect a presence; by a sense of unease that will afflict the traveller unwise enough to pause to drink from the fountain in the square that still gushes spring water from a faucet stuck in a stone lion's mouth. A cat prowls in a weedy garden; he grins and spits, arches his back, bounces away from an intangible on four fear-stiffened legs. Now all shun the village below the château in which the beautiful somnambulist helplessly perpetuates her ancestral crimes.

Wearing an antique bridal gown, the beautiful queen of the vampires sits all alone in her dark, high house under the eyes of the portraits of her demented and atrocious ancestors, each one of whom, through her, projects a baleful posthumous existence; she counts out the Tarot cards, ceaselessly construing a constellation of possibilities as if the random fall of the cards on the red plush tablecloth before her could precipitate her from her chill, shuttered room into a country of perpetual summer and obliterate the perennial sadness of a girl who is both death and the maiden.

Her voice is filled with distant sonorities, like reverberations in a cave: now you are at the place of annihilation, now you are at the place of annihilation. And she is herself a cave full of echoes, she is a system of repetitions, she is a closed circuit. 'Can a bird sing only the song it knows or can it learn a new song?' She draws her long, sharp fingernail across the bars of the cage in which her pet lark sings, striking a plangent twang like that of the plucked heartstrings of a woman of metal. Her hair falls down like tears.

The castle is mostly given over to ghostly occupants but she herself has her own suite of drawing room and bedroom. Closely barred shutters and heavy velvet curtains keep out every leak of natural light. There is a round table on a single leg covered with a red plush cloth on which she lays out her inevitable Tarot; this room is never more than faintly illuminated by a heavily shaded lamp on the mantelpiece and the dark red figured wallpaper is obscurely, distressingly patterned by the rain that drives in through the neglected roof and leaves behind it random areas of staining, ominous marks like those left on the sheets by dead lovers. Depredations of rot and fungus everywhere. The unlit chandelier is so heavy with dust the individual prisms no longer show any shapes; industrious spiders have woven canopies in the corners of this ornate and rotting place, have trapped the porcelain vases on the mantelpiece in soft grey nets. But the mistress of all this disintegration notices nothing.

She sits in a chair covered in moth-ravaged burgundy velvet at the low, round table and distributes the cards; sometimes the lark sings, but more often remains a sullen mound of drab feathers. Sometimes the Countess will wake it for a brief cadenza by strumming the bars of its cage; she likes to hear it announce how it cannot escape.

She rises when the sun sets and goes immediately to her table where she plays her game of patience until she grows hungry, until she becomes ravenous. She is so beautiful she is unnatural; her beauty is an abnormality, a deformity, for none of her features exhibit any of those touching imperfections that reconcile us to the imperfection of the human condition. Her beauty is a symptom of her disorder, of her soullessness.

The white hands of the tenebrous belle deal the hand of destiny. Her fingernails are longer than those of the mandarins of ancient China and each is pared to a fine point. These and teeth as fine and white as spikes of spun sugar are the visible signs of the destiny she wistfully attempts to evade via the arcana; her claws and teeth have been sharpened on centuries of corpses, she is the last bud of the poison tree that sprang from the loins of Vlad the Impaler who picnicked on corpses in the forests of Transylvania.

The walls of her bedroom are hung with black satin, embroidered with tears of pearl. At the room's four corners are funerary urns and bowls which emit slumbrous, pungent fumes of incense. In the centre is an elaborate cata-falque, in ebony, surrounded by long candles in enormous silver candlesticks. In a white lace négligé stained a little with blood, the Countess climbs up on her catafalque at dawn each morning and lies down in an open coffin.

A chignoned priest of the Orthodox faith staked out her wicked father at a Carpathian crossroad before her milk teeth grew. Just as they staked him out, the fatal Count cried: 'Nosferatu is dead; long live Nosferatu!' Now she possesses all the haunted forests and mysterious habitations of his vast domain; she is the hereditary commandant of the army of shadows who camp in the village below her château, who penetrate the woods in the form of owls, bats and foxes, who make the milk curdle and the butter refuse to come, who ride the horses all night on a wild hunt so they are sacks of skin and bone in the morning, who milk the cows dry and, especially, torment pubescent girls with fainting fits, disorders of the blood, diseases of the imagination.

But the Countess herself is indifferent to her own weird authority, as if she were dreaming it. In her dream, she would like to be human; but she does not know if that is possible. The Tarot always shows the same configuration: always she turns up La Papesse, La Mort, La Tour Abolie, wisdom, death, dissolution.

On moonless nights, her keeper lets her out into the garden. This garden, an exceedingly sombre place, bears a strong resemblance to a burial ground and all the roses her dead mother planted have grown up into a huge, spiked wall that incarcerates her in the castle of her inheritance. When the back door opens, the Countess will sniff the air and howl. She drops, now, on all fours. Crouching, quivering, she catches the scent of her prey. Delicious crunch of the fragile bones of rabbits and small, furry things she pursues with fleet, four-footed speed; she will creep home, whimpering, with blood smeared on her cheeks. She pours water from the ewer in her bedroom into the bowl, she washes her face with the wincing, fastidious gestures of a cat.

The voracious margin of huntress's nights in the gloomy garden, crouch and pounce, surrounds her habitual tormented somnambulism, her life or imitation of life. The eyes of this nocturnal creature enlarge and glow. All claws and teeth, she strikes, she gorges; but nothing can console her for the ghastliness of her condition, nothing. She resorts to the magic comfort of the Tarot pack and shuffles the cards, lays them out, reads them, gathers them up with a sigh, shuffles them again, constantly constructing hypotheses about a future which is irreversible.

An old mute looks after her, to make sure she never sees the sun, that all day she stays in her coffin, to keep mirrors and all reflective surfaces away from her – in short, to perform all the functions of the servants of vampires. Everything about this beautiful and ghastly lady is as it should be, queen of night, queen of terror – except her horrible reluctance for the role.

Nevertheless, if an unwise adventurer pauses in the square of the deserted village to refresh himself at the fountain, a crone in a black dress and white apron presently emerges from a house. She will invite you with smiles and gestures; you will follow her. The Countess wants fresh meat. When she was a little girl, she was like a fox and contented herself entirely with baby rabbits that squeaked piteously as she bit into their necks with a nauseated voluptuousness, with voles and field-mice that palpitated for a bare moment between her embroidress's fingers. But now she is a woman, she must have men. If you stop too long beside the giggling fountain, you will be led by the hand to the Countess's larder.

All day, she lies in her coffin in her négligé of blood-stained lace. When the sun drops behind the mountain, she yawns and stirs and puts on the only dress she has, her mother's wedding dress, to sit and read her cards until she grows hungry. She loathes the food she eats; she would have liked to take the rabbits home with her, feed them on lettuce, pet them and make them a nest in her red-and-black chinoiserie escritoire, but hunger always overcomes her. She sinks her teeth into the neck where an artery throbs with fear; she will drop the deflated skin from which she has extracted all the nourishment with a small cry of both pain and disgust. And it is the same with the shepherd boys and gipsy lads who, ignorant or foolhardy, come to wash the dust from their feet in the water of the fountain; the Countess's governess brings them into the drawing room where the cards on the table always show the Grim Reaper. The Countess herself will serve them coffee in tiny cracked, precious cups, and little sugar cakes. The hobbledehoys sit with a spilling cup in one hand and a biscuit in the other, gaping at the Countess in her satin finery as she pours from a silver pot and chatters distractedly to put them at their fatal ease. A certain desolate stillness of her eyes indicates she is inconsolable. She would like to caress their lean brown cheeks and stroke their ragged hair. When she takes them by the hand and leads them to her bedroom, they can scarcely believe their luck.

Afterwards, her governess will tidy the remains into a neat pile and wrap it in its own discarded clothes. This mortal parcel she then discreetly buries in the garden. The blood on the Countess's cheeks will be mixed with tears; her keeper probes her fingernails for her with a little silver toothpick, to get rid of the fragments of skin and bone that have lodged there.

Fee fie fo fum
I smell the blood of an Englishman.

One hot, ripe summer in the pubescent years of the present century, a young officer in the British army, blond, blue-eyed, heavy-muscled, visiting friends in Vienna, decided to spend the remainder of his furlough exploring the little-known uplands of Romania. When he quixotically decided to travel the rutted cart-tracks by bicycle, he saw all the humour of it: 'on two wheels in the land of the vampires'. So, laughing, he sets out on his adventure.

He has the special quality of virginity, most and least ambiguous of states: ignorance, yet at the same time, power in potentia, and, furthermore, unknowingness, which is not the same as ignorance. He is more than he knows – and has about him, besides, the special glamour of that generation for whom history has already prepared a special, exemplary fate in the trenches of France. This being, rooted in change and time, is about to collide with the timeless Gothic eternity of the vampires, for whom all is as it has always been and will be, whose cards always fall in the same pattern.

Although so young, he is also rational. He has chosen the most rational mode of transport in the world for his trip round the Carpathians. To ride a bicycle is in itself some protection against superstitious fears, since the bicycle is the product of pure reason applied to motion. Geometry at the service of man! Give me two spheres and a straight line and I will show you how far I can take them. Voltaire himself might have invented the bicycle, since it contributes so much to man's welfare and nothing at all to his bane. Beneficial to the health, it emits no harmful fumes and permits only the most decorous speeds. How can a bicycle ever be an implement of harm?

A single kiss woke up the Sleeping Beauty in the Wood.

The waxen fingers of the Countess, fingers of a holy image, turn up the card called Les Amoureux. Never, never before . . . never before has the Countess cast herself a fate involving love. She shakes, she trembles, her great eyes close beneath her finely veined, nervously fluttering eyelids; the lovely cartomancer has, this time, the first time, dealt herself a hand of love and death.

> Be he alive or be he dead
> I'll grind his bones to make my bread.

At the mauvish beginnings of evening, the English m'sieu toils up the hill to the village he glimpsed from a great way off; he must dismount and push his bicycle before him, the path too steep to ride. He hopes to find a friendly inn to rest the night; he's hot, hungry, thirsty, weary, dusty . . . At first, such disappointment, to discover the roofs of all the cottages caved in and tall weeds thrusting through the piles of fallen tiles, shutters hanging disconsolately from their hinges, an entirely uninhabited place. And the rank vegetation whispers, as if foul secrets, here, where, if one were sufficiently imaginative, one could almost imagine twisted faces appearing momentarily beneath the crumbling eaves . . . but the adventure of it all, and the consolation of the poignant brightness of the hollyhocks still bravely blooming in the shaggy gardens, and the beauty of the flaming sunset, all these considerations soon overcame his disappointment, even assuaged the faint unease he'd felt. And the fountain where the village women used to wash their clothes still gushed out bright, clear water; he gratefully washed his feet and hands, applied his mouth to the faucet, then let the icy stream run over his face.

When he raised his dripping, gratified head from the lion's mouth, he saw, silently arrived beside him in the square, an old woman who smiled eagerly, almost conciliatorily at him. She wore a black dress and a white apron, with a housekeeper's key ring at the waist; her grey hair was neatly coiled in a chignon beneath the white linen headdress worn by elderly women of that region. She bobbed a curtsy at the young man and beckoned him to follow her. When he hesitated, she pointed towards the great bulk of the mansion above them, whose façade loured over the village, rubbed her stomach, pointed to her mouth, rubbed her stomach again, clearly miming an invitation to supper. Then she beckoned him again, this time turning determinedly upon her heel as though she would brook no opposition.

A great, intoxicated surge of the heavy scent of red roses blew into his face as soon as they left the village, inducing a sensuous vertigo; a blast of rich, faintly corrupt sweetness strong enough, almost, to fell him. Too many roses. Too many roses bloomed on enormous thickets that lined the path, thickets bristling with thorns, and the flowers themselves were almost too luxuriant, their huge congregations of plush petals somehow obscene in their excess, their whorled, tightly budded cores outrageous in their implications. The mansion emerged grudgingly out of this jungle.

In the subtle and haunting light of the setting sun, that golden light rich with nostalgia for the day that is just past, the sombre visage of the place, part manor house, part fortified farmhouse, immense, rambling, a dilapidated eagle's nest atop the crag down which its attendant village meandered, reminded him of childhood tales on winter evenings, when he and his brothers and sisters scared themselves half out of their wits with ghost stories set in just such places and then had to have candles to light them up newly terrifying stairs to bed. He could almost have regretted accepting the crone's unspoken invitation; but now, standing before the door of time-eroded oak while she selected a huge iron key from the clanking ringful at her waist, he knew it was too late to turn back and brusquely reminded himself he was no child, now, to be frightened of his own fancies.

The old lady unlocked the door, which swung back on melodramatically creaking hinges, and fussily took charge of his bicycle, in spite of his protests. He felt a certain involuntary sinking of the heart to see his beautiful two-wheeled symbol of rationality vanish into the dark entrails of the mansion, to, no doubt, some damp outhouse where they would not oil it or check its tyres. But, in for a penny, in for a pound – in his youth and strength and blond beauty, in the invisible, even unacknowledged pentacle of his virginity, the young man stepped over the threshold of Nosferatu's castle and did not shiver in the blast of cold air, as from the mouth of a grave, that emanated from the lightless, cavernous interior.

The crone took him to a little chamber where there was a black oak table spread with a clean white cloth and this cloth was carefully laid with heavy silverware, a little tarnished, as if someone with foul breath had breathed on it, but laid with one place only. Curiouser and curiouser; invited to the castle for dinner, now he must dine alone. All the same, he sat down as she had bid him. Although it was not yet dark outside, the curtains were closely drawn and only the sparing light trickling from a single oil lamp showed him how dismal his surroundings were. The crone bustled about to get him a bottle of wine and a glass from an ancient cabinet of wormy oak; while he bemusedly drank his wine, she disappeared but soon returned bearing a steaming platter of the local spiced meat stew with dumplings, and a shank of black bread. He was hungry after his long day's ride, he ate heartily and polished his plate with the crust, but this coarse food was hardly the entertainment he'd expected from the gentry and he was puzzled by the assessing glint in the dumb woman's eyes as she watched him eating.

But she darted off to get him a second helping as soon as he'd finished the first one and she seemed so friendly and helpful, besides, that he knew he could count on a bed for the night in the castle, as well as his supper, so he sharply reprimanded himself for his own childish lack of enthusiasm for the eerie silence, the clammy chill of the place.

When he'd put away the second plateful, the old woman came and gestured he should leave the table and follow her once again. She made a pantomime of drinking; he deduced he was now invited to take after-dinner coffee in another room with some more elevated member of the household who had not wished to dine with him but, all the same, wanted to make his acquaintance. An honour, no doubt; in deference to his host's opinion of himself, he straightened his tie, brushed the crumbs from his tweed jacket.

He was surprised to find how ruinous the interior of the house was – cobwebs, worm-eaten beams, crumbling plaster; but the mute crone resolutely wound him on the reel of her lantern down endless corridors, up winding staircases, through the galleries where the painted eyes of family portraits briefly flickered as they passed, eyes that belonged, he noticed, to faces, one and all, of a quite memorable beastliness. At last she paused and, behind the door where they'd halted, he heard a faint, metallic twang as of, perhaps, a chord struck on a harpsichord. And then, wonderfully, the liquid cascade of the song of a lark, bringing to him, in the heart – had he but known it – of Juliet's tomb, all the freshness of morning.

The crone rapped with her knuckles on the panels; the most seductively caressing voice he had ever heard in his life softly called out, in heavily accented French, the adopted language of the Romanian aristocracy: 'Entrez.'

First of all, he saw only a shape, a shape imbued with a faint luminosity since it caught and reflected in its yellowed surfaces what little light there was in the ill-lit room; this shape resolved itself into that of, of all things, a hoop-skirted dress of white satin draped here and there with lace, a dress fifty or sixty years out of fashion but once, obviously, intended for a wedding. And then he saw the girl who wore the dress, a girl with the fragility of the skeleton of a moth, so thin, so frail that her dress seemed to him to hang suspended, as if untenanted in the dank air, a fabulous lending, a self-articulated garment in which she lived like a ghost in a machine. All the light in the room came from a low-burning lamp with a thick greenish shade on a distant mantelpiece; the crone who accompanied him shielded her lantern with her hand, as if to protect her mistress from too suddenly seeing, or their guest from too suddenly seeing her.

So that it was little by little, as his eyes grew accustomed to the half-dark, that he saw how beautiful and how very young the bedizened scarecrow was, and he thought of a child dressing up in her mother's clothes, perhaps a child putting on the clothes of a dead mother in order to bring her, however briefly, to life again.

The Countess stood behind a low table, beside a pretty, silly, gilt-and-wire birdcage, hands outstretched in a distracted attitude that was almost one of flight; she looked as startled by their entry as if she had not requested it. With her stark white face, her lovely death's head surrounded by long dark hair that fell down as straight as if it were soaking wet, she looked like a shipwrecked bride. Her huge dark eyes almost broke his heart with their waiflike, lost look; yet he was disturbed, almost repelled, by her extraordinarily fleshy mouth, a mouth with wide, full, prominent lips of a vibrant purplish-crimson, a morbid mouth. Even – but he put the thought away from him immediately – a whore's mouth. She shivered all the time, a starveling chill, a malarial agitation of the bones. He thought she must be only sixteen or seventeen years old, no more, with the hectic, unhealthy beauty of a consumptive. She was the châtelaine of all this decay.

With many tender precautions, the crone now raised the light she held to show his hostess her guest's face. At that, the Countess let out a faint, mewing cry and made a blind, appalled gesture with her hands, as if pushing him away, so that she knocked against the table and a butterfly dazzle of painted cards fell to the floor. Her mouth formed a round 'o' of woe, she swayed a little and then sank into her chair, where she lay as if now scarcely capable of moving. A bewildering reception. Tsk'ing under her breath, the crone busily poked about on the table until she found an enormous pair of dark green glasses, such as blind beggars wear, and perched them on the Countess's nose.

He went forward to pick up her cards for her from a carpet that, he saw to his surprise, was part rotted away, partly encroached upon by all kinds of virulent-looking fungi. He retrieved the cards and shuffled them carelessly together, for they meant nothing to him, though they seemed strange playthings for a young girl. What a grisly picture of a capering skeleton! He covered it up with a happier one – of two young lovers, smiling at one another, and put her toys back into a hand so slender you could almost see the frail net of bone beneath the translucent skin, a hand with fingernails as long, as finely pointed, as banjo picks.

At his touch, she seemed to revive a little and almost smiled, raising herself upright.

'Coffee,' she said. 'You must have coffee.' And scooped up her cards into a pile so that the crone could set before her a silver spirit kettle, a silver coffee pot, cream jug, sugar basin, cups ready on a silver tray, a strange touch of elegance, even if discoloured, in this devastated interior whose mistress ethereally shone as if with her own blighted, submarine radiance.

The crone found him a chair and, tittering noiselessly, departed, leaving the room a little darker.

While the young lady attended to the coffee-making, he had time to contemplate with some distaste a further series of family portraits which decorated the stained and peeling walls of the room; these livid faces all seemed contorted with a febrile madness and the blubber lips, the huge, demented eyes that all had in common bore a disquieting resemblance to those of the hapless victim of inbreeding now patiently filtering her fragrant brew, even if some rare grace has so finely transformed those features when it came to her case. The lark, its chorus done, had long ago fallen silent; no sound but the chink of silver on china. Soon, she held out to him a tiny cup of rose-painted china.

'Welcome,' she said in her voice with the rushing sonorities of the ocean in it, a voice that seemed to come elsewhere than from her white, still throat. 'Welcome to my château. I rarely receive visitors and that's a misfortune since nothing animates me half as much as the presence of a stranger . . . This place is so lonely, now the village is deserted, and my one companion, alas, she cannot speak. Often I am so silent that I think I, too, will soon forget how to do so and nobody here will ever talk any more.'

She offered him a sugar biscuit from a Limoges plate; her fingernails struck carillons from the antique china. Her voice, issuing from those red lips like the obese roses in her garden, lips that do not move – her voice is curiously disembodied; she is like a doll, he thought, a ventriloquist's doll, or, more, like a great, ingenious piece of clockwork. For she seemed inadequately powered by some slow energy of which she was not in control; as if she had been wound up years ago, when she was born, and now the mechanism was inexorably running down and would leave her lifeless. This idea that she might be an automaton, made of white velvet and black fur, that could not move of its own accord, never quite deserted him; indeed, it deeply moved his heart. The carnival air of her white dress emphasized her unreality, like a sad Columbine who lost her way in the wood a long time ago and never reached the fair.

'And the light. I must apologize for the lack of light . . . a hereditary affliction of the eyes . . .'

Her blind spectacles gave him his handsome face back to himself twice over; if he presented himself to her naked face, he would dazzle her like the sun she is forbidden to look at because it would shrivel her up at once, poor night bird, poor butcher bird.

Vous serez ma proie.

You have such a fine throat, m'sieu, like a column of marble. When you came through the door retaining about you all the golden light of the summer's day of which I know nothing, nothing, the card called 'Les Amoureux' had just emerged from the tumbling chaos of imagery before me; it seemed to me you had stepped off the card into my darkness and, for a moment, I thought, perhaps, you might irradiate it.

I do not mean to hurt you. I shall wait for you in my bride's dress in the dark.

The bridegroom is come, he will go into the chamber which has been prepared for him.

I am condemned to solitude and dark; I do not mean to hurt you.

I will be very gentle.

(And could love free me from the shadows? Can a bird sing only the song it knows, or can it learn a new song?)

See, how I'm ready for you. I've always been ready for you; I've been waiting for you in my wedding dress, why have you delayed for so long . . . it will all be over very quickly.

You will feel no pain, my darling.

She herself is a haunted house. She does not possess herself; her ancestors sometimes come and peer out of the windows of her eyes and that is very frightening. She has the mysterious solitude of ambiguous states; she hovers in a no-man's land between life and death, sleeping and waking, behind the hedge of spiked flowers, Nosferatu's sanguinary rosebud. The beastly forebears on the walls condemn her to a perpetual repetition of their passions.

(One kiss, however, and only one, woke up the Sleeping Beauty in the Wood.)

Nervously, to conceal her inner voices, she keeps up a front of inconsequential chatter in French while her ancestors leer and grimace on the walls;

however hard she tries to think of any other, she only knows of one kind of consummation.

He was struck, once again, by the birdlike, predatory claws which tipped her marvellous hands; the sense of strangeness that had been growing on him since he buried his head under the streaming water in the village, since he entered the dark portals of the fatal castle, now fully overcame him. Had he been a cat, he would have bounced backwards from her hands on four fear-stiffened legs, but he is not a cat: he is a hero.

A fundamental disbelief in what he sees before him sustains him, even in the boudoir of Countess Nosferatu herself; he would have said, perhaps, that there are some things which, even if they *are* true, we should not believe possible. He might have said: it is folly to believe one's eyes. Not so much that he does not believe in her; he can see her, she is real. If she takes off her dark glasses, from her eyes will stream all the images that populate this vampire-haunted land, but, since he himself is immune to shadow, due to his virginity – he does not yet know what there is to be afraid of – and due to his heroism, which makes him like the sun, he sees before him, first and foremost, an inbred, highly strung girl child, fatherless, motherless, kept in the dark too long and pale as a plant that never sees the light, half-blinded by some hereditary condition of the eyes. And though he feels unease, he cannot feel terror; so he is like the boy in the fairy tale, who does not know how to shudder, and not spooks, ghouls, beasties, the Devil himself and all his retinue could do the trick.

This lack of imagination gives his heroism to the hero.

He will learn to shudder in the trenches. But this girl cannot make him shudder.

Now it is dark. Bats swoop and squeak outside the tightly shuttered windows. The coffee is all drunk, the sugar biscuits eaten. Her chatter comes trickling and diminishing to a stop; she twists her fingers together, picks at the lace of her dress, shifts nervously in her chair. Owls shriek; the impedimenta of her condition squeak and gibber all around us. Now you are at the place of annihilation, now you are at the place of annihilation. She turns her head away from the blue beams of his eyes; she knows no other consummation than the only one she can offer him. She has not eaten for three days. It is dinner-time. It is bed-time.

> Suivez-moi.
> Je vous artendais.
> Vous serez ma proie.

The raven caws on the accursed roof. 'Dinner-time, dinner-time,' clang the portraits on the walls. A ghastly hunger gnaws her entrails; she has waited for him all her life without knowing it.

The handsome bicyclist, scarcely believing his luck, will follow her into her bedroom; the candles around her sacrificial altar burn with a low, clear flame, light catches on the silver tears stitched to the wall. She will assure him, in the very voice of temptation: 'My clothes have but to fall and you will see before you a succession of mysteries.'

She has no mouth with which to kiss, no hands with which to caress, only the fangs and talons of a beast of prey. To touch the mineral sheen of the flesh revealed in the cool candle gleam is to invite her fatal embrace; in her low, sweet voice, she will croon the lullaby of the House of Nosferatu.

Embraces, kisses; your golden head, of a lion, although I have never seen a lion, only imagined one, of the sun, even if I've only seen the picture of the sun on the Tarot card, your golden head of the lover whom I dreamed would one day free me, this head will fall back, its eyes roll upwards in a spasm you will mistake for that of love and not of death. The bride-groom bleeds on my inverted marriage bed. Stark and dead, poor bicyclist; he has paid the price of a night with the Countess and some think it too high a fee while some do not.

Tomorrow, her keeper will bury his bones under her roses. The food her roses feed on gives them their rich colour, their swooning odour, that breathes lasciviously of forbidden pleasures.

> Suivez-moi.
> 'Suivez-moi!'

The handsome bicyclist, fearful for his hostess's health, her sanity, gingerly follows her hysterical imperiousness into the other room; he would like to take her into his arms and protect her from the ancestors who leer down from the walls.

What a macabre bedroom!

His colonel, an old goat with jaded appetites, had given him the visiting card of a brothel in Paris where, the satyr assured him, ten louis would buy just such a lugubrious bedroom, with a naked girl upon a coffin; offstage, the brothel pianist played the *Dies Irae* on a harmonium and, amidst all the perfumes of the embalming parlour, the customer took his necrophiliac pleasure of a pretended corpse. He had good-naturedly refused the old man's offer of such an initiation; how can he now take criminal advantage of the disordered girl with fever-hot, bone-dry, taloned hands and eyes that deny all the erotic promises of her body with their terror, their sadness, their dreadful, balked tenderness?

So delicate and damned, poor thing. Quite damned.

Yet I do believe she scarcely knows what she is doing.

She is shaking as if her limbs were not efficiently joined together, as if she might shake into pieces. She raises her hands to unfasten the neck of her dress and her eyes well with tears, they trickle down beneath the rim of her dark glasses. She can't take off her mother's wedding dress unless she takes off her dark glasses; she has fumbled the ritual, it is no longer inexorable. The mechanism within her fails her, now, when she needs it most. When she takes off the dark glasses, they slip from her fingers and smash to pieces on the tiled floor. There is no room in her drama for improvisation; and this unexpected, mundane noise of breaking glass breaks the wicked spell in the room, entirely. She gapes blindly down at the splinters and ineffectively smears the tears across her face with her fist. What is she to do now?

When she kneels to try to gather the fragments of glass together, a sharp sliver pierces deeply into the pad of her thumb; she cries out, sharp, real. She kneels among the broken glass and watches the bright bead of blood form a drop. She has never seen her own blood before, not her *own* blood. It exercises upon her an awed fascination.

Into this vile and murderous room, the handsome bicyclist brings the innocent remedies of the nursery; in himself, by his presence, he is an exorcism.

He gently takes her hand away from her and dabs the blood with his own handkerchief, but still it spurts out. And so he puts his mouth to the wound. He will kiss it better for her, as her mother, had she lived, would have done.

All the silver tears fall from the wall with a flimsy tinkle. Her painted ancestors turn away their eyes and grind their fangs.

How can she bear the pain of becoming human?

The end of exile is the end of being.

He was awakened by larksong. The shutters, the curtains, even the long-sealed windows of the horried bedroom were all opened up and light and air streamed in; now you could see how tawdry it all was, how thin and cheap the satin, the catafalque not ebony at all but black-painted paper stretched on struts of wood, as in the theatre. The wind had blown droves of petals from the roses outside into the room and this crimson residue swirled fragrantly about the floor. The candles had burnt out and she must have set her pet lark free because it perched on the edge of the silly coffin to sing him its ecstatic morning song. His bones were stiff and aching, he'd slept on the floor with his bundled-up jacket for a pillow, after he'd put her to bed.

But now there was no trace of her to be seen, except, lightly tossed across the crumpled black satin bedcover, a lace négligé lightly soiled with blood, as it might be from a woman's menses, and a rose that must have come from the fierce bushes nodding through the window. The air was heavy with incense and roses and made him cough. The Countess must have got up early to enjoy the sunshine, slipped outside to gather him a rose. He got to his feet, coaxed the lark on to his wrist and took it to the window. At first, it exhibited the reluctance for the sky of a long-caged thing, but, when he tossed it up on to the currents of the air, it spread its wings and was up and away into the clear blue bowl of the heavens; he watched its trajectory with a lift of joy in his heart.

Then he padded into the boudoir, his mind busy with plans. We shall take her to Zurich, to a clinic; she will be treated for nervous hysteria. Then to an eye specialist, for her photophobia, and to a dentist to put her teeth into better shape. Any competent manicurist will deal with her claws. We shall turn her into the lovely girl she is; I shall cure her of all these nightmares.

The heavy curtains are pulled back, to let in brilliant fusillades of early morning light; in the desolation of the boudoir, she sits at her round table in her white dress, with the cards laid out before her. She has dropped off to sleep over the cards of destiny that are so fingered, so soiled, so worn by constant shuffling that you can no longer make the image out on any single one of them.

She is not sleeping.

In death, she looked far older, less beautiful and so, for the first time, fully human.

I will vanish in the morning light; I was only an invention of darkness.

And I leave you as a souvenir the dark, fanged rose I plucked from between my thighs, like a flower laid on a grave. On a grave.

My keeper will attend to everything.

Nosferatu always attends his own obsequies; she will not go to the graveyard unattended. And now the crone materialized, weeping, and roughly gestured him to begone. After a search in some foul-smelling outhouses, he discovered his bicycle and, abandoning his holiday, rode directly to Bucharest where, at the poste restante, he found a telegram summoning him to rejoin his regiment at once. Much later, when he changed back into uniform in his quarters, he discovered he still had the Countess's rose, he must have tucked it into the breast pocket of his cycling jacket after he had found her body. Curiously enough, although he had brought it so far away from Romania, the flower did not seem to be quite dead and, on impulse, because the girl had been so lovely and her death so unexpected and pathetic, he decided to try and resurrect her rose. He filled his tooth glass with water from the carafe on his locker and popped the rose into it, so that its withered head floated on the surface.

When he returned from the mess that evening, the heavy fragrance of Count Nosferatu's roses drifted down the stone corridor of the barracks to greet him, and his spartan quarters brimmed with the reeling odour of a glowing, velvet, monstrous flower whose petals had regained all their former bloom and elasticity, their corrupt, brilliant, baleful splendour.

Next day, his regiment embarked for France.

DRACULA

6d.

BY

BRAM
STOKER

6d.

WESTMINSTER

Archibald Constable & Co Ltd

2 WHITEHALL GARDENS

BIBLIOGRAPHY AND ACKNOWLEDGMENTS

On vampirism in general Montague Summers's *The Vampire: His Kith and Kin* (1928) and *The Vampire in Europe* (1929) and Dudley Wright's *Vampires and Vampirism* (1914) are unreliable, and have for too long been treated as gospel. Tony Faivre's *Les Vampires* (1962) and Sturm and Volker's excellent *Von denen Vampiren oder Menschensaugern* (1973) are both much more scholarly, and can be trusted more than the (many) Summers derivatives. On the lore of blood in general, the most readable (and wide-ranging) account is Earle Hackett's *Blood: The Paramount Humour* (1973). On the erotic angle, Ornella Volta's *Il Vampiro* (1962) is interesting (if a little strange at times) and has some extraordinary illustrations (translated, without these, 1965). Also Robert Eisler's *Man into Wolf* (1951) – especially the notes. On premature burial (and related matters), Lyall Watson's *Romeo Error* (1974) synthesizes the literature.

Information on the Enlightenment and the vampire can be found in the following sources: Tournefort's *Voyage* (translated 1741), Calmet's *Treatise* (most accessible in Christmas's *The Phantom World*, 1858), the report on Paole (reprinted in Faivre and Sturm and often adapted), the *Gentleman's Magazine* (March and May 1732), *The Craftsman* (20 May 1732,) *Applebee's Journal* (27 May 1732), the *London Journal* (11 March 1732, the first English account), *Harleian Miscellany* (1745, reprinting a manuscript – by 'Three English Gentlemen' – of 1734), Horace Walpole's *Correspondence* (a letter of 16 January 1786, which claims that King George II had 'had no doubt of the existence of vampires . . .'), d'Argens's *Lettres Juives* (or *The Jewish Spy*, 1738, translated 1739–40 – partly anthologized in Calmet), the report by van Swieten (reprinted in French by Volta and Riva in *Histoires de Vampires*, 1961), the report by Prospero Lambertini (Pope Benedict) (also in Volta and Riva), Diderot's *Encyclopédie* (article on 'Vampire'), Voltaire's *Dictionnaire Philosophique* (any edition with the supplement), Rousseau's 'Lettre à Christophe de Beaumont' (Pléiade, vol. iv, 1969) and the first draft of his *Émile* (*Profession de Foi*, ed.

Masson, 1914), and Charles Nodier's *Infernalia* (1825) – an anthology (the second, after Calmet), which is also useful on the more ephemeral Ruthven items of early 1820s Paris. Calmet's *Treatise* anthologizes various French reports about 1732 (such as the *Dutch Gleaner*, March 1732, and the *Mercure Historique et Politique*, October 1736), as well as containing extracts from Tournefort, d'Argens, etc. Plus many other eighteenth-century reports, periodicals, memoirs and travel books.

On pseudo-science and the pre-Romantics, Auguste Viatte's two-volume *Sources Occultes du Romantisme*, 1770–1829 (rev. ed. 1969), is still useful (and a key source on Nodier and his ilk); Robert Darnton's *Mesmerism and the End of Enlightenment* (1968) is terrific and all too brief.

On vampires in literature, Propp's *Morphologie du Conte* (rev. ed. 1965) and Todorov's *Introduction à la Littérature Fantastique* (1970) are the best for methodology (although Todorov's ideas have more recently been questioned). Most of the actual stories are listed in my 'Vampire Mosaic' (see pages 68–93, where the interesting items are marked with an asterisk). It would be impossible to list all of them (newly discovered stories – many of them trash – turn up every year, from obscure Victorian periodicals, the Parlour Novelist series, Railway Travellers' collections, reprinted selections from periodicals, and so on). An example of the most ephemeral type (which did not qualify for my 'Mosaic') is Whyte Melville's otherwise quite amusing *Bones and I or the Skeleton at Home* (Ch. 4, 'A Vampire', in which 'Madame de St Croix' destroys the Hungarian Count V   ). This is (like countless others) at best 'symptomatic' of the popularity of the Medusa in the 1880s and 1890s. The most useful general commentaries on the vampire in literature include Sturm and Volker (see above), Varma's *Gothic Flame* (1957), Varma and Carter's introductions to the Arno edition of *Varney the Vampyre* (1970), Scarborough's *Supernatural in Modern Fiction* (1917), Birkhead's *Tale of Terror* (1921), Summers's *Gothic Quest* (1938), Lovecraft's *Supernatural Horror in Literature* (1945), Penzoldt's *Supernatural in Fiction* (1952), Caillois's *Au Coeur du Fantastique* (1965), Pirie's *Heritage of Horror* (1973) and, of course, Praz's *Romantic Agony* (rev. ed. 1970, with a new Foreword by Frank Kermode). For dreams, Hayter's *Opium and the Romantic Imagination* (1968) is the best.

On that 'wet, ungenial summer', the primary sources include letters, journals or diaries by Byron, Shelley, Mary Godwin/Shelley and, of course, Polidori. Also the famous Introduction to the popular edition of *Frankenstein* (1831, abridged) by Mary Shelley, and Lady Caroline Lamb's *Glenarvon* (1816). Stendhal wrote a first-hand account of an 'incident' between Bryon and Polidori, which occurred four months after the ghost-story session in Milan. Of the secondary sources, the most useful are three articles by Henry Viets on Polidori (1961 and 1969), and the work of James Rieger. It was Reiger who first suggested that Mary Shelley's account of the genesis of *Frankenstein* might be inaccurate (in *Studies in English Literature*, 1963, and *The Heresies of Shelley*, 1967) and, using his thesis as a starting point, I have extended it (with some further information) to apply to the origins of *The Vampyre*. Rieger is also challenging on Shelley's hand in a draft version of *Frankenstein* (in his introduction to the 1818 edition, 1974). Other useful secondary sources include Marchand and Moore on Byron, Small, Spark, Nitchie and, especially, Norman on Mary Shelley (whose short stories have been collected by Charles Robinson, 1976 – they are mostly unmemorable), Ash on Polidori and various biographies of Shelley (the most substantial being by Richard Holmes). To fill out the picture, memoirs and letters by the friends of Byron and Shelley are also interesting. Polidori's MD thesis (in Latin) is kept in Edinburgh University Library. On the Ruthven syndrome, key sources still include Edmond Estève's *Byron et le Romantisme Français* (1929). Also the various novels, stories, plays, poems and operas that were derived from *The Vampyre* (most of which are available in the British Library), plus Richard Switzer's *Lord Ruthven and the Vampires* (*French Review*, 29, 1955).

On penny-dreadfuls in general, and Rymer in particular, Louis James's *Fiction for the Working Man* (1963) and *Print and the People* (1976) are far and away the best sources, although Dalziel's *Popular Fiction a Hundred Years Ago* (1958) and Altick's *English Common Reader* (1957) are also useful. On Rymer, A. Johanssen's *House of Beadle and Adams* (1950) and T. Catling's *Life's Pilgrimage* (1911) provide background detail about biography and the 'Salisbury Square' school respectively, while Rymer's own article on 'Popular Writing' (*Queen's Magazine*, which he was editing at the time, 1842) gives a good idea of his early views on penny-bloods. The pamphlets put out by 'good causes', using the *Feast of Blood* format, are all in collections in the British Library.

Standard biographies are useful for information on Dumas père, Hoffmann, Alexis Tolstoy, Fitz-James O'Brien (who has something of a cult following in France, where there are good editions of his complete stories), Huysmans, Baudelaire, Gautier (some of whose tales have been translated by Richard Holmes) and most of the well-known authors mentioned in my 'Mosaic'. Neither of the biographies of Bram Stoker (Harry Ludlam, 1962; Daniel Farson, 1975) is really adequate. Some of the wilder assertions about Stoker's 'trauma' are contained in the *British Journal of Medical Psychology*, 1973 (Seymour Shuster's article) and Dr J. S. Bierman's *Dracula: Prolonged Childhood Illness and the Oral Triad*. Ludlam's is the better of the two biographies, but Stoker still remains a mystery. Books by and about the Irving regime at the Lyceum (especially in the twilight years) sometimes reveal much more. These include Stoker's own *Reminiscences*, Laurence Irving's biography and virtually anything on Ellen Terry. Of Stoker's other novels and stories (many of which really are second rate), the interesting ones include *Under the Sunset* (a collection of whimsical children's stories, 1882), *The Jewel of Seven Stars* (an Egyptian mummy story, concerning the resurrection of Queen Tara and revealing Stoker's interest in Egyptian archaeology, 1903), *The Lady of the Shroud* (about a Balkan princess who pretends to be a vampire, owing much to Anthony Hope, 1909), *The Lair of the White Worm* (concerning the exploits of Lady Arabella March, who transmutes into a giant snake, living 'amid a mass of slime' down a deep well-hole – a field day for sexologists, 1911) and *Dracula's Guest* (a collection of his best short stories, published posthumously in April 1914 by Stoker's widow, Florence, and often since – the title story appears on pages 397–409). As interesting as any of these (from the point of view of Stoker the man) is an article he published in the *Nineteenth Century* magazine (1908) on censorship: 'If the plague-spot continues to enlarge, a censorship there must be ... women are the worst offenders in this form of breach of moral law ... A close analysis will show that the only emotions which in the long run harm are those arising from sex impulses ...' Another piece of evidence for the 'repression' thesis about *Dracula*.

On the sources for *Dracula*, Devendra Varma was the first to mention Burton and Rossetti (although he does not specifically refer to Hall Caine's *Recollections*) in *The Vampire's Bedside Companion* (1975 – otherwise not very useful); another connection with the Pre-Raphaelites occurred in 1897, when Philip Burne-Jones (a friend of the Stoker family) exhibited the painting *The Vampire* (female variety, of course) at the time *Dracula* was published; Charles Collins (*A Feast of Blood*) resurrected *The Mysterious Stranger* from where Montague Summers had buried him; of the spate of books on Vlad the Impaler (and on *Dracula*), by far the best are the work of Leonard Wolf (*A Dream of Dracula*, 1972; *The Annotated Dracula*, 1975). Wolf's reading of *Dracula* is subtle, and I am indebted to it (even if our conclusions differ). Apart from these, the books on Vlad are not particularly useful, and in any case the connection is tenuous. The best (which is really on Dracula-*ism*) is Gabriel Ronay's *Dracula Myth* (1972). My views on the others, and on the 'Vlad syndrome', have been expressed clearly enough in a review article (*London Magazine*, June 1974). For *historical* purposes, the standard work on Vlad Tepes is now Gianfranco Giraudo's *Drakula: Contributi alla storia delle idee politiche nell' Europa Orientale alla svolta del XV secolo* (1972), and the pioneering articles by Grigore Nandris (1959, 1966) are still key sources. Some of the Vlad pamphlets have been translated and appear in Appendices I to III of Raymond McNally and Radu Florescu, *In Search of Dracula* (1972). For the books that Stoker himself used, see pages 352–93. On the politics of *Dracula*, articles by Stein and Gattegno (*Littérature*, December 1972) are useful.

The most reliable perspectives on the novel include the researches and commentaries of Richard Dalby (*Bram Stoker: a Bibliography of First Editions*, 1983, and *Dracula's Brood*, 1987), Clive Leatherdale (*Dracula: the Novel and the Legend*, 1985, and *The Origins of Dracula*, 1987) and James B. Twitchell (*The Living Dead: a Study of the Vampire in Romantic Literature*, 1981, and *Dreadful Pleasures: an Anatomy of Modern Horror*, 1985). A. N. Wilson's comments are from his Introduction to the World's Classics edition of *Dracula* (1983). Studies of vampires in the eighteenth century include Paul Barber's *Vampires, Burial and Death* (1988), M. R. Brownell's *Pope and the Vampires in*

Germany (*Eighteenth Century Life,* June 1976), and my own researches (with Robert Wokler) for 'From the Orang-utan to the Vampire: Towards an Anthropology of Rousseau' (in *Rousseau after 200 Years,* 1982). On vampires and Ireland, Richard Ellmann's *Oscar Wilde* (1987) and my own *Vampirism and Irish Bureaucracy* (*Bristol University Newsletter,* with Kieran Flanagan, May 1979) have punctured the surface, as it were. Raymond McNally and Radu Florescu's two books *The Essential Dracula* (1979) and *Dracula: Prince of Many Faces* (1989) have promoted the Vlad theme. And Franco Moretti's *Signs Taken for Wonders* (1983), especially the chapter 'Dialectic of Fear', has further explored the politics of *Dracula.* Joseph S. Bierman's *Genesis and Dating of Dracula from Bram Stoker's Working Notes* (*Notes and Queries,* January–February 1977) revealed the existence of Stoker's *Dracula* papers.

Apart from all these printed sources, the following people – given in no particular order here – helped me at various stages and I would like warmly to thank them: Grey Gowrie (the current Lord Ruthven, who has more of a sense of humour than the original one), Theo Brown (for her inexhaustible knowledge of folklore motifs and her kindness in sharing it), Christopher Lee (for his encouragement at an early stage), Brian J. Frost (for his assistance over one or two tricky bibliographical problems), John Eggeling and the late Vernon Lay (both of whom sold me a lot of books and gave useful advice on bibliography), Edward Horesh (who helped me through the Talmud and *Das Kapital*), Iain Cassie (who directed an independent film which turned into the BBC2 documentary in which I first tried out my ideas), Jean Théodorides (who put me on to the rabies connection), my brother Nicholas Frayling (who took time off from his parish duties to help sort out the theology), Angela Carter (who discussed the magic and the myth, at the very witching time of night), E. F. Bleiler (who questioned the Tieck attribution of *Wake Not the Dead*), Tim Cribb (who found the *Household Words* reference – an intriguing one), Ivor Stoker Dixon (who pointed me towards the Wagner connection and other thoughts about Bram), Robert James Leake (of the Dracula Society), and Gillian Plummer and Barbara Berry (who typed the final text, from a manuscript even more untidy than Bram Stoker's). Finally, the staff at the Rosenbach Museum and Library, Philadelphia, permitted me to study in detail Bram Stroker's working notes and research notes in their reading room. Although they were unable at that stage to grant me permission to quote the manuscripts *in extenso* (I had to paraphrase), the staff were very helpful. Thanks also to the long-suffering staff in the British Library, Cambridge University Library, the Warburg Institute, Edinburgh University Library, the Bibliothèque Nationale and the Bibliothèque Publique et Universitaire in Geneva; they were sometimes apprehensive about the type of book I was requesting, but they were always supportive.

Christopher Frayling, 1990

ADDITIONAL BIBLIOGRAPHY (2016)

When earlier versions of *Vampyres* were first published, Gothic and neo-Gothic literature were not as fashionable as they are today. In fact, librarians in the British Library used to give me strange looks when I ordered some of the choicer titles. Today, it is difficult to find young literary scholars in the British Library who are *not* researching aspects of the Gothic. I have often been told, at conferences, that *Vampyres* helped to pave the way for the current academic and literary interest in the subject, which is flattering. This revised and updated version has benefited from many books and articles that have recently been published, as part of this Gothic Revival; this move from marginal to mainstream. There have been two biographies of Bram Stoker – by Barbara Belford (1996) and Paul Murray (2004) – and one biographical study by Peter Haining and Peter Tremayne (1997), plus Jeffrey Richards's monumental biography of *Henry Irving* (2005). Stoker's scissors-and-paste dramatized version of *Dracula* has been located and published by Sylvia Starshine (1997); his *Notes for Dracula* have been issued in full, with facsimiles (ed. Robert Eighteen-Bisang and Elizabeth Miller, 2008); his abridged paperback version of 1901 has been reprinted; his Dublin journal has appeared (ed. Elizabeth Miller and Dacre Stoker, 2012); good critical editions of *Dracula* have been published (notably by Penguin Classics, 2003; ed. Leslie Klinger 2008; and ed. Clive Leatherdale 1998); and the manuscript corrected for the typesetters has surfaced (described in ed. Bruce Francis: the *Book Sail Catalogue*, 1984). Jarlath Killeen has edited a volume of centenary Stoker essays. Whole books have been devoted to critical debates surrounding the significance of the text, including *Bram Stoker Dracula: a Reader's Guide* (ed. William Hughes, 2009) and Elizabeth Miller's *Dracula: Sense and Nonsense* (2000). Mary Shelley's manuscript 'Frankenstein Notebooks' of 1816–17 have been well edited by Charles E. Robinson (Garland, 1996).

There have been numerous anthologies of vampire stories, including *The Vampire Omnibus* (ed. Peter Haining, 1995), *The Mammoth Book of Dracula* (ed. Stephen Jones, 1997), *Dracula's Guest: a Connoisseur's Collection* (ed. Michael Sims, 2010), *Vampires: Classic Tales* (ed. Mike Ashley, 2011) and *In the Shadow of Dracula* (eds Leslie S. Klinger and Jeff Conner, 2011). I have been indebted to these, in updating my 'Vampire Mosaic'. Bram Stoker's work as a theatre critic has been studied in Catherine Wynne's *Bram Stoker, Dracula and the Victorian Gothic Stage* (2013); Roy Foster's collection *Paddy and Mr Punch* (1995) contains an important article on 'Protestant Magic' focusing on Maturin, Le Fanu, Stoker, crumbling Irish mansions and ancestral curses; the political context has been explored in David Glover's *Vampires, Mummies and Liberals* (1996); the Irish background in Luke Gibbons's *Gaelic Gothic* (2004) and Joseph Valente's *Dracula's Crypt* (2002); and Robert Mighall's *A Geography of Victorian Gothic Fiction* (1999) includes material on *Vampires and Victorians*. The 'Lord Ruthven' phenomenon has been dissected by Roxana Stuart in *Stage Blood: Vampires of the 19th-Century Stage* (1994).

On vampire fiction in general, the successes of *Interview* (and sequels), *Buffy*, *True Blood* and the *Twilight Saga*, and assorted box sets, have led to the publication of numerous collections of essays, and books – usually with an emphasis on the current concerns of gender, identity and race. On Angela Carter's *The Lady of the House of Love*, there are good editions of her collection of stories *The Bloody Chamber* (introduced by Helen Simpson, 2006; and Marina Warner, 2012); for more background on the genesis of *The Lady* – and my role in it – see Christopher Frayling: *Inside the Bloody Chamber* (2015).

As well as these printed sources, warm thanks go to Roy Foster, Jarlath Killeen, Elizabeth Miller, Paul Murray, Catherine Wynne, Derek Towers –

who directed my *Nightmare* series on BBC Television – and, once again, to Grey Gowrie, Mrs Thatcher's Minister for the Arts, poet and direct descendant of Lord Ruthven . . .

SOURCES OF ILLUSTRATIONS

a = above, b = below, l = left, r = right

2 National Gallery of Art, Washington, DC Rosenwald Collection (1951.10.470); **10** British Library Board/Topfoto; **121** Royal Collection, London. Photo akg-images/De Agostini Picture Library; **122a** Mary Evans Picture Library, London; **122b** Photo akg-images; **123, 124** National Portrait Gallery, London; **125** British Library, London; **126** Victoria & Albert Museum, London; **127** Private collection; **128al** British Library, London; **128ar, 128bl, 128br** British Library Board/Topfoto; **201al, 201bl** Bibliothèque nationale de France, Paris; **201ar** Wellcome Library, London; **201br** Herzog August Bibliothek, Wolfenbüttel, Germany; **202a** Detroit Institute of Arts. Founders Society Purchase with funds from Mr and Mrs Bert L. Smokler and Mr and Mrs Lawrence A. Fleischman (55.5A); **202b** Andrew Edmunds, London; **203al** British Museum, London; **203ar** National Gallery of Art, Washington, DC Rosenwald Collection (1943.3.4711.qq); **203b** University of Tennessee, Chattanooga Library; **204** Tate, London; **205al** Photo akg-images; **205ar** Los Angeles County Museum of Art. Gift of Michael G. Wilson (M.81.313.86); **205b** Bibliothèque nationale de France, Paris; **206a** Private collection; **206b** Private collection/Look and Learn/Bridgeman Images; **207** Munch Museum, Oslo. Photo akg-images/Erich Lessing; **208** Munch Museum, Oslo. Photo Scala, Florence; **289** Photo akg-images/British Library, London; **290al** Sutcliffe Gallery, Whitby; **290ar** Whitby Public Library; **290b** Sutcliffe Gallery, Whitby; **291al, 291ar** The Rosenbach of the Free Library of Philadelphia; **291bl** Hulton-Deutsch Collection/Corbis; **291br** The Rosenbach of the Free Library of Philadelphia; **292** Lord Chamberlain's Collection of Plays, British Library, London; **293al** Victoria & Albert Museum, London; **293ar** Private collection; **293b** *Tatler*, October 1902; **294** Rider & Son, London, 1916. Courtesy Mark Terry Facsimile Dust Jackets L.L.C.; **295** Routledge, London, 1914. Courtesy Mark Terry Facsimile Dust Jackets L.L.C.; **296** Grosset & Dunlap, New York, 1931. Courtesy Mark Terry Facsimile Dust Jackets L.L.C.; **377** *Nosferatu* (1922). Directed by F. W. Murnau. Prana-film; **378–79** *Vampyr* (1932). Directed by Carl Dreyer. Dreyer-Tobis-Klangfilm/The Kobal Collection; **380al** *Dracula* (1931). Directed by Tod Browning. Universal Pictures. Bridgeman Images; **380ar** *Horror of Dracula* (1958). Directed by Terence Fisher. Hammer/The Kobal Collection; **380b** *Mark of the Vampire* (1935). Directed by Tod Browning. Bridgeman Images; **381a** *Blood and Roses* (1960). Directed by Roger Vadim. Film Ege/Documento/The Kobal Collection; **381b** *The Vampire Lovers* (1970). Directed by Roy Ward Baker. Hammer/AIP/The Kobal Collection; **382al** *Black Sabbath* (1964). Directed by Mario Bava. AIP/The Kobal Collection; **382ar** *Nosferatu* (1979). Directed by Werner Herzog. AF archive/Alamy Stock Photo; **382b** *Bram Stoker's Dracula* (1992). Directed by Francis Ford Coppola. Zoetrope/Columbia Tri-Star Films. Photos 12/Alamy Stock Photo; **383al** *Interview with the Vampire* (1994). Directed by Neil Jordan. Geffen Pictures/The Kobal Collection/ Francois Duhamel; **383ar** *Buffy the Vampire Slayer* (1997, first season television series). Directed by Joss Whedon. Moviestore collection Ltd/Alamy Stock Photo; **383bl** *Let The Right One In* (2008). Directed by Thomas Alfredson. Fido Film AB/The Kobal Collection; **383br** *Shadow of the Vampire* (2000). Directed by E. Elias Merhige. BBC/Delux/Metrodome. Private collection; **384** *Twilight* (2008). Directed by Catherine Hardwicke. Summit Entertainment/The Kobal Collection; **454** Photo PVDE/Bridgeman Images